C000181702

# New Collected Poems

LES MURRAY, born in 1938, grew up on a dairy farm at Bunyah on the north coast of New South Wales. Since 1971 he has made literature his full-time career. Carcanet publish *Translations from the Natural World* (1993), *Subhuman Redneck Poems* (1996, awarded the T.S. Eliot Prize), *Conscious and Verbal* (1999), *Learning Human: New Selected Poems* (2001), *Poems the Size of Photographs* (2002) and his essays and prose writings *The Paperbark Tree* (1992). His verse novel *Fredy Neptune* appeared in 1998, when Murray also received the Queen's Gold Medal for Poetry.

Also by Les Murray from Carcanet

*Selected Poems*
*Translations from the Natural World*
*Subhuman Redneck Poems*
*Fredy Neptune*
*Conscious and Verbal*
*Learning Human: New Selected Poems*
*Poems the Size of Photographs*

Essays
*The Paperbark Tree*

As editor
*Fivefathers*

# New Collected Poems

LES MURRAY

CARCANET

This edition first published in Great Britain in 2003 by
Carcanet Press Limited
Alliance House
Cross Street
Manchester M2 7AQ

First published in Australia by Duffy & Snellgrove, Sydney, 2002

A CIP catalogue record for this book is available from the British Library
ISBN 1 85754 623 7

The publisher acknowledges financial assistance from the Arts Council of England

Printed and bound in England by SRP Ltd, Exeter

To the glory of God

# CONTENTS

*from* THE DAYLIGHT MOON, 1987

from TRANSLATIONS FROM
THE NATURAL WORLD, 1992

from CONSCIOUS AND VERBAL, 1999

# THE BURNING TRUCK

FOR MRS MARGARET WELTON

It began at dawn with fighter planes:
they came in off the sea and didn't rise,
they leaped the sandbar one and one and one
coming so fast the crockery they shook down
off my kitchen shelves was spinning in the air
when they were gone.

They came in off the sea and drew a wave
of lagging cannon-shells across our roofs.
Windows spat glass, a truck took sudden fire,
out leaped the driver, but the truck ran on,
growing enormous, shambling by our street-doors,
coming and coming ...

By every right in town, by every average
we knew of in the world, it had to stop,
fetch up against a building, fall to rubble
from pure force of burning, for its whole
body and substance were consumed with heat
but it would not stop.

And all of us who knew our place and prayers
clutched our verandah-rails and window-sills,
begging that truck between our teeth to halt,
keep going, vanish, strike ... but set us free.
And then we saw the wild boys of the street
go running after it.

And as they followed, cheering, on it crept,
windshield melting now, canopy-frame a cage
torn by gorillas of flame, and it kept on
over the tramlines, past the church, on past
the last lit windows, and then out of the world
with its disciples.

*1*

## TABLEAU IN JANUARY

January, noon. The idle length of a street ...
There is more light than world, and what few outlines
Persist forget their meaning in the heat.

The metal sea's too bright to walk upon.
Thoughts pass, and figment shops, and random glimmers
From crystals in the concrete, and oiled swimmers.
The sky does not exist when it's outshone.

On the dazed white sand, umbrellas stiffly lean
To pose and impose their shade upon the shifting
Languor of bodies and glare, and all the sifting
Motes of dim music mingled with the scene
Fade into summer, January, drifting ...

Things drift apart, significances fade.
The returning street, once blue, is taut with azure
Tension between persistence and erasure.
In the cool of doorways, shirts drink lemonade.

January, noon. The unreal, idle street.
There is more light than world. The poet, smiling,
Takes his soft lines and bends them till they meet.


## THE TRAINEE, 1914

Ah, I was as soiled as money, old as rag,
I was building a humpy beside a gully of woes,
Till the bump of your drum, the fit of your turned-up hat
Drew me to eat your stew, salute your flag

And carry your rifle far away to your wars:
Is war very big? As big as New South Wales?

# THE WIDOWER IN THE COUNTRY

I'll get up soon, and leave my bed unmade.
I'll go outside and split off kindling wood
from the yellow-box log that lies beside the gate,
and the sun will be high, for I get up late now.

I'll drive my axe in the log and come back in
with my armful of wood, and pause to look across
the Christmas paddocks aching in the heat,
the windless trees, the nettles in the yard …
and then I'll go in, boil water and make tea.

This afternoon, I'll stand out on the hill
and watch my house away below, and how
the roof reflects the sun and makes my eyes
water and close on bright webbed visions smeared
on the dark of my thoughts to dance and fade away.
Then the sun will move on, and I will simply watch,
or work, or sleep. And evening will come on.

Getting near dark, I'll go home, light the lamp
and eat my corned-beef supper, sitting there
at the head of the table. Then I'll go to bed.
Last night I thought I dreamed – but when I woke
the screaming was only a possum ski-ing down
the iron roof on little moonlit claws.


# NOONDAY AXEMAN

Axe-fall, echo and silence. Noonday silence.
Two miles from here, it is the twentieth century:
cars on the bitumen, powerlines vaulting the farms.
Here, with my axe, I am chopping into the stillness.

Axe-fall, echo and silence. I pause, roll tobacco,
twist a cigarette, lick it. All is still.
I lean on my axe. A cloud of fragrant leaves
hangs over me moveless, pierced everywhere by sky.

Here, I remember all of a hundred years:
candleflame, still night, frost and cattle bells,
the draywheels' silence final in our ears,
and the first red cattle spreading through the hills

and my great-great-grandfather here with his first sons,
who would grow old, still speaking with his Scots accent,
having never seen those highlands that they sang of.
A hundred years. I stand and smoke in the silence.

A hundred years of clearing, splitting, sawing,
a hundred years of timbermen, ringbarkers, fencers
and women in kitchens, stoking loud iron stoves
year in, year out, and singing old songs to their children

have made this silence human and familiar
no farther than where the farms rise into foothills,
and, in that time, how many have sought their graves
or fled to the cities, maddened by this stillness?

Things are so wordless. These two opposing scarves
I have cut in my red-gum squeeze out jewels of sap
and stare. And soon, with a few more axe-strokes,
the tree will grow troubled, tremble, shift its crown

and, leaning slowly, gather speed and colossally
crash down and lie between the standing trunks.
And then, I know, of the knowledge that led my forebears
to drink and black rage and wordlessness, there will be silence.

After the tree falls, there will reign the same silence
as stuns and spurs us, enraptures and defeats us,
as seems to some a challenge, and seems to others
to be waiting here for something beyond imagining.

Axe-fall, echo and silence. Unhuman silence.
A stone cracks in the heat. Through the still twigs, radiance
stings at my eyes. I rub a damp brow with a handkerchief
and chop on into the stillness. Axe-fall and echo.

The great mast murmurs now. The scarves in its trunk
crackle and squeak now, crack and increase as the hushing
weight of high branches heels outward, and commences
tearing and falling, and the collapse is tremendous.

Twigs fly, leaves puff and subside. The severed trunk
slips off its stump and drops along its shadow.
And then there is no more. The stillness is there
as ever. And I fall to lopping branches.

Axe-fall, echo and silence. It will be centuries
before many men are truly at home in this country,
and yet, there have always been some, in each generation,
there have always been some who could live in the presence of silence.

And some, I have known them, men with gentle broad hands,
who would die if removed from these unpeopled places,
some again I have seen, bemused and shy in the cities
you have built against silence, dumbly trudging through noise

past the railway stations, looking up through the traffic
at the smoky halls, dreaming of journeys, of stepping
down from the train at some upland stop to recover
the crush of dry grass underfoot, the silence of trees.

Axe-fall, echo and silence. Dreaming silence.
Though I myself run to the cities, I will forever
be coming back here to walk, knee-deep in ferns,
up and away from this metropolitan century,

to remember my ancestors, axemen, dairymen, horse-breakers,
now coffined in silence, down with their beards and dreams,
who, unwilling or rapt, despairing or very patient,
made what amounts to a human breach in the silence,

made of their lives the rough foundation of legends –
men must have legends, else they will die of strangeness –
then died in their turn, each, after his own fashion,
resigned or agonized, from silence into great silence.

Axe-fall, echo and axe-fall. Noonday silence.
Though I go to the cities, turning my back on these hills,
for the talk and dazzle of cities, for the sake of belonging
for months and years at a time to the twentieth century,

the city will never quite hold me. I will be always
coming back here on the up-train, peering, leaning
out of the window to see, on far-off ridges,
the sky between the trees, and over the racket
of the rails to hear the echo and the silence.

I shoulder my axe and set off home through the stillness.


## THE AWAY-BOUND TRAIN

FOR CON KIRILOFF

I stand in a house of trees, and it is evening:
at the foot of the stairs, a creek runs grey with sand.

A rocking, unending dim sound,
a racket as if of a train,
wears through my sleep, and I wake
to find it late afternoon

at which I sit up, rub my eyes –
beneath us, the carriage-wheels moan
on their winter-wet, wind-polished rails,
but the train hurries on, hurries on.

The loco horn beams out its admonition
at a weatherboard village standing on the fields.

The near hills rise steeply and fall,
the hills farther off settle down:
I light up a cigarette, wipe
my breath from the cold window-pane.

The upland farms are all bare,
except where dark, storm-matted fern
has found its way down from the heights,
or landslides have brought down raw stone

for, outside, it's silent July,
when wet rocks stare from the hills
and thistles grow, and the rain
walks with the wind through the fields –

and this is my country, passing by me forever:
beyond these hills and paddocks lies the world.

Outside, it is timeless July,
when horses' hoofs puncture the chill
green ground, mud dogging their steps,
and summer's plough sleeps in the barn,

when rabbits camp up in the mouths
of flooded burrows, and dogs
under creekbanks wince at the thump
of a gun fired close to the earth.

The cold time, the season of clouds
beyond the end of the year,
when boxwood chunks glare in the stove –
but that is the past. I am here.

I look across the clear, receding landscape:
from a distant ridge, a horseman eyes the train.

The train never slackens its speed:
and iron bridge echoes, is gone,
on the far bank, twilit and tall,
the green timber gathers us in.

And we dash through the forest, my face,
reflected, wanders and sways
on the glass of the windowpane, and
I press my nose to my nose ...

the loco horn sounds far across the uplands:
a man with no past has all too many futures.

I take out a book, read a phrase
five times – and put the book down.
The window-sash chatters. My mind
trails far in the wake of the train

where, away in the left-behind hills,
through paddock and cattlecamp I
go drifting down valleys towards
the peopled country of sleep ...

I wait in the house. It is raining in the forest.
If I move or speak, the house will not be there.


## SPRING HAIL

    This is for spring and hail, that you may remember:
    for a boy long ago, and a pony that could fly.

We had huddled together a long time in the shed
in the scent of vanished corn and wild bush birds,
and then the hammering faltered, and the torn
cobwebs ceased their quivering and hung still
from the nested rafters. We became uneasy
at the silence that grew about us, and came out.

The beaded violence had ceased. Fresh-minted hills
smoked, and the heavens swirled and blew away.
The paddocks were endless again, and all around
leaves lay beneath their trees, and cakes of moss.
Sheep trotted and propped, and shook out ice from their wool.
The hard blue highway that had carried us there
fumed as we crossed it, and the hail I scooped
from underfoot still bore the taste of sky
and hurt my teeth, and crackled as we walked.

    This is for spring and hail, that you may remember
    a boy long ago, and a pony that could fly.

With the creak and stop of a gate, we started to trespass:
my pony bent his head and drank up grass
while I ate ice, and wandered, and ate ice.
There was a peach tree growing wild by a bank
and under it and round, sweet dented fruit
weeping pale juice amongst hail-shotten leaves,
and this I picked up and ate till I was filled.

I sat on a log then, listening with my skin
to the secret feast of the sun, to the long wet worms
at work in the earth, and, deeper down, the stones
beneath the earth, uneasy that their sleep
should be troubled by dreams of water soaking down,
and I heard with my ears the creek on its bed of mould
moving and passing with a mothering sound.

>   This is for spring and hail, that you may remember
>   a boy long ago on a pony that could fly.

My pony came up then and stood by me,
waiting to be gone. The sky was now
spotless from dome to earth, and balanced there
on the cutting-edge of mountains. It was time
to leap to the saddle and go, a thunderbolt whirling
sheep and saplings behind, and the rearing fence
that we took at a bound, and the old, abandoned shed
forgotten behind, and the paddock forgotten behind.
Time to shatter peace and lean into spring
as into a battering wind, and be rapidly gone.

It was time, high time, the highest and only time
to stand in the stirrups and shout out, blind with wind
for the height and clatter of ridges to be topped
and the racing downward after through the lands
of floating green and bridges and flickering trees.
It was time, as never again it was time
to pull the bridle up, so the racketing hooves

fell silent as we ascended from the hill
above the farms, far up to where the hail
formed and hung weightless in the upper air,
charting the birdless winds with silver roads
for us to follow and be utterly gone.

    This is for spring and hail, that you may remember
    a boy and a pony long ago who could fly.


# DRIVING THROUGH SAWMILL TOWNS

*1*

In the high cool country,
having come from the clouds,
down a tilting road
into a distant valley,
you drive without haste. Your windscreen parts the forest,
swaying and glancing, and jammed midday brilliance
crouches in clearings ...
then you come across them,
the sawmill towns, bare hamlets built of boards
with perhaps a store,
perhaps a bridge beyond
and a little sidelong creek alive with pebbles.

*2*

The mills are roofed with iron, have no walls:
you look straight in as you pass, see lithe men working,

the swerve of a winch,
dim dazzling blades advancing
through a trolley-borne trunk
till it sags apart
in a manifold sprawl of weatherboards and battens.

The men watch you pass:
when you stop your car and ask them for directions,
tall youths look away –
it is the older men who
come out in blue singlets and talk softly to you.

Beside each mill, smoke trickles out of mounds
of ash and sawdust.

3

You glide on through town,
your mudguards damp with cloud.
The houses there wear verandahs out of shyness,
all day in calendared kitchens, women listen
for cars on the road,
lost children in the bush,
a cry from the mill, a footstep –
nothing happens.

The half-heard radio sings
its song of sidewalks.

Sometimes a woman, sweeping her front step,
or a plain young wife at a tankstand fetching water
in a metal bucket will turn round and gaze
at the mountains in wonderment,
looking for a city.

4

Evenings are very quiet. All around
the forest is there.
As night comes down, the houses watch each other:
a light going out in a window here has meaning.

You speed away through the upland,
glare through towns
and are gone in the forest, glowing on far hills.

On summer nights
ground-crickets sing and pause.
In the dark of winter, tin roofs sough with rain,
downpipes chafe in the wind, agog with water.
Men sit after tea
by the stove while their wives talk, rolling a dead match
between their fingers,
thinking of the future.


## EVENING ALONE AT BUNYAH

*1*

My father, widowed, fifty-six years old,
sits washing his feet.
The innocent sly charm
is back in his eye of late years, and tonight
he's going dancing.

*I wouldn't go tonight,* he says to me
by way of apology. *You sure you won't come?*
*What for?* I ask. *You know I only dance
on bits of paper.* He nods and says, *Well, if
any ghosts come calling, don't let 'em eat my cake.*

I bring him a towel and study his feet afresh:
they make my own feel coarse. They are so small,
so delicate he can scarcely bear to walk
barefoot to his room to find his dancing shoes
and yet all day he works in hobnailed boots
out in the forest, clearing New South Wales.

No ghosts will come, Dad. I know you dote on cake.
I know how some women who bake it dote on you.
It gets them nowhere.
You are married still.

2

Home again from the cities of the world.
Cool night, and the valley relaxes after heat,
the earth contracts, the planks of the old house creak,
making one more adjustment, joist to nail,
nail to roof, roof to the touch of dew.

Smoke stains, rafters, whitewash rubbed off planks ...
yet this is one house that Jerry built to last:
when windstorms came, and other houses lost
roofs and verandahs, this gave just enough
and went unscathed, for all the little rain
that sifted through cracks, the lamps puffed out by wind
sucked over the wallplate, and the occasional bat
silly with fear at having misplaced the dark.

When I was a child, my father was ashamed
of this shabby house. It signified for him
hard work and unjust poverty. There would come
a day when he'd tear it down and build afresh.
The day never came. But that's another poem.

No shame I felt in those days was my own.
It can be enough to read books and camp in a house.
Enough, at fourteen, to watch your father sit
at the breakfast table nursing his twelve-gauge
shotgun, awaiting the doubtful reappearance
of a snake's head at a crack in the cement
of the skillion fireplace floor.

The blood's been sluiced
away, and the long wrecked body of the snake
dug out and gone to ash these thirteen years,
but the crack's still there,
and the scores the buckshot ripped beside the stove.

3

There is a glow in the kitchen window now
that was not there in the old days. They have set
three streetlights up along the Gloucester road
for cows to stray by, and night birds to shun,
for the road itself's not paved, and there's no town
in the valley yet at all.
It is hoped there will be.

Today, out walking, I considered stones.
It used to be said that I must know each one
on the road by its first name, I was such a dawdler,
such a head-down starer.
I picked up
a chunk of milk-seamed quartz, thumbed off the clay,
let the dry light pervade it and collect,
eliciting shifting gleams, revealing how
the specific strength of a stone fits utterly
into its form and yet reflects the grain
and tendency of the mother-lode, the mass
of a vanished rock-sill tipping one small stone
slightly askew as it weighs upon your palm,
and then I threw it back towards the sun
to thump down on a knoll
where it may move a foot in a thousand years.

Today, having come back, summer was all mirror
tormenting me. I fled down cattle tracks
chest-deep in the earth, and pushed in under twigs
to sit by cool water speeding over rims
of blackened basalt, the tall light reaching me.

Since those moth-grimed streetlamps came,
my dark is threatened.

4

I stand, and turn, and wander through the house,
avoiding those floorboards that I know would creak,
to the other verandah. Here is where I slept,
and here is where, one staring day, I felt
a presence at my back, and whirled in fright
to face my father's suit, hung out to air.

This country is my mind. I lift my face
and count my hills, and linger over one:
Deer's, steep, bare-topped, where eagles nest below
the summit in scrub oaks, and where I take
my city friends to tempt them with my past.

Across the creek and the paddocks of the moon
four perfect firs stand dark beside a field
lost long ago, which holds a map of rooms.
This was the plot from which we transplants sprang.
The trees grew straight. We burgeoned and spread far.
I think of doors and rooms beneath the ground,
deep rabbit rooms, thin candlelight of days ...
and, turning quickly, walk back through the house.

5

Night, and I watch the moonrise through the door.
Sitting alone's a habit of mind with me ...
for which I'll pay in full. That has begun.
But meanwhile I will sit and watch the moon.

My father will be there now, at a hall
in the dark of the country, shining at the waltz,
spry and stately, twirling at formal speeds
on a roaring waxed-plank floor.
The petrol lamps
sizzle and glare now the clapping has died down.
They announce some modern dance. He steps outside
to where cigarettes glow sparsely in the dark,
joins some old friends and yarns about his son.

Beneath this moon, an ancient radiance comes
back from far hillsides where the tall pale trunks
of ringbarked trees haphazardly define
the edge of dark country I could not afford
to walk in at night alone
lest I should hear
the barking of dogs from a clearing where no house
has ever stood, and, walking down a road
in the wilderness, meet a man who waited there
beside a creek to tell me what I sought.

Father, come home soon.
Come home alive.


## THE PRINCES' LAND

FOR VALERIE, ON HER BIRTHDAY

Leaves from the ancient forest gleam
in the meadow brook, and dip, and pass.
Six maidens dance on the level green,
a seventh toys with an hourglass,

letting fine hours sink away,
turning to sift them back again.
An idle prince, with a cembalo,
sings to the golden afternoon.

Two silver knights, met in a wood,
tilt at each other, clash and bow.
Upon a field semé of birds
Tom Bread-and-Cheese sleeps by his plough.

But now a deadly stillness comes
upon the brook, upon the green,
upon the seven dancing maids,
the dented knights are dulled to stone.

The hours in the hourglass
are stilled to fine fear, and the wood
to empty burning. Tom the hind
walks in his sleep in pools of blood.

The page we've reached is grey with pain.
Some will not hear, some run away,
some go to write books of their own,
some few, as the tale grows cruel, sing Hey

but we who have no other book
spell out the gloomy, blazing text,
page by slow page, wild year by year,
our hope refined to what comes next,

and yet attentive to each child
who says he's looked ahead and seen
how the tale will go, or spied
a silver page two pages on,

for, as the themes knit and unfold,
somewhere far on, where all is changed,
beyond all twists of grief and fear,
we look to glimpse that land again:

the brook descends in music through
the meadows of that figured land,
nine maidens from the ageless wood
move in their circles, hand in hand.

Two noble figures, counterchanged,
fence with swift passion, pause and bow.
All in a field impaled with sun
the Prince of Cheese snores by his plough.

Watching bright hours file away,
turning to sift them back again,
the Prince of Bread, with a cembalo
hums to the golden afternoon.

## ILL MUSIC

My cousin loved the violin
and played it gracefully in tune
except when, touching certain chords,
he fell down, shrieked and bit at boards
till blood and froth stood on his chin.

Some talked of Providence, or sin,
or feared the rot had now got in
to a family tree once pruned with swords –
but these are words.

And Jim said little when his kin
found a place to place him in,
nor did he ever tell his guards
how notes may run, and catch, and veer towards
that pitch where shrieks and suns begin –
for these are words.


## TROOP TRAIN RETURNING

Beyond the Divide
the days become immense,
beyond our war
in the level lands of wheat,
the things that we defended are still here,
the willow-trees pruned neatly cattle-high,
the summer roads where far-back bullock drays
foundered in earth and mouldered into yarns.
From a ringbarked tree, as we go cheering by
a tower and a whirlwind of white birds,
as we speed by
with a whistle for the plains.

On kitbags in the aisle, old terrors doze,
clumsy as rifles in a peacetime train.

Stopped at a siding
under miles of sun,
I watched a friend I mightn't see again
shyly shake hands, becoming a civilian,
and an old Ford truck
receding to the sky.

I walk about. The silo, tall as Time,
casts on bright straws its coldly southward shade.

All things are spaced out here
each in its value.
The pepper-trees beside the crossroads pub
are dim with peace,
pumpkins are stones
in fields so loosely green.

In a little while, I'll be afraid to look
out for my house and the people that I love,
they have been buried in the moon so long.

Beyond all wars
in the noonday lands of wheat,
the whistle summons shouters from the bar,
refills the train with jokes and window noise.
This perfect plain
casts out the things we've done
as we jostle here, relaxed as farmers, smoking,
held at this siding
till the red clicks green.


## BLOOD

Pig-crowds in successive, screaming pens
we still to greedy drinking, trough by trough,
tusk-heavy boars, fat mud-beslabbered sows:
Gahn, let him drink, you slut, you've had enough!

Laughing and grave by turns, in milky boots,
we stand and yarn, and whet our butcher's knife,
sling cobs of corn – Hey, careful of his nuts!
It's made you cruel, all that smart city life.

In paper spills, we roll coarse, sweet tobacco.
That's him down there, the one we'll have to catch,
that little Berkshire with the pointy ears.
I call him Georgie. Here, you got a match?

The shadow of a cloud moves down the ridge,
on summer hills, a patch of autumn light.
My cousin sheathes in dirt his priestly knife.
They say pigs see the wind. You think that's right?

I couldn't say. It sounds like a fair motto.
There are some poets – Right, he's finished now.
Melon-sized and muscular, with shrieks
the pig is seized and bundled anyhow

his twisting strength permits, then sternly held.
My cousin tests his knife, sights for the heart
and sinks the blade with one long, even push.
A wild scream bursts as knife and victim part

and hits the showering heavens as our beast
flees straight downfield, choked in his pumping gush
that feeds the earth, and drags him to his knees –
Bleed, Georgie, pump! And with a long-legged rush

my cousin is beside the thing he killed
and pommels it, and lifts it to the sun:
I should have knocked him out, poor little bloke.
It gets the blood out if you let them run.

We hold the dangling meat. Wet on its chest
the narrow cut, the tulip of slow blood.
We better go. We've got to scald him next.
Looking at me, my cousin shakes his head:

What's up, old son? You butchered things before …
it's made you squeamish, all that city life.
Sly gentleness regards me, and I smile:
You're wrong, you know. I'll go and fetch the knife.

I walk back up the trail of crowding flies,
back to the knife which pours deep blood, and frees
sun, fence and hill, each to its holy place.
Strong in my valleys, I may walk at ease.

A world I thought sky-lost by leaning ships
in the depth of our life – I'm in that world once more.
Looking down, we praise for its firm flesh
the creature killed according to the Law.


## THE ABOMINATION

Long before dawn, I rose by Paddy's Lantern,
lit up my own and walked through miles of dew
with my striding shadow, adze and burlap bag
to check my traps. The woods were cold and deep,
the fence on the ridgeline tingled, wet with stars.

Away below, in a gully facing in
towards the dark, a stumphole fire glowed
but I looked away and went on with my round,
killing each rabbit with a practised chop
and dropping it, still straining, in my bag.

A winding course of unhurried killings led
me down the dark to my farthest trap, which lay
a short walk from the fire. Here I killed
one final time, and slung my heavy bag
to approach the blaze – as I had known I would.

Behind the black terrazzo of old heat
light glared from crumbling pits. Old roots are tough
but when they catch, their blinding rings inch deep
and rage for months and suck your breath away
if you kneel before them too long, peering in ...

as I knew I had by the pallor of the sky.
Scrambling up to go, I told myself
no harm in this. I was just looking down
to see how far back the earth might be unsafe.
It wouldn't do to break through on such heat.

Budded with light on light, the butts of glare
in their fire-burrows were a deeper fact
that stared down my evasions, and I found
a rabbit in my hands and, in my mind,
an ancient thing. And it was quickly done.

Afterwards, I tramped the smoking crust
heavily in on fire, stench and beast
to seal them darkly under with my fear
and all the things my sacrifice might mean,
so hastily performed past all repair.


## ONCE IN A LIFETIME, SNOW

FOR CHRIS AND MARY SHARAH

Winters at home brought wind,
black frost and raw
grey rain in barbed-wire fields,
but never more

until the day my uncle
rose at dawn
and stepped outside – to find
his paddocks gone,

his cattle to their hocks
in ghostly ground
and unaccustomed light
for miles around.

And he stopped short, and gazed
lit from below,
and half his wrinkles vanished
murmuring *Snow*.

A man of farm and fact
he stared to see
the facts of weather raised
to a mystery

white on the world he knew
and all he owned.
Snow? Here? he mused. I see.
High time I learned.

Here, guessing what he meant
had much to do
with that black earth dread old men
are given to,

he stooped to break the sheer
crust with delight
at finding the cold unknown
so deeply bright,

at feeling it take his prints
so softly deep,
as if it thought he knew
enough to sleep,

or else so little he
might seek to shift
its weight of wintry light
by a single drift,

perceiving this much, he scuffed
his slippered feet
and scooped a handful up
to taste, and eat

in memory of the fact
that even he
might not have seen the end
of reality ...

Then, turning, he tiptoed in
to a bedroom, smiled,
and wakened a murmuring child
and another child.


## RECOURSE TO THE WILDERNESS

FOR PETER BARDEN

Towards the end of the long Australian peace
when I was a twenty-two-year-old with failings,
ostentatious, untravelled, with a gift for dependence,
penury had grown stale; my childhood was in danger,
so I preceded you, in all but spirit,
to the Outside country
where the sealed roads end,
the far, still Centre.

Today, a sequence from that equivocal season
danced in my memory:
I saw myself away in South Australia,
still a novice, but learning,
having already felt frost through my blanket,
learned how to dig a hip-hole, to sleep quickly,
how to camp in good cover, especially in cities.
A month from home, barely,
and I'd even made a beginning

in the more advanced, more fruitful major subjects:
jettisoning weight, non-planning, avoidance of thought
in favour of landscape, stones and the travelling sky.

All that day, I had traversed the German country
– vast fields of September, distant adobe houses –
hungry, such was my mood, for the exotic,
I'd listened for German in casual talk overheard
in winecellar towns at peace with their horizons.

Now it was night. Damp furrows smelt of spring,
cool iron and thistle-stems. Far-off windows shone
approaching, receding. Cars dipped below the world's edge
on unknown roads.

And I walked on and on
upbraiding myself with melancholy pleasure
for past insufficiencies, future humiliations:
*You are always at fault. Nor will this ever change,*
*etcetera, etcetera.*

Later that night
the horror of Hell stared down at me for a great time,
silent, with horns,
till I reared awake, and found
myself bedded down on hay in a dawn-wet paddock
with twenty curious rams foregathered round me.

Under that augury, I hitchhiked on all that day
out of the fenced and fertile south-east districts
and, just on sundown, entered the waterless kingdom.

      o

In the silent lands
time broadens into space.
Approaching Port Augusta, going on,
iron-brown and limitless, the plains
were before me all day. Burnt mountains fell behind
in the glittering sky.

At dawn, the sun would roll up from his lair
in the kiln-dry lake country, fire his heat straight through
the blind grey scrub, awaken me beside wheeltracks
and someone's car, and I would travel on.

At noon, far out in a mirage, I would brew
tea with strangers, yarn about jobs in the North
which I meant not to get
and, chewing quietly, watch maybe an upstart
dust-devil forming miles off, going high
to totter, darken
and, quite suddenly, vanish,
leaving a formless, thinning stain on the heavens.

Where the spirits of sea-cliffs
hovered on the plain
I would remember routines we had invented
for putting spine into shapeless days: the time
we passed at a crouching trot down Wynyard Concourse
telling each other in loud mock-Aranda and gestures
what game we were tracking down what haunted gorge,
frivolous games
but they sustained me like water,

they, and the is-ful ah!-nesses of things.


## THE COMMERCIAL HOTEL

Days of asphalt-blue and gold
murmurous with stout and flies,
lorries bought, allotments sold,

and recent heroes, newly old,
stare at their beer with bloating eyes.
Days of asphalt-blue and gold

dim to saloon bars, where unfold
subtleties of enterprise,
lorries bought, allotments sold,

where, with fingers burnt, the bold
learn to be indirect, and wise.
Days of asphalt-blue and gold

confirm the nation in its mould
of wages, contract and supplies,
lorries bought, allotments sold,

and the brave, their stories told,
age and regard, without surmise,
days of asphalt-blue and gold
lorries bought, allotments sold.


## THE INCENDIARY METHOD

Hungry that year
for a quick resolution
a blasting reply
to clean out the mind
of the year's slow piling
of question on question
I fumbled a match
and lit the grey, tattered
fuse of a paperbark
tree in the swamps
and watched it howl up
a tower of flame,
sweet oil and smuts
for my summer banner
over the pools
and startled beasts
feeding on rushes.

The fire swarmed
and then petered out
in a trickle of remnant
sparks and small candles
and I said to myself
in the guilt of my gleeful
search for more tea-trees
with tarpaper trunks,
there are more ways than one
of cleansing the spirit
and while I may know
this way can burn cities
it won't burn them here
in the dark of this swamp
a sixty-foot blaze
in the dark of this poem
with only beasts watching
over the pools
and smoking rushes.


## AN ABSOLUTELY ORDINARY RAINBOW

The word goes round Repins,
the murmur goes round Lorenzinis,
at Tattersalls, men look up from sheets of numbers,
the Stock Exchange scribblers forget the chalk in their hands
and men with bread in their pockets leave the Greek Club:
There's a fellow crying in Martin Place. They can't stop him.

The traffic in George Street is banked up for half a mile
and drained of motion. The crowds are edgy with talk
and more crowds come hurrying. Many run in the back streets
which minutes ago were busy main streets, pointing:
There's a fellow weeping down there. No one can stop him.

The man we surround, the man no one approaches
simply weeps, and does not cover it, weeps
not like a child, not like the wind, like a man
and does not declaim it, nor beat his breast, nor even
sob very loudly – yet the dignity of his weeping

holds us back from his space, the hollow he makes about him
in the midday light, in his pentagram of sorrow,
and uniforms back in the crowd who tried to seize him
stare out at him, and feel, with amazement, their minds
longing for tears as children for a rainbow.

Some will say, in the years to come, a halo
or force stood around him. There is no such thing.
Some will say they were shocked and would have stopped him
but they will not have been there. The fiercest manhood,
the toughest reserve, the slickest wit amongst us

trembles with silence, and burns with unexpected
judgements of peace. Some in the concourse scream
who thought themselves happy. Only the smallest children
and such as look out of Paradise come near him
and sit at his feet, with dogs and dusty pigeons.

Ridiculous, says a man near me, and stops
his mouth with his hands, as if it uttered vomit –
and I see a woman, shining, stretch her hand
and shake as she receives the gift of weeping;
as many as follow her also receive it

and many weep for sheer acceptance, and more
refuse to weep for fear of all acceptance,
but the weeping man, like the earth, requires nothing,
the man who weeps ignores us, and cries out
of his writhen face and ordinary body

not words, but grief, not messages, but sorrow,
hard as the earth, sheer, present as the sea –
and when he stops, he simply walks between us
mopping his face with the dignity of one
man who has wept, and now has finished weeping.

Evading believers, he hurries off down Pitt Street.


## WORKING MEN

Seeing the telegram go limp
and their foreman's face go grey and stark,
the fettlers, in their singlets, led him
out, and were gentle in the dark.


## A WALK WITH O'CONNOR

A winter's day of wind, and no horizon.
Out of the vagueness, breakers on cold grey sand.
Leaving Bondi behind, we followed the dim coast south
over tongues of land
between the Pacific and the red-tiled homes,
exulted our way over heights with talk of heroes,
disputed down through scrub to famous coves
and scaled low cliffs, position by quotation,
hand over hand.

At Waverley, where the gravestones stop at the brink,
murmuring words, to the rebel's tomb we went,
an exile's barrow of Erin-go-bragh and pride
in grey-green cement:
we examined the harps, the hounds, the lists of the brave
and, reading the Gaelic, constrained and shamefaced, we tried
to guess what it meant
then, drifting away,
translated Italian off opulent tombstones nearby
in our discontent.

On a farther beach, though,
where mile-long water, folding, crashed on sand
with a shudder of glee
we caught up drift battens, invoking Cuchulain sent mad,
and fought with the sea,
persuading each other that, in our own lives, this
was how it might be,
how, in the nature of purpose and of men,
it might well be.

But farther again
in a place of thorn and cliff
discussing ways
with nightfall closing in
we came to the old forts with their low tomb doors,
ladders of rust, gaunt casemates loud with wind
and the stench of man
and we spoke of the gun crews and the great oiled guns
that all the heydays of our childhood war
had never once engaged an enemy
or made much more than urgent spouts of boil
far out on the shining grid
of a fire-plan ...

I looked at O'Connor
and he spoke to me,
but these were as many aspects of our quest,
I mean the Quest that summons all true men,
as that evening's light
permitted us to see.


SENRYU

Just two hours after
Eternal Life pills came out
someone took thirty.

# THE BALLAD TRAP

In the hanging gorges
the daring compact wears thin,
picking meat from small skeletons,
counting damp notes in a tin,

the rifle birds ringing at noon
in the steep woods,
hard-riding boys dazed at the brink
of their attitudes,

the youngest wheedling for songs,
his back to the night,
dark mountains the very English
for souring delight:

Remember the Escort? Remember
lamps long ago
and manhood filched from the horse police
and a name from Cobb and Co.

Their metre hobbled, the horses
hump their dark life,
longing for marriage, the tall man
sharpens his knife –

Yes, let us sing! cries the Captain
while we have breath.
Better, God knows, than this thinking.
The ballad ends with their death.

# HAYFORK POINT

Dazzling blue eyes
of winter stare from the box-trees
the shadows of barns are thin with frosted straw.

All over the country
the dented light of milk cans.

Cold proteins cling
to the wet-lipped cane-knife blocking
swedes by the sty for a tumult of fat squealers.
For the mouths of following cattle, boys on tractors
bayonet green stacks and hoy them down the sky
green spinning in air.
The bull, looking up,
is drenched in flying meadow.

Pinched hours pass
and farmers lug dull cans
but magpies, dismissing weight, lift over stones now
alighting on wires ever farther off
to balance at behests
of song, and spring

for something has turned
and from the heavens, gently
invisibly, gently
grass goes on falling.


# THE FIRE AUTUMN

The walls of the country this year, the forest escarpments,
the seacoast stump-mountains are fired with amber and buff
like autumn in the Jura, October legends of fall,
some hilltops are sailing the storm-rains with almost bare poles
and the logs that still smoulder in gullies are not far from mist.

Up the steep timber roads, though, in under the heights
you are too close for charm. The fire-killed leaves stick unmoved
like the scales of monsters that lived at too blinding a pitch
to stay in existence. The ruins of bullock-bell trails
are bared to midsummer. The froth of rain rots on black bark.
We have heard that the smoke from this coast was seen far out over
the curve of the earth, on the open Pacific, on islands.
We know certain colours and cooling nuances are gone,
much birdsong, too, some millions of wealth, a few persons
baked in sheet iron. The word *sylvan* cracks in the sun.

But this is order. This is the fire autumn
in the ancient of rocks, the paradise of lost eons.
We have been to see autumn in Europe. It is beautiful but
humanized to despair in those poor remnant woods
with tourist paths leading to every clump of Waldeinsamkeit.
The great year of man has entered a burning season:
the chainsaw, junked beercans, newsprint, the torrents of birth
are one fire with that great autumn the North world conducts
through her nation-states, through the unuttered minds of officials
with every fuel from oil to musicians to fields.
In the year of the moon-shot, the column of Trajan at Rome,
kept prisoner by the Italian government, as Greece
holds the Parthenon (they are not of our world, these monuments)
murmured to us, *Your masters are burning the earth
to keep it in flight round not even the Sun any more
but that sheer point that even the Daystar (mostly) obeys
at the heart of their gravities. The point is smaller than Man
and they're desperate with joy. They have overcome dignity.*
The spiralling captives continued their motionless climb.

Since mankind went critical, time is a fiery screen
on which all the scenes we may call the world play at once,
housewives in the sky, jets over bullock-carts, music,
the updraft of real things drawn spinning into the act
rattles our brains. Reentering calm, some burn up.
Murder forms out of nothing in streets unspeakably adult.

The clatter of fallout scares soldiers from under your clothes.
Of the wealthy, so many are living now in the future
that wombs become wardrobes. Only the poor need be born.

And yet, in clothes that come boxed from that whirlwind
we have walked out among the great aircraft that bend the horizon,
growing ever more beautiful for ever more prodigious flight.
We have handled the taut, racked machine-guns that shot war to shreds
and, circling their complex near-absolute fitness of form
over the mass mud-graves, some have felt themselves leap
clean over the apple-bough wheels of the great star factory.

The cesspools of maturity are heaving with those who leap short.
Some are citing as Europe's last knowledge (Oh burning Israel)
that nothing not founded upon the irrational can stand,
but some land in good country at a venture of kindness
and such is the humour, the grace of the Infinite Man,
that in towns grown at ease with their landscapes, strolling, they find
old cars, weatherboards, dumb oildrums standing in grass
have come into truth as firmly almost as mountains.
Things lacking this radiance not wholly of light, this silence
of momentous containment, the Unrevealed Torah of objects,
spin with the world. They are deadly. On girls bored to sleep
they beget fibro children who wither youth into days.

But some who come to our country as being the farthest
out on earth towards the country they sought
are waiting to hear, where they lie in their deckchairs and graves,
that, with distance, the serious laws of the universe change,
and more, growing native, still find the limitless country
too near for speech. The dignity growing on trees
in the drystick forests, the mines in the waste land, the stones,
is not solar, nor deeply mortal. In dour shirtsleeve joy
they answer the Sun of a universe where it is clear
that this earth is continuous with nothing but the unknown.

Like a distant coast beyond shimmer, too still for cloud,
the trees of my forests and breakaway mountains are feathering
with gold of emergence, with claret, cerise, liquid green,
faint blues fat with powder, new leaves clustered thick down the length
of charcoal-stiff bark. Brush water is licking stones clean.
The tracks of birds glitter. Blunt mountains steer towards noon
and all down December, black thaw will be riding the streams.
For this also is order. This is a farther season
in the ancient of rocks, the paradise of far eons,
and I am asking the dead to wait, with forgiveness,
the innocent planets are grinding their keepers to gold.


## THE CANBERRA REMNANT

Eavesdropping rain
a quiet car
a sense of mountains
in the air,

dark houses sleeping
beneath the freez-
ing drip of Europ-
ean trees,

lost paddock and stone
under the lake
and only a few
souls still awake

to polish a bead,
to turn a page,
to label a fly
or a golden age

in a thousand redeeming
projects they
keep safe from the Government
of the Day.

# TOWARD THE IMMINENT DAYS

FOR GEOFF AND SALLY LEHMANN

*1*

Midmorning, September, and red tractors climb
on a landscape wide as all forgiveness. Clouds
in the west horizon, parrots twinkling down
on Leary's oats, on Stewarts' upturned field –

good friends are blood relations that you choose.
The phrase discovers me in the heart of farmland
harpstringing fences, coming back into my life.
A thick coin flips out of my mouth, I leap over thistles

and I think of your wedding, I make it shine among trees
in a vast evening cattlecamp lit by jewelled pendants, by plates,
by brass lamps suspended on trace chains at great height.
The beams of carlights conjure our bustling assembly.

Now the minister comes, with rapid changes of car,
and all of us, painters, centurions in mufti, horses,
lawyers discoursing on sheepback, all drink up quickly,
the hush of Queensland falling on sculptress and ghost.

As the words begin, your pledges rising, whole branches
of blossom appear on the tree your lives have reached,
from out of sight of land, an incredibly high
hymeneal piping makes my wineglass sing –

or so I choose to remember it in the country
and from that glass I'll drink your health always,
recalling your abundant house, the dancing,
your shovelled cake rich as the history of Calabria.

2

Topping ridges, considering some poor late gift
(my gifts this year are so very nearly ineffable)
I think of a day too great for the calendar numbers
that, faintest in winter, grows like a buried moon,

a radiant season swelling through the horizons
beyond September, mortality crumbling down
till on summer mornings, a farm boy can see through the hills
the roots of pumpkin-vines knotting clean under New England.

With Advent so near beneath a man's pitchfork,
the wild and paddocks rising into each other
in the whole green crescent of the tented air,
to keep the dead at peace, wise farmers talk drought,

Hanrahan's comfort – but wheat is crowding through cities.
Cabinet ministers pace in the light of Canowindra
as cattle cross on the stockroutes, a commonwealth walking,
young men leap rivers and, lounging in grasses that threaten

the smaller brick towns, they long for a splendid alert.
Only marriage will save them. The hills are so riddled with fun
that timber dance-halls hide out in the ruins of whisky
and Holdens surging from under barns at midday

are buffed by almost uncontainable winds
for the woman of seed who is the landscape is seizing
all things in her gift. Verandahs sail home on the hills
till the imminent day is burned remote by the sun.

3

Singing, All living are wild in the imminent days,
I walk into furrows end-on and they rise through my flesh
burying worlds of me. It is the clumsiest dancing,
this walking skewways over worm-ocean that heaps

between skid and crumble with lumped stones in ambush for feet
but it marches with seed and steadiness, knowing the land.
As the dogs set out from the house, minute, black, running,
I am striding on over the fact that it is the earth

that holds our mark longest, that soil dug never returns
to primal coherence. Dead men in the fathoms of fields
sustain without effort millennial dark columns
and to their suspension, the crystal centuries come –

But now I am deep in butter-thick native broom
wading, sky-happy, a cotton-bright drover of bees.
As I break out of flowers, the dogs who have only
chaos for language, and territory dense in their fur,

mob me, leaping, and I am too merry with farms
not to run with them, to trample my shadow on sticks:
outpacing dignity, I collide with sheer landscapes
dancing with dogs in the rain of information.

4

In my aunt's house, the milk jug's beaded crochet cover
tickles the ear. We've eaten boiled things with butter.
Pie spiced like islands, dissolving in cream, is now
dissolving in us. We've reached the teapot of calm.

The table we sit at is fashioned of three immense
beech boards out of England. The minute widths of the years
have been refined in the wood by daughters' daughters.
In the year of Nelson, I notice, the winter was mild.

But our talk is cattle and cricket. My quiet uncle
has spent the whole forenoon sailing a stump-ridden field
of blady-grass and Pleistocene clay never ploughed
since the world's beginning. The Georgic furrow lengthens

in ever more intimate country. But we're talking bails,
stray cattle, brands. In the village of Merchandise Creek
there's a post in a ruined blacksmith shop that bears
a charred-in black-letter script of iron characters,

hooks, bars, conjoined letters, a weird bush syllabary.
It is the language of property seared into skin
but descends beyond speech into the muscles of cattle,
the world of feed as it shimmers in cattle minds.

My uncle, nodding, identifies the owners
(I gather M-bar was mourned by thousands of head).
It has its roots in meadows deeper than Gaelic,
my uncle's knowledge. Farmers longest in Heaven

share slyly with him in my aunt's grave mischievous smile
that shines out of every object in my sight
in these loved timber rooms at the threshold of grass.
The depth in this marriage will heal the twentieth century.

5

Broad afternoon. The hired boy and I
stack saccaline in the hammer-mill by the sheds
till the air is coarse with silage. Clouds of fowls
and black, shape-shifting turkeys frisk our output

but we are watching how my cousins flare
around the cowbails, yarding up fresh milkers,
knee-gripping buckets (strophe, antistrophe);
no primitive bush pumpkin eaters here,

these are prosperous, well-mannered children,
gentle with cows. Even the youngest's a dairyman
concerned with his poddy-calves. No one here will be
a visitor gnawed by lifelong celebration.

We look at them. Even the hired boy knows,
at his age, that freedom is memory. He sees hope
in asking me about cities. How can I tell him
the cities are debris driven by explosions

whose regulation takes a merciless cunning?
I love my cities too well not to start at least there.
I turn his question away, out into the hills
where the bold rabbit-shooter may learn his life from a pool

*or consider the turkeys* (their splendour coherent with filth)
*if they mistake your toes for corn, look out!*
*my grandfather vomited once and our fowls got blind drunk* –
I rack my past for a health the boy can use.

6

In the land of cows-to-milk
there was once a wobbly calf
and he grew to be a bull
scraping up armorial dirt
with a pedigree to bellow
in the bullness of his season
and we used to chase him home –
whoa back bull!
through our neighbours' flagrant fences
till my father linked a chain
round his horns to catch and lead:
You will save your herd-improvements
for our own herd, mister bull!
He was docile for a time
till he found he was the strong one
and began to trot – whoa bull!

Whoa bull – and the running started
as depicted in the friezes.
Loop his chain around a sapling
(wrench of splinters) try a tree!

Block him, yard him, bloody bull,
I'll sell you for dogmeat, screamed
my short-legged father, clinging, swinging
on the chain and prancing faster
than the sons of man can run
skipping on the ringbarked hills
stumbling, leaping on the mountains.
Jersey farmer, Jersey bull
raging under the horizons
until, sometime after dark,
soaked with tropic and Antarctic
spray and dust of Innamincka
in murderous mutual respect
man and bull would stagger home
linked, supporting one another
wheezing Corn, moaning Supper
shedding forests from their chain.

When you see him, ask my father.

7

Dog roses, wild clematis, indigo
crossing the creek on my mind's feet, though,
I walk on home where the stars are thinnest, glancing
back at the village with one human house

that is my uncle's farm. Nightjars glide through me,
snipping winged ants. Into the brimming hills
cattle graze beyond the human marriages,
and the one-globe kitchen windows, miles apart,

approach the quiet of boats far out on the year
whose wake is all that will persist of them.
What lasts is the voyage of families down their name.
Houses pass into Paradise continually,

voices, loved fields, all wearing away into Heaven.
As the cornplanter sings out to the rising month
bush-hidden creeks in the rabbit country wash
like a clear stone in my mind, the heavenly faculty.

Hiles' paddock leans on its three-strand fence in the dark
bending the road a little with its history.
Our lives are refined by remotest generations.
Months late, I catch up with your wedding once again,

the candles laughter chicken-legs speeches champagne
I pass with a wave (lifting a friend from the wheeltracks)
and full of a lasting complicity, old henchman,
about the life of this world, strike home over grass.

For your wedding, I wish you the frequent image of farms.


## LAMENT FOR THE COUNTRY SOLDIERS

The king of honour, louder than of England,
cried on the young men to a gallant day
and ate the hearts of those who would not go

for the gathering ranks were the Chosen Company
that each man in his lifetime seeks, and finds,
some for an hour, some beyond recall.

When to prove their life, they set their lives at risk
and in the ruins of horizons died
one out of four, in the spreading rose of their honour

they didn't see the badge upon their hat
was the ancient sword that points in all directions.
The symbol hacked the homesteads even so.

The static farms withstood it to the end,
the galloping telegrams ceasing, the exchanges
ringing no more in the night of the stunned violin,

43

and in the morning of insult, the equal remember
ribaldry, madness, the wire jerking with friends,
ironic salutes for the claimants of the fox-hunt

as, camped under tin like rabbiters in death's gully,
they stemmed the endless weather of grey men and steel
and, first of all armies, stormed into great fields.

But it was a weight beyond speech, the proven nation,
on beasts and boys. Newborn experiment withered.
Dull horror rotting miles wide in the memory of green.

Touching money, the white feather crumpled to ash,
cold lies grew quickly in the rank decades
as, far away, the ascendant conquered courage,

as we debauched the faith we were to keep
with the childless singing on the morning track,
the Sportsmen's Thousand leaping on the mountains,

now growing remote, beneath their crumbling farms,
in the district light, their fading companies
with the king of honour, deeper than of England

though the stones of increase glitter with their names.


## THE CONQUEST

Phillip was a kindly, rational man:
Friendship and Trust will win the natives, Sir.
Such was the deck the Governor walked upon.

One deck below, lieutenants hawked and spat.
One level lower, and dank nightmares grew.
Small floating Englands where our world began.

o

And what was trust when the harsh dead swarmed ashore
and warriors, trembling, watched the utterly strange
hard clouds, dawn beings, down there where time began,

so alien the eye could barely fix
blue parrot-figures wrecking the light with change,
man-shapes digging where no yam roots were?

o

The Governor proffers cloth and English words,
the tribesmen defy him in good Dhuruwal.
Marines stand firm, known warriors bite their beards.

Glass beads are scattered in that gulf of style
but pickpockets squeal, clubbed in imagination,
as naked Indians circle them like birds.

o

They won't Respond. They threaten us. Drive them off.
In genuine grief, the Governor turns away.
Blowflies form trinkets for a harsher grief.

As the sickness of the earth bites into flesh
trees moan like women, striplings collapse like trees –
fever of Portsmouth hulks, the Deptford cough.

o

It makes dogs furtive, what they find to eat
but the noonday forest will not feed white men.
Capture some Natives, quick. Much may be learned

indeed, on both Sides. Sir! And Phillip smiles.
Two live to tell the back lanes of his smile
and the food ships come, and the barracks rise as planned.

o

And once again the Governor goes around
with his Amity. The yeasts of reason work,
triangle screams confirm the widening ground.

45

No one records what month the first striped men
mounted a clawing child, then slit her throat
but the spear hits Phillip with a desperate sound.

o

The thoughtful savage with Athenian flanks
fades from the old books here. The sketchers draw
pipe-smoking cretins jigging on thin shanks

poor for the first time, learning the Crown Lands tune.
The age of unnoticed languages begins
and Phillip, recovering, gives a nodded thanks.

o

McEntire speared! My personal Huntsman, speared!
Ten Heads for this, and two alive to hang!
A brave lieutenant cools it, bid by bid,

to a decent six. The punitive squads march off
without result, but this quandong of wrath
ferments in slaughters for a hundred years.

o

They couldn't tell us how to farm their skin.
They camped with dogs in the rift glens of our mind
till their old men mumbled who the stars had been.

They had the noon trees' spiritual walk.
Pathetic with sores, they could be suddenly not,
the low horizon strangely concealing them.

o

A few still hunt way out beyond philosophy
where nothing is sacred till it is your flesh
and the leaves, the creeks shine through their poverty

or so we hope. We make our conquests, too.
The ruins at our feet are hard to see.
For all the generous Governor tried to do

the planet he had touched began to melt
though he used much Reason, and foreshadowed more
before he recoiled into his century.


## THE BALLAD OF JIMMY GOVERNOR

H.M. PRISON, DARLINGHURST, 18TH JANUARY 1901

You can send for my breakfast now, Governor.
The colt from Black Velvet's awake
and the ladies all down from the country
are gathered outside for my sake.

Soon be all finished, the running.
No tracks of mine lead out of here.
Today, I take that big step
on the bottom rung of the air
and be in Heaven for dinner.
Might be the first jimbera there.

The Old People don't go to Heaven,
good thing. My mother might meet
that stockman feller her father
and him cut her dead in the street.
Mother, today I'll be dancing
your way and his way on numb feet.

But a man's not a rag to wipe snot on,
I got that much into their heads,
them hard white sunbonnet ladies
that turned up their short lips and said
my wife had a slut's eye for colour.
I got that into their head

and the cow-cockies' kids plant up chimneys
they got horse soldiers out with the Law
after Joe and lame Jack and tan Jimmy –
but who learnt us how to make war
on women, old men, babies?
It ain't all one way any more.

The papers, they call us bushrangers:
that would be our style, I daresay,
bushrangers on foot with our axes.
It sweetens the truth, anyway.
They don't like us killing their women.
Their women kill us every day.

And the squatters are peeing their moleskins,
that's more than a calf in the wheat,
it's Jimmy the fencer, running
along the top rail in the night,
it's the Breelong mob crossing the ranges
with rabbitskins soft on their feet.

But now Jack in his Empire brickyard
has already give back his shoes
and entered the cleanliness kingdom,
the Commonwealth drums through the walls
and I'm weary of news.

I'm sorry, old Jack, I discharged you,
you might have enjoyed running free
of plonk and wet cornbags and colour
with us pair of outlaws. But see,
you can't trust even half a whitefeller.
You died of White Lady through me.

They tried me once running, once standing:
one time ought to do for the drop.
It's more trial than you got, I hear, Joe,
your tommyhawk's chipped her last chop.
I hope you don't mind I got lazy
when the leaks in my back made me stop.

If any gin stands in my print
I'll give her womb sorrow and dread,
if a buck finds our shape in the tussocks
I'll whiten the hair in his head,
but a man's not a rag to wipe boots on
and I got that wrote up, bright red,

where even fine ladies can read it
who never look at the ground
for a man that ain't fit to breed from
may make a terrible bound
before the knacker's knife gets him.
Good night to you, father. Sleep sound.

Fetch in my breakfast, Governor,
I have my journey to make
and the ladies all down from the country
are howling outside for my sake.


## SMLE

*1*

January, heat. Raw saplings stand like cattle
in the distance of farms. Cornfields out there decaying
to slatternly paper in the blacksnake days ...
Perched in this tree against the eastern sun

I am watching the shallows where my cousins toss
slow-sinking bait, small things that try to swim.
The river burns my face. Islands of wind –
my shot surrounds me, flooding upward, knocking

birds by the hundreds from the swamp-oak fringe
to cry and escape the wave that fades and fades.
Yelling Three! my cousins, wading out, Four!
and I skither down barefeet-first where flung-out mullet

almost move. The utter weight that annulled them
will not stop. It burns them hugely with grass
in the numb dimension, gill-furrows ravaged by specks
their fins fibrillate. They are swimming away in their muscles

but what has remained of the universe won't give –
we strip a swamp-oak branch to thread them on
and revert to farmers. I eject a spent shell,
a tang of brass, a seed that will not grow

2

except in solitude. My Lee Enfield goes home
slung athwart my shoulder, heavy as talent.
Neither a musket, the weapon of masses by rank,
nor a machine-gun, guardian of statistics,

it points at country where it is roughly at home
in obsolescence. Pity the road-signs that lead
into that legend of billy tea, post-and-rail fence
and jackaroo, pulped in the wired slough at Pozières,

the acceptable shillings. Bayonet-lug to butt-plate,
impassive as the true touchstone, you gleam, old rifle,
tall as my hip. I almost followed you once.
I have new masters now, though. They are rewriting the world.

They make me homesick for honour, that terrible country
the poor still believe in. But let's evade the modernities,
mechanical recoil, furious cycle of gas.
Much that you taught me I have slowly learned,

the way you could contain insupportable pressure
just long enough is still germane to my shoulder
like the line of your sights on a plane above your stock
and the burned steel light in your barrel, a rational abyss –

3

I think it is under the Pyrenees, that city.
A gunsmith is shaping a spiral tube from flat steel;
Homage, murmur the killed, to Catalonia
and the Prussian needles are witching the peasants to clay

but Copernicus' wheel is cutting the grooves that expelled us
to whistle up nations in deep glades of the world.
Not by the plough alone did the grain cities come.
Landtaker's title I sing, and its fulminate seal.

At Bunker Hill, though, on a bright day, the wind in the lanes
is freezing squire and scullion clean through their jack.
The men on the hillside are enjoying their skill
as much as their principles. But all servility reels

from the shock of that day. There is almost a moment,
a longbow time of voices speaking equality
and candid with weapons. Oh where will the poor gibbet hide?
They'll sentence me next time, growls Ben Hall. So I'll earn it.

The man with the rifle reversed and black-powder beard
has the air of one looking farther into republics.
Thanks for the arms, Colonel. We'll know when to salute
and the delegates saying We'll have no earlier gods.

These things were the New World. It lasted as long as the wilds.
Now the addicts of wheels, dug in out of sight beneath boredom,
are hiding their children for safety among the ascendancies.
The New World erodes through plastic and joins the dark stream.

The children are way ahead with their mullet emblem.
Forward, the Murrays! In the mountain country
above the farms, I could hold out, eat birds –
I smile away the small madness of preparation,

replacing the bolt. Less easy to smile away man-sized
kangaroos spurting, downed statesmen kicking like deer
in the poisonous ruin of courage we have achieved.
The moon-shot loose in my pocket, I walk among trees.

4

Unlocking, they rise in me, the deep-stacked rifles,
Mauser, Garand, Carcano, Dreyse, Lebel,
straight pull and falling block, Mannlicher's clip ...
rifles, at such attention all their days,

what else could come out of them but death?
And there is no machine unquestioned by their oiled
and summary grace. Your rod and staff, old Cain,
have battered us human. How few can stand even that.

Only boys argue, or cheer, hearing weapons condemned:
the invocation shines clearly enough between cries.
How many are there could bear the vision of history,
let alone Nature? Grooved turn-bolt receiver, tongued sear.

For many boys, it is the first pressure of history,
not to say power, a rifle slapped in their hands
whose steel eye calibrates the windage of politics
as that other eye is said to measure love

by wise adolescents in a belt-fed epoch.
The aimed jets whining, the boys facing front on new grass
glory in the green vortex that whirls them away.
The spirit of ultimate ground on the wreckage of green

is metal and wood, as ever, in two bloody hands.
Of those who shoot, some few are riflemen.
Cold claimants mine their Versailles from the fat of the rest.
I would pay many gold teeth for a softer conviction.

5

There are humans truly unwarlike. They live well guarded.
They are protected by everything on earth.
It is the far rim of things their chimneys sustain
from the warrior pent among soldiers, the corporal suddenly

leading his company, the naked youth trap-shooting Turks.
There are also wolves in sheep country who recommend grass
and salvations so avid that blood squeezes out between verbs.
The nation-states examine their entrails in fear.

War is wasted, the General cries, on civilians
but I saw a black angel dancing in war-surplus
shouting Let wars break out of the circle of war!
The man of foresight, quiet beneath bricks, rewarding

human exposure, smiles. His fingers select
a mint brass clip, the nails of Christ and two spares.
So honour's abolished – and we are still in the world.
There will be cover for him in the leafless centuries.

I part the grass very gently, I hide among towns
and Browning, Tokarev, Vetterli, Mondragón
consider the works of their fingers. One checks an alignment,
one fits a return-spring. Absorbed as the stainers of glass.

6

Rolling straight over my Enfield's human dimensions
under the farmer's barbed wire into the road
where tractors are passing, I scale a ripe scree of melons
and wave to the driver good-day! My rifle lies down,

a sudden lurch half-buries it under rotundities.
And perhaps indeed it will be as easy as that,
perhaps the mountains will strip off their rocks and cry Kiss me!
or the grocer turned spirit unravel his gut without pain.

If not, the rocket will have to lie down with the lamb.
I wave at the wings to the right and left of mankind:
only the politics come out either end, boys!
The farmer smiles, imagines I'm swatting something.

I choose for my rising to be a son of that place
where rifle and sword are stars of our evolution,
steel of our own sphere. You have to be almost a person
to use either rightly according to its nature

and ever to use a rifle as less than it is,
as truncheon, quarterstaff, musket, symbol, display,
belongs to tyranny. There's a scale closer to peace
on my rear sight than any tout's elevation.

January, heat. In the circle of live and dead farms
I stack the wholly obedient person of death
up high in the house out of child-reach
and go to eat fish with my remaining compatriots.


## VINDALOO IN MERTHYR TYDFIL

The first night of my second voyage to Wales,
tired as rag from ascending the left cheek of Earth,
I nevertheless went to Merthyr in good company
and warm in neckclothing and speech in the Butcher's Arms
till Time struck us pintless, and Eddie Rees steamed in brick lanes
and under the dark of the White Tip we repaired shouting

to I think the Bengal. I called for curry, the hottest,
vain of my nation, proud of my hard mouth from childhood,
the kindly brown waiter wringing the hands of dissuasion
O vindaloo, sir! You sure you want vindaloo, sir?
But I cried Yes please, being too far in to go back,
the bright bells of Rhymney moreover sang in my brains.

Fair play, it was frightful. I spooned the chicken of Hell
in a sauce of rich yellow brimstone. The valley boys with me
tasting it, croaked to white Jesus. And only pride drove me,
forkful by forkful, observed by hot mangosteen eyes,
by all the carnivorous castes and gurus from Cardiff
my brilliant tears washing the unbelief of the Welsh.

Oh it was a ride on Watneys plunging red barrel
through all the burning ghats of most carnal ambition
and never again will I want such illumination
for three days on end concerning my own mortal coil
but I signed my plate in the end with a licked knife and fork
and green-and-gold spotted, I sang for my pains like the free
before I passed out among all the stars of Cilfynydd.


## INCORRIGIBLE GRACE

Saint Vincent de Paul, old friend,
my sometime tailor,
I daresay by now you are feeding
the rich in Heaven.


## WALKING TO THE CATTLE PLACE

A MEDITATION

*At once I came into a world wherein I recovered my full being.*

– *Tagore*


### 1. Sanskrit

Upasara, the heifer after first mating,
adyaśvīnā, the cow about to calve, strīvatsā
the cow who has borne a heifer calf (atrināda
the calf newly born). I will smuggle this sūtra.

Around the sleeping house, dark cattle rubbing
off on stiff corner joists their innocent felt
and the house is nudged by a most ancient flow.
I will wake up in a world that hooves have led to.

To be of Europe also is a horn-dance,
cattle-knowledge. Even here, where Europa,
dumped rusty in her disgrace, gathered childhood afresh
by the draywheels' mercy, on creeks of the far selections.

Before the moon, away out, a rogue heifer dings
her bell on strained wire. A wrangling dry tintinnation
tells me she's through, and struggling on to her hooves.
She will never pierce the greater grid she has conjured.

But, a vulgar fruit of the Disruption, to talk
as if salvation were the soul's one food.
Today for no sin much, neither killing a brahmin
nor directly a cow, I will follow cattle.


## 2. Birds in Their Title Work Freeholds of Straw

At the hour I slept
kitchen lamps were sending out barefoot children
muzzy with stars and milk thistles
stoning up cows.
They will never forget their quick-fade cow-piss slippers
nor chasing such warmth over white frost, saffron to steam.
It will make them sad bankers.
It may subtly ruin them for clerks
this deeply involved unpickable knot of feeling
for the furred, smeared flesh of creation, the hate, the concern.
Viciously, out of sight, they pelt cows with stove-lengths
and hit them with pipes,
and older brothers sometimes, in more frenzied guilt,
have rancid, cracked eyes.
The city man's joke doesn't stretch to small minotaur bones.

But strange to think, as the dairy universe
reels from a Wall Street tremor, a London red-shift
on the flesh-eating graphs
and no longer only the bright and surplus children
get out of these hills,
how ghostly cows must be crowding the factory floors now

and licking black turbines
for the spectral salt
till the circuit-breaker's stunning greenhide crack
sears all but wages.

o

In the marginal dialect of this valley
(Agen my son grows up, tourists won't hear it)
udders are *elders*.

It was very bad news for the Kirk:
old men of the hard grey cloth, their freckled faces
distended, squeezing grace through the Four Last Things
in a Sabbath bucket.
I can tell you sparetime childhoods force-fed this
make solid cheese, but often strangely veined.
I'm thinking of aunts who had telescopes to spot
pregnancies, inside wedlock or out
(there is no life more global than a village)
and my father's uncles, monsters of hospitality.

Perhaps we should forget the seven-day-week tinned bucket
and the little children dead beat at their desks –
*Caesar got up and Milked then he Got his soldiers* –
but birds in their title work freeholds of straw
and the eagle his of sky.

Dripstone for Caesar.


## 3. The Names of the Humble

Fence beyond fence from breakfast
I climb through into my thought
and watch the slowing of herds into natural measures.

Nose down for hours, ingesting grass, they breathe grass,
trefoil, particles, out of the soft-focus earth
dampened by nose-damp. They have breathed great plateaux to dust.

But a cow's mouth circling on feed, the steady radius
shifting (dry sun) as she shifts,
subsumes, say, two-thirds of mankind. Our cities, our circles.

They concede me a wide berth at first. I go on being harmless
and some graze closer, gradually. It is like watching
an emergence. Persons.

Where cattletracks mount
boustrophedon to the hills
I want to discern the names of all the humble.

      o

A meaningful lack in the mother-tongue of factories:
how do you say *one* cattle? Cow, bull, steer
but nothing like *bos. Cattle* **is** *chattel*, is owned

by man the castrator,
body and innocence, cud and death-bellow and beef.
Bush people say *beast*, and mean no more fabulous creature
and indeed, from the moon to the alphabet, there aren't many.
Surely the most precious Phoenician cargo
was that trussed rough-breathing ox turned dawnward to lead
all Europe's journey.

      o

Far back as I can glimpse with descendant sight,
beyond roads or the stave-plough, there is a boy on cold upland,
gentle tapper of veins, a blood-porridge eater,
his ringlets new-dressed with dung, a spear in his fist,

it is thousands of moons to the cattle-raid of Cooley

but we could still find common knowledge, verb-roots
and noun-bark enough for an evening fire of sharing
cattle-wisdom,

though it is a great year yet
till Prithu will milk from the goddess (*O rich in cheer, come!*)
and down through his fingers into the rimmed vessel earth

grain and food-gardens.
We are entirely before
the seed-eater towns.

o

A sherry-eyed Jersey looks at me. Fragments of thoughts
that will not ripple together worry her head

it is sophistication trying to happen

there's been betrayal enough, and eons enough.
Or no more than focus, then,
trying to come up as far as her pupils.

Her calm gifts all central,
her forehead a spiked shield to wolves
she bobs in her hull-down affinities.
The knotted sway pole along which her big organs hang
(it will offer them ruthlessly downward when knob joints cave in)
rests unafraid in enzyme courtesies, though,

steadier than cognitions speckling brains.

Since I've sunk my presence into the law
that every beast shall be apportioned space
according to display, I unfurl a hand.

She dribbles, informing
her own weighted antique success,
and stays to pump the simpler, infinite herbage.

o

Her Normandy bones
the nap of her Charolais colour

the ticks on her elder are such
muscatels of good blood.

If I envy her one thing
it is her ease with this epoch.
A wagtail switching left-right, left-right on her rump.

Where cattletracks climb
rice-terrace-wise to the hills
I want to speak the names of all the humble.


## 4. The Artery

It is patience and stalks in the wide house of cattle
the zenith warming to unswallow stowage
and quietly chew. It is uttermost custom,
the day of these beings who licked the glimmering ice
from the north returning world, from the still man-figures.

But mouths stop suddenly. Heads turn. A roan bullock sound –
thin leather sniping them, the driven beef mob, oncoming,
is filling the road, dog-harried, fence-deflected
up shallow cuttings, down them, their elegant squeeze-shaped
hoofs swirl up a sky bath stockmen, wheeling, don't venerate

and, indecisive, the cows run, stopping. A freshet
that will not carry these with it is going down-country
to the slowing saleyard pools, the bare holding lakes
and then in great spurts to the ocean without limits.
Come back, mother cows. Plates flower for these children.

They are going to the plains of cash and the captive bolt,
to the clotted panic, the eunuch mounting in crushes, écoutez
mugir ces atroces abats: see, brains, where man's hunger
whirrs in the firmament. They are taken up flying
stately in the feathers of the knives, they are shown dominion

before, to the last lymph tear, they are chilled from dripping
and marbled in their fat they are pillars of the city
till out of cool rooms they crowd into our veins
through the sawdust gate. Soutine was mad three days
painting a bull suspended in loud strange honour,

till the police smashed in, and the huge meat gagged down landings.
It is near the bone, it is black as the Angus studbook
the thought of this comedy feeding our muscles. The dead
upright are buffoons, they nudge their own tragedy. Meet
it probably isn't, to prod a dance from hung haunches

in metres invented for reasons of bouphonia,
but I wouldn't chop prose for it, facing it. My stature.
More than cattle are pent in the long crush of the roads
but a whistling butcher may slice through the tears in things
and a poor man savour them. It was this horror,
beyond the great ice, that launched us. Luscious bone-fruit.
What silk will tie this artery of knowledge?


## 5. Death Words

Beasts, cattle, have words, neither minor nor many.
The most frightening comes with a sudden stilt jump: the blood-moan
straight out of earth's marrow, that *clameur*, huge-mouthed,
raised when they nose death at one of their own

and only then. The whole milking herd at that cry
will come galloping, curveting, fish-leaping in furious play-steps
on the thunderstruck paddock, horning one another. A hock dance.
A puddle of blood will trigger it, even afterbirth.

They make the shield-wall over it, the foreheads jam down
on where death has stuck, as if to horn to death Death
(dumb rising numerous straw-trace). They pour out strength
enormously on the place, heap lungs' heat on the dead one.

It is one word they enact in the horn-gate there
and the neighbour herds all running to join in it
hit the near fences, creaking. We've unpicked many million
variants from our own like wake. This is a sample.

Roughly all at once, though, from the last-comers inward
the bunched rite breaks up. They grow aimless, calm down
in straggling completion. You might say Eat, missa est.
It is uttered just once for each charnel. They will feed

a tongue's nub away from then on. Their word of power
is formal, terrible, but, for an age now, stops there.
At best, ours ramify still. Perhaps God is inevitable.
He will not necessarily come, though, again, in our species.


## 6. *The Commonwealth of Manu*

AFTER A DISCUSSION WITH WALTER DAVIS

Just for a moment
it seemed true of our country equally:
Brahmin, Kshatriya,
Vaishya, Shudra,
the four castes in our country, too, plus such as myself
and the genuine black men.

Brahmins? Yes, certainly.
Warriors, too, faintly honoured. (In April, their feast.)
Then merchants and drudges. A vast majority drudges
to tighten one bolt all day, and remember equality.

Vaishya, though, merchant, lowest of the twice-born,
consider his dominance:
the whole nation turning on him,
his the government, his the laws, his the profits,

his systems the System.
All his, the glory of goods
to make silent the rivers, to level the untidy hills,
a dispensation not found in the laws of Manu.

Who, in the old country, stands as god to those merchants?
Ganesha mainly, isn't it, the elephant-headed,
he whose steed is a rat, Ganesha the greedy one,
overcomer of obstacles?

Consider the elephant,
thick-skinned, intelligent vast,
the beast of long affection, long revenge,
capable of absorbing a whole pond.
Unable to jump. And very private at love.

Ganesha the god, provider of unearned good luck,
has a lovable tusk, and a cobra for a belt.
His other face is failure,
insanity, death.
Men dream they are swimming the wind.
Under this aspect, called Ganapati, he can
sometimes be appeased by a sacrifice of morals.

Just for a moment, it seemed so patently true,
considered without charity,
that this thread of Krishna I am spinning faltered,

this thread, these cattle.


## 7. Stockman Songs

Going to Rubuntja, the cattle-train. Banging two trailers.
Going empty to Urubuntja. Whipping like a duelling spear, but noisy.

    o

The artesian bore, that iron waterhole, that flowering water-bush;
thirsty calves come around. It dances on, stamping up steam.

    o

Cattle trailing to Rubuntja. Dotted on the sand-plain, tjaanaa

    o

My wife's uncle Blue-tongue Lizard. He tastes of spinifex.
I chased him under the flat rocks there near Anakota.

    o

The clumsy bull, see! He's written a cheque on that cow's flank,
in the dust of her flank, on the fur, a long water cheque.

o

My sad big horse. Men noticed his testicles. Horse.

o

Look out, kangaroos! Jimmy Kulnma is casting lead fingers
in the sand, for his brown gun. Look out, kangaroos!

o

The iron waterhole, the iron gnamma-hole,
like a fat pigeon fluffing up, preening all day long.

o

How they howl, burning, how they fly, the cone-haired initiands;
falling, they are grass-trees on Tnorula, they are palms in Pmolangkinja.

o

Cattle walking to Rubuntja, roan among the leopardwood trees.


## 8. The Bush

*'The boss at home, Missus?' A man couldn't tell suitors from buyers –*
*I could. They were shyer – Then you put your saddles in store –*
*And you kissed me once and started naming the sires*
*you'd give the boys home from agistment at Grammar and Shore –*

The moon dipper, poured, is rising out of late rain,
the wind also rising confirms the bed of the house.
Old fencers sleep straight. The feeding dams ripple and blur.
The white bull of Wagga goes into the mountains again.

*– And that was your father. The second time I dared call*
*he frogmarched me into the library, gnawed his moustache:*
*See you were wounded. He poured out two Haigs. I hope*
*you're still in a state to show our young filly the bush?*

Fifty years' blue ribbons dimming the hall
– *And are we weary of showing each other the bush?*


## 9. *Poley Bullock Couplets*

Old Poley, pin bullock. The round one has left me slack here.
It is a kind of rest, this waiting, at pasture.

o

The first stones that Wheel broke, setting out, were my sex –
to think before me he was no more than a paradox.

o

Horses? Weak-boned screamers, all farting and zest.
When I followed war, it was the long stay: conquest.

o

I was most kin to humans when we trudged bedraggled,
one hide to the common rain, neither leading nor led.

o

The keenest whip-hands were those with stripes to pass on
but their yarn was right: a bull's breath will kill oxen.

o

I feed with man's foster mother. Dim company for her,
I wait for my one child, the wheel, to roll free of power.


## 10. *The Boeotian Count*

       Maudie
         Maisie
     Shit-in-the bail
   Quince
       Blossom        Daisy
         shy Abigail
    Primavera
       Strawberry           Doris

one with a twostroke udd-
        ah          Marrabel         Arabelle
     Horace                       huge Onnanolia
           dear
      Kayleen     little
  Glory                        flies
       Calico       please
         Chloreen    spare Anatolia
        Ambidextra
IRON for creatures who    Portia
slobber at extra            Persia
   teats
   on the sly     swish!
                   in my eye
      full of KNOTS    bastard!
  if the milk's ropy   incontinent Sadie
stone an old lady
(quiet, you filth
        how come you crossed water?)
  Oh   be kind, then, to Rose
               Gopi
    and Rose's  daughter
     lame
               Utopie
  slavename
        earnotch   ring
  brandname
               the far crows
              are
Bottla      boys who knew horsewords
       all died for the King   sleepy
  Corka
            Nugget
  Biddy
   Sheila        Jerusalem
      Boxy
    Janet
Hafod           Joanie Walker
   boys who scorn cowtalk

gladden the bayonet
Hendre                                        Silkie
PetuniaPecuniaRegynaMahalia
Godsend            li
                   Lily              Meg
                   li
         sundry         Bulleero
              (lay glossolalia)
                             Brindle-
-down-from-the-moon
Hool 'em up, Nipper
                        more milkers than Brown
                     more points than the warriors
                        this infinite muster
                   the Cape        Ungundhlovu
                     the royal kraal of Ulster
              nurses of Camembert
              King of Franks
         and that staunch spreidh of
                   cantons,
              I give you thanks
Moocher
                   and Dopey        old Cornucopie
                   and Honeycomb              rainbeaded
                                        and warm
              I pray that Hughie
                   will send you
                        safe home
              where ploughing is playing
         where Karma is Līlā.


## 11. Novilladas Democráticas

The fancy rider sent his Texan boots
to the showground fence to warn off polished wood.

Hearing talk of a princely purse, the bullock
was riddling trucks with his sad Mongol bow.


67

Filtering through the chrome and rust horizon
came boys and bark and shirts of landless red.

When the rider nocked the quarrel of his skill
the first leap slipped the dust of all his driving

moons travelled beneath him. His sex hit mountains and threads.
The bullock tried to explode in burgundy spittle

the state borders looping over him flourished their wheels
the sun in a frenzy was rhythmically tearing its clothes

his rapid brim cooled Brunette Downs. A moleskin pigeon
was trying to fly five ways from the roof of the sea

and the watchers strangled gnarled and woollen beasts
yelling Huge! The monster was jumping a jack-knife

and a number of hands into the wall of the country.
Burlesque sounds out of horses, men running like grass.

For a while, one human burned to be extinct
as longhorns. But a clown persuaded him.

The Skuthorpe rider, next up, picked his words
with a match. Beauty! Give him the wild cow's milk!

A derelict spirit begged to drink from swords
but was dismissed to futures of glazed paper.

## 12. Hall's Cattle

*Returning in chagrin from that defeat, Sir Frederick (Pottinger) consoled himself by ordering his men to burn down Sandy Creek homestead and to shut Hall's and McGuire's cattle in the mustering paddock to starve ... Hall went back to the smoking ruins of his home and the stinking corpses of his cattle: 'There's no evidence to try you on, my man, but in the meantime this will teach you a lesson.'*

*– J. S. Manifold,* Who Wrote the Ballads

Upwind on Sandy Creek, cooking
not meat in a three-legged pot,
the future's oldest vessel,
sit McGuire and Hall.

Rails mortised in ironbark,
no special engine,
summoned this ruin within scent of water.
Rails regular as caste

in a tidy mind.
The homestead of course ash.
If he lacked hide before
he has a huge start now, Hall, home from acquittal.

*For little enough, for a phrase of Kerry grammar*
*those English bailiff's bastards triced up Father*
*and learnt him how to sing his hundred lines*
*of the Hanover anthem ...*

*So they did mine*
*but he was Devon.*
Flies, humming, trinket blue and poison green –
*I know little of Ireland.*

Yes, police-baronet Pottinger
the drafting paddock poles
knock, splinter and rebound.
Poor starving heads.

*They'll sentence me next time.*
*They have sentenced our sort*
*and all I know is this life.*
*I know nothing of America.*

The water trough chamois'd smooth
with the last saliva, flies' foretaste.
When the dingoes hit
there is gargling for tongues.

*Bushrangering isn't my work*
*but work is in prison*
*and the volunteer warders*
*have disgraced all reason.*

When crows scatter down,
black fence sitters, meaning to stay,
they hack the bulbed eyes out first –
a day comes a man stops saying luck.

*I'm thinking of a caper*
*to get them laughed out of the world,*
*a little war without deaths –*
*they are not worth lives.*

Upwind of Cubbin Bin, slamming
the lid back on steam
in a three-legged vessel, Ben Hall
sits by his farm

and, rising, shakes mountains and watches
blue sergeants rage in their chains
the straight man's out on the moonlight side
and holidays shake from his reins.

It is a day for the poor,
their own saddle on a blood horse,
as the bush flies breed
to feed on noble brains.

## 13. Boöpis

Coming out of reflections
I find myself in the earth.
                    My cow going on
into the creek from this paspalum-thatched tunnel-track
divides her hoofs among the water's impediments,
clastic and ungulate stones.
                       She is just deep
enough to be suckling the stream when she drinks from it.

Wetted hooves, like hers,
incised in the alluvium
this grave's-width ramp up through the shoulder of the bank
but cattle paunches with their tongue-mapped girths also
brushed in glazes,
easements and ample places
at the far side of things from subtractive plating of spades
or the vertical silvers a coffin will score, sinking.

North, the heaped districts, and south
there'd be at least a Pharaoh's destruction of water
suspended above me in this chthonic section.
Seeds fall in here from the poise
of ploughland, grass land.
                    I could be easily
foreclosed to a motionless size in the ruins of gloss.

The old dead, though, are absorbed, becoming strata.
The crystals, too, of glaze or matt, who have
not much say in a slump
seem coolly balanced toward me.
                    At this depth among roots
I thank God's own sacrifice
that I am not here with seeds and a weighty request
from the upper fields,
my own words constrained with a cord.
Not being that way, if I met the lady of summer,
the beautiful cow-eyed one, I would be saying:

Madam, the children of the overworld
cannot lay down their instruments at will.
Babel in orbit maps the hasty parks,
missile and daisy scorn the steady husbands
and my countrymen mix green with foreign fruit.


## 14. *The Pure Food Act*

Night, as I go into the place of cattle.

Night over the dairy
the strainers sleeping in their fractions,
vats
and the mixing plunger, that dwarf ski-stock, hung.

On the creekstone cement
water driven hard through the Pure Food Act
dries slowest round tree-segment stools,
each buffed
to a still bum-shine,
sides calcified with froth.

Country disc-jocks
have the idea. Their listeners aren't all human.
Cows like, or let their milk for, a firm beat
nothing too plangent (diesel bass is good).
Sinatra, though, could calm a yardful of horns
and the Water Music
has never yet corrupted honest milkers
in their pure food act.

The quiet dismissal switching it off, though,
and carrying the last bucket, saline-sickly
still undrinkable raw milk to pour in high
for its herringbone and cooling pipe-grid
fall
to the muscle-building cans.

His wedding, or a war,
might excuse a man from milking

but milk-steeped hands are good for a violin
and a cow in rain time is
a stout wall of tears.

But I'm britching back.

I let myself out through the bail gate.
Night, as I say.
Night, as I go out to the place of cattle.


## 15. Gōlōka

Their speech is a sense of place
night makes remote
lucerne fields in the dark hills are renamed
Moorea, Euboea.

That bull invoking Mundubbera, Karuah
and Speewah, now, Speewah
is trying his sultanate out on infinite space.

Sleepy, lingually liquescent.
It is a delectation, the matter of rock-salt,
a drawn, sparkling mouth

squaremouth, though, for the mother
mourning at the five-bar
gate for her tongue-sculpted, milky one
manhandled to the mad chute, steel-barred,
gone above gears.

No. Calling back the lost ones
is long, but not weak.
Older than crying, and less for yourself.

When heifers processing
the planet's uncountable crop
butt, or show horns, glower, jump fur-marred aside
and afterwards lick
they are establishing

the order of precedence of the Sun King's court
a needed concern
the risen will have cast off.

Effacing the cave-clay hand
from the shoulders of cattle, and the pet cattle-names
from the souls of slaves,
will be night work for us before that wide enablement.

What I know, says the man
who has come out of his house,
is nothing recent. An old song and an ancient one.

The ancient tune is faint (fainter still, the kings in her)
but it keeps me farming
rather than raping, or embalming, the land.
The other's the New World. We won't be peasants again.

Children are leaping
and wives are setting out cakes on trestle tables
(cuisine is class, but cookery is cake)
Camerons with Schultzes Breens married Crowhursts Joy
turned Catholic
the meaning of lists a weave we are cruellest maintaining it
a tissue wider than countries it carries all blood
it must only change slowly. Disorder is drawn to the gaps
the more we expect it we would love to be honest
but we know when to be.
This is community. Courage had better be real.

A black woman murmurs:
The Son of God, he said all hidden things would come out
he wasn't nervous.

A cornbag quilt and an aeroplane to sow clover
suit my breed of jokes
says the strong man facing the moon.
We'll suffer culture for some of our devilry yet
as Athens comes for our hide, or sends Arcadia.
Consequences hurt worse, but they impoverish less
being Nature.

I stand to one side of this night work
wishing it ease
for the minuscule stitch of baptismal clothes to tip through it
and five-course breakfasts eaten with great knives.

Through fences mended
with bedsprings, for intransigence,
and out between tussocks come all the tame and wild cattle
with their boat-prow briskets and brow-whorls and
prehuman gifts:
rank loyalty ritual
curiosity, frenzy, affection, remembrance of ambush
and their farther own: ear-focus, digestion of hard sugar,
a nose for oestrus.

The moon rides herd on a tide of fertile crescents.
Right among the tables people are touching the cattle
not mastering. Meeting.
They mingle and they take steps
humans laugh cattle nuzzle fur shifts over joints and no voice
pretends a transaction.
Humped decorum, cows pee. Charlie's Wain in the sky full of grass
sprinkles the creatures
all here are flesh of heaven as roughly as stones.

When Cloven Hoof and Wheel made war on a chair
the Hoof was burned to hide the holes in his back
that was indeed war
good people resigned from dancing and lived in the air
much wearing of black
then madness was easy. That day crumbles here. More future
in a little girl feeding the clean beasts rainbow cake.

o

Scattered, at the nub of things,
over that blood-and-dung mirror-floor, the leaf-giving
earth, men and bulls,

they of Murcia, they of Nîmes, the Nandi bull, the white bull
of Washpool, and he of the Cassidys, and they of the
drinkers of *bikavér*
they are single beyond counting; the people and the horned
people stand
in the sad forbearance
of those inescapably armed.

I am looking at the place where the names well out of field stone,
at the feared successor of plenty, the place like curved water.
In the fullness of work, it is health to see this,
the cattle-sphere fitting the green
and hard yellow worlds.

I am looking at equality where it seeks no victories.

o

The delivered stampede
continuing around me in feasting, the herds graze among us
in planetary dispersions. A Xhosa herdkeeper
salutes me, with his spoon:
Xho, eater from tins!

Xhe! I wholly agree,
sitting on cram-full bags.
There's also drinking from a jar. The depôt pleasures.
What better in Carthage or Rome
when they became cover?

*The king of justice (human)*
*would not enter Paradise without the lost, or his dog*
– living and work are one thing, or the rivers die,
my neighbour's wife's saying,
a blackfellow told me tonight, and I knew. I knew.
Dozens of us clasp hands with her, for courage.

Laughter, away down the creek
gradually less competitive:
the literal disports.

76

Nearer sit poncho-wrapped figures
sipping through silver tubes. Antique, polite,
they would insult you first.
They are sizing up ringers (whose weapons would be improvised)
and the ringers themselves are praising this inside country.
Yes. Nice patch of storm.

Hard men, talking places
on a night-watch track:
Camooweal. Caaguazú.
Rectangular grind of cattle jaws all around them.

The houses of humans walking home in dew-dark
are hillsides apart.
As I enter my own, the moon is coming weather
and the sun dry honey
in every cell of the wood.

I have travelled one day.


# JÓZSEF

M.J.K. 1882–1974 IN PIAM MEMORIAM

You ride on the world-horse once
no matter how brave your seat
or polished your boots, it may gallop you
into undreamed-of fields

but this field's outlandish: Australia!
To end in this burnt-smelling, blue-hearted
metropolis of sore feet and trains
(though the laughing bird's a good fellow).

Outlandish not to have died
in king-and-kaiserly service,
dismounted, beneath the smashed guns
or later, with barons and credit

after cognac, a clean pistol death.
Alas, a small target, this heart.
Both holes were in front, though, entry
and exit. I learned to relish that.

Strange not to have died with the Kingdom
when Horthy's fleet sank, and the betting
grew feverish, on black and on red,
to have outlived even my Friday club

and our joke: *senilis senili
gaudet*. I bring home coffee now.
Dear God, not one café in this place,
no Andrássy-street, no Margaret's Island …

no law worth the name: they are British
and hangmen and precedent-quibblers
make rough jurisprudence at best.
*Fairness*, of course; that was their word.

I don't think Nature speaks English.
I used to believe I knew enough
with *gentleman*, *whisky*, *handicap*
and perhaps *tweed*. French lacked all those.

I learned the fine detail at seventy
out here. Ghosts in many casinos
must have smiled as I hawked playing cards
to shady clubs up long stairways

and was naturalized by a Lord Mayor
and many bookmakers, becoming a
New Australian. My son claims he always
was one. We had baptized him Gino

in Hungary. His children are natives
remote as next century. My eyes
are losing all faces, all letters,
the colours go, red, white, now green

into Hungary, Hungary of the poplar trees
and the wide summers where I am young
in uniform, riding with Nelly,
the horseshoes' noise cupping our speeches.

I, Mórelli József Károly,
once attorney, twice gunshot, thrice rich,
my cigarettes, monogrammed, from Kyriazi,
once married (dear girl!) to a Jew

(gaining little from that but good memories
though my son's uniforms fitted her son
until it was next year in Cape Town)
am no longer easy to soften.

I will eat stuffed peppers and birds' milk,
avoid nuns, who are monstrous bad luck,
write letters from memory, smoke Winstons
and flex my right elbow at death

and, more gently, at living.


## FOLKLORE

What are the sights of our town?

Well, there is that skeleton they hang
some nights in the bar of the Rest
and everyone laughing in whispers
the barmaid broke down one time, laughing.
The cord goes up through the ceiling
to the undersprings of the big
white bed in the Honeymoon Suite
and when those bones even jiggle
there's cheers (and a donnybrook once)
and when they joggle, there's whooping
and folk stalking out in emotions

and when they dance – hoo, when they dance!
he knows every tune on the honeymoon
flute, does the hollow-hipped fellow.
There are a few, mind, who drink on
straight through it all. Steady drinkers.
Up over the pub there's the sky
full of stars, as I have reflected
outside, while guiding the course of my
thoughts. Some say there's a larger
cord goes up there, but I doubt it
I mean
but then I'm no dancer.

Besides that, there's meatworks and mines.


# THE POLICE: SEVEN VOICES


## 1. The Knuckle Garden

*In the city of Cargo*
*at the very centre of it*
*is the Knuckle Garden*

*Alibis melt off like grease*
*names, causes, soak into the tiles*
*in the Knuckle Garden*

*This garden is kept by blue serge*
*men with thick pocketknife nails*
*and impatient fellows*

*Their opinions are petrol, and steel,*
*blurred elastic, and knowing the time,*
*they are wholly practical*

*With strong lights to shine through hard men*
*and hoses – men have died fighting those,*
*Laocoöns, distending*

Men have died of falling downstairs
have ruptured their spleen eating pies
have confessed to God's death

And women have bled from soul-searching
but let us, however altered
the shape of our smiles, be content

For factory whistles would choke
and the flag catch afire from its stars
without these ministers

Nor would the great Cargo come
or keep on its shelves, without
the Knuckle Garden.


## 2. Plainclothes Park

Thinking my old thought in the eye-stinging dark:
the Motive Revealer. People are so undeclared.
A button, now, on a unit in your pocket –
I was wiring that airy device in the mid-city park.

There'd be luminous face colours. Visible only to you.
Green for lying, yellow when you had them scared.
Violence? Red. When a man reached intense pink, you'd hit him
first. Or change tack. I've had various meanings for blue …

The man sitting next to me thought his kink out loud:
*The body – you know? There are design flaws God left
hanging. Too many non-overridable programmes.
Why shouldn't we will new teeth, new hair, new organs?*

*Will-overrides, friend. We need to start working on these,
and shielding. Good God! All that soft rippable belly
without a bone casque. And non-retractable genitals!*
My trouble, I muttered, is with doubt, not knees.

His face was no colour that betokens guilt
but I questioned him (and I think he questioned me).
No result. He left the park shortly after
and vanished from sight in the city we had built.


## 3. Discontent, Reading Conan Doyle

CI: the detectives. After the age of belief
we're what happened to mystery. Our model explainaway trade
brings complex relief.

Not quite your suave Sherlocks, we know
fences, sperm, payoffs, the squalor of minds, and where
the husbands go.

The gentlemen Sherlocks
trail their gentlemen quarry, one case at a time.
Let us touch our forelocks.

From cars, under glass
we watch the citizens: Touchables and Not
is our theory of class.

The uniform branch have their mystery, the Peace:
shall meaning be slow, at home, at the factory, at church
or loose in the streets?

We still defend logic –
try bringing a fat man down off a love-death pact
and you learn about magic –

but our mystery's the Score
that is, knowing it. Which is the Upper Hand.
That's to say, the Law.

Not of course for some.
Say the Law's a regent till the King comes back
if he does come.

Reading modern stuff at times
you'd think all crime was protest, or illusion –
we should charge the victims.

Doubts, then, and changes:
don't ever book on them. The old sleuths dealt, like us,
only with strangers

so if we're sent
to interview you, in especially the poorer suburbs,
don't run. Don't quote the law. If you're a man

be in employment.


## 4. Rostered Duty

This is the hour the Crucified Bludger is fed
a tin dish held to his mouth and his night's stain hosed down
before he is driven slow-slow through the fibro-tile streets
and the message gets through to moaners, to oversleepers,
to migrants who dream dark police, to blokes thinking Sickie.

This is the hour the hurrying frowners at railway
stations don't look but all read his placard: WORK-SHY.
Soon, outside factory and depot, flies supping his wounds,
he will be ignored by staff, by management, by unions,
all too mature to look. Very few people focus,

not the realists, nor the long planners, not the fellows
with trades in demand, nor the ones proud they can shovel
as much as God's truck can dump; self-provers and winners
never see him at all, and talk about him constantly.
But everyone knows the form: on a quiet day

passing Hey Folks PLANETWIDE Pow! Discounts / Trade Ins!
I've been known to say to the salesfolk there not looking
*Gooday, how's the carrot?* Yes, I've had my turn,
served my tour with the Bludger. Every policeman does one.
I've picked airgun slugs out of him, tuned his trannie on race days,

heard him howl in the truck bay, echoing the oil drums.
I've supervised him and his wife on a visiting day –
*No madam we can't let him down* – and had her scream
into my face ME! *crucify ME, God damn you!*
At least it's intense. Jail is drearier employment.

When he'd get randy we'd turn him face to the van.
I think of him often, spread-Andrewed on four bolts
parked facing the sea for a treat of a summer evening
(when he bit my hand to the bone he saw more sunsets).
I remember him watching the big ships loading bales

and unloading bales, as the radio quacked Production.
*This is a shop, boys, not a nation,* a man said,
making a gesture. A poet growled *Misemployment*
but poets are kids. A thousand fellows in ties
picking flyspecks from pepper with fine Government needles

or that's what it looked like said *No time to be choosy.*
*Unless he's got a job,* smiled the chief clerk, *he can't have one.*
It was interesting duty, travelling with the Bludger,
more to the point than backing up wives and collectors
and once you've done it, you're never, like they say, off duty.


5. *The Lips Move During Anointing*

FOR FR EDMUND CAMPION

Stopped
        tilted
                watching a ditch
digger's family eat, in a window,
                        miles on –
blue metal gums my draining reasons
wait
    there'll be time for doubling my tongue
back, in,
        and the bucket and the raincoat
I'm trying to say

on-the-spot dignity Walther speed
                              docked
my imaginary body
streaming hurt at the sky like headlights
I'm trying to SAY
                    that shame, rolling, boot-walloping
into the sniggers of gambling men tankwater
drinkers pill burners
                    I'll be with long gone
horse police in their own steel, made dance
or wire stretched between trees,
that story
I was the scorer you didn't call sport
to blunt men up against the numbers
poor is still
                              Christ
                    and not money-poor now
I was a copper, not ever a policeman
a john served right on a lorry's tray
I was the joker who made numbers win
I'm learning pity
                    rougher than shear
watching those ones
                         my glazing angle.
I would feed them from my own plate
set aside even fact, with good losing, not
doing my job with a score for a vision
which makes a cop of any fellow
                              unfix me, but, then
from my slewed skidding. I
will, bare-eyed, see them
                         anyway, a long time
happy with lamp pickles worn faces, no one
stacking on the realities
chipped star of black tea
I was a toddler under sad calendars
there, before winning
                    walk, don't spill

85

this, in my chinstrap cup under the oilskins, this
decency, shape
                    there'll be no columns
in justice.
            No setup.


## 6. The Breach

I am a policeman
it is easier to make me seem an oaf
than to handle the truth

I came from a coaldust town
when I was seventeen, because there was nothing
for a young fellow there

the Force drew me because of a sense I had
and have grown out of
I said to Ware once, Harry, you're the best
cop of the lot: you only arrest falls
he was amused

I seem to be making an inventory of my life
but in that house opposite, first floor
there is a breach
and me, in this body I am careful with,
I'm going to have to enter that house soon

and stop that breach

it is a bad one people could fall through
we know that three have
and he's got a child poised

I have struck men in back rooms late at night
with faces you could fall a thousand feet down
and I've seen things in bowls

the trick is not to be a breach yourself
and to stop your side from being one
I suppose

the sniper Spiteri, when I was just out of cadets –
some far-west cockies' boys straight off the sheep train
came up with their .303s and offered to help
they were sixteen years old

we chased them away, not doubting for a minute
they could do what they said
bury your silver the day we let that start

now I've said my ideals

Snowy cut, snow he cut ...
A razor-gang hood my uncle claims he met
is running through my mind
in Woolloomooloo, wet streets, the nineteen twenties
dear kind Snowy Cutmore

Snowy cuts no more
he was a real breach

also, on our town, I
remember the old hand bowsers, that gentle apop-
lexy of benzine in the big glass heads
twenty years since I saw them

There's a moment with every man who has started a stir
when he tires of it, wants to put it aside
and be back, unguilty, that morning, pouring the milk

that is the time to separate him from it
if I am very good I'll judge that time
just about right

the ideal is to keep the man and stop
the breach
that's the high standard

but the breach must close

if later goes all right
I am going to paint the roof of our house
on my day off.


## 7. Sergeant Forby Lectures the Cadets

Old Warwick, the husband, scratched his head:
they'd run off together, was all he knew.
He didn't know where.
Most would have said where.
He had no theories about the horse.

We stood round it,
the trackers drowsing.

*Our witnesses reckon they told the boarder*
*you knew, and would shoot him.*

He had no views on that.
They went off together. *I told them Get,*
*her and him.*

Then some fool poked the horse with a stick.
It bowled us, gagging, clean off the hill.

Country people aren't keen on decay
too many midsummer funerals, I guess,
of beasts, and men. Too many feeds
of ptomaine mutton in the heat
sweets from the handy home botulin kit.
No market for jugged hare or ripe cheese
among that sort.

We had some sort of case:
opportunity, motive, shot horse
but Warwick's counsel made mince of it.
Without bodies, the onus was on us
(I hope the Onus comes on him
some dark night)
but he was right.

And Warwick got off.
He was ten minutes gone
when the answer hit me like a brick:
country people aren't keen on decay
of course!

And we dug under the horse.

The secret of our profession, this:
we dig under the horse.
Dismiss.


## AQUALUNG SHINTO

FOR CHRIS KOCH

All day above the Japanese fleet,
the zenith sun between the islands
unmoving. We were after the flagship

and kept diving, finding tackle
jettisoned in her agony. My
shadow over the sand floor curved

on chain, on wavering metal forms,
Don saying *Be careful of any ammo,
it could still give us the instant bends.*

We were following the logic
of a dying ship among islands: here
he would have considered beaching her, here
the sub may have come for the admiral. We dived

in lucid water, tracing down
the death-hours of an Imperial captain
thirty years wiser than we were

in settling steel, in shouting men
in – reached after final avalanche cruising –
a peaceful Sun, that shapelessness.

We would come up from the dreamlight plane
and eat meals aboard the boat
*Where we want her to lie, I guess,*

*is a place neither dry nor drowned*
*where we could drift in Dante-style*
*and observe grotesques of courage*

*performed by knights of bushido in*
*tight black jackets. Quintessence movies.*
I finished my can. *I would go up*

*to Yamada and address him: Captain*
*I was born in 'thirty-eight*
*please give me what you own of me.*

Those days, below in the sharks' kingdom,
I kept remembering the iron ore ports
the black ships feeding at all times

and ore dust the colour of dried blood
on every object. Baseball Maru,
have you jettisoned anything

but the sword-wearers? That direct style?
(OVERACHIEVERS ARE JAPANESE
I wrote in pentel ink on the bulkhead.)

The water was layered like a pearl
clear-opaque-clear as I swam down
thinking of Marines twenty years in hiding
in dugouts, eating tadpole mush,
waiting to fight, treasuring a mortar

young men approaching fifty still
begging pardon, not having flown winged bombs

NIHON, the ultimate taut ship ...
It shamed our carefully dazzle-painted
sanity. Don below me bubbled.
We were close to the flagship now
by the debris. Her presence was
longing for form. Her own. Again.
Aloud in my head I told myself
she would rise if I clapped my hands:

towering superstructure, respectable
maritime-power lines – all just
askew by a fraction from machine history

in the copyist's deadness which betrays
cherishment of carp flags and tea brushes
design like poems in a culture-language.

At night, weighing the heart of it:
*We are as easy to recruit*
*as ever,* Don said,
*but harder to command.*

*We are almost free of the State*
*almost clear, again, of armies.*
*It is time to oppress the State.*

*I think that is the history*
*of the rest of this century: cavaliers.*
*Were you romantic about cavaliers?*

*In the end it may be safer.*
*Defaming the high words – honour, courage –*
*has not stopped us. It has made us mad*

*we are maddened by a dumb spirit.*
I lay there also musing. Waves.
Mishima died. Screams from Lod airport ...

*In the one entirely native*
*and wisest Japanese faith,* I said,
*a mirror hangs before sanctuaries.*

*Oh Zen makes colonials of a few*
*but each people has its proper Shinto*
*distinctive as verandah beams*

*hard to join as a stranger's childhood.*
*What withers us is that Australia*
*is a land of shamefaced shrines.*

*Perhaps,* I went on, *the history coming*
*is just more peoples passing for white,*
*fronting for themselves in English*

*and preserving their life in a closing fraction*
*from which leap unbelievably savage*
*flames. Which was your major point.*

Imminent below us those nights, big
as an undersea ridge between the islands
a battleship of the Kongo class

was sending out her crew like waves:
*Your fathers killed us, their minds aloof*
*from us in war as in any peace*

*and we were bringing pine-needle cakes, fox stories.*

# THE CANBERRA SUBURBS' INFINITE EXTENSION

Citizens live in peace and honour
in Pearce and Higgins and O'Connor,
Campbellites drive Mercedes-Benzes,
lobbyists shall multiply in Menzies –
but why not name suburbs for ideas
which equally have shaped our years?

I shall play a set of tennis
in the gardens of Red Menace

Shall I scorn to plant a dahlia
in the soil of White Australia?

Who will call down Lewis Mumford
on the streets of Frugal Comfort?

*Oh live in Fadden and be content:*
*everywhere's Environment.*


# THINKING ABOUT ABORIGINAL LAND RIGHTS, I VISIT THE FARM I WILL NOT INHERIT

Watching from the barn the seedlight and nearly-all-down
Currents of a spring day, I see the only lines bearing
consistent strain are the straight ones: fence, house corner,
outermost furrows. The drifts of grass coming and canes
are whorled and sod-bunching, are issuant, with dusts.
The wind-lap outlines of lagoons are pollen-concurred
and the light rising out of them stretches in figments and wings.
The ambient day-tides contain every mouldering and oil
that the bush would need to come back right this day,
not suddenly, but all down the farm slopes, the polished shell barks

flaking, leaves noon-thin, with shale stones and orchids at foot
and the creek a hung gallery again, and the bee trees unrobbed.
By sundown it is dense dusk, all the tracks closing in.
I go into the earth near the feed shed for thousands of years.

# THEIR CITIES, THEIR UNIVERSITIES

The men of my family danced a reel with sugar
    for two generations.
Robbie Burns was involved, that barley spirit
and history, and their fathers' voyage out
    but that is a novel.
The past explains us and it gets our flesh.

You find most older Murray houses
    girt in some glitter
of bottle-glass in the paddocks, rum necks and whisky ghosts,
Wolfe's dark Aromatic Schnapps mostly grassroots-under now
    and insulin, insulin
as if to help the earth digest such crystals,
the thousand year jag, the gullies of downtrodden light.

    It was in these spirits
that Veitch rode the frisky stick horse: *Go in, Mrs Maurer!*
    *he's shying at ye!*
and Sam towed Reggie-Boy shrieking behind his big Dodge
    in the splintering sulky.

It was through these that Hughie tumbled off his mare
    on the heirloom fiddle
and uncle Jock Clark danced Whee! in the shopping-day street
    prick burst from his trousers
asperging the people, a boneless arm limber as Jock
    and Burns got misquoted.

      o

From the photograph, they look at me. Intelligent book-shy faces.
The scrolls of their fiddles curl at me, the pipe smoke goes up
fuzzy as the toddler who moved, or the man who shook his head
    at a fly
and smeared his last chance at history. The day is a bright one,

the golden wedding of Bella and John Allan,
old Bunyah Johnnie, seated here past the end
of his fabulous hospitality: *small table at Murrays*
*today. Only twenty-six, not counting family* –
That homestead is long gone – *man should hae led trumps* –
and the times are flattening down. The ringbarked Twenties.

My great-grandfather John
is remembering what it is to conquer country:
    brush soil upturned,
thin-legged black people who would show you fruit,
a house set fair to a track to capture company.

Isabella, shrunken in silks, is holding minds with him
    (they are first cousins)
*Gey strange it is, my hands free all day long now*
*of flour, milk, feathers. We never had to stint.*
    *Thank God for that, John.*

John Murray of Bunyah, born in a Biscay storm,
    my offshore Basque
    and thriftless as Montrose.

            o

The drinking Murrays. They were rarely brutal.
It wasn't Murrays who rode the policeman with spurs
or gelded the half-witted youth to spare him problems
    but trotting through town
whips coiled and pipes alight, drawing revellers to them
and holding forth on music and seeds and the wurrld
    in their fathers' accent
and going home after three nights, cooeeing abstemious
settlers from bed to hooting strathspey contests

and holding Saturday dances from Thursday night on
with their children milking a hundred cows in jig time
and schottische time, as the fiddlers raised the sun,
    that was the notion.

    After the heights
Grandfather, crossed, would upend the breakfast table
    and then his breakfast:
*Father's sick. Walk quiet. He'll draw the whip on you.*
He has been out of Sense and Worth in timber rooms
where men make bets and spittle beads, whooping their Lallans,
and night-sugar world where Burns is an evil spirit
    and self a form of anger.

                    o

Aunts with a nose for sin, young chaps with haircuts
combed like an open ginger book, pretty girls like a leafed one
relax from their poses, stroll off into marriages, deaths.

    Here at the focus
the sun goes under the paddocks, though, and pipers
are bulging the house with their summoned howling tune
and the drinkers, the brothers, candles in their hands,
are kneeling on the floor to judge the tramping beat
    and the style of it:
    *The big bloke's stepping fine!*

And Veitch is confiding the hard drink to get into
a man is the second one. He means, for subversion.
    Veitch's shield against
inspectors, collectors, police is a happy day
that leaves them sitting about, hiccuping and ashamed
or lurching from their cars miles off, ashamed, hiccuping.

Wives and sisters are forbidden the shamanism of glass;
    they go busy, or proud
or brandish the Word, that soured woman's weapon
cold-hammered by Knox, fresh-honed by the Wee Free Kirk,
    hard splinter of that Faith
    which overcame religion,

but the patriarchs are keeping their own time
like a door in the farm-dull days, and separate as logic.
    Boys nodding in cars outside
the pubs work promised ground they will not inherit.
It distils too sweet. Though it is all their wages.
They hear their lives going wheedle-and-away
on the four strained wires of a fiddle, in a spent tradition
*Good on ye, Allan!* and singing with no terms.
*Scotland is a place Dad goes when he drinks rum*
    but their feet are tapping.

They wasted their lands for that (and for all that)
    the redhaired Murrays.
The reasons are a novel, incomplete as cultures
now everywhere become. It is almost overt now:

        we are going to the cause
        not coming from it.


## KISS OF THE WHIP

In Cardiff, off Saint Mary's Street,
there in the porn shops you could get
a magazine called Kiss of the Whip.
I used to pretend I'd had poems in it.

Kiss of the Whip. I never saw it.
I might have encountered familiar skills
having been raised in a stockwhip culture.
Grandfather could dock a black snake's head,

Stanley would crack the snake for preference
leap from his horse grab whirl and jolt!
the popped head hummed from his one-shot slingshot.
The whips themselves were black, fine-braided,

arm-coiling beasts that could suddenly flourish
and cut a cannibal strip from a bull
(millisecond returns) or idly behead an
ant on the track. My father did that.

A knot in the lash would kill a rabbit.
There were decencies: good dogs and children
were flogged with the same·lash doubled back.
A horsehair plait on the tip for a cracker

sharpened the note. For ten or twelve thousand
years this was the sonic barrier's
one human fracture. Whip-cracking is that:
thonged lightning making the leanest thunder.

When black snakes go to Hell they are
affixed by their fangs to carved whip-handles
and fed on nothing but noonday heat,
sweat and flowing rumps and language.

They writhe up dust-storms for revenge
and send them roaring where creature comfort's
got with a touch of the lash. And that
is a temple yard that will bear more cleansing

before, through droughts and barracks, those
lax, quiet-speaking, sudden fellows
emerge where skill unbraids from death
and mastering, in Saint Mary's Street.


## ON THE WRECKAGE OF A HIJACKED AIRLINER

How did the Oriental
curse go, again? May you live
in literary times?

## ESCAPING OUT THERE

With clutch-slip and tappet-noise
we rotate the Shell station
a Royal Mail Reo
bus gathering speed through the last
sleeve-pluck of motels.
I was right to turn inland from here.

Dressed by two clotheslines
by noon I'll be famous throughout
the birthday-call networks.
Police bikes will leap headlands for me
and feel under paddocks
but I will be away out.

The people around me
restore me like colours. Their heads
are full of quiet electrified porridge and blood
I almost can't bear how delicate the webbings
of their lives are in there, the cattle and front yards and psalms.
The men wear the old war haircuts of this century
and the women's waves are no longer the newest idea.

The driver is practising grips
for his wrestle with ranges
we are leaving the parts where Please and Excuse Me are said
the man up front of me
hands his wife to one side as gently as crockery
getting down their bags.

The hills are coming around us like calves
to a rattled milk bucket
the plovers and waves step away at the crossings we reach.
The offsider can hit drum letterboxes and dogs
with papers and the mail.
He discusses his family, using racehorse names:
Prince Rajah's his eldest, I think. Dickie's Pride is his wife.

The windscreen is filled half the time with nothing but sky
we are getting well out.
Farm people step down
at Howards and Scobies and Where the Old School Got Burnt.
At All the Bloodwoods
and at the Flying-Fox Cooking-Place
timber people step down.
There are no people now at Praising White Moth Larvae
and no one gets off Where the Big Red Bull Went Over.
I wouldn't either.

But crossing that crest, the second sight comes upon us:
*You would never again*, the rabbiter's wife says to me,
*you've grew out of it.*
*They should be thumped, but in hot blood*, says the fencer,
*none of this ten-years-cold-steel stuff*
*you young bastard.*

I am over the crest
and going on where unadmitted grandmothers
make farms easy-going
and cornbag quilts cover more than kids of a three-dog
winter's night.
I will go on from there to where the west wind rises
further east, the gorge is so far back
and take a job out there with a lazy man.

When strangers come, I'll slope steeply down and grow trees.
My name will rub off out there on the lips of the watershed
and when I am fine as cloud-webbing, I will drift
vaguely down valleys,
me, or my water, if it comes to that,
into further lives.

I will make good ancestors.

# PORTRAIT OF THE AUTIST AS
# A NEW WORLD DRIVER

A car is also
a high-speed hermitage. Here
only the souls of policemen can get at you.
Who would put in a telephone,
that merciless foot-in-the-door
of realities, realties?

Delight of a stick-shift –
farms were abandoned for these pleasures. Second
to third in this Mazda is a stepped inflection
third back to first at the lights
a concessive
V of junction.

Under the overcoming
undiminishing sky you are scarcely supervised:
you can let out language
to exercise, to romp in the grass beyond Greek.
You can rejoice in tongues,
orotate parafundities.

They simplify
who say the Artist's a child
they miss the point closely: an artist
even if he has brothers, sisters, spouse
is an only child.

Among the self-taught
the loners, chart-freaks, bush encyclopedists
there are protocols, too: we meet
gravely as stiff princes, and swap fact:
*Did you know some bats can climb side on?*

Mind you, Hitler was one of us.
He had a theory. We also count stern scholars
in whose disputes you almost hear the teenage
hobbyist still disputing proof and mint
and wheelmen who murmur *Suffering is bourgeois.*

But swapping cogs to pass a
mountainous rig and its prime mover, I
reflect that driving's a mastery the mastered
are holding on to.
It has gone down among the ancient crafts
to hide in our muscles.

Indeed, if you asked
where the New World is, I'd have to answer
he is in his car
he is booming down the highways
in that funnel of blue-green-gold, tree-flecked and streaming
light that a car is always breaking out of –

    We didn't come of
    the New World, but we've owned it.
    From a steady bang, ever more globes, flying outward;
    strange tunings are between us.
    Of course we love our shells: they make the anthill
    bearable. Of course the price is blood.

## COMPANY

Where two or three
are gathered together, that
is about enough.

## CYCLING IN THE LAKE COUNTRY

Dried phlegm of lakes
that die of thirst. Burnt umber
dust, wind-smoothed, on glue.
Miles across, cattle-coloured
are the plains of Ryoanji.

Lakes of craze-brick. The salt
detailing around mallee islands
is two brush-hairs thick
(the galvanized salt farther out
sustains mirage islands).

No ruins in Australia?
Here are the ruins of seas
and ruins in the mouth:
the place-names here are now
pronounced in English.

Choking beasts to kill time
the particulate, millionfold
lake basins, wind-topped,
are eon-strength ocean paste
awaiting pole-melt and rains.

    o

This angelic free walking:
in a long meditation of shores
far-reachingly stepping
I cross the immense north stations
ahead of blown grass.

Passing smoke-coloured emus:
the Army, with Lewis guns,
once fought that lot in the wheat country.
Throat-talking sandgropers, they rise
dangling medals of clay.

No man ever composed
a sacred song. The honey ant,
euro and wagtail fathers brought them forth
thigh-slapping in showers of selves,
lying down, being outcrops.

When the humans reeled
under violence, they gave boys'
foreskins to the hawk men
on the whirlwind ground.
Age-long, it sufficed us.

o

The free-leaping spirit
hunters and white men with wheels
have one fact in common:
heat, flies and self-doubt
fall away from a man dressed in speed.

Roused by the full moon
I ride on along
the wire coasts of the outstation paddocks,
those seas of tranquillity,
in daylight, dry land.

The hull-down homestead passes me, miles off
*'I knew you were missing the sea,*
*love, that first year.'*
*They lie, embraced, their backs to history*
*she listens to the sea in his chapped ear.*

o

The war is farmers and miners. Both sides own me.
Big wheels revolve, and my mother's Cornish dad
comes into mind: he coughs up red and black,
dying, before my day,
on the Hunter fields.

The gold rushes conquered the world
most work, most love
most art is mining now.
The mullock is still
literal in Kalgoorlie.

Hearing the word *gentleman*
in a public bar there
I recognize a line of evolution
we thought to secure with a distant crown
lest it outgrew privilege.

In Kalgoorlie, though, I meet
a blind gem cutter. She
can put any stone to her cheek
name it and grade it.
She has no fear of cold stones at her cheek.

o

The light-wheeled VeeJays of
Kambalda Yacht Club
set spinnakers and career off
ages into the blue.
There is, naturally, a Commodore.

The day I reach Kambalda
some revenant waters still lie
thumbnail-deep, off the causeway
the sky floating there vast as Huron
but flesh shows between waves.

In sheltered, warm plasma
I dive to ring-finger depth,
no unwelcome settler.
A span deeper, and gravity's
calf begins sucking my hand.

o

Lionel Brockman hides his wife
and children in several stones
and watches from a finch as I camp.
*I don't understand the world,*
I confess, to coax them.

They are wise to fight shy.
Trees withdrew from my kind
when we said Tactics.
Nor is our takeover smell lessened, now that art
is not culture, but a culture.

I have been drunk in towns
built out of defiance of taste
which is to say, Europe.
I have rolled in the fact
and made a jingling sound.

Who am I to throw clay
at a Valiant abandoned in glare
stripped raw and daubed CONSTIPATED – CAN'T PASS A THING
we are a colloquial nation
most colonial when serious.

I am drawn to the noble mad, but
they betray evolution:
they do not lie, or joke.
One I met on the Goldfields would have it honour was sperm
and sadism a preference.

At birth, each Australian
receives a stout bullshit gauge
made of mulga from here
double-edged, emblematic
it is his to break.

*Country the forceful can*
*wreck but not reach*
*shall welcome the calm man*
*with nothing to teach,*
I sing to Brockman in the mulga forest.

o

Out here, the trees
grow coolly under the earth
and the bush is branches.
Something crashes away
in a dream of tall woods.

Going south all day
I think about the Republic.
I will improve my silence and listen to lives.
Those who would listen
have always been the Republic.

I rest, and my two wheels
continue as if the plains sloped
south, as the map falls.
Sunrise and sunset ride over me,
unending wheels.

     o

The Tuareg say
God made the desert last
as his most spacious great hall
to withdraw in from creation.
He is receding north now.

Limestone plain. The round lakes
clutch bulrushes at their deep point
bayonet-stiff between rains
the bottoms shelve in months and days of chalk
white circling rings. Impenetrable hollows.

Riding at noon
the great paddocks swimming with heat
I come to a stone hut. It is hard to think there,
the walls drip with laughter,
the tank, the yards, the downed fence cower with laughter.

     o

Young man in a ute:
*I'm from over in New South. I bought this block.*
A lifetime of work stares at him off the leaves.
In Sydney they keep a black stump with a share
and handles. The first plough on this continent.

*In Esperance, I reached a final lake*
*cupped in rough talcum.*
*Soft facepowder bloom made all the hanging country*
*faintly peach. Downward among cloud-wools*
*I had for long moments*

*a more-than-perfect self*
*refined by the lands*
*in mourning for the sea.*
*We bobbed at each other as the coast wind passed*
*the drive-in, and found us.*


## SIDERE MENS EADEM MUTATO

A SPIRAL OF SONNETS FOR ROBERT ELLIS

Out of the Fifties, a time of picking your nose
while standing at attention in civilian clothes,
we travelled luxury class in our drift to the city
not having a war, we went to university.
We learned to drink wine, to watch Swedish movies, and pass
as members, or members-in-law, of the middle class
but not in those first days when, stodge-fed, repressed,
curfewed and resented, we were the landladies' harvest.
I had meant to write a stiff poem about that, to be
entitled NOTES FROM THE HOUSE OF MRS HARVEY
it might have been unkind, in part – but then, to be honest
one did evict me for eating my dessert first
and even from the kindliest, we were
estranged, as from parents, in a green Verona,

o

a nail-biting fiefdom of suede boots, concupiscence, tea,
a garden pruned by the *Herald* angels yearly.
In that supermarket of styles, with many a setback
we tried everything on, from Law School Augustan to rat pack
and though in Chinese my progress was smooth up to *K'ung*
and in German I mastered the words that follow *Achtung*
in my slow-cycling mind an eloquence not yet articulate
was trying to say Youth. This. I will take it straight.
And you were losing your bush millenarian faith – I
remember your dread of the Wrath on first tasting coffee.
We were reading Fisher Library, addressing gargoyles on the stair,
drafting self after self on Spir-O-Bind notepaper
as the tidal freshers poured in, with hard things to learn
in increasing droves they were getting off at Redfern.

o

Literate Australia was British, or babu at least,
before Vietnam and the American conquest
career had overwhelmed learning most deeply back then:
a major in English made one a minor Englishman
and woe betide those who stepped off the duckboards of that.
Slacking and depth were a single morass. But a spirit
of unresolved life caught more and more in its powerful
field. It slowed their life to bulk wine and pool.
Signals had to be found. The day you gave up fornication
we took your WetChex and, by insufflation,
made fat balloons of them, to glisten aloft in the sun
above the Quad, the Great Hall, the Carillon –
and that was Day One in the decade of chickens-come-home
that day kids began smoking the armpit hairs of wisdom.

o

It is some while since we roomed at Bondi Beach
and heard the beltmen crying each to each.
Good friends we made while snatching culture between
the cogs of the System (they turned slower then)
reemerge, and improve as their outlines grow more clear
(but where's Lesley now? and Jacqueline, what of her?).
Academe has grown edgier. Many still drowse in the sun
but *intellect* sounds like the cocking of a sten gun.

Remember urbanity, by which our time meant
allusion to little-known Names in a special accent?
It persists – but war's grown; war, snarling out of that trip
in which Freud and Marx are left and right thongs in a goosestep.
Mind you, Jane Fonda plays in it too. It's fairly thin war.
The tiger is real, and in pain. He is fed on paper.

o

When the decorous towers were shaken by screams and bare hands
they deserved to be shaken. They had sought to classify humans.
The kids were constructing a poem of feathers and pain,
a prayer, a list, a shriek, it reached no resolution
except to stay crucial. Their prophets said different things:
Pour wax on the earth. Beat spirals into rings.
But though they shamed Magog their father and crippled his war
their own gnawed at them. They colonized one another.
With the cameras running, somehow the beat had to go on
(in times of trend, death comes by relegation)
but selfhood kept claiming the best people hand over fist
in a few months a third of mankind had been called fascist –
as the music slowed, the big track proved to be
'Fantasia of the World as a Softened University'.

o

Some things did change. Middle-class girls learned to swear,
men walked on the face of the moon once the Pill had tamed her
and we entered our thirties. No protest avails against that.
The horror of Time is, people don't snap out of it.
Now student politicoes well known in our day
have grown their hair two inches and are running the country.
Revolution's established. There will soon be degrees
conferred, with fistshake and speech, by the Dean of Eumenides.
The degree we attained was that brilliant refraction of will
that leaves one in several minds when facing evil.
It's still being offered. The Church of Jesus and Newman
did keep some of us balanced concerning the meanings of *human*
that greased golden term (all the rage in the new demiurgy)
though each new Jerusalem tempts the weaker clergy.

o

Academe has gained ground. She is the great house of our age,
replacing Society, granting the entree to privilege
likewise a museum, of peoples, of scholars, of writing –
vampires at times may tend an iron lung.
Her study is fashion, successive lock-gates leaking Time
she loves this new goddess for whom abortion is orgasm,
the talkative one. Nothing, now, less intense
could thrill an elite above unwilled experience.
When our elders, the castes who live by delegation,
turned in, like unlicensed guns, imagination,
thought, spirit, ideals to the all-wise University
there were aspects of learning they did not foresee
like being called the Masses, Funny Little Men
who live in the Suburbs and resemble Eichmann.

o

Academe is the class struggle, and whatever side
prevails will be hers. But I'm no alma-matricide
her task's also central: not making chemists and lawyers
but getting the passionate through their mating-and-war-years
to compromise. Remember? These shibboleths seem very real
in the light of a burning green stick. But where death's not literal
grace must be discerning. We have seen noble minds become rabid
and, as democrats, treat the Union stewards like dirt –
doctrine takes such a long view, especially in colonies,
that I'm grateful, like you, for downtown and country-town eyes
that glint and stay subtle while knowledge is power and foreign
through these, and some clowning, we master generalization
that blade of Caesarean rebirth which, day after day,
freed words in us. And cut our homes away.

o

That's the nub and the cork of it. Most rhymes in -ism and -ation
are nothing but cabals, though, out to take over the nation
compared with true persons: with Peter who sought gallant war,
with Herr Doktor Kurt H., who was a Siegfried-figure
by his own admission, with Vanessa Max Lawrence Penny
of *Honi Soit* then – they were our peerless company –
with Duncan the Sydney historian, who in an Australian course might send off the First Fleet by August:

and Dave Croll who died of a train, having seen much reality
these dine with my uncles and hills in the restaurant of memory
(which is also a starship, a marriage, a crystal of heaven)
with the droll men of Physics who one day would capture the Quark
with Germaine a few tables off winning a hard conversation
and Lex who cried *Poetry is not the wine but the cognac* …


## THE BROAD BEAN SERMON

Beanstalks, in any breeze, are a slack church parade
without belief, saying *trespass against us* in unison,
recruits in mint Air Force dacron, with unbuttoned leaves.

Upright with water like men, square in stem-section
they grow to great lengths, drink rain, keel over all ways,
kink down and grow up afresh, with proffered new greenstuff.

Above the cat-and-mouse floor of a thin bean forest
snails hang rapt in their food, ants hurry through several dimensions:
spiders tense and sag like little black flags in their cordage.

Going out to pick beans with the sun high as fence-tops, you find
plenty, and fetch them. An hour or a cloud later
you find shirtfulls more. At every hour of daylight

appear more that you missed: ripe, knobbly ones, fleshy-sided,
thin-straight, thin-crescent, frown-shaped, bird-shouldered,
    boat-keeled ones,
beans knuckled and single-bulged, minute green dolphins at suck,

beans upright like lecturing, outstretched like blessing fingers
in the incident light, and more still, oblique to your notice
that the noon glare or cloud-light or afternoon slants will uncover

till you ask yourself Could I have overlooked so many, or
do they form in an hour? unfolding into reality
like templates for subtly broad grins, like unique caught expressions,

like edible meanings, each sealed around with a string
and affixed to its moment, an unceasing colloquial assembly,
the portly, the stiff, and those lolling in pointed green slippers ...

Wondering who'll take the spare bagfulls, you grin with happiness
– it is your health – you vow to pick them all
even the last few, weeks off yet, misshapen as toes.


## THE ACTION

*We have spoken of the Action,*
*the believer-in-death, maker of tests and failures.*
*It is through the Action*
*that the quiet homes empty, and barrack beds fill up, and cities*
*that are cover from God.*
*The Action, continual breakthrough,*
*cannot abide slow speech. It invented Yokels,*
*it invented the Proles, who are difficult/noble/raffish,*
*it invented, in short, brave Us and the awful Others.*
*The smiling Action*
*makes all things new: its rites are father-killing,*
*sketching of pyramid plans, and the dance of Circles.*

Turning slowly under trees, footing off the river's linen
to come into shade – some waterhens were subtly
edging away to their kampongs of chomped reeds –
eel-thoughts unwound through me. At a little distance
I heard New Year children slap the causeway.
                                        Floating
in Coolongolook River, there below the junction
of Curreeki Creek,
                        water of the farms upheld me.


113

*We were made by the Action:*
*the apes who agreed to speech ate those who didn't,*
*Action people tell us.*
*Rome of the waterpipes came of the Action, lost it,*
*and Louis' Versailles, in memory of which we mow grass.*
*Napoleon and Stalin were, mightily, the Action.*
*All the Civilizations, so good at royal arts and war*
*and postal networks –*
*it is the myriad Action*
*keeps them successive, prevents the achievement for good*
*of civilization.*

Wash water, cattle water, irrigation-pipe-tang water
and water of the Kyle,
                         the chainsaw forests up there
where the cedar getter walks at night with dangling pockets,
water of the fern-tree gushers' heaping iron,
water of the bloodwoods, water of the Curreeki gold rush,
water of the underbrush sleeping shifts of birds
all sustained me,
                   thankful for great dinners
that had made me a lazy swimmer, marvellous floater,
looking up through the oaks
                              to the mountain Coolongolook,
the increase-place of flying-fox people, dancers –

*Now talk is around of a loosening in republics,*
*retrievals of subtle water: all the peoples*
*who call themselves The People,*
*all the unnoticed cultures,*
*remnants defined by a tilt in their speech, traditions*
*that call the stars, say, Great Bluff, Five Hounds of Oscar,*
*the High and Low Lazies,*
*spells, moon-phase farming – all these are being canvassed.*
*The time has come round for republics of the cultures*
*and for rituals, with sound: the painful washings-clean*
*of smallpox blankets.*
*It may save the world,*
*or be the new Action.*

                                                    Leaves
were coming to my lips, and the picnic on the bank
made delicious smoke.
                        Soon, perhaps, I'd be ready
to go and eat steak amongst Grandmother's people,
talk even to children,
                        dipping my face again
I kneaded my muscles, softening the Action.


## THE EDGE OF THE FOREST

The edge of the forest, hard smoke beyond the paddocks
frays back and is there. Cutters go out through it,
come in again on the ringbarked slopes, down the fence lines.

– *You have to send flooded gum quick. It don't stay flooded –*
*ironbark's a bugger to bark if it comes dry weather –*
the man sitting next to me knows inside the forest.

He has his praise out there. Two taps on a trunk
and he can tell you its life. Steering the chainsaw
he can drop a tree on a cigarette paper. His billets

bumped, loading, ring like gongs; they win prizes.
*Tallowwood's lovely: it has a deep like fat.*
He has raised trucks out of swamp with his quick chain-cunning.

He loves praise, hoards it. The tic's become hereditary.
His arts are the waltz, cards, company, ripostes:
*Easy seen you're not two-faced. You wouldn't wear that one.*

But at sixty-five, they take your life away.
If work has been shelter, they let in the winter
if work has been drudgery, night mocks the late-freed man
if work has been proof they take the glass away.

At four years old, he was milking easy cows
and was put to the plough at fourteen, the day after school.
Hauling timber with the teams, trusted in cattle dealing

he worked, then and always – long in lieu of pay –
for a sign of love from his irritable father,
the planter of flasks. His nightmare, strawed with praise.

The years hurry by. He was facing the bad birthday.
Neighbours talked heart. They tell you when to die
in a community. Thus when the Company, in person,

told him *Stay on: you're our best man*, some custom
and cliché were bent. It was a commutation.
Life. Life given back. Almost a father speaking.

He will come and go for years yet through the edge of the forest.


# LACHLAN MACQUARIE'S FIRST LANGUAGE

*The Governor and the seer are talking at night in a room
beyond formality. They are not speaking English.*
What like were Australians, then, in the time to come?
They had lost the Gaelic in them. It had become

like a tendon a man has no knowledge of in his body
but which puzzles his bending, at whiles, with a flexing impulse.
They'd wide cities, dram-shops, carriages with wings –
all the visions of Dun Kenneth. The singing at a ceilidh

lacked unison, though: each man there bellowing out of him
and his eyes undirected. Had they become a nation?
They had, and a people. A verandah was their capitol
though they spoke of a town where they kept the English seasons.

I heard different things: a farmer was telling his son
trap rabbits and sell the skins, then you can buy your
Bugs Bunny comics! – I didn't understand this. All folk there,
except the child-hating ones, were ladies and gentlemen.

# THE EUCHRE GAME

*So drunk he kept it at tens – and the bloody thing lost!*
*he bought a farm out of it.* Round the battered formica
table the talk is luck more than justice, justice
being the politics of a small child's outcry.

The subtlest eyes in the Southern Hemisphere look at
the cards in front of them. *Well I'll go alone.*
Outside the window, passionfruit flowers are blooming
singly together. Many are not in the sun.

Men lose a trick, deal a fresh hand. Intelligence here
is interest and the refusal of relegation;
those who conceive it chance-fixed to their benefit also
believe in justice. Some of them are what remains of

the Revolution. *Hey, was that for us?* Footsteps
recede down the hall. One looks at the window, three smile:
*Europeans! you're all suffering-snobs. Who's away?*
The game's loosely sacred: luck is being worked at.

# THE MITCHELLS

I am seeing this: two men are sitting on a pole
they have dug a hole for and will, after dinner, raise
I think for wires. Water boils in a prune tin.
Bees hum their shift in unthinning mists of white

bursaria blossom, under the noon of wattles.
The men eat big meat sandwiches out of a styrofoam
box with a handle. One is overheard saying:
*drought that year. Yes. Like trying to farm the road.*

The first man, if asked, would say *I'm one of the Mitchells.*
The other would gaze for a while, dried leaves in his palm,
and looking up, with pain and subtle amusement,

say *I'm one of the Mitchells*. Of the pair, one has been rich
but never stopped wearing his oil-stained felt hat. Nearly everything
they say is ritual. Sometimes the scene is an avenue.


## THE FLYING-FOX DREAMING

Now that the west
is lighting in under leaves
and Hookfoot the eagle
has gone from over the forest
there is no sound except the
tree-foxes, unwrapping from rest:

finger-winged night workers
who will soon beat up in tens
and thousands out of this daylong head-down city;
in the offing of scents above earth, they will cast for grown
and native fruit, and home in down-country for miles
on the ripe tree beacons.

Upside down all their days
Antipodean,
night wardrobes their singleness for them. Each bat, alone,
puts off crowding and chatter, once above the perches
he becomes the unfolded, far-speeding, upward-sidestepping,
nightowl-outflying one.

Here, one, his fur ballast
dropped among weeds in its tightening parchment, also
disproves a bush story: they don't excrete through the mouth
to satisfy gravity. All down the valley of fig
and flying-fox men, the lights now of towns are beginning
to gleam. They will burn late. It goes on being appropriate,

even the dead one becoming a clenched oval stone
*now clear of all twig-arrest, free of clambering dinners,*
*free at last of dawns' dazzling comedowns. Windrowing east*
*over the farms, adroit*
*at wingshrink turns*
*he is topping the nectar time, and the pollen harvest,*
*going on out continually over horizons.*


## VISITING ANZAC IN THE YEAR OF METRICATION

Gelibolu, Chanakkale –
there's no place called *Gallipoli*
down there, where the summer fires strip
the hills of scrub and rosemary.

Old wire snags the steeps like thorn
and human bones come out of the clay
where squatters' and selectors' boys
and the aghas' sons and their peasant boys

met in a raked boot-scrambling roar
and the *sooling* prints turned black with names
when currents drifted the landing buoys
to the heights of thyme and rosemary.

      o

Things sticking out jag at the mind,
Tooths' bottles, messtins, vertebrae
laid down in the bonzer *stoushing* days
the *spirited* and *clean-cut* days

up where the laddering trenches clung
and gravel flew in hobnailed sprays
where ripped and screaming chaps found out
that fellow humans really would,

where crimson-tidemarked puttees bore
histories of crowding in the sea
below the chirrup-haunted thyme,
burst entrails, shell-brass, rosemary.

o

When hard-case jokes and frantic help
poured content into noble sieves
that human lives cannot keep filled
it was the day of *turning round*,

when, firing, wags might turn around
and yell *How's that?* and in a push
a hundred jokers might turn round
and sprawl, and leap. Towns died of that

and the bush went underground:
the nation stalled in elegy
with a Day for massing through the streets
in pub time, wearing rosemary.

o

At Lone Pine and the Nek, the spinner
has scattered his cranial shilling bets
the king-and-country stones up there
mark no one's grave (Islam burns crosses).

Bowled Walers and stumped Victorians lie
in those broken hills inextricably
with their adversary, who was no less brave.
The misemployed, undone by courage,

have become the Unsaluting Army
and buttoned boys, for all their trades,
are country again, and that funny Missus
Porter's not yet changed poetry.

o

White bones, inconsolable proof
high scree, incomparable test –
on both points, class warfare has raged
but the war-pipes sail through jam-packed streets

where everyone is turning round:
old men and the ageing wear bright coins
and plain men and battlers' sons are proud
and the *flash* still trust extremity.

Our continent is uncrowded space,
a subtler thing than history.
The Day of our peace will need a native
herb that out-savours rosemary.

o

Down in the flatlands, coming away,
torn cotton bloomed in the few scratch fields
and conscripts on bivouac jogged by,
the Hittite face, the Turan face –

down there, in a day of rabid peace
and wartime love, one thought of how,
to farm blokes, war is Sudden City.
The newchums learned the tram-routes well

but disaster is all our brotherhood,
starved height, incomparable friends,
this is the reign of the measuring god,
this is the pit of rosemary.

o

High, near-Port Lincoln light. Harsh places.
This is the day of Freedom, too –
like the sardine tin lid tied
to the hawk's tail, life presents new faces.

Those shelterless hardscrabble cols
where even the Heads get *knocked* were best
assaulted in youth: we were handiest,
the climbing was overt and in vogue

and done with friends, in company.
Pioneering there, building with planks,
we showed the *battler* style to Death
amongst hoarse screams and rosemary.


# THE POWERLINE INCARNATION

When I ran to snatch the wires off our roof
hands bloomed teeth shouted I was almost seized
held back from this life
                          O flumes    O chariot reins
you cover me with lurids deck me with gaudies feed
my coronal    a scream sings in the air
above our dance    you slam it to me with farms
that you dark on and off numb hideous strong friend
Tooma and Geehi freak and burr through me
rocks fire-trails damwalls mountain-ash trees slew
to darkness through me    I zap them underfoot
with the swords of my shoes
                          I am receiving mountains
piloting around me    Crackenback    Anembo
the Fiery Walls    I make a hit in towns
I've never visited: smoke curls lightbulbs pop grey
discs hitch and slow    I plough the face of Mozart
and Johnny Cash    I bury and smooth their song
I crack it for copper links and fusebox spiders
I call my Friend from the circuitry of mixers
whipping cream for a birthday    I distract the immortal
Inhuman from hospitals
                          to sustain my jazz
and here is Rigel in a glove of flesh
my starry hand discloses smoke, cold Angel.

Vehicles that run on death come howling into
our street with lights a thousandth of my blue
arms keep my wife from my beauty    from my species
the jewels in my tips
                    I would accept her in
blind white remarriage    cover her with wealth
to arrest the heart    we'd share Apache leaps
crying out *Disyzygy!*
                    shield her from me, humans
from this happiness I burn to share    this touch
sheet car    live ladder    wildfire garden shrub –
away off I hear the bombshell breakers thrown
diminishing me    a meaninglessness coming
over the circuits
                    the god's deserting me
but I have dived in the mainstream    jumped the graphs
I have transited the dreams of crew-cut boys named Buzz
and the hardening music
                    to the big bare place
where the strapped-down seekers, staining white clothes, come
to be shown the Zeitgeist
                    passion and death my skin
my heart all logic    I am starring there
and must soon flame out
                    having seen the present god
It who feels nothing    It who answers prayers.


SYDNEY AND THE BUSH

When Sydney and the Bush first met
there was no open ground
and men and girls, in chains and not,
all made an urgent sound.

Then convicts bled and warders bred,
the Bush went back and back,
the men of Fire and of Earth
became White men and Black.

123

When Sydney ordered lavish books
and warmed her feet with coal
the Bush came skylarking to town
and gave poor folk a soul.

Then bushmen sank and factories rose
and warders set the tone –  ·
the Bush in quarter-acre blocks
helped families hold their own.

When Sydney and the Bush meet now
there is antipathy
and fashionable suburbs float
at night, far out to sea.

When Sydney rules without the Bush
she is a warders' shop
with heavy dancing overhead
the music will not stop

and when the drummers want a laugh
Australians are sent up.
When Sydney and the Bush meet now
there is no common ground.


## THE RETURNEES

As we were rowing to the lakes
our oars were blunt and steady wings

the tanbark-coloured water was
a gruel of pollen: more coming down
hinted strange futures to our cells

the far hills ancient under it
the corn flats black-green under heat
were cut in an antique grainy gold

it was the light of Boeotian art.

o

Bestowing tourbillons that drowned
the dusty light we had used up
pulling the distance to us, we
were conscious of a lifelong sound

on everything, that low fly-humming
melismatic untedious endless
note that a drone-pipe-plus-chants or

(shielding our eyes, rocking the river)

a ballad – some ballads – catch, the one
some paintings and many yarners summon
the ground-note here of unsnubbing art

cicadas were in it, and that Gothic
towering of crystals in the trees
Jock Neilson cutting a distant log

o

still hearing, we saw a snake ahead
winding, being his own snorkel

aslant in the swimming highlights, only
his head betrayed him, leading two
ripples and a scaled-down swirl. We edged

closer, were defied and breathed at.
A migrant, perhaps? a pioneer?
or had a kookaburra dropped
him, missing the organ-busting ground
and even the flat of the drinking-ground?

                    o

Touching the oars and riding, we
kept up with the blunt, heat-tasting head
debating its life, and sparing it

which is the good of Athens. Where
the rotted milk-wharf took the sun
flint-hard on top, dappling below

(remembered children danced up there
spinning their partners, the bright steel cans.
A way of life. But a way of life.)

the snake rose like a Viking ship
signed mud with a scattering flourish and
was into the wale of potato ground

like a whip withdrawn. We punted off.

                    o

Oar-leather jumping in spaced kicks
against the swivel-screw of rowlocks
we hauled the slow bush headlands near

drinking beer, and talking a bit

such friendliness shone into us, such
dry complex cheer, insouciant calm

out of everything, the brain-shaped trees
the wrinkling middle gleam, the still
*indifferently well-wooded* hills, it was

like rowing to meet your very best
passionately casual and dead friends
and feast with them on a little island

or an angel leaning down to one
queuing on the Day, to ask
*what was the best throw that you did?*

that note, raised to the pitch of tears:
tower of joking, star of skill,
gate of sardonyx and worn gold

*Black men and Rosenberg and I*
*have beliefs in common,* I exclaimed

and you were agreeing that Mao Tse-tung
had somehow come to Dunsinane –

      o

any more heightening and it would
have been a test, but the centre we
had stirred stopped down again, one notch

to happiness, and we were let dip
our points in the wide stopped water and
reclaim our motion. Bloodwood trees

round there were in such a froth of bloom
their honey dripped on shale and gummed
blady-grass in wigwams and ant-towns

sweetness, infusing, followed us
*Reality is somebody's,* you said
with a new and wryly balanced smile

*We're country, and Western,* I replied.

## SPURWING PLOVER

Foiled hunters sulk homewards at dusk

and the plover, among bitten grass
and the puffed felt of cattle manure
has made his white head and chest
a peg, or a mushroom. His greys
and dark tints are tucked in the gloom.

It is a discipline test
his still white. It faces sharp critics.
Those fellows are burning to shoot:

they'd like the stiff crack in the air
and your struggles, plover, much more
than ever your family-defending
quick dives, or your dinnerplate-scraping
sad cry: *turkey work! turkey work!*


## LACONICS: THE FORTY ACRES

We have bought the Forty Acres,
prime bush land.

If Bunyah is a fillet
this paddock is the eye.

The creek half-moons it,
log-deep, or parting rocks.

The corn-ground by now
has had forty years' grassed spell.

Up in the swamp
are paperbarks, coin-sized frogs –

The Forty, at last,
our beautiful deep land

it was Jim's, it was Allan's,
it was Reg's, it is Dad's –

Brett wanted it next
but he'd evicted Dad:

for bitter porridge
many cold returns.

That interior machine-gun,
my chainsaw, drops dead timber.

Where we burn the heaps
we'll plant kikuyu grass.

Ecology? Sure.
But also husbandry.

And the orchard will go there,
and we'll re-roof the bare pole barn.

Our croft, our Downs,
our sober, shining land.


CREEPER HABIT

On Bennelong Point
a two-dimensional tree
drapes the rock cutting.

Bird-flecked, self-espaliered
it issues out of the kerb
feeding on dead sparks
of the old tram depot;

a fig, its muscles
of stiffened chewing gum grip
the flutings and beads
of the crowbar-and-dynamite wall.

The tree has height and extent
but no roundness. Cramponned in cracks
its branches twine and utter
coated leaves.

With half its sky blank rock
it has little choice.
It has climbed high from a tiny sour gall
and spreads where it can,
feeding its leaves on the light
of North Shore windows.


## TANKA: THE COFFEE SHOPS

Lorenzini's, Vadim's,
Rowe Street, and Repin's upstairs,
all shuttered and gone.
The coffee shops vanished
just as they'd conquered the world.


## THE GALLERY

Stale pasture, midsummer
    going down to the canopy
    that is under the paddocks

tristania trees, laurinas, water gums
are a sinewy corps
    beneath their loot of rosettes

floodwrack hangs jammed
in the lillipilli boughs
    it is campfires fixed above ground
it is wet-season beards

    through root-stumbling cattletrack
doors, below the landscape
to the pavement, cracked floor
    and the bouldery parterres

    bulltussocks ostend
    fierce wheat-heads of their bloom

dead-end water breeds

    still-purposeful water finds ways
    between rock, and the light
    hangs quivering all day.

In the inwardness
it is twilit and tall,
inleaning, with stilled sway.
Flies stay out in the farms.

Parrots sweep in here
from the hacking gunshot corn
for their sip of ancient
and way along the gallery
a great white-cedar tree,
Melia azedarach, burns
in a Christmas of sun.

    The creek is a vein
    like every stream on earth
    going back to the heart

but the gallery's a bridge
of the forest across cleared land,
battalions sheltering
out of the chainsaw age here.

The cool of high country
marches west with the galleries
shade, verticals, complexity
hide out from the plains inside
half-day horizons

whisky of the high
peat maltings, smuggled out
under Antarctic beeches,
runoff from the white man's tent,
washes one's feet here

black thwarts, branched tackle
rotting where they paused
on their way to the lagoons
    deflect and bridge
the fish-scummed spider pools

rust drip, glass gravel,
kingfisher, robin, wren.

All tumbled together, in the vanished flood,
eel bones, the rock of horror,
                        style-test of fellows
and the rock of God who does not rescue flesh.

This skeleton river, soil-shadow feeding the farms:
to be under these terraces
                        understanding your life
that is more than half gone, and your friends dismarrying,

to be here with your country, that will waken when it wakens,
that won't be awakened by contempt
                        or love;
to know you may live and die in colonial times.

rock-bar of quartz
why should your life go well?

rock-bench of basalt
do we know everything yet?

despair and attitudes
might be licensed then

oar-bench of mahogany
is all the evidence in?

courage and largesse
of hope may, till then, be licensed

in the middle of the world

Out of the ochre-mined
farm gullies, milky blood
and bottles creep in
but the creek is irreverent
in its riddling way:

*when they stole my hat*
*I hid beneath a stone*
*and I starved their corn*
*and when I got strong*
*I ate the bastards' corn*

but the gallery's the interchange
of some primal worlds
it points out of every
evergreen island,
                    it is
greater than hedgerows
where doomed pets hang on
against autumn cultures;
it leads inland to the heart.

And climbing up, out
through liana cordage, boot-slipping
   on humus, under panicles,
   acmena and syzygium trunks, you

come into the place where fathers and children are sitting
around under paperbark trees. They are eating wrapped tucker
and God-enclosed melons. The daylight moon is rising
over the shoulder of towns, it is putting on flesh
and seeds; it will ripen smoke-red above the white farms.


# EMPLOYMENT FOR THE CASTES IN ABEYANCE

I was a translator at the Institute:
fair pay, clean work, and a bowerbird's delight
of theory and fact to keep the forebrain supple.

I was Western Europe. *Beiträge, reviste,*
*dissertaties, rapports* turned English under my
one-fingered touch. Teacup-and-Remington days.

It was a job like Australia: peace and cover,
a recourse for exiles, poets, decent spies,
for plotters who meant to rise from the dead with their circle.

I was getting over a patch of free-form living:
flat food round the midriff, long food up your sleeves –
castes in abeyance, we exchanged these stories.

My Chekhovian colleague who worked as if under surveillance
would tell me tales of real life in Peking and Shanghai
and swear at the genders subsumed in an equation.

The trade was uneasy about computers, back then:
if they could be taught not to render, say, *out of sight*
*out of mind* as *invisible lunatic*

they might supersede us – not
because they'd be better. More on principle.
Not that our researchers were unkindly folk:

one man on exchange from Akademgorod
told me about Earth's crustal plates, their ponderous
inevitable motion, collisions that raised mountain chains,

the continents rode on these Marxian turtles, it seemed;
another had brought slow death to a billion rabbits,
a third team had bottled the essence of rain on dry ground.

They were translators, too, our scientists:
they were translating the universe into science,
believing that otherwise it had no meaning.

Leaving there, I kept my Larousse and my Leutseligkeit
and I heard that machine translation never happened:
language defeated it. We are a language species.

I gather this provoked a shift in science,
that having become a side, it then changed sides
and having collapsed, continued at full tempo.

Prince Obolensky succeeded me for a time
but he soon returned to Fiji to teach Hebrew.
In the midst of life, we are in employment:

seek, travel and print, seek-left-right-travel-and-bang
as the Chinese typewriter went which I saw working
when I was a translator in the Institute.


# THE CARDIFF COMMONWEALTH ARTS FESTIVAL
# POETRY CONFERENCE 1965, RECALLED

Three a.m., Tiger Bay. In the only
club still open, the Sheik's Tent,
James McAuley and two Welsh students
are discussing enjambment.

135

Uptown, the Bomb Culture's just opened
its European run,
discounting many things on its counter:
calm tradition is one;

here, though, cheesecloth, fuzzed menace and Sin
are all mortified to death
to find themselves kindly dismissed
for talk of Wordsworth;

the Pleasure Principle's looking quite haggard,
belching whisky, sweating scent,
the belly dancers rhythmically twitching,
pallid boughs in a current.


## DRIVING TO THE ADELAIDE FESTIVAL 1976 VIA THE MURRAY VALLEY HIGHWAY

A long narrow woodland with channels, reentrants, ponds:
the Murray's a mainstream with footnotes, a folklorists' river.

The culture, on both banks, is pure Victoria:
the beer, the footy, the slight earnest flavour, the cray.

Some places there's a man-made conventional width of water
studded with trunks; a cold day in the parrots' high rooms.

Walking on the wharf at Echuca, that skyscraper roof:
sixty feet down timber to a dry-season splash.

In the forest there are sudden cliffs: dusty silken water
moving away: the live flow is particle-green.

Billabongs are pregnant with swirls, and a sunken road
of hyacinth leads to an eerie noonday corner.

Ships rotting in the woods, ships turning to silt in blind channels;
one looked like a bush pub impelled by a combine header.

Out in the wide country, channels look higher than the road
even as you glance along them. Salt glittering out there.

Romance is a vine that survives in the ruins of skill:
inside the horizon again, a restored steamboat, puffing.

Thinking, at speed among lakes, of a time beyond denim
and the gardens of that time. Night-gardens. Fire gardens.

Crazed wood, brushed chars, powder-blue leaves. Each year the purist
would ignite afresh with a beerbottle lens, a tossed bumper –

Heading for a tent show, thinking stadium thoughts,
a dense bouquet slowing the van through the province of sultanas.


## THE BULADELAH-TAREE HOLIDAY SONG CYCLE

*1*

The people are eating dinner in that country north of Legge's Lake;
behind flywire and venetians, in the dimmed cool, town people eat Lunch.
Plying knives and forks with a peek-in sound, with a tuck-in sound,
they are thinking about relatives and inventory, they are talking about
    customers and visitors.
In the country of memorial iron, on the creek-facing hills there,
they are thinking about bean plants, and rings of tank water, of growing
    a pumpkin by Christmas;
rolling a cigarette, they say thoughtfully Yes, and their companion nods,
    considering.
Fresh sheets have been spread and tucked tight, childhood rooms have
    been seen to,

for this is the season when children return with their children
to the place of Bingham's Ghost, of the Old Timber Wharf, of the
    Big Flood That Time,
the country of the rationalized farms, of the day-and-night farms,
    and of the Pitt Street farms,
of the Shire Engineer and many other rumours, of the tractor crankcase
    furred with chaff,

137

the places of sitting down near ferns, the snake-fear places, the
    cattle-crossing-long-ago places.

2

It is the season of the Long Narrow City; it has crossed the Myall, it
    has entered the North Coast,
that big stunning snake; it is looped through the hills, burning all night
    there.
Hitching and flying on the downgrades, processionally balancing on
    the climbs,
it echoes in O'Sullivan's Gap, in the tight coats of the flooded-gum trees;
the tops of palms exclaim at it unmoved, there near Wootton.
Glowing all night behind the hills, with a north-shifting glare, burning
    behind the hills;
through Coolongolook, through Wang Wauk, across the Wallamba,
the booming tarred pipe of the holiday slows and spurts again; Nabiac
    chokes in glassy wind,
the forests on Kiwarrak dwindle in cheap light; Tuncurry and Forster
    swell like cooking oil.
The waiting is buffed, in timber villages off the highway, the waiting is
    buffeted:
the fumes of fun hanging above ferns; crime flashes in strange windscreens,
    in the time of the Holiday.
Parasites weave quickly through the long gut that paddocks shine into;
powerful makes surging and pouncing: the police, collecting Revenue.
The heavy gut winds over the Manning, filling northward, digesting the
    towns, feeding the towns;
they all become the narrow city, they join it;
girls walking close to murder discard, with excitement, their names.
Crossing Australia of the sports, the narrow city, bringing home the
    children.

3

It is good to come out after driving and walk on bare grass;
walking out, looking all around, relearning that country.
Looking out for snakes, and looking out for rabbits as well;
going into the shade of myrtles to try their cupped climate, swinging by
    one hand around them,

in that country of the Holiday ...
stepping behind trees to the dam, as if you had a gun,
to that place of the Wood Duck,
to that place of the Wood Duck's Nest,
proving you can still do it; looking at the duck who hasn't seen you,
the mother duck who'd run Catch Me (broken wing) I'm Fatter
    (broken wing), having hissed to her children.

4

The birds saw us wandering along.
Rosellas swept up crying out *we think we think*; they settled farther along;
knapping seeds off the grass, under dead trees where their eggs were,
    walking around on their fingers,
flying on into the grass.
The heron lifted up his head and elbows; the magpie stepped aside a bit,
angling his chopsticks into pasture, turning things over in his head.
At the place of the Plough Handles, of the Apple Trees Bending Over,
    and of the Cattlecamp,
there the vealers are feeding; they are loosely at work, facing everywhere.
They are always out there, and the forest is always on the hills;
around the sun are turning the wedgetail eagle and her mate, that dour
    brushhook-faced family:
they settled on Deer's Hill away back when the sky was opened,
in the bull-oak trees way up there, the place of fur tufted in the grass,
    the place of bone-turds.

5

The Fathers and the Great-grandfathers, they are out in the paddocks
    all the time, they live out there,
at the place of the Rail Fence, of the Furrows Under Grass, at the place
    of the Slab Chimney.
We tell them that clearing is complete, an outdated attitude, all over;
we preach without a sacrifice, and are ignored; flowering bushes grow
    dull to our eyes.
We begin to go up on the ridge, talking together, looking at the
    kino-coloured ants,
at the yard-wide sore of their nest, that kibbled peak, and the workers
    heaving vast stalks up there,

the brisk compact workers; jointed soldiers pour out then, tense with acid;
several probe the mouth of a lost gin bottle;
*Innuendo*, we exclaim, *literal minds!* and go on up the ridge, announced
   by finches;
passing the place of the Dingo Trap, and that farm hand it caught, and
   the place of the Cowbails,
we come to the road and watch heifers,
little unjoined Devons, their teats hidden in fur, and the cousin with
   his loose-slung stockwhip driving them.
We talk with him about rivers and the lakes; his polished horse is
   stepping nervously,
printing neat omegas in the gravel, flexing its skin to shake off flies;
his big sidestepping horse that has kept its stones; it recedes gradually,
   bearing him;
we murmur *stone-horse* and *devilry* to the grinners under grass.

6

Barbecue smoke is rising at Legge's Camp; it is steaming into the
   midday air,
all around the lake shore, at the Broadwater, it is going up among the
   paperbark trees,
a heat-shimmer of sauces, rising from tripods and flat steel, at that place
   of the cone shells,
at that place of the Seagrass, and the tiny segmented things swarming in
   it, and of the Pelican.
Dogs are running around disjointedly; water escapes from their mouths,
confused emotions from their eyes; humans snarl at them Gwanout and
   Hereboy, not varying their tone much;
the impoverished dog people, suddenly sitting down to nuzzle themselves;
   toddlers side with them:
toddlers, running away purposefully at random, among cars, into big
   drownie water (come back, Cheryl-Ann!).
They rise up as charioteers, leaning back on the tow-bar; all their
   attributes bulge at once:
swapping swash shoulder-wings for the white-sheeted shoes that bear
   them,
they are skidding over the flat glitter, stiff with grace, for once not
   travelling to arrive.

From the high dunes over there, the rough blue distance, at length they
    come back behind the boats,
and behind the boats' noise, cartwheeling, or sitting down, into the lake's
    warm chair;
they wade ashore and eat with the families, putting off that uprightness,
    that assertion,
eating with the families who love equipment, and the freedom from
    equipment,
with the fathers who love driving, and lighting a fire between stones.

7

Shapes of children were moving in the standing corn, in the child-
    labour districts;
coloured flashes of children, between the green and parching stalks,
    appearing and disappearing.
Some places, they are working, racking off each cob like a lever, tossing
    it on the heaps;
other places, they are children of child-age, there playing jungle:
in the tiger-striped shade, they are firing hoehandle machine-guns,
    taking cover behind fat pumpkins;
in other cases, it is Sunday and they are lovers.
They rise and walk together in the sibilance, finding single rows irksome,
    hating speech now,
or, full of speech, they swap files and follow defiles, disappearing and
    appearing;
near the rain-grey barns, and the children building cattleyards beside
    them;
the standing corn, gnawed by pouched and rodent mice; generations
    are moving among it,
the parrot-hacked, medicine-tasselled corn, ascending all the creek flats,
    the wire-fenced alluvials,
going up in patches through the hills, towards the Steep Country.

8

Forests and State Forests, all down off the steeper country; mosquitoes
    are always living in there:
they float about like dust motes and sink down, at the places of the
    Stinging Tree,

141

and of the Staghorn Fern; the males feed on plant-stem fluid, absorbing
that watery ichor;
the females meter the air, feeling for the warm-blooded smell, needing
blood for their eggs.
They find the dingo in his sleeping-place, they find his underbelly and
his anus;
they find the possum's face, they drift up the ponderous pleats of the fig
tree, way up into its rigging,
the high camp of the fruit bats; they feed on the membranes and ears of
bats; tired wings cuff air at them;
their eggs burning inside them, they alight on the muzzles of cattle,
the half-wild bush cattle, there at the place of the Sleeper Dump, at the
place of the Tallowwoods.
The males move about among growth tips; ingesting solutions, they
crouch intently;
the females sing, needing blood to breed their young; their singing is in
the scrub country;
their tune comes to the name-bearing humans, who dance to it and
irritably grin at it.

9

The warriors are cutting timber with brash chainsaws; they are trimming
hardwood pit-props and loading them;
*Is that an order?* they hoot at the peremptory lorry driver, who laughs;
he is also a warrior.
They are driving long-nosed tractors, slashing pasture in the dinnertime
sun;
they are fitting tappets and valves, the warriors, or giving finish to a
surfboard.
Addressed on the beach by a pale man, they watch waves break and
are reserved, refusing pleasantry;
they joke only with fellow warriors, chaffing about try-ons and the
police, not slighting women.
Making Timber a word of power, Con-rod a word of power, Sense a
word of power, the Regs. a word of power,
they know belt-fed from spring-fed; they speak of being *stiff*, and
being *history*;
the warriors who have killed, and the warriors who eschewed killing,

the solemn, the drily spoken, the life peerage of endurance; drinking
water from a tap,
they watch boys who think hard work a test, and boys who think it is
not a test.

10

Now the ibis are flying in, hovering down on the wetlands,
on those swampy paddocks around Darawank, curving down in ragged
dozens,
on the riverside flats along the Wang Wauk, on the Boolambayte
pasture flats,
and away towards the sea, on the sand moors, at the place of the
Jabiru Crane;
leaning out of their wings, they step down; they take out their
implement at once,
out of its straw wrapping, and start work; they dab grasshopper and
ground-cricket
with nonexistence ... spiking the ground and puncturing it ...
they swallow down the outcry of a frog;
they discover titbits kept for them under cowmanure lids, small
slow things.
Pronging the earth, they make little socket noises, their thoughtfulness
jolting down and up suddenly;
there at Bunyah, along Firefly Creek, and up through Germany,
the ibis are all at work again, thin-necked ageing men towards
evening; they are solemnly all back
at Minimbah, and on the Manning, in the rye-and-clover irrigation fields;
city storemen and accounts clerks point them out to their wives,
remembering things about themselves, and about the ibis.

11

Abandoned fruit trees, moss-tufted, spotted with dim lichen paints;
the fruit trees of the Grandmothers,
they stand along the creekbanks, in the old home paddocks, where
the houses were,
they are reached through bramble-grown front gates, they creak at
dawn behind burnt skillions,

143

at Belbora, at Bucca Wauka, away in at Burrell Creek,
    at Telararee of the gold-sluices.
The trees are split and rotten-elbowed; they bear the old-fashioned
    summer fruits,
the annual bygones: china pear, quince, persimmon;
the fruit has the taste of former lives, of sawdust and parlour song,
    the tang of Manners;
children bite it, recklessly,
at what will become for them the place of the Slab Wall, and of the
    Coal Oil Lamp,
the place of moss-grit and swallows' nests, the place of the Crockery.

12

Now the sun is an applegreen blindness through the swells, a white
    blast on the sea face, flaking and shoaling;
now it is burning off the mist; it is emptying the density of trees, it is
    spreading upriver,
hovering about the casuarina needles, there at Old Bar and Manning
    Point;
flooding the island farms, it abolishes the milkers' munching breath
as they walk towards the cowyards; it stings a bucket here, a teacup there.
Morning steps into the world by ever more southerly gates; shadows
    weaken their north skew
on Middle Brother, on Cape Hawke, on the dune scrub toward Seal Rocks;
steadily the heat is coming on, the butter-water time, the clothes-
    sticking time;
grass covers itself with straw; abandoned things are thronged with spirits;
everywhere wood is still with strain; birds hiding down the creek galleries,
    and in the cockspur canes;
the cicada is hanging up her sheets; she takes wing off her music-sheets.
Cars pass with a rational zoom, panning quickly towards Wingham,
through the thronged and glittering, the shale-topped ridges, and the
    cattlecamps,
towards Wingham for the cricket, the ball knocked hard in front of
    smoked-glass ranges, and for the drinking.
In the time of heat, the time of flies around the mouth, the time of the
    west verandah;
looking at that umbrage along the ranges, on the New England side;

clouds begin assembling vaguely, a hot soiled heaviness on the sky, away
there towards Gloucester;
a swelling up of clouds, growing there above Mount George, and above
Tipperary;
far away and hot with light; sometimes a storm takes root there, and fills
the heavens rapidly;
darkening, boiling up and swaying on its stalks, pulling this way and that,
blowing round by Krambach;
coming white on Bulby, it drenches down on the paddocks, and on the
wire fences;
the paddocks are full of ghosts, and people in cornbag hoods approaching;
lights are lit in the house; the storm veers mightily on its stem, above the
roof; the hills uphold it;
the stony hills guide its dissolution; gullies opening and crumbling down,
wrenching tussocks and rolling them;
the storm carries a greenish-grey bag; perhaps it will find hail and send it
down, starring cars, flattening tomatoes,
in the time of the Washaways, of the dead trunks braiding water, and of
the Hailstone Yarns.

13

The stars of the holiday step out all over the sky.
People look up at them, out of their caravan doors and their campsites;
people look up from the farms, before going back; they gaze at their year's
worth of stars.
The Cross hangs head-downward, out there over Markwell;
it turns upon the Still Place, the pivot of the Seasons, with one shoulder
rising:
'Now I'm beginning to rise, with my Pointers and my Load ...'
hanging eastwards, it shines on the sawmills and the lakes, on the glasses
of the Old People.
Looking at the Cross, the galaxy is over our left shoulder, slung up highest
in the east;
there the Dog is following the Hunter; the Dog Star pulsing there above
Forster; it shines down on the Bikies,
and on the boat-hire sheds, there at the place of the Oyster; the place of
the Shark's Eggs and her Hide;
the Pleiades are pinned up high on the darkness, away back above the
Manning;

they are shining on the Two Blackbutt Trees, on the rotted river wharves,
    and on the towns;
standing there, above the water and the lucerne flats, at the place of
    the Families;
their light sprinkles down on Taree of the Lebanese shops, it mingles with
    the streetlights and their glare.
People recover the starlight, hitching north,
travelling north beyond the seasons, into that country of the Communes,
    and of the Banana:
the Flying Horse, the Rescued Girl, and the Bull, burning steadily above
    that country.
Now the New Moon is low down in the west, that remote direction of the
    Cattlemen,
and of the Saleyards, the place of steep clouds, and of the Rodeo;
the New Moon who has poured out her rain, the moon of the
    Planting-times.
People go outside and look at the stars, and at the melon-rind moon,
the Scorpion going down into the mountains, over there towards
    Waukivory, sinking into the tree-line,
in the time of the Rockmelons, and of the Holiday ...
the Cross is rising on his elbow, above the glow of the horizon;
carrying a small star in his pocket, he reclines there brilliantly,
above the Alum Mountain, and the lakes threaded on the Myall River,
    and above the Holiday.


## THE SWARM

*Of late there has been some loose talk about Australia becoming a republic ...*
                                        – Governor-General Sir John Kerr, 1976

On a stone wall, adrift from their hive
seeking shelter away from the wind
of a bitter blue day, this tight swarm
of brown English bees is adhering.

Poor monarchists, clumped round their queen,
they look like a furry, half-risen
loaf of gingerbread dough, with transparent
mica scales crusted on it: worn wings.

That animal, made up of lives,
drones, queen, dispensable workers –
we feel almost tempted to stroke it
but we know the terror, the venom

in those many clenched loyalists, whose rote
runs simply *Some eat the royal jelly:*
*most do not. This is Right. Work and die.*
What is, is, the clustered swarm murmurs.

Oh it is, some cool men with a smoke-pot
might smirk, and box them. Not us, though.
We must love and bypass them, like Nature,
since *springtime* or *freedom* would be loose talk indeed.


# FOUR GAELIC POEMS


## 1. Free Kirk Cemetery, Northern New South Wales

I farmed in the land
of Lazy Fair.

Pipe-music and dancing
when I was young;

lamplight and wireless
as I grew older.

Rabbits shot in a flood
rabbits eaten in drought-time.

Now inside a fence
psalm-flattened silence.

## 2. A Skirl for Outsets

The sea smooths a page of its folio
and another page:
I lie in the lee of high sand
earning my wage;

pale child of the sunburnt clans
I lie covered there
and try out this pibroch-baseline
on the air:

*Purest moment of all venture*
*is the beginning,*
*recruits stepping out, tanned and sure,*
*who, stepping, sing.*

*It is the first depth of voyage*
*after stowing all aboard,*
*a moment, on deck, and on the bridge,*
*and the lengthening forward.*

And then there's the density of
fraught thresholds in
first love, and in first real love.
Some cross them again.

We are mad for fresh starts, for leaps forward,
for this vertigo;
for new Angles, and recycled Breakthroughs,
the 1912 Show,

for the terrorist's clenched joy
when told he, or she,
is to move at the vortex of things
with the Chosen Company.

Connoisseurship of outsets
is required, perhaps,
to say what is shrouds in all this,
what is silk, what straps:

I have loved the absorbed angel
Preparation, and that charge
that gathers in maps, stores, field-glasses
and attracts a charge:

the squadron, the Core Group, the Movement,
*Sinn Fein amháinn!* –
how briefly we knew not to join
was best for man.

The swimmer into cleanness leaping
spurns the shore,
exultant, out of gravity, acclaimed,
upright in water,

*and this is the way the worlds end*
*after space, after sense:*
*not by the tin bowl, nor the Bomb,*
*but by Significance.*


## 3. The Gum Forest

After the last gapped wire on a post,
homecoming for me, to enter the gum forest.

This old slow battlefield: parings of armour,
cracked collars, elbows, scattered on the ground.

New trees step out of old: lemon and ochre
splitting out of grey everywhere, in the gum forest.

In there for miles, shade track and ironbark slope,
depth casually beginning all around, at a little distance.

Sky sifting, and always a hint of smoke in the light;
you can never reach the heart of the gum forest.

In here is like a great yacht harbour, charmed to leaves,
innumerable tackle, poles wrapped in spattered sail,
or an unknown army in reserve for centuries.

Flooded-gums on creek ground, each tall because of each.
Now a blackbutt in bloom is showering with bees
but warm blood sleeps in the middle of the day.

The witching hour is noon in the gum forest.
Foliage builds like a layering splash: ground water
drily upheld in edge-on, wax-rolled, gall-puckered
leaves upon leaves. The shoal life of parrots up there.

Stone footings, trunk-shattered. Non-human lights.
Enormous abandoned machines. The mysteries of the gum forest.

Delight to me, though, at the water-smuggling creeks,
health to me, too, under banksia candles and combs.

A wind is up, rubbing limbs above the bullock roads;
mountains are waves in the ocean of the gum forest.

I go my way, looking back sometimes, looking round me;
singed oils clear my mind, and the pouring sound high up.

Why have I denied the passions of my time? To see
lightning strike upward out of the gum forest.


*4. Elegy for Angus Macdonald of Cnoclinn*

The oldest tree in Europe's lost
a knotty branch it could ill spare
to make a hump in Sydney ground,
not for the first time. No. But the last.
A genus of honey bees has died out,
a strain that came to us from the lost world.

Anger at that coarse canting fool
who tried to bury you meanings and all
under his turnip-cairn of texts
– you with the knowledge, he with the talk –
kept us from tears, the day you rode
down ropes in your chest of polished wood.

You were as strange in our waters as
the Atlantis-reef Rocabarraidh. Students,
we came for ancestral language, but you,
no teacher of grammar, gave us lore,
a sight down usages to the Bronze Age
and an ideal from then, older than Heaven,
the 'harmony of the men of peace'.

The highest folk culture in the West
and terms from a lost, non-Greek Agora
mingled in you, our giver of words:
*feallsanachd, oine, foidhirlisg.*
Late on and far from heirs, you wrote
your oral learning down in a book,
a dense heaped Cadbury Hill of a book,

the history of your island, songs
and steadings of Heisgir under the sea,
black crimes from the Age of Forays, wise
folk government in the Lordship of the Isles,
astronomy and logic of the men
who taught in that curious late druidical
university of the White Mountain;

you were oath-bound to transmit these things
and you did transmit them. The book remains,
cranky, magnificent, pregnant with rethinkings
as the Watts Towers or Fort's museum,
a Celtic history indeed, a line –
for this is the meaning of the drowned lands –
by which to haul from the conqueror's sea
of myth, our alternative antiquity.

Teacher of my heart, you'll not approve
my making this in the conqueror's language
(though Calgacus used their Latin finely:
'You have made a desert and called it peace').
Even the claim I make at times
to writing Gaelic in English words
would make you sniff (but also smile),

but my fathers were Highlanders long ago
then Borderers, before this landfall
– 'savages' once, now we are 'settlers'
in the mouth of the deathless enemy –
but I am seized of this future now.
I am not European. Nor is my English.

And perhaps you too were better served here
than in Uist of the Sheldrakes and the tides
watching the old life fade, the *toradh*,
the good, go out of the island world.
Exile's a rampart, sometimes, to the past,
a distiller of spirit from bruised grains;
this is a meaning of the New World.

The good does not go out of the past.
Angles of the moving moon and sun
elicit fresh lights from it continually;
now, in the new lands, everyone's Ethnic
and we too, the Scots Australians, who've been
henchmen of much in our self-loss
may recover ourselves, and put off oppression.

This, then, for the good you put on us,
round-tower of Gaelic, grand wrongheaded one,
now you have gone to the dark crofts:
the oldest tree in Europe's shed
a seed to us – and the Otherworld
becomes ancestral, a code of history,
a style of fingering, an echo of vowels,
honey that comes to us from the lost world.

# RAINWATER TANK

Empty rings when tapped give tongue,
rings that are tense with water talk:
as he sounds them, ring by rung,
Joe Mitchell's reddened knuckles walk.

The cattledog's head sinks down a notch
and another notch, beside the tank,
and Mitchell's boy, with an old jack-plane,
lifts moustaches from a plank.

From the puddle that the tank has dripped
hens peck glimmerings and uptilt
their heads to shape the quickness down;
petunias live on what gets spilt.

The tankstand spider adds a spittle
thread to her portrait of her soul.
Pencil-grey and stacked like shillings
out of a banker's paper roll

stands the tank, roof-water drinker.
The downpipe stares drought into it.
Briefly the kitchen tap turns on
then off. But the tank says Debit, Debit.


# THE FUTURE

There is nothing about it. Much science fiction is set there
but is not about it. Prophecy is not about it.
It sways no yarrow stalks. And crystal is a mirror.
Even the man we nailed on a tree for a lookout
said little about it; he told us evil would come.
We see, by convention, a small living distance into it
but even that's a projection. And all our projections
fail to curve where it curves.
                                It is the black hole
out of which no radiation escapes to us.

The commonplace and magnificent roads of our lives
go on some way through cityscape and landscape
or steeply sloping, or scree, into that sheer fall
where everything will be that we have ever sent there,
compacted, spinning – except perhaps us, to see it.
It is said we see the start.
                                    But, from here, there's a blindness.
The side-heaped chasm that will swallow all our present
blinds us to the normal sun that may be imagined
shining calmly away on the far side of it, for others
in their ordinary day. A day to which all our portraits,
ideals, revolutions, denim and deshabille
are quaintly heartrending. To see those people is impossible,
to greet them, mawkish. Nonetheless, I begin:
'When I was alive – '
                          and I am turned around
to find myself looking at a cheerful picnic party,
the women decently legless, in muslin and gloves,
the men in beards and weskits, with the long
cheroots and duck trousers of the better sort,
relaxing on a stone verandah. Ceylon, or Sydney.
And as I look, I know they are utterly gone,
each one on his day, with pillow, small bottles, mist,
with all the futures they dreamed or dealt in, going
down to that engulfment everything approaches;
with the man on the tree, they have vanished into the Future.


## COWYARD GATES

I saw from the road last time, our house
is all down now.
I didn't go to look.

My cousin had prised the last sheet iron off
the rafters of our sleep
and winced the wall-studs down.

He didn't want an untidy widower ageing
on his new farm.
I'll want the timber for cowyard gates, he said.

The floor joists will persist awhile
and the fireplace, that pack-ice of concrete, stained
with the last spilt fat.
I didn't go to look.

I had said goodbye to that house many times
and so helped it fall.
I have even ransacked it,
carried off slants of sunlight and of wind
that used to strike through the bedroom planking, blades
against the upstart.

Many feelings are suspended:
the front verandah feeling, looking away at the west,
the back verandah feeling, wet boards, towel on its nail,
all widowed in the air,

but, half demolished, it was almost an eddy
standing there on the ridge,
memory and loss in a grove of upright boards.

Now Time's free to dissipate all the days trapped there:
books in the sleepout, green walling of branches around
our Christmas table, my mother placing and placing
a tin ring on scone-dough, telling me about French.
The first weeks of her death.

Suppertime lamp,
full moon through the loungeroom door.
I did not go to look.

# IMMIGRANT VOYAGE

My wife came out on the *Goya*
in the mid-year of our century.

In the fogs of that winter
many hundred ships were sounding;
the DP camps were being washed to sea.

The bombsites and the ghettoes
were edging out to Israel,
to Brazil, to Africa, America.

The separating ships were bound away
to the cities of refuge
built for the age of progress.

Hull-down and pouring light
the tithe-barns, the cathedrals
were bearing the old castes away.

    o

Pattern-bombed out of babyhood,
Hungarians-become-Swiss,
the children heard their parents:
Argentina? Or Australia?
Less politics, in Australia ...

Dark Germany, iron frost
and the waiting many weeks
then a small converted warship
under the moon, turning south.

Way beyond the first star
and beyond Cape Finisterre
the fishes and the birds
did eat of their heave-offerings.

    o

The *Goya* was a barracks:
mess-queue, spotlights, tower,
crossing the Middle Sea.

In the haunted blue light
that burned nightlong in the sleeping-decks
the tiered bunks were restless
with coughing, demons, territory.

On the Sea of Sweat, the Red Sea,
the flat heat melted even
dulled deference of the injured.
Nordics and Slavonics
paid salt-tax day and night, being
absolved of Europe

but by the Gate of Tears
the barrack was a village
with accordions and dancing
(Fräulein, kennen Sie meinen Rhythmus?)
approaching the southern stars.

                    o

Those who said Europe
has fallen to the Proles
and the many who said
we are going for the children,

the nouveau poor
and the cheerful shirtsleeve Proles,
the children, who thought
No Smoking signs meant men
mustn't dress for dinner,

those who had hopes
and those who knew that they
were giving up their lives

were becoming the people
who would say, and sometimes urge,
in the English-speaking years:
we came out on the *Goya*.

       o

At last, a low coastline,
old horror of Dutch sail-captains.

Behind it, still unknown,
sunburnt farms, strange trees, family jokes
and all the classes of equality.

As it fell away northwards
there was one last week for songs,
for dreaming at the rail,
for beloved meaningless words.

Standing in to Port Phillip
in the salt-grey summer light
the village dissolved
into strained shapes holding luggage;

now they, like the dour
Australians below them, were facing
encounter with the Foreign
where all subtlety fails.

       o

Those who, with effort,
with concealment, with silence, had resisted
the collapsed star Death,
who had clawed their families from it,
those crippled by that gravity

were suddenly, shockingly
being loaded aboard lorries:
They say, another camp –
One did not come for this –

As all the refitted
ships stood, oiling, in the Bay,
spectres, furious and feeble,
accompanied the trucks through Melbourne,

resignation, understandings
that cheerful speed dispelled at length.

That first day, rolling north
across the bright savanna,
not yet people, but numbers.
Population. Forebears.

　　　　o

Bonegilla, Nelson Bay,
the dry-land barbed wire ships
from which some would never land.

In these, as their parents
learned the Fresh Start music:
physicians nailing crates,
attorneys cleaning trams,
the children had one last
ambiguous summer holiday.

Ahead of them lay
the Deep End of the schoolyard,
tribal testing, tribal soft-drinks,
and learning English fast,
the Wang-Wang language.

Ahead of them, refinements:
thumbs hooked down hard under belts
to repress gesticulation;

ahead of them, epithets:
wog, reffo, Commo Nazi,
things which can be forgotten
but must first be told.

And farther ahead
in the years of the Coffee Revolution
and the Smallgoods Renaissance,
the early funerals:

the misemployed, the unadaptable,
those marked by the Abyss,

friends who came on the *Goya*
in the mid-year of our century.


## THE CRAZE FIELD

These lagoons, these watercourses,
streets of the underworld.
Their water has become the trees that stand along them.

Below root-revetments, in the circles of the water's recession
the ravines seem thronged with a legacy of lily pads.
Earth curls and faintly glistens, scumbled painterly and peeling.

Palates of drought-stilled assonance,
they are cupped flakes of grit, crisps of bottom, dried meniscus
lifted at the edges.

Abstracts realized in slime. Shards of bubble, shrivelled viscose
of clay and stopped life:
the scales of the water snake have gone to grey on this channel.

o

Exfoliate bark of the rain tree, all the outer
plaques have a jostling average size.
It is a kind of fire, the invention of networks.

Water's return, however gradual (and it won't be)
however gentle (it won't be) would not re-lay all seamless
this basal membrane;
it has borne excess of clarity.

This is the lush sheet that overlay the first cities,
the mother-goddess towns, but underlay them first;
this they had for mortar.

Laminar, half detached, these cusps are primal tissue,
foreshadowings of leaf, pottery, palimpsest,
the Dead Lagoon Scrolls.

In this hollow season
everything is perhaps to be recapitulated,
hurriedly, approximately. It is a kind of fire.
Saturate calm is all sprung, in the mother country.

> o

The lagoon-bed museums meanwhile have a dizzy stillness
that will reduce, with all the steps that are coming,
to meal, grist, morsels.
Dewfall and birds' feet have nipped, blind noons have nibbled
this mineral matzoh.

The warlike peace-talking young, pacing this dominion
in the beautiful flesh that outdoes their own creations,
might read gnomic fragments:

> *corr    lux    Romant    irit*

or fragmentary texts:

> *who lose belief in God will not only believe*
> *in anything. They will bring blood offerings to it.*

Bones, snags, seed capsules,
intrinsic in the Martian central pan,
are hidden, in the craze, under small pagoda eaves.

# FOR A JACOBITE LADY

Proud heart, since the light of making lace
for an exiled prince died in your eyes
it is above two centuries.

Your Cause grew literary as it died;
it was Gothic in classicizing times
and a wilder gothic extinguished it,

but you are there in the heat of it,
codes, glasses, the waiting on Versailles,
the sin of hope that eats the heart.

Your needle has left what it could trace:
your life's thread, in endless free returns,
making little subjoined worlds of grace.

That was monarchy. At its defeat
earth fell against heaven, and everyone
was exposed to glory in the street.

I write you this from the Land of Peace,
the Plain of Sports of the vision poems;
your wars drove us here; we possess it now.

We are descendants. As was our one Prince.
Not over the water, but in the wine,
he is more assailed now, since more visible,

freed from the robes of any court.
Causes are our courts; they try our lives,
and dispose of them, to prove their own

as if to see both sides of death
truly, at once, in their due weight
were not reserved to the consummate.

# THE GRASSFIRE STANZAS

August, and black centres expand on the afternoon paddock.
Dilating on a match in widening margins, they lift
a splintering murmur; they fume out of used-up grass
that's been walked, since summer, into infinite swirled licks.

The man imposing spring here swats with his branch, controlling it:
only small things may come to a head, in this settlement pattern.

Fretted with small flame, the aspiring islands leave
odd plumes behind. Smuts shower up every thermal
to float down long stairs. Aggregate smoke attracts a kestrel.

Eruption of darkness from far down under roots
is the aspect of these cores, on the undulating farmland;
dense black is withered into web, inside a low singing;
it is dried and loosened, on the surface; it is made weak.

The green feed that shelters beneath its taller death yearly
is unharmed, under new loaf soot. Arriving hawks teeter
and plunge continually, working over the hopping outskirts.

The blackenings are balanced, on a gradient of dryness
in the almost-still air, between dying thinly away
and stripping the whole countryside. Joining, they never gain
more than they lose. They spread away from their high moments.

The man carries smoke wrapped in bark, and keeps applying it
starting new circles. He is burning the passive ocean
around his ark of buildings and his lifeboat water.

It wasn't this man, but it was man, sing the agile
exclamatory birds, who taught them this rapt hunting
(strike! in the updrafts, snap! of hardwood pods).
Humans found the fire here. It is inherent. They learn,
wave after wave of them, how to touch the country.

Sterilizing reed distaffs, the fire edges on to a dam;
it circuits across a cow-track; new surf starts riding outward
and a nippy kestrel feeds from its foot, over cooling mergers.

It's the sun that is touched, and dies in expansion, mincing,
making the round dance, foretelling its future, driving
the frantic lives outwards. The sun that answers the bark tip
is discharged in many little songs, to forestall a symphony.

Cattle come, with stilted bounding calves. They look across the
ripple lines of heat, and shake their armed heads at them;
at random, then, they step over. Grazing smudged black country
they become the beasts of Tartarus. Wavering, moving out over
dung-smouldering ground still covered with its uncovering.


## HOMAGE TO THE LAUNCHING-PLACE

Pleasure-craft of the sprung rhythms, bed,
            kindest of quadrupeds,
you are also the unrocking boat
            that moves on silence.

Straining hatchway into this world,
            you sustain our collapses
above earth; guarantor of evolution,
            you are our raised base-line.

Resisting gravity, for us and in us,
            you form a planet-wide
unobtrusive discontinuous platform,
            a layer: the mattressphere,
pretty nearly our highest common level
            (tables may dispute it).

Muscles' sweatprinted solace,
godmother of butt-stubbing dreams,
            you sublimate, Great Vehicle,
all our upright passions;
            midwife of figuring, and design,
you moderate them wisely;
            aiming solitude outwards, at action,
you sigh Think some more. Sleep on it ...

Solitude. Approaching rest
Time reveals her oscillation
            and narrows into space;
            there is time in that dilation:
            Mansions. Defiles. Continents.
            The living and the greatly living,
            objects that take sides,
            that aren't morally neutral –

you accept my warm absence
            there, as you will accept,
one day, my cooling presence.

            I loved you from the first, bed,
doorway out of this world;
            above your inner springs
I learned to dig my own.

            Primly dressed, linen-collared one,
you look so still, for your speed,
            shield that carries us to the fight
            and bears us from it.

# FIRST ESSAY ON INTEREST

Not usury, but interest. The cup slowed in mid-raise,
the short whistle, hum, the little forwards shift
mark our intake of that non-physical breath

which the lungs mimic sharply, to cancel the gap in pressure
left by our self vanishing into its own alert –
A blink returns us to self, that intimate demeanour

self-repairing as a bow-wave. What we have received
is the ordinary mail of the otherworld, wholly common,
not postmarked divine; no one refuses delivery,

not even the eagle, her face fixed at heavy Menace:
*I have juices to sort the relevant from the irrelevant;*
even her gaze may tilt left, askance, aloof, right,
fixing a still unknown. Delaying huge flight.

Interest. Mild and inherent with fire as oxygen,
it is a sporadic inhalation. We can live long days
under its surface, breathing material air

then something catches, is itself. Intent and special silence.
This is interest, that blinks our interests out
and alone permits their survival, by relieving

us of their gravity, for a timeless moment;
that centres where it points, and points to centring,
that centres us where it points, and reflects our centre.

It is a form of love. The everyday shines through it
and patches of time. But it does not mingle with these;
it wakens only for each trace in them of the Beloved.

And this breath of interest is non-rhythmical;
it is human to obey, humane to be wary of rhythm
as tainted by the rallies, as marching with the snare drum.
The season of interest is not fixed in the calendar cycle;

it pulls towards acute dimensions. Death is its intimate.
When that Holland of cycles, the body, veers steeply downhill
interest retreats from the face; it ceases to instill
and fade, like breath; it becomes a vivid steady state

that registers every grass-blade seen on the way,
the long combed grain in the steps, free insects flying;
it stands aside from your panic, the wracked disarray;
it behaves as if it were the part of you not dying.

Affinity of interest with extremity
seems to distil to this polar disaffinity
that suggests the beloved is not death, but rather
what our death has hidden. Which may be this world.


## THE FISHERMEN AT SOUTH HEAD

They have walked out as far as they can go on the prow of the continent,
on the undercut white sandstone, the bowsprits of the towering headland.
They project their long light canes
or raise them up to check and string, like quiet archers.
Between casts they hold them couched,
a finger on the line, two fingers on a cigarette, the reel cocked.

They watch the junction of smooth blue with far matt-shining blue,
the join where clouds enter,
or they watch the wind-shape of their nylon
bend like a sail's outline
south towards, a mile away, the city's floating gruel
of gull-blown effluent.

Sometimes they glance north, at the people on that calf-coloured edge
lower than theirs, where the suicides come by taxi
and stretchers are winched up
later, under raining lights
but mostly their eyes stay level with the land-and-ocean glitter.

Where they stand, atop the centuries
of strata, they don't look down much
but feel through their tackle the talus-eddying
and tidal detail of that huge simple pulse
in the rock and their bones.

Through their horizontal poles they divine the creatures of ocean:
a touch, a dip, and a busy winding death gets started;
hands will turn for minutes, rapidly,
before, still opening its pitiful doors, the victim
dawns above the rim, and is hoisted in a flash above the suburbs
– or before the rod flips, to stand
trailing sworn-at gossamer.

On that highest dreadnought scarp, where the terra cotta
waves of bungalows stop, suspended at sky,
the hunters stand apart.
They encourage one another, at a distance, not by talk

but by being there, by unhooking now and then
a twist of silver for the creel, by a vaguely mutual
zodiac of cars TV windcheaters.
Braced, casual normality. Anything unshared,
a harlequin mask, a painted wand flourished at the sun,
would anger them. It is serious to be with humans.


THE DOORMAN

The man applying rules to keep me out
knows if I have to deal with him the rules
apply to me. I am to be kept out.
Naïve to think that he respects the rules;
he knows their purpose. Complicity is out:
if I were his sort I would know the rules.

His genes have seeped down a hundred centuries;
in a slave-ship's hold they pooled to form his eyes,
on a Sunday-school mop they collected to a face
and they formed a skin in the dry air of a palace.
In stripes, in armour, in pinstripes, he stays the same man
and I know his sister, that right-thinking woman.

He is a craftsman, and these are his tools:
unyielding correctness, thin mouth, a nose for clout,
modulations of boredom (let the blusterers threaten).
He guards the status quo as he guards mankind's salvation
and those he protects need never learn the rules:
his contempt is reserved for those who are In, and Out.


## ANTHROPOMORPHICS

Outside the serious media, the violence of animals
is often like a sad cartoon. Tom catches Jerry
and one of them grows less cute, glibbed with saliva,
shivering, darting. But Tom keeps his appealing intent look.
Similarly the snake, having struck and left you with it,
flourishes off quickly, his expression if anything self-righteous.
Hunting, we know, is mostly a form of shopping
where the problem's to make the packages hold still;
Death's best for that, though cheetahs have been seen feeding
on the bulk of a gazelle while the raised head end still bleated:
it was like the companionable sacking of a small Norse ship.
Even with sex, the symbolic beasts can be unreliable:
the great bull, mounting, cramps his lungs on her knobbed spine
and looks winded and precarious. He is more sexual walking.
I praise, nonetheless, our humane and Scythian arts.

# THE NEW MORETON BAY

(ON THE CONVERSION TO CATHOLICISM OF THE POET KEVIN HART)

A grog-primed overseer, who later died,
snapped at twenty convicts gasping in a line
*That pole ain't heavy! Two men stand aside!*
and then two more, *And, you, pop-eyes! And you!*
– until the dozen left, with a terrible cry,
broke and were broken
beneath the tons of log they had stemmed aloft desperately.

Because there is no peace in this world's peace
the timber is to carry. Many hands heave customarily,
some step aside, detained by the Happiness Police
or despair's boutiques; it is a continual sway –
but when grace and intent
recruit a fresh shoulder, then we're in the other testament
and the innocent wood lifts line-long, with its leaves and libraries.


# THE SYDNEY HIGHRISE VARIATIONS


*1. Fuel Stoppage on Gladesville Road Bridge
in the Year 1980*

So we're sitting over our sick beloved engine
atop a great building of the double century
on the summit that exhilarates cars, the concrete vault on its thousands
of tonnes of height, far above the tidal turnaround.

Gigantic pure form, all exterior, superbly uninhabited
or peopled only by transients at speed, the bridge
is massive outline.

It was inked in by scaffolding and workers.
Seen from itself, the arch
is an abstract hill, a roadway up-and-over without country,
from below, a ponderous grotto, all entrance and vast shade
framing blues and levels.
From a distance, the flyover on its vaulting drum
is a sketched stupendous ground-burst, a bubble raising surface
or a rising heatless sun with inset horizons.

Also it's a space-probe,
a trajectory of strange fixed dusts, that were milled,
boxed with steel rod mesh and fired, in stages,
from sandstone point to point. They docked at apogee.

It feels good. It feels right.
The joy of sitting high is in our judgement.
The marvellous brute-force effects of our century work.
They answer something in us. Anything in us.


## 2. View of Sydney, Australia, from Gladesville Road Bridge

There's the other great arch eastward, with its hanging highways;
the headlands and horizons of packed suburb, white among bisque-fired;
    odd smokes rising;
there's Warrang, the flooded valley, that is now the ship-chained Harbour,
recurrent everywhere, with its azure and its grains;
ramped parks, bricked containers,
verandahs successive around walls,
and there's the central highrise, multi-storey, the twenty-year countdown,
the new city standing on its haze above the city.

        Ingots of sheer
        affluence poles
        bomb-drawing grid
        of columnar profit
        piecrust and scintillant
        tunnels in the sky
        high window printouts
        repeat their lines
        repeat their lines

credit conductors
repeat their lines
bar graphs on blue
glass tubes of boom
in concrete wicker
each trade Polaris
government Agena
fine print insurrected
tall drinks on a tray

All around them is the old order: brewery brick terrace hospital
horrible workplace; the scale of the tramway era,
the peajacket era, the age of the cliff-repeating woolstores.
South and west lie the treeless suburbs, a mulch of faded flags,
north and partly east, the built-in paradise forest.


## 3. The Flight from Manhattan

It is possible the heights of this view are a museum:
though the highrise continues desultorily along some ridges,
    canned Housing, Strata Title,
    see-through Office Space,
    upright bedsteads of Harbour View,
    residential soviets,
the cranes have all but vanished from the central upsurge.

    Hot-air money-driers,
    towering double entry,
    Freud's cobwebbed poem
    with revolving restaurant,
they took eighty years to fly here from Manhattan
these variant towers. By then, they were arriving everywhere.

    In the land of veneers,
    of cladding, of Cape Codding
    (I shall have Cape Codded)
    they put on heavy side.

The iron ball was loose in the old five-storey city
clearing bombsites for them. They rose like nouveaux accents
and stilled, for a time, the city's conversation.

    Their arrival paralleled
    the rise of the Consumers
    gazing through themselves
    at iconoclasms, wines,
    Danish Modern ethics.

Little we could love expanded to fill the spaces
of high glazed prosperity. An extensive city
that had long contained the dimensions of heaven and hell
couldn't manage total awe at the buildings of the Joneses.

    Their reign coincided
    with an updraft of Ideology,
    that mood in which the starving
    spirit is fed upon the heart.

Employment and neckties and ruling themes ascended
into the towers. But they never filled them.
Squinting at them through the salt
and much-washed glass of her history, the city kept her flavour
fire-ladder high, rarely above three storeys.

In ambiguous battle at length, she began to hedge
the grilles of Aspiration. To limit them to standing
on economic grounds. With their twists of sculpture.

On similar grounds we are stopped here, still surveying
the ridgy plain of houses. Enormous. England's buried Gulag.
The stacked entrepôt, great city of the Australians.

## 4. The C19-20

The Nineteenth Century. The Twentieth Century.
There were never any others. No centuries before these.
Dante was not hailed in his time as an Authentic
Fourteenth Century Voice. Nor did Cromwell thunder, *After all,
in the bowels of Christ, this* is *the Seventeenth Century!*

The two are one aircraft in the end, the C19-20,
capacious with cargo. Some of it can save your life,
some can prevent it.
The cantilevered behemoth
is fitted up with hospitals and electric Gatling guns
to deal with recalcitrant and archaic spirits.

It rose out of the Nineteenth, steam pouring from venturi
and every man turning hay with a wooden fork
in the Age of Piety (A.D. or B.C.) wants one
in his nation's airline. And his children dream of living
in a palace of packing crates beside the cargo terminal:
No one will see! Everything will be surprises!

Directly under the flightpath, and tuned to listening,
we hear the cockpit traffic, the black box channel
that can't be switched off: Darwinians and Lawrentians
are wrestling for the controls,
*We must take her into Space! / We must fly in potent circles!*


## 5. The Recession of the Joneses

The worldwide breath of Catching Up
may serve to keep the mighty, slowing
machine aloft beyond our lifetime:
nearly all of the poor are blowing.

The soaring double century
might end, and mutate, and persist;
as we've been speaking, the shadows of
bridges, cranes, towers have shifted east.

When we create our own high style
skill and the shadow will not then part;
as rhetoric would conceal from art
effort has at best a winning margin.

The sun, that is always catching up
with night and day and month and year,
blazes from its scrolled bare face: *To be
solar, I must be nuclear* –

Six hundred glittering and genteel towns
gathered to be urban in plein air,
more complex in their levels than their heights
and vibrant with modernity's strange anger.


## QUINTETS FOR ROBERT MORLEY

Is it possible that hyper-
ventilating up Parnassus
I have neglected to pay tribute
to the Stone Age aristocracy?
 I refer to the fat.

We were probably the earliest
civilized, and civilizing, humans,
the first to win the leisure,
sweet boredom, life-enhancing sprawl
 that require style.

Tribesfolk spared us and cared for us
for good reasons. Our reasons.
As age's counterfeits, forerunners of the city,
we survived, and multiplied. Out of self-defence
 we invented the Self.

It's likely we also invented some of love,
much of fertility (see the Willensdorf Venus)
parts of theology (divine feasting, Unmoved Movers)
likewise complexity, stateliness, the ox-cart
    and self-deprecation.

Not that the lists of pugnacity are bare
of stout fellows. Ask a Sumo.
Warriors taunt us still, and fear us:
in heroic war, we are apt to be the specialists
    and the generals.

But we do better in peacetime. For ourselves
we would spare the earth. We were the first moderns
after all, being like the Common Man
disqualified from tragedy. Accessible to shame, though,
    subtler than the tall,

we make reasonable rulers.
Never trust a lean meritocracy
nor the leader who has been lean;
only the lifelong big have the knack of wedding
    greatness with balance.

Never wholly trust the fat man
who lurks in the lean achiever
and in the defeated, yearning to get out.
He has not been through our initiations,
    he lacks the light feet.

Our having life abundantly
is equivocal, Robert, in hot climates
where the hungry watch us. I lack the light step then too.
How many of us, I wonder, walk those streets
    in terrible disguise?

So much climbing, on a spherical world;
had Newton not been a mere beginner at gravity
he might have asked how the apple got up there
in the first place. And so might have discerned
    an ampler physics.


## BENT WATER IN THE TASMANIAN HIGHLANDS

Flashy wrists out of buttoned grass cuffs, feral whisky burning gravels,
jazzy knuckles ajitter on soakages, peaty cupfuls, soft pots overflowing,
setting out along the great curve, migrating mouse-quivering water,
mountain-driven winter water, in the high tweed, stripping off its
    mountains
to run faster in its skin, it swallows the above, it feeds where it is fed on,
it forms at many points and creases outwards, pleated water
shaking out its bedding soil, increasing its scale, beginning the headlong
– Bent Water, you could call this level
between droplet and planetary, not as steered by twisting beds laterally
but as upped and swayed on its swelling and outstanding own curvatures,
its floating top that sweeps impacts sidelong, its event-horizon,
a harelip round a pebble, mouthless cheeks globed over a boulder, a
finger's far-stretched holograph, skinned flow athwart a snag
– these flexures are all reflections, motion-glyphs, pitches of impediment,
say a log commemorated in a log-long hump of wave,
a buried rock continually noted, a squeeze-play
through a cracked basalt bar, maintaining a foam-roofed two-sided
overhang of breakneck riesling; uplifted hoseless hosings, fully circular
    water,
flattened water off rock sills, sandwiched between an upper
and a lower whizzing surface, trapped in there with airy scatter
and mingled high-speed mirrorings; water groined, produced and spiralled
– Crowded scrollwork from events, at steepening white velocities
as if the whole outline of the high country were being pulled out
along these joining channels, and proving infinite, anchored deeply as it
is in the groundwater scale, in the silence around racy breccia
yet it is spooling out; the great curve, drawing and driving,
of which these are the animal-sized swells and embodiments
won't always describe this upland; and after the jut falls, the inverse

towering on gorges, these peaks will be hidden beneath
rivers and tree-bark, in electricity, in cattle, on the ocean
– Meditation is a standing wave, though, on the black-green inclines
of pouring and cascading, slate-dark rush and timber-worker's tea
bullying the pebble-fans; if we were sketched first at this speed,
sheaths, buttocks, wings, it is mother and history and swank here
till our wave is drained of water. And as such it includes the writhing
down in a trench, knees, bellies, the struggling, the slack bleeding
remote enough perhaps, within its close clean film,
to make the observer a god; do we come here to be gods?
or to watch an alien pouring down the slants of our anomaly
and be hypnotized to rest by it? So much detail's unlikely, for hypnosis;
it looks like brotherhood sought at a dreamer's remove
and, in either view, laws of falling and persistence:
the continuous ocean round a planetary stone, braiding uptilts
after swoops, echo-forms, arches built from above and standing
on flourish, clear storeys, translucent honey-glazed clerestories –


# EQUANIMITY

Nests of golden porridge shattered in the silky-oak trees,
cobs and crusts of it, their glory-box;
the jacarandas' open violet immensities
mirrored flat on the lawns,
weighted by sprinklers; birds, singly and in flocks
hopping over the suburb, eating, as birds do, in detail
and paying their peppercorns;
talk of 'the good life' tangles love with will

however; if we mention it, there is more to say:
the droughty light, for example, at telephone-wire
height above the carports, not the middle-ground
distilling news-photograph light of a smoggy Wednesday,
but that light of the north-west wind, hung on the sky
like the haze above cattleyards;
hungry mountain birds, too, drifting in for food, with the sound
of moist gullies about them, and the sound of the pinch-bar;
we must hear the profoundly unwished

garble of a neighbours' quarrel, and see repeatedly
the face we saw near the sportswear shop today
in which mouth-watering and tears couldn't be distinguished.

Fire-prone place-names apart
there is only love; there are no Arcadias.
Whatever its variants of meat-cuisine, worship, divorce,
human order has at heart
an equanimity. Quite different from inertia, it's a place
where the churchman's not defensive, the indignant aren't on
        the qui vive,
the loser has lost interest, the accountant is truant to remorse,
where the farmer has done enough struggling-to-survive
for one day, and the artist rests from theory –
where all are, in short, off the high comparative horse
of their identity.
Almost beneath notice, as attainable as gravity, it is
a continuous recovering moment. Pity the high madness
that misses it continually, ranging without rest between
assertion and unconsciousness,
the sort that makes Hell seem a height of evolution.
Through the peace beneath effort
(even within effort: quiet air between the bars of our attention)
comes unpurchased lifelong plenishment;
Christ spoke to people most often on this level
especially when they chattered about kingship and the Romans;
all holiness speaks from it.

From the otherworld of action and media, this
interleaved continuing plane is hard to focus:
we are looking into the light –
it makes some smile, some grimace.
More natural to look at the birds about the street, their life
that is greedy, pinched, courageous and prudential
as any on these bricked tree-mingled miles of settlement,
to watch the unceasing on-off
grace that attends their nearly every movement,
the same grace moveless in the shapes of trees
and complex in our selves and fellow walkers: we see it's indivisible

and scarcely willed. That it lights us from the incommensurable
we sometimes glimpse, from being trapped in the point
(bird minds and ours are so pointedly visual):
a field all foreground, and equally all background,
like a painting of equality. Of infinite detailed extent
like God's attention. Where nothing is diminished by perspective.


## THE FOREST HIT BY MODERN USE

The forest, hit by modern use,
stands graced with damage.
                                     Angled plaques
tilt everywhere, with graphic needle crowns
and trinket saps fixed round their year;
vines spiderweb, flowering, over smashed
intricacies; long rides appear.

Dense growths that were always underbrush
expand in the light, beside bulldozers'
imprinted machine-gun belts of spoor.

Now the sun's in, through breaks and jags,
culled slopes are jammed with replacement; green
and whipstick saplings, every one out
to shade the rest to death.
                                 Scabbed chain
feeds leaf-mould its taut rain-cold solution;
bared creeks wash gold; kingfishers hover.

There is still great height: all through the hills
spared hierarchs toughen to the wind
around the punk hearts that got them spared
and scatter seed down the logging roads.

Grease-fungi, scrolls, clenched pipes of bark:
the forest will now be kept like this
for a long time. There are rooms in it
and, paradox for mystery, birds
too tiny, now that we see them, for
their amplitude and carrying flash of song.

On a stump, a sea eagle eats by lengths
their enemy, a coil-whipping dry land fish,
and voids white size to make room for it.

## SHOWER

From the metal poppy
this good blast of trance
arriving as shock, private cloudburst blazing down,
worst in a boarding-house greased tub, or a barrack with competitions,
best in a stall, this enveloping passion of Australians:
tropics that sweat for you, torrent that braces with its heat,
inflames you with its chill, action sauna, inverse bidet,
sleek vertical coruscating ghost of your inner river,
reminding all your fluids, streaming off your points, awakening
the tacky soap to blossom and ripe autumn, releasing the squeezed
    gardens,
smoky valet smoothing your impalpable overnight pyjamas off,
pillar you can step through, force-field absolving love's efforts,
nicest yard of the jogging track, speeding aeroplane minutely
steered with two controls, or trimmed with a knurled wheel.
Some people like to still this energy and lie in it,
stirring circles with their pleasure in it – but my delight's that toga
worn on either or both shoulders, fluted drapery, silk whispering
    to the tiles

with its spiralling frothy hem continuous round the gurgle-hole;
this ecstatic partner, dreamy to dance in slow embrace with
after factory-floor rock, or even to meet as Lot's abstracted
merciful wife on a rusty ship in dog latitudes,
sweetest dressing of the day in the dusty bush, this persistent
time-capsule of unwinding, this nimble straight well-wisher.
Only in England is its name an unkind word;
only in Europe is it enjoyed by telephone.


## THE QUALITY OF SPRAWL

Sprawl is the quality
of the man who cut down his Rolls-Royce
into a farm utility truck, and sprawl
is what the company lacked when it made repeated efforts
to buy the vehicle back and repair its image.

Sprawl is doing your farming by aeroplane, roughly,
or driving a hitchhiker that extra hundred miles home.
It is the rococo of being your own still centre.
It is never lighting cigars with ten-dollar notes:
that's idiot ostentation and murder of starving people.
Nor can it be bought with the ash of million-dollar deeds.

Sprawl lengthens the legs; it trains greyhounds on liver and beer.
Sprawl almost never says Why not? with palms comically raised
nor can it be dressed for, not even in running shoes worn
with mink and a nose ring. That is Society. That's Style.
Sprawl is more like the thirteenth banana in a dozen
or anyway the fourteenth.

Sprawl is Hank Stamper in *Never Give an Inch*
bisecting an obstructive official's desk with a chainsaw.
Not harming the official. Sprawl is never brutal
though it's often intransigent. Sprawl is never Simon de Montfort
at a town-storming: Kill them all! God will know his own.
Knowing the man's name this was said to might be sprawl.

Sprawl occurs in art. The fifteenth to twenty-first
lines in a sonnet, for example. And in certain paintings;
I have sprawl enough to have forgotten which paintings.
Turner's glorious *Burning of the Houses of Parliament*
comes to mind, a doubling bannered triumph of sprawl –
except, he didn't fire them.

Sprawl gets up the nose of many kinds of people
(every kind that comes in kinds) whose futures don't include it.
Some decry it as criminal presumption, silken-robed Pope Alexander
dividing the new world between Spain and Portugal.
If he smiled *in petto* afterwards, perhaps the thing did have sprawl.

Sprawl is really classless, though. It's John Christopher Frederick Murray
asleep in his neighbours' best bed in spurs and oilskins
but not having thrown up:
sprawl is never Calum who, drunk, along the hallways of our house,
reinvented the Festoon. Rather
it's Beatrice Miles going twelve hundred ditto in a taxi,
No Lewd Advances, No Hitting Animals, No Speeding,
on the proceeds of her two-bob-a-sonnet Shakespeare readings.
An image of my country. And would that it were more so.

No, sprawl is full-gloss murals on a council-house wall.
Sprawl leans on things. It is loose-limbed in its mind.
Reprimanded and dismissed
it listens with a grin and one boot up on the rail
of possibility. It may have to leave the Earth.
Being roughly Christian, it scratches the other cheek
and thinks it unlikely. Though people have been shot for sprawl.

# THREE POEMS IN MEMORY OF MY MOTHER, MIRIAM MURRAY NÉE ARNALL

BORN 23.5.1915, DIED 19.4.1951

## Weights

Not owning a cart, my father
in the drought years was a bowing
green hut of cattle feed, moving,
or gasping under cream cans. No weight
would he let my mother carry.

Instead, she wielded handles
in the kitchen and dairy, singing often,
gave saucepan-boiled injections
with her ward-sister skill, nursed neighbours,
scorned gossips, ran committees.

She gave me her factual tone,
her facial bones, her will,
not her beautiful voice
but her straightness and her clarity.

I did not know back then
nor for many years what it was,
after me, she could not carry.


## Midsummer Ice

Remember how I used
to carry ice in from the road
for the ice chest, half running,
the white rectangle clamped in bare hands
the only utter cold
in all those summer paddocks?

How, swaying, I'd hurry it inside
en bloc and watering, with the butter
and the wrapped bread precarious on top of it?
'Poor Leslie,' you would say,
'your hands are cold as charity – '
You made me take the barrow
but uphill it was heavy.

We'd no tongs, and a bag
would have soaked and bumped, off balance.
I loved to eat the ice,
chip it out with the butcher knife's grey steel.
It stopped good things rotting
and it had a strange comb at its heart,
a splintered horizon rife with zero pearls.

But you don't remember.
A doorstep of numbed creek water the colour of tears
but you don't remember.
I will have to die before you remember.


*The Steel*

I am older than my mother.
Cold steel hurried me from her womb.
I haven't got a star.

What hour I followed
the waters into this world
no one living can now say.
My zodiac got washed away.

The steel of my induction
killed my brothers and sisters;
once or twice I was readied for them

and then they were not mentioned
again, at the hospital
to me or to the visitors.
The reticence left me only.

I think, apart from this,
my parents' life was happy,
provisional, as lives are.

Farming spared them from the war,
that, and an ill-knit blue shin
my father had been harried back

to tree-felling with, by his father
who supervised from horseback.
The times were late pioneer.

So was our bare plank house
with its rain stains down each crack
like tall tan flames,
magic swords, far matched perspectives:

it reaped Dad's shamed invectives –
Paying him rent for this shack!
The landlord was his father.

But we also had fireside ease,
health, plentiful dinners, the radio;
we'd a car to drive to tennis.

Country people have cars
for more than shopping and show,
our Dodge reached voting age, though,
in my first high school year.

I was in the town at school
the afternoon my mother
collapsed, and was carried from the dairy.
The car was out of order.

The ambulance was available
but it took a doctor's say-so
to come. This was refused.
My father pleaded. Was refused.

The doctor wanted details
but my father could only say
*A bad turn. She's having a bad turn!*
the words his culture
could allow on a party-line phone.

At length a neighbour nurse
produced the jargon: haemorrhage,
miscarriage, and the ambulance
was swiftly on its way.

The time all this took didn't pass,
it spread through sheets, unstoppable.
Thirty-seven miles to town
and the terrible delay.

Little blood brother, blood sister,
I don't blame you.
How can you blame a baby?
or the longing for a baby?

Little of that week
comes back. The vertigo,
the apparent recovery –
She will get better now.
The relapse on the Thursday.

In school and called away
I was haunted, all that week,
by the spectre of dark women,
Murrays dressed in midday black

who lived on the river islands
and are seen only at funerals;
their terrible weak authority.

Everybody in the town
was asking me about my mother;
I could only answer childishly
to them. And to my mother,

and on Friday afternoon
our family world
went inside itself forever.

Sister Arnall, city girl
with your curt good sense,
were you being the nurse
when you let them hurry me?
being responsible

when I was brought on to make way
for a difficult birth in that cottage hospital
and Mrs Cheers' child stole my birthday?

Or was it our strange diffidence,
unworldly at a pinch, unresentful
of being a case among cases,

a relative, wartime sense,
modern, alien to fuss,
that is not in the Murrays?

I don't blame the Cheers boy's mother:
she didn't put her case.
It was the steel proposed
reasonably, professionally,
that became your sentence

but I don't decry unselfishness:
I'm proud of it. Of you.
Any virtue can be fatal.

In the event, his coming gave no trouble
but it might have, I agree;
nothing you agreed to harmed me.
I didn't mean to harm you
I was a baby.

For a long time, my father
himself became a baby
being perhaps wiser than me,
less modern, less military;

he was not ashamed of grief,
of its looking like a birth
out through the face

bloated, whiskery, bringing no relief.
It was mainly through fear
that I was at times his father.
I have long been sorry.

Caked pans, rancid blankets,
despair and childish cool
were our road to Bohemia
that bitter wartime country.

What were you thinking of,
Doctor MB, BS?
Were you very tired?
Did you have more pressing cases?

Know panic when you heard it:
Oh you can bring her in!
Did you often do
diagnosis by telephone
while not knowing rural language?

Perhaps we wrong you,
make a scapegoat of you;
perhaps there was no stain
of class in your decision,

no view that two framed degrees
outweighed a dairy.
It's nothing, dear:
just some excited hillbilly –

As your practice disappeared
and you were cold-shouldered in town
till you broke and fled,
did you think of the word *Clan*?

It is an antique
concept. Not wholly romantic.
More, I think, my mother
was well loved. And people

stopped trusting their lives
to the one who understood anguish
only in translation.
I can forgive you. It was
cold steel that you blundered on.

Thirty-five years on earth:
that's short. That's short, Mother,
as the lives cut off by war

and the lives of spilt children are short.
Justice wholly in this world
would bring them no rebirth
nor restore your latter birthdays.
How could that be justice?

My father never quite
remarried. He went back
by stages of kindness to me
to the age of lonely men,
of only men, and men's company

that is called the Pioneer age.
Snig chain and mountain track;
he went back to felling trees

and seeking justice from his
dead father. His only weakness.
One's life is not a case

except of course it is.
Being just, seeking justice:
they were both of them right,
my mother and my father.

There is justice, there is death,
humanist: you can't have both.
Activist, you can't serve both.
You do not move in measured space.

The poor man's anger is a prayer
for equities Time cannot hold
and steel grows from our mother's grace.
Justice is the people's otherworld.


## MACHINE PORTRAITS WITH
## PENDANT SPACEMAN

FOR VALERIE

The bulldozer stands short as a boot on its heel-high ripple soles;
it has toecapped stumps aside all day, scuffed earth and trampled rocks
making a hobnailed dyke downstream of raw clay shoals.
Its work will hold water. The man who bounced high on the box
seat, exercising levers, would swear a full frontal orthodox
oath to that. First he shaved off the grizzled scrub
with that front-end safety razor supplied by the school of hard knocks
then he knuckled down and ground his irons properly; they copped many
    a harsh rub.
At knock-off time, spilling thunder, he surfaced like a sub.

    o

Speaking of razors, the workshop amazes with its strop,
its elapsing leather drive-belt angled to the slapstick flow
of fast work in the Chaplin age; tightened, it runs like syrup,
streams like a mill-sluice, fiddles like a glazed virtuoso.
With the straitlaced summary cut of Sam Brownes long ago
it is the last of the drawn lash and bullocking muscle
left in engineering. It's where the panther leaping, his swift shadow
and all such free images turned plastic. Here they dwindle, dense with oil,
like a skein between tough factory hands, pulley and diesel.

                    o

Shaking in slow low flight, with its span of many jets,
the combine seeder at nightfall swimming over flat land
is a style of machinery we'd imagined for the fictional planets:
in the high glassed cabin, above vapour-pencilling floodlights, a hand,
gloved against the cold, hunts along the medium-wave band
for company of Earth voices; it crosses speech garble music –
the Brandenburg Conch the Who the Illyrian High Command –
as seed wheat in the hoppers shakes down, being laced into the thick
night-dampening plains soil, and the stars waver out and stick.

                    o

Flags and a taut fence discipline the mountain pasture
where giant upturned mushrooms gape mildly at the sky
catching otherworld pollen. Poppy-smooth or waffle-ironed, each armature
distils wild and white sound. These, Earth's first antennae
tranquilly angled outwards, to a black, not a gold infinity,
swallow the millionfold numbers that print out as a risen
glorious Apollo. They speak control to satellites in high
bursts of algorithm. And some of them are tuned to win
answers to fair questions, viz. What is the Universe in?

                    o

How many metal-bra and trumpet-flaring film extravaganzas
underlie the progress of the space shuttle's Ground Transporter Vehicle
across macadam-surfaced Florida? Atop oncreeping house-high panzers,
towering drydock and ocean-liner decks, there perches a gridiron football
field in gradual motion; it is the god-platform; it sustains the bridal
skyscraper of liquid Cool, and the rockets borrowed from the Superman
and the bricked aeroplane of Bustout-and-return, all vertical,

conjoined and myth-huge, approaching the starred gantry where human
lightning will crack, extend, and vanish upwards from this caravan.

o

Gold-masked, the foetal warrior
unslipping on a flawless floor,
I backpack air; my life machine
breathes me head-Earthwards, speaks the Choctaw
of tech-talk that earths our discipline –

but the home world now seems outside-in;
I marvel that here background's so fore
and sheathe my arms in the unseen

a dream in images unrecalled
from any past takes me      I soar
at the heart of fall on a drifting line

this is the nearest I have been
to oneness with the everted world
the unsinking leap      the stone unfurled

o

In a derelict village picture show I will find a projector,
dust-matted, but with film in its drum magazines, and the lens
mysteriously clean. The film will be called *Insensate Violence*,
no plot, no characters, just shoot burn scream beg claw
bayonet trample brains – I will hit the reverse switch then, in conscience,
and the thing will run backwards, unlike its coeval the machine-gun;
blood will unspill, fighters lift and surge apart; horror will be undone
and I will come out to a large town, bright parrots round the saleyard pens
and my people's faces healed of a bitter sophistication.

o

The more I act, the stiller I become;
the less I'm lit, the more spellbound my crowd;
I accept all colours, and with a warming hum
I turn them white and hide them in a cloud.
To give long life is a power I'm allowed
by my servant, Death. I am what you can't sell

at the world's end – and if you're still beetle-browed
try some of my treasures: an adult bird in its shell
or a pink porker in his own gut, Fritz the Abstract Animal.

o

No riddles about a crane. This one drops a black clanger on cars
and the palm of its four-thumbed steel hand is a raptor of wrecked tubing;
the ones up the highway hoist porridgy concrete, long spars
and the local skyline; whether raising aloft on a string
bizarre workaday angels, or letting down a rotating
man on a sphere, these machines are inclined to maintain
a peace like world war, in which we turn over everything
to provide unceasing victories. Now the fluent lines stop, and strain
engrosses this tower on the frontier of junk, this crane.

o

Before a landscape sprouts those giant stepladders that pump oil
or before far out iron mosquitoes attach to the sea
there is this sortilege with phones that plug into mapped soil,
the odd gelignite bump to shake trucks, paper scribbling out serially
as men dial Barrier Reefs long enfolded beneath the geology
or listen for black Freudian beaches; they seek a miles-wide pustular
rock dome of pure Crude, a St Paul's-in-profundis. There are many
wrong numbers on the geophone, but it's brought us some distance,
    and by car.
Every machine has been love and a true answer.

o

Not a high studded ship boiling cauliflower under her keel
nor a ghost in bootlaced canvas – just a length of country road
afloat between two shores, winding wet wire rope reel-to-reel,
dismissing romance sternwards. Six cars and a hay truck are her load
plus a thoughtful human cast which could, in some dramatic episode,
become a world. All machines in the end join God's creation
growing bygone, given, changeless – but a river ferry has its timeless mode
from the grinding reedy outset; it enforces contemplation.
We arrive. We traverse depth in thudding silence. We go on.

# THE INTERNATIONAL POETRY
# FESTIVALS THING

Those conventions of the trade
in affluent stone cities:
we travel to them up the long shaft
polished by Europe's victims;

since few books can ascend that,
we walk out past the airport submachine-guns
carrying the mirrors we hold up
to the life of our people.

Those scenes at the first
usually luxurious breakfast:
*Ciao Allen! Zhenia moi!*
polished brevity of attention,
hooded senior repartee,
witty switching of small table flags

but always the unspoken
question, too: how many
divisions, with that fellow?

You notice, on lone walks,
how the city was rebuilt.
Yet you do the unspeakable

among competitive nonchalances
and the polite who've seen Hell:
you are unguarded.
No one is that distinguished!

At last the readings,
super-cool or impassioned recitals
very largely of subtitles
even in fair translation.

Hour on stylish hour of it:
*Who is to read now – the Pole?*
*No, the opposite Pole –*
Nothing worthwhile is lost:
the poetry is in print somewhere.

And afterwards, always,
an Englishman quoting cliché
with a heavy archness,
often doing it out of friendliness.

Some things do get through,
your relief at quiet praise
tells you how unguarded
you really were not, previously.

To your terror, you find
you have earned the admiration
of that bright girl who
for always coming down on one side
you had nicknamed Winter Sunlight:

now you may have to say it –
*il me serait trop*
*distingué, ton prolétariat –*

Meanwhile, the spirit follows
its curious own nose
collecting, for its lasting life,
south sun. A Gothic square.
Café lamps. Two conversations.
Icecreamed tongues in the horse chestnut trees.

Declining, conjugating,
the week ends in embraces
of love, of career,
*Will you be now in Cambridge?*
in real regard and book exchanges.

And we carry home our sleek
mirrors cram-full of chic
to show our people.


## LITTLE BOY IMPELLING A SCOOTER

Little boy on a wet pavement
near nightfall, balancing his scooter,
his free foot spurning it along,
his every speeding touchdown
striking a match of spent light,
the long concrete patched with squeezed-dry impacts
coming and going, his tyres' rubber edge
splitting the fine water. He jinks the handlebars
and trots around them, turning them
back, and stamps fresh small impulsions
maddeningly on and near, off and behind
his earlier impulses.
                            Void blurring pavement stars,
void blurring wheel-noise, uneven with hemmed outsets
as the dark deepens over town. To bear his rapture,
to smile, to share in it, require attitudes
all remote from murder,
watching his bowed intent face and slackly trailing
sudden pump leg passing and hemm! repassing
under powerlines and windy leaves
and the bared night sky's interminable splendours.

# SELF-PORTRAIT FROM A PHOTOGRAPH

If this picture has survived
its subject's absorption in the absolute
which is either God or death

it will first have been obsolete
for many years, till its style
was wholly defused, its life

glazed over by pathos, by summary
and it could grow timeless,
a midcentury face, taken late in that century.

A high hill of photographed sun-shadow
coming up from reverie, the big head
has its eyes on a mid-line, the mouth
slightly open, to breathe or interrupt.

The face's gentle skew to the left
is abetted, or caused, beneath the nose
by a Heidelberg scar, got in an accident.
The hair no longer meets across the head

and the back and sides are clipped ancestrally
Puritan-short. The chins are firm and deep
respectively. In point of freckling
and bare and shaven skin is just over

halfway between childhood ginger
and the nutmeg and plastic death-mottle
of great age. The large ears suggest more
of the soul than the other features:

dull to speech, alert to language,
tuned to background rustle, easily agonised,
all too fond of monotony, they help
keep the eyes, at their sharpest, remote,

half-turned to another world
that is poorer than this one, but contains it.
The short bulb nose is propped firmly
by flesh ridges. In decline, slow or steep,

this face might have wrinkled copiously
by the shoalwater webbing near the eyes.
With temples this military-naked
you see muscles chewing in the head.

That look of dawning interest, or objection
in which we glimpse dread of dentists,
could be shifting to enjoy a corny joke
out of friendship, or in reflex defiance

of claimant Good Taste and display;
such moods were one edge of his loyalty.
Another is the biceps tourniquet
of rolled sleeves, just out of frame,

a fashion of darkening carriers,
farmers, labourers and their sons
for more than a century.

Wardrobe, this precise relation
between a pinstriped business shirt
and its absent tie can never be recaptured,

and slighter factors, in this drapery and skin:
like impulses deflected by the saints
they end here, short of history.

# THE HYPOGEUM

Below the moveable gardens of this shopping centre
down concrete ways
                    to a level of rainwater,
a black lake glimmering among piers, electric lighted,
windless, of no depth.
                    Rare shafts of daylight
waver at their base. As the water is shaken, the few
cars parked down here seem to rock. In everything
there strains that silent crash, that reverberation
which persists in concrete.
                    The cardboard carton
Lorenzo's Natural Flavour Italian Meat Balls has foundered
into a wet ruin. Dutch Cleanser is propped at a high
featureless wall. Self-raising Flour is still floating
and supermarket trolleys hang their inverse harps,
silver leaking from them.
                    What will help the informally religious
to endure peace? Surface water dripping into
this underworld makes now a musical blip,
now rings from nowhere.
                    Young people descending the ramp
pause at the water's brink, banging their voices.


# AN IMMORTAL

Beckoner of hotheads, brag-tester, lord of the demi-suicides,
in only one way since far before Homer have you altered:
when now, on wry wheels still revolving, the tall dust showers back
and tongue-numbing Death stills a screaming among the jagged images,
you disdain to strip your victims' costly armour, bright with fire and duco,
or even to step forth, visible briefly in your delusive harness,
glass cubes whirling at your tread, the kinked spear of frenzy in your hand.

Do you appear, though, bodily to your vanquished challengers
with the bare face of the boy who was large and quickest at it,
the hard face of the boss and the bookie, strangely run together,
the face of the expert craftsman, smiling privately, shaking his head?
Are you sometimes the Beloved, approaching and receding through
    the glaze?
Or is this all merely cinema? Are your final interviews wholly personal
and the bolt eyes disjunct teeth blood-vomit all a kind mask lent by
    physics?

We will never find out, living. The volunteers, wavering and firm,
and the many conscripted to storm the house of meaning
have stayed inside, with the music. Or else they are ourselves,
sheepish, reminiscent, unsure how we made it past the Warrior
into our lives – which the glory of his wheeled blade has infected
so that, on vacant evenings, we may burn with the mystery of his face,
his speed, his streetlights pointing every way, his unbelief in joking.


## SECOND ESSAY ON INTEREST: THE EMU

Weathered blond as a grass tree, a huge Beatles haircut
raises an alert periscope and stares out
over scrub. Her large olivine eggs click
oilily together; her lips of noble plastic
clamped in their expression, her head-fluff a stripe
worn mohawk style, she bubbles her pale-blue windpipe:
the emu, *Dromaius novaehollandiae*,
whose stand-in on most continents is an antelope,
looks us in both eyes with her one eye
and her other eye, dignified courageous hump,
feather-swaying condensed camel, Swift Courser of New Holland.

Knees backward in toothed three-way boots, you stand,
Dinewan, proud emu, common as the dust
in your sleeveless cloak, returning our interest.
Your shield of fashion's wobbly: You're Quaint, you're Native,

even somewhat Bygone. You may be let live –
but beware: the blank zones of Serious disdain
are often carte blanche to the darkly human.
Europe's boats on their first strange shore looked humble
but, Mass over, men started renaming the creatures.
Worship turned to interest and had new features.
Now only life survives, if it's made remarkable.

Heraldic bird, our protection is a fable
made of space and neglect. We're remarkable and not;
we're the ordinary discovered on a strange planet.
Are you Early or Late, in the history of birds
which doesn't exist, and is deeply ancient?
My kinships, too, are immemorial and recent,
like my country, which abstracts yours in words.
This distillate of mountains is finely branched, this plain
expanse of dour delicate lives, where the rain,
shrouded slab on the west horizon, is a corrugated revenant
settling its long clay-tipped plumage in a hatching descent.

Rubberneck, stepped sister, I see your eye on our jeep's load.
I think your story is, when you were offered
the hand of evolution, you gulped it. Forefinger and thumb
project from your face, but the weighing palm is inside you
collecting the bottletops, nails, wet cement that you famously swallow,
your passing muffled show, your serially private museum.
Some truths are now called *trivial*, though. Only God approves them.
Some humans who disdain them make a kind of weather
which, when it grows overt and widespread, we call *war*.
There we make death trivial and awesome, by rapid turns about,
we conscript it to bless us, force-feed it to squeeze the drama out;

indeed we imprison and torture death – this part is called *peace* –
we offer it murder like mendicants, begging for significance.
You rustle dreams of pardon, not fleeing in your hovercraft style,
not gliding fast with zinc-flaked legs dangling, feet making high-tensile
seesawing impacts. Wasteland parent, barely edible dignitary,
the disinterested spotlight of the lords of interest

and gowned nobles of ennui is a torch of vivid arrest
and blinding after-darkness. But you hint it's a brigand sovereignty
after the steady extents of God's common immortality
whose image is daylight detail, aggregate, in process yet plumb
to the everywhere focus of one devoid of boredom.


## A RETROSPECT OF HUMIDITY

All the air conditioners now slacken
their hummed carrier wave. Once again
we've served our three months with remissions
in the steam and dry iron of this seaboard.
In jellied glare, through the nettle-rash season,
we've watched the sky's fermenting laundry
portend downpours. Some came, and steamed away,
and we were clutched back into the rancid
saline midnights of orifice weather,
to damp grittiness and wiping off the air.

Metaphors slump irritably together in
the muggy weeks. Shark and jellyfish shallows
become suburbs where you breathe a fat towel;
babies burst like tomatoes with discomfort
in the cotton-wrapped pointing street markets;
the lycra-bulging surf drips from non-swimmers
miles from shore, and somehow includes soil.
Skins, touching, soak each other. Skin touching
any surface wets that and itself
in a kind of mutual digestion.
Throbbing heads grow lianas of nonsense.

It's our annual visit to the latitudes
of rice, kerosene and resignation,
an averted, temporary visit
unrelated, for most, to the attitudes
of festive northbound jets gaining height –

closer, for some few, to the memory
of ulcers scraped with a tin spoon
or sweated faces bowing before dry
where the flesh is worn inside out,
all the hunger-organs clutched in rank nylon,
by those for whom exhaustion is spirit:

an intrusive, heart-narrowing season
at this far southern foot of the monsoon.
As the kleenex flower, the hibiscus
drops its browning wads, we forget
annually, as one forgets a sickness.
The stifling days will never come again,
not now that we've seen the first sweater
tugged down on the beauties of division
and inside the rain's millions, a risen
loaf of cat on a cool night verandah.


## FLOWERING EUCALYPT IN AUTUMN

That slim creek out of the sky
the dried-blood western gum tree
is all stir in its high reaches:

its strung haze-blue foliage is dancing
points down in breezy mobs, swapping
pace and place in an all-over sway

retarded en masse by crimson blossom.
Bees still at work up there tack
around their exploded furry likeness

and the lawn underneath's a napped rug
of eyelash drift, of blooms flared
like a sneeze in a redhaired nostril,

minute urns, pinch-sized rockets
knocked down by winds, by night-creaking
fig-squirting bats, or the daily

parrot gang with green pocketknife wings.
Bristling food for tough delicate
raucous life, each flower comes

as a spray in its own turned vase,
a taut starburst, honeyed model
of the tree's fragrance crisping in your head.

When the Japanese plum tree
was shedding in spring, we speculated
there among the drizzling petals

what kind of exquisitely precious
artistic bloom might be gendered
in a pure ethereal compost

of petals potted as they fell.
From unpetalled gum-debris
we know what is grown continually,

a tower of fabulous swish tatters,
a map hoisted upright, a crusted
riverbed with up-country show towns.


## THE CHIMES OF NEVERWHERE

*How many times did the Church prevent war?*
*Who knows? Those wars did not occur.*
*How many numbers don't count before ten?*
*Treasures of the Devil in Neverwhere.*

The neither state of Neverwhere
is hard to place as near or far
since all things that didn't take place are there
and things that have lost the place they took:

Herr Hitler's buildings, King James' cigar,
the happiness of Armenia,
the Abelard children, the Manchus' return
are there with the Pictish Grammar Book.

The girl who returned your dazzled look
and the mornings you might have woke to her
are your waterbed in Neverwhere.
There shine the dukes of Australia

and all the great poems that never were
quite written, and every balked invention.
There too are the Third AIF and its war
in which I and boys my age were killed

more pointlessly with each passing year.
There too half the works of sainthood are
the enslavements, tortures, rapes, despair
deflected by them from the actual

to beat on the human-sacrifice drum
that billions need not die to hear
since Christ's love of them struck it dumb
and his agony keeps it in Neverwhere.

*How many times did the Church bring peace?*
*More times than it happened. Leave it back there:*
*the children we didn't let out of there need it,*
*for the Devil's at home in Neverwhere.*

# THE SMELL OF COAL SMOKE

John Brown, glowing far and down,
wartime Newcastle was a brown town,
handrolled cough and cardigan, rain on paving bricks,
big smoke to a four-year-old from the green sticks.
Train city, mother's city, coming on dark,
Japanese shell holes awesome in a park,
electric light and upstairs, encountered first that day,
sailors and funny ladies in Jerry's Fish Café.

It is always evening on those earliest trips,
raining through the tram wires where blue glare rips
across the gaze of wonderment and leaves thrilling tips.
The steelworks' vast roofed débris unrolling falls
of smoky stunning orange, its eye-hurting slump walls
mellow to lounge interiors, cut pile and curry-brown
with the Pears-Soap-smelling fire and a sense of ships
mourning to each other below in the town.

This was my mother's childhood and her difference,
her city-brisk relations who valued Sense
talking strike and colliery, engineering, fowls and war,
Brown's grit and miners breathing it, years before
as I sat near the fire, raptly touching coal,
its blockage, slick yet dusty, prisms massed and dense
in the iron scuttle, its hammered bulky roll
into the glaring grate to fracture and shoal,

its chips you couldn't draw with on the cement
made it a stone, tar crockery, different –
and I had three grandparents, while others had four:
where was my mother's father, never called Poor?
In his tie and his Vauxhall that had a boat bow
driving up the Coalfields, but where was he now?
Coal smoke as much as gum trees now had a tight scent
to summon deep brown evenings of the Japanese war,

to conjure gaslit pub yards, their razory frisson
and sense my dead grandfather, the Grafton Cornishman,
rising through the night schools by the pressure in his chest
as his lungs creaked like mahogany with the grains of John Brown.
His city, mother's city, at its starriest
as swearing men with doctors' bags streamed by toward the docks
past the smoke-frothing wooden train that would take us home soon
with our day-old Henholme chickens peeping in their box.


## THE MOUTHLESS IMAGE OF GOD
## IN THE HUNTER-COLO MOUNTAINS

Starting a dog, in the past-midnight suburbs, for a laugh,
barking for a lark, or to nark and miff, being tough
or dumbly meditative, starting gruff, sparking one dog off
almost companionably, you work him up, playing the rough riff
of punkish mischief, get funky as a poultry-farm diff
and vary with the Prussian note: *Achtung! Schar, Gewehr' auf!*
starting all the dogs off, for the tinny chain reaction and stiff
far-spreading music, the backyard territorial guff
echoing off brick streets, garbage cans, off every sandstone cliff
in miles-wide canine circles, a vast haze of auditory stuff
with every dog augmenting it, tail up, mouth serrated, shoulder ruff
pulsing with its outputs, a continuous clipped yap from a handmuff
Pomeranian, a Labrador's ascending fours, a Dane grown great enough
to bark in the singular, many raffish bitzers blowing their gaff
as humans raise windows and cries and here and there the roof
and you barking at the epicentre, you, putting a warp to the woof,
shift the design with a throat-rubbing lull and ill howl,
dingo-vibrant, not shrill, which starts a howling school
among hill-and-hollow barkers, till horizons-wide again a tall
pavilion of mixed timbres is lifted up eerily in full call
and the wailing takes a toll: you, from playing the fool,
move, behind your arch will, into the sorrow of a people.

o

And not just one people. You've entered a sound-proletariat
where pigs exclaim *boff-boff!* making off in fright
and fowls say *chirk* in tiny voices when a snake's about,
quite unlike the rooster's *Chook Chook*, meaning look, a good bit:
hens, get stoock into it! Where the urgent boar mutters *root-root*
to his small harassed sow, trotting back and forth beside her, *rut-rut*
and the she-cat's curdling *Mao?* where are kittens? mutating to *prr-mao*,
come along, kittens, are quite different words from *prr-au*,
general-welcome-and-acceptance, or extremity's portmanteau *mee-EU!*
Active and passive at once, the boar and feeding sow
share a common prone *unh*, expressing repletion and bestowing it,
and you're where the staid dog, excited, emits a mouth-skirl
he was trying to control, and looks ashamed of it
and the hawk above the land calls himself Peter P. P. Pew,
where, far from class hatred, the rooster scratches up some for you
and edgy plovers sharpen their nerves on a blurring wheel.
Waterbirds address you in their neck-flexure language, hiss and bow
and you speak to each species in the seven or eight
planetary words of its language, which ignore and include the detail
God set you to elaborate by the dictionary-full
when, because they would reveal their every secret,
He took definition from the beasts and gave it to you.

    o

If at baying time you have bayed with dogs and not humans
you know enough not to scorn the moister dimensions
of language, nor to build on the sandbanks of Dry.
You long to show someone non-human the diaphragm-shuffle
which may be your species' only distinctive cry,
the spasm which, in various rhythms, turns our face awry,
contorts speech, shakes the body, and makes our eyelids liquefy.
Approaching adulthood, one half of this makes us shy
and the other's a touchy spear-haft we wield for balance.
Laughter-and-weeping. It's the great term the small terms qualify
as a whale is qualified by all the near glitters of the sea.

Weightless leviathan our showering words overlie and modify,
it rises irresistibly. All our dry-eyed investigations
supply that one term, in the end; its occasions multiply,
the logics issue in horror, we are shattered by joy
till the old prime divider bends and its two ends unify
and the learned words bubble off us. We laugh because we cry:
the crying depth of life is too great not to laugh
but laugh or cry singly aren't it: only mingled are they spirit
to wobble and sing us as a summer dawn sings a magpie.
For spirit is the round earth bringing our flat earths to bay
and we're feasted and mortified, exposed to those momentary Heavens
which, speaking in speech on the level, we work for and deny.


## TIME TRAVEL

FOR DANIEL

To revisit the spitfire world
of the duel, you put on a suit
of white body armour, a helmet
like an insect's composite eye
and step out like a space walker
under haloed lights, trailing a cord.

Descending, with nodding foil in hand
towards the pomander-and-cravat sphere
you meet the Opponent, for this journey
can only be accomplished by a pair
who semaphore and swap quick respect
before they set about their joint effect

which is making zeroes and serifs so
swiftly and with such sprung variety
that the long steels skid, clatter, zing,
switch, batter, bite, kiss and ring
in the complex rhythms of that society
with its warrior snare of comme il faut

that has you facing a starched beau
near stable walls on a misty morning,
striking, seeking the surrender in him,
the pedigree-flaw through which to pin him,
he probing for your own braggadocio,
confusion, ennui or inner fawning –

Seconds, holding stakes and cloths, look grim
and surge a step. Exchanges halt
for one of you stands, ageing horribly,
collapses, drowning from an entry
of narrow hurt. The other gulps hot chocolate
a trifle fast, but talking nonchalant –

a buzzer sounds. Heads are tucked
under arms, and you and he swap
curt nods in a more Christian century.


## THREE INTERIORS

The mansard roof of the Barrier Industrial Council's
pale-blue Second Empire building in Broken Hill
announces the form of a sprightly, intricately painted
pressed metal ceiling, spaciously stepped and tie-beamed
high over the main meeting hall. The factual light
of the vast room is altered, in its dusty rising
toward that coloured mime of myriadness, that figured
carpet of the mind, whose marvel comes down the clean walls
almost to the shoulder-stain level, the rubbings of mass defiance
which circle the hall miner-high above worn-out timber flooring.
Beauty all suspended in air – I write from memory
but it was so when we were there. A consistent splendour,
quite abstract, bloc-voted, crystalline with colour junctions
and regulated tendrils, high in its applied symphonic theory
above the projection hatch, over sports gear and the odd steel chair
marooned on the splintery extents of the former dance floor.

o

The softly vaulted ceiling of St Gallen's monastic library
is beautifully iced in Rococo butter cream with scrolled pipework
surf-dense around islands holding russet-clad, vaguely heavenly
personages who've swum up from the serried volumes below.
The books themselves, that vertical live leather brickwork,
in the violin-curved, gleaming bays, have all turned their backs
on the casual tourist and, clasped in meditation, they pray
in coined Greek, canonical Latin, pointed Hebrew.
It is an utterly quiet pre-industrial machine room
on a submarine to Heaven, and the deck, the famous floor
over which you pad in blanket slippers, has flowed in
honey-lucent around the footings, settled suavely level and hardened:
only the winding darker woods and underwater star-points
of the parquetry belie that impression. What is below
resembles what's above, but just enough, as cloud-shadow,
runways and old lake shores half noticed in mellow wheat land.

o

The last interior is darkness. Befuddled past-midnight
fear, testing each step like deep water, that when you open
the eventual refrigerator, cold but no light will envelop you.
Bony hurts that persuade you the names of your guides now
are balance, and gravity. You can fall up things, but not far.
A stopping, teeming caution. As of prey. The dark is arbitrary
delivering wheeled smashes, murmurings, something that scuttled,
doorjambs without a switch. The dark has no subject matter
but is alive with theory. Its best respites are: no surprises.
Nothing touching you. Or panic-stilling chance embraces.
Darkness is the cloth for pained eyes, and lovely in colour,
splendid in the lungs of great singers. Also the needed matrix
of constellations, flaring Ginzas, desert moons, apparent snow,
verandah-edged night rain. Dark is like that: all productions.
Almost nothing there is caused, or has results. Dark is all one interior
permitting only inner life. Concealing what will seize it.

# MORSE

Tuckett. Bill Tuckett. Telegraph operator, Hall's Creek,
which is way out back of the Outback, but he stuck it,
quite likely liked it, despite heat, glare, dust and the lack
of diversion or doctors. Come disaster you trusted to luck,
ingenuity and pluck. This was back when nice people said pluck,
the sleevelink and green eyeshade epoch.
                                        Faced, though, like Bill Tuckett
with a man needing surgery right on the spot, a lot
would have done their dashes. It looked hopeless (dot dot dot)
Lift him up on the table, said Tuckett, running the key hot
till Head Office turned up a doctor who coolly instructed
up a thousand miles of wire, as Tuckett advanced slit by slit
with a safety razor blade, pioneering on into the wet,
copper-wiring the rivers off, in the first operation conducted
along dotted lines, with rum drinkers gripping the patient:
d-d-dash it, take care, Tuck!
                                And the vital spark stayed unshorted.
Yallah! breathed the camelmen. Tuckett, you did it, you did it!
cried the spattered la-de-dah jodhpur-wearing Inspector of Stock.
We imagine, some weeks later, a properly laconic
convalescent averring Without you, I'd have kicked the bucket ...

From Chungking to Burrenjuck, morse keys have mostly gone silent
and only old men meet now to chit-chat in their electric
bygone dialect. The last letter many will forget
is dit-dit-dit-dah, V for Victory. The coders' hero had speed,
resource and a touch. So ditditdit daah for Bill Tuckett.


# LATE SNOW IN EDINBURGH

Snow on the day before Anzac!
A lamb-killing wind out of Ayr
heaped a cloud up on towering Edinburgh
in the night, and left it adhering
to parks and leafing trees in the morning,
a cloud decaying on the upper city,

on the stepped medieval skyscrapers there,
cassata broadcast on the lower city
to be a hiss on buzzing cobblestones
under soaped cars, and cars still shaving.

All day the multiplying whiteness
persisted, now dazzling, now resumed
into the spectral Northern weather,
moist curd out along the Castle clifftops,
linen collar on the Mound, pristine pickings
in the Cowgate's blackened teeth, deposits
in Sir Walter Scott's worked tusk, and under
the soaked blue banners walling Princes Street.
The lunchtime gun fired across dun distances
ragged with keen tents. By afternoon, though,
derelicts sleeping immaculate in wynds
and black areas had shrivelled to wet sheep.
Froth, fading, stretched thinner on allotments.

As the melting air browned into evening
the photographed city, in last umber
and misty first lights, was turning into
the stones in a vast furrow. For that moment
half a million moved in an earth cloud
harrowed up, damp and fuming, seeded
with starry points, with luminous still patches
that wouldn't last the night. No Anzac Day
prodigies for the visitor-descendant.
The snow was dimming into Spring's old
Flanders jacket and frieze trousers. Hughie Spring
the droll ploughman, up from the Borders.

# ART HISTORY: THE SUBURB OF SURREALLS

We dreamed very wide awake
those days, for obedience's sake:

*In the suburb of Surrealls*
*horse families board the airline bus*
*to sell packages of phlegm.*
*My notebook is hugely swollen.*
*For some reason I am American.*

Such dreaming is enforceable.
Everyone became guarded;
a tinkling of symbols was heard.
It's the West occupying the dreamworld
because the East has captured reason,
some said. Many ceased to listen.

In fact we'd gone to the dream
for supplies of that instant
paint of the twilight kingdom
which colours every object
supernal, deeply important.
Spirit-surrogate. We even synthesised it.

Exposed to the common air, it
weathered quickly to the tone
of affectless weird despair,
elegant barely contained anger
our new patrons demanded
when we had trained them to it.

False dreamings are imperial
but we couldn't disappoint them
(Few others now read us by choice.
*Woolf! Woolf!* our master's voice).

To be fair, many of us
had now joined the creative class
and become our masters
– but the paint, when stolen
and breathed straight from the tin,
gave a noble deathly rush
that replaced imagination.


## THE DIALECTIC OF DREAMS

Dream harbours Sin, and Innocence, and Magic,
re-stews mundane cabbage, stacks a shifting Tarot,
equivocates naïvely about Death, the secular Absolute –

things Rationality, the replacement aristocrat
approves only for enhancement. By midday
it has clarified its twinship with that relic –

but it comes round again, by deep night at the latest,
in a skin boat sailing on the blood
for dream lives its life engorged. It owns tumescence,

makes eerie conquests, can engender children –
though few who see the sun. The real takes some joint permission
and all of ourself not in the dream lies flaccid.

Every night, stepped mast or unfurled sail,
we reach a land where nothing is held trivial.

o

Real dreams are from home • back there. The light as it was,
will be, might have been • all the receding dream-tenses.

The dreamer is even yourself • or you're aware it is.
There in the action, unsafe • greater than the action, passive,

rarely uttering, in the endless • preparations, for horror, for happiness, those appalling formulae • other-directed at us

which may persist as salt foam • on the margin of lapsed scenes
or, like the filmed cities, be resumed • into their own presence.

And that otherworld incongruence • spindling faintly through the day,
heightening thought, blanking it • silvering, beckoning away:

preternatural, those interiors • half-recalled by consciousness,
they were never in this world • not in your life, those wet bossed lanes.

Yet this is the heart of work • *the human sage, the butterfly*
to be conscious at the source of worlds • rapt, raising the ante.

                    o

The daylight oil, the heavier grade of Reason,
reverie's clear water, that of the dreamworld ocean
agitate us and are shaken, forming the emulsion

without which we make nothing much. Not art,
not love, not war, nor its reasoned nightmare methods,
not the Taj, not our homes, not the Masses or the gods

– but the fusion persists in the product, not in us.
A wheel shatters, drains our pooled rainbow. It was a moment:
the world is debris and museum of that moment,

its prospectus and farm. The wheel is turned by this engine.
I think of the people and buildings in a business street,
how they lack a perfect valve to take on and release

unceasing fusions. And will be pulled down for it,
their walls dreamed on in the milk of obsolete children.

                    o

Dream surrounds, is infused with this world. It is not subordinate.
We come from it; we live at tangents and accords with it; we go
back into it, at last, through the drowsing torture chambers to it.

We have gills for dream-life, in our head; we must keep them wet
from the nine-nights' immense, or dreams will emerge bodily, and
    enforce it.
Hide among or deny the shallow dreadful ones, and they may stay out:

moor things in Heaven and earth then, Ratio, anyhow you can
because dream's the looseleaf book, not of fiction, but of raw Pretend,
incalculable as this world when the God of Mercy intervened often.

It is the free splitting from God that parts Nature from dream.
They refresh each other with bafflement, each as the other's underground
freeing lives to be finite, because more; to be timeless, yet pure
    preparation –

while those spaces, sacred as the poor, of the haloed russet kingdom
are tigers impelling us, full of futures and pasts, toward a present.


## SATIS PASSIO

Elites, levels, proletariat:
the uniting cloth crowns
of Upper and Lower Egypt
suggests theories of poetry
which kindness would accept
to bestow, like Heaven, dignity
on the inept and the ept,
one Papuan warrior's phallocrypt
the soaring equal of its fellowcrypt.

By these measures, most knowledge
in our heads is poetry,
varied crystals of detail, chosen
by dream-interest, and poured spirally
from version to myth, with spillage,
from theory to history
and, with toppings-up, to story,

not metered, lined or free
but condensed by memory
to roughly vivid essences:
most people's poetry is now this.
Some of it is made by poets.

God bless the feral poetries,
littératures and sensibilities,
theory, wonder, the human gamut
leaping cheerfully or in heavy earnest
– but there is this quality to art
which starts, rather than ends, at the gist.
Not the angle, but the angel.

Art is what can't be summarised:
it has joined creation from our side,
entered Nature, become a fact
and acquired presence,
more like ourselves or any subject
swirled around, about, in and out,
than like the swirling poetries.

Art's best is a standing miracle
at an uncrossable slight distance,
an anomaly, finite but inexhaustible,
unaltered after analysis
as an ancient face.

Not the portrait of one gone
merely, no pathos of the bygone
but a section, of all that exist,
a passage, a whole pattern
that has shifted the immeasurable
first step into Heaven.
A first approximation.
Where is Heaven? Down these roads.

The fine movement of art's face
before us is a motionless traffic
between here and remote Heaven.
It is out through this surface,
we may call it the Unfalling Arrow,
this third mode, and perhaps by art first
that there came to us the dream-plan
of equality and justice,
long delayed by the poetries –

but who was the more numinous,
Pharaoh or the hunted Nile heron?
more splendid, the iris or Solomon?
Beauty lives easily with equities
more terrible than theory dares mean.
Of the workers set free to break stone
and the new-cracked stone, which is more luminous?

God bless the general poetries?
This is how it's done.


## FLOOD PLAINS ON THE COAST FACING ASIA

Hitching blur to a caged propeller
with its motor racket swelling
barroom to barrage, our aluminium
airboat has crossed the black coffee
lagoon and swum out onto
one enormous crinkling green.
Now like a rocket loudening
to liftoff, it erects the earsplitting
wigwam we must travel in
everywhere here, and starts skimming
at speed on the never-never
meadows of the monsoon wetland.

Birds lift, scattering before us
over the primeval irrigation,
leaf-running jacanas, twin-boomed
with supplicant bare feet for tails;
knob-headed magpie geese
row into the air ahead of us;
waterlilies lean away, to go
under as we overrun them
and resurrect behind us.
We leave at most a darker green
trace on the universal glittering
and, waterproof in cream and blue,
waterlilies on their stems, circling.

Our shattering car
crossing exposed and seeping spaces
brings us to finely stinking places,
yet whatever riceless paddies
we reach, of whatever grass,
there is always sheeting spray
underhull for our passage;
and the Intermediate Egret leaps
aloft out of stagnant colours
and many a double-barrelled crossbow
shoots vegetable breath emphatically
from the haunts of flaking buffalo;
water glinting everywhere, like ice,
we traverse speeds humans once reached
in such surroundings mainly
as soldiers, in the tropic wars.

At times, we fold our windtunnel
away, in its blackened steel sail
and sit, for talk and contemplation.
For instance, off the deadly islet,
a swamp-surrounded sandstone knoll
split, cabled, commissured
with fig trees' python roots.
Watched by distant plateau cliffs
stitched millennially in every crevice

with the bark-entubed dead
we do not go ashore.
Those hills are ancient stone gods
just beginning to be literature.

We release again the warring sound
of our peaceful tour, and go sledding
headlong through mounded paperbark
copses, on reaches of maroon
grit, our wake unravelling
over green curd where logs lie digesting
and over the breast-lifting deeps
of the file snake, whom the women here
tread on, scoop up, clamp head-first in their teeth
and jerk to death, then carry home as meat.

Loudest without speech, we shear
for miles on the paddock of nymphaeas
still hoisting up the paired pied geese,
their black goslings toddling below them.
We, a family with baby and two friends,
one swift metal skin above the food-chains,
the extensible wet life-chains of which
our civility and wake are one stretch,
the pelicans circling over us another
and the cat-napping peace of the secure,
of eagles, lions and two-year-old George
asleep beneath his pink linen hat as
we enter domains of flowering lotus.

In our propeller's stiffened silence
we stand up among scalloped leaves
that are flickering for hundreds of acres
on their deeper water. The lotus
prove a breezy nonhuman gathering
of this planet, with their olive-studded
rubbery cocktail glasses, loose carmine roses,
salmon buds like the five-fingertips-joined
gesture of summation, of *ecco!*
waist-high around us in all their greenery

on yeasty frog water. We receive this
sidelong, speaking our wiry language
in which so many others ghost and flicker.

We discuss Leichhardt's party and their qualities
when, hauling the year 1845
through here, with spearheads embedded in it,
their bullock drays reached and began skirting
this bar of literal water
after the desert months which had been
themselves a kind of swimming,
a salt undersea plodding, monster-haunted
with odd very pure surfacings.
We also receive, in drifts of calm
hushing, which fret the baby boy,
how the fuzzed gold innumerable cables
by which this garden hangs skyward
branch beneath the surface, like dreams.

The powerful dream of being harmless,
the many chains snapped and stretched hard for that:
both shimmer behind our run back
toward the escarpments where stallion-eyed
Lightning lives, who'd shiver all heights
down and make of the earth
one oozing, feeding peneplain.
Unprotected Lightning: there are his wild horses
and brolgas, and far heron not rising.
Suddenly we run over a crocodile.
On an unlilied deep, bare even
of minute water fern, it leaped out,
surged man-swift straight under us. We ran over it.
We circle back. Unhurt, it floats, peering
from each small eye turret, then annuls
buoyancy and merges subtly under,
swollen leathers becoming gargoyle stone,
chains of contour, with pineapple abdomen.

# CUMULUS

Repeatedly out of grazed plateaux, the Dividing
Range assumes, soaring after gliding,
into high countries, not peaked but cumulus
in evergreen black and mossy bleached khaki
out under antarctic grey and razory blues,
horizons above the nation, now visited rarely
except in polemic hiking, or on the ski niveaux.
We turned away to ochre and surf sands long ago
and secret cattleyards never formed a traceable city.

White cloud still assembles daily along each island
far above our South Sea levels. Mist forest, tussock sops
under redoubled height drink fog along the Tops
and newly earthed rivers edge out of sphagnum overloads
to shin down human clay and unhuman cobbled roads
to the short east, to the brown west ocean of land;
the cello necks of tree ferns spread as they come uncurled
and screech-red parrots fly, with many stops,
toward the beech trees of the southern world.

On the varying heights where stupendous heights are brewed
out of clear air by pitch and altitude
few have yet lived, in all the centuries. Some have stayed.
Many themes attended the hibernation of Ned Kelly:
the fat moth-feast of the tribes, whip bird and rifle bird,
moleskin prospectors each working his vein of solitude;
Thunderbolt emerging from the wet cave of his treasure
sights a coach down through timber, spurs into ballad measure –
but these disappear down the crumples of the possum-skin rug,

the great ravines of catchment. Jindabygone, Adamemory.
Of Governors fleeing heat on the hill stations, we recall Jimmy,
but the sleepout in the dark ranges has weakened its tug
and retreat is continually modelled. Our plateau capital
avoids its own heights and nearby mountains. They are all

cloud-shadowed with new dry forest. The vixen feeds her cubs,
and kangaroos fold down to graze, above the human suburbs.
Neither fantasy nor fear has built an eagle's nest fortress
to top our nonfiction poetry. We've put the wild above us.


# FEDERATION STYLE ON THE NORTHERN RIVERS

And entering on the only smooth road
this steamer glides past the rattling shipyard
where they're having the usual Aboriginal
whale-feast in reverse, with scaffolding and planking;
engine smoke marching through blue sheoak trees
along the edge of Jack Robertson farms,
the river opens and continually opens

and lashed on deck, a Vauxhall car,
intricate in brass, with bonnet grooves,
a bulb to squawk, great guillotine levers,
high diamond-buttoned leather club chairs
and dressing-table windscreen to flash afar:
in British cherry metal, detailed in mustard
it cruises up country with a moveless wheel.

In the town it approaches, a Habsburg-yellow store
Provisions – Novelties – J. Cornwell Prop.
contains a knot of debt that has reached
straining point, tugging between many poor
selector farmers and several not necessarily
rich city suppliers. Mobilised, it can tear
the store apart, uproot many families

and tomorrow the auditor will be in town
and the car will be parked just where he comes
after a prolonged hilarious midday dinner
*I see your town's acquired a motor –*
*You fancy those beasts, do you, Stickney?*
One face grows inspired, in step with the other.
*What is that sly joker Cornwell at?*

asks the Bank of Australasia's swank bow window:
*How can he have afforded a motor?*
but a schooner bee deflects the questioner.
*Would you like to take a spin in her,*
*Stickney? – I daresay your books will wait*
*for half an hour ...* One mounts from the left,
one hoists the crankhandle. Directly, indirectly

they wind down the street over horsemanures
of varying fatness, past the Coffee Palace
unconcerned with ales – *Stickney, you're a marvel!*
*Just aim her straight and don't shout Whoa!*
*Tread on that to slow her: don't tug the wheel –*
Children running, neighbours cheering, *Go it, Jim!*
Mr Cornwell lifts his hat to the faces greeting him.

Smashing water-windows along the parallel
wheeltracks of the cart-cut river road
they pass the deeply laden Cornwell shop-boat
*Turn inland here: we will have drier going.*
*I agree she'd be a buy, Stickney: I'd have to think –*
Think how to waste more afternoon
with the tall affection of local tales:

*... And old Tom Beattie managing himself*
*along, like a bad horse; you hear him curse it:*
*Hold up, you bugger! Walk! –* Mr Cornwell,
*we should get back, to your ledgers. – Yes.*
*Take the left fork two miles on. A shortcut –*
The shortcut ends in blackpudding bog
and no country curricles bowling by it.

*Dear God, Cornwell, I must catch tomorrow's boat!*
but heaving, corduroying, pole-levering all fail
and Cornwell must vanish through the rung timber.
For Stickney there will now accrue a wait
heavy as blacksoil around buried wheels.
Shanks' pony? Not I. Not through snaky bush.
He watches a swamp pheasant's sailing flight,

and on the creekbank, in a place where cattle,
and white man's firesticks, can't come
he finds a child's small bowerbird farm:
scraped roads, wharf, little twig cattleyards,
clay beasts. A new world, already immemorial.
He will tighten his coat against evening chill
long before Cornwell reappears with helpers.

That night the yellow store will burn
in a jammed eye-parching abolishment of proof
and the car, strangely spotless, will not be harmed.
Tomorrow the innocent owner will collect it.
The steamer hoots. *Cornwell, now that you're*
*safely ruined: where did you go yesterday?*
*– I had to dodge certain bandicoot farms*

*where the little ones bolt up under the house*
*at the sight of a stranger. I've never cared*
*to be a stranger who threatens children.*
They part, across water, with the ghost of a salute.
Certain surnames will now survive in the district.
As the town declines through the mulberry years
Cornwell will receive odd grateful sovereigns.
The rebuilt store will be kept by a Hogan.


EASTER 1984

When we saw human dignity
healing humans in the middle of the day

we moved in on him slowly
under the incalculable gravity

of old freedom, of our own freedom,
under atmospheres of consequence, of justice

under which no one needs to thank anyone.
If this was God, we would get even.

And in the end we nailed him,
lashed, spittled, stretched him limb from limb.

We would settle with dignity
for the anguish it had caused us,

we'd send it to be abstract again,
we would set it free.

      o

But we had raised up evolution.
It would not stop being human.

Ever afterwards, the accumulation
of freedom would end in this man

whipped, bloodied, getting the treatment.
It would look like man himself getting it.

He was freeing us, painfully, from freedom,
justice, dignity – he was discharging them

of their deadly ambiguous deposit,
remaking out of them the primal day

in which he was free not to have borne it
and we were free not to have done it,

free never to torture man again,
free to believe him risen.


## PHYSIOGNOMY ON THE SAVAGE MANNING RIVER

Walking on that early shore, in our bodies,
the autumn ocean has become wasp-waisted:
a scraped timber mansion hung in showering
ropework is crabbing on the tide's flood,
swarming, sway, and shouting,
entering the rivermouth over the speedy bar.

As it calms into the river, the Tahitian
helmsman, a pipe-smoking archer,
draws and tightens the wheel. The spruce captain
meanwhile celebrates the bohème of revolutions
with a paper cigarette, and the carpenter,
deepwater man, combs his sulky boy's hair.

*Seo abhainn mar loch* – the polished river is indeed
like a loch, without flow, clear to the rainforest islands
and the Highland immigrants on deck, remarking it,
keep a hand, or a foot, on their bundles and nail-kegs.
No equipment is replaceable: there's only one of anything,
experience they will hand down.

Beyond the river brush extends the deserted
Aboriginal hunting park. There is far less blue
out in the grassland khaki than in our lifetime
though the hills are darkening, sprinkling outward,
closing on crusted lagoons. Nowhere a direct line;
no willows yet, nor any houses.
Those are in the low hills upriver.
Beyond are the ranges, edge over edge, like jumbled sabres.

Crocodile chutes slant out of the riverbank forest
where great logs have been launched.
It is the feared long-unburnable
dense forest of the dooligarl. The cannibal solitary
humanoid of no tribe. Here, as worldwide, he and she
are hairy, nightmare-agile, with atavisms of the feet.
Horror can be ascribed and strange commissions given
to the fireless dooligarl. Killer, here, of gingery bat-hunters.

Tiptoeing after its slung leadline, the ship moves forward
for hours into the day. Raising the first dogleg paddocks,
the first houses, the primal blowflies.
Soup and clothing
boil in a fire-hut, in cauldrons slung on steel saws
there where next century's pelicans will haunt the Fish Cooperative.

The gossip on the river is all Miss Isabella Kelly:
triumphing home with her libel case now won
and, for her months in jail, a thousand pounds compensation;
she has found her stations devastated:
yards smashed, homestead burnt, cattle lifted
(irrecoverable nods are winked here).
Now she has sailed to England in her habitual
infuriated self esteem.
She will have Charles Dickens write her story.
Voices, calling God to forgive them, wish her drownded.

Isabella Mary Kelly. The shadowy first landholder.
Now she has given the district a larger name
to drop than her own. She, who rode beside
her walking convicts three days through the wilderness
to have them flogged half-insane in proper form
at Port Macquarie and Raymond Terrace
then walked them immediately back,
her crosshatched alleged harem,
she who told the man who dragged her from swift floodwater
'You waste your gallantry. You are still due a lashing.
Walk on, croppy.'

Isabella Kelly, of the sidesaddle acerbities,
grazier and pistol shot
throned and footless in her hooped midcentury skirts,
for some years it has been she,
and perhaps it really was she, who had the deadly crystals
mixed into scones for the natives at Belbora,
Miss Kelly all alone. The colonies' earlier Kelly.
Jilted in Dublin – or is that an acanthus leaf
of motivation, modelled over something barer?
Suddenly her time has passed.
Death in a single room in chilly Sydney
still lies ahead – and being confused with Kate Kelly –
but she has moved already into her useful legend.

Now up every side creek a youth in a cabbagetree hat
is rocking like a steersman, feinting like a boxer:
every stone of gravel must go a round or two
in a circling dish, and the pouring of waters be adjusted.

The same on every track round the heads of rivers:
men escaping the black mills
and families tired of a thousand years' dim tenancy
are entering the valley beside their jolting stacks;
there is even the odd spanker,
reins in hand behind trotters, on a seat like a chocolate éclair,
though he is as yet rare;
more are riding through horse-high grass, and into timber
that thickens, like work, to meet their mighty need of it.

The ship is tied up meanwhile in a sort
of farmyard dockland:
pigs under the wharf, saddles, pumpkin patches, corn boats.
The men unloading her, who never doff their shirts,
are making whips of tin;
this one who has worn the white clay girdle of the Bora,
of sung rebirth, now plies a lading hook
to keep his Kentish wife.
At spell-oh time, they will share a pipe of tobacco
which she has shaved from the succulent twist with her case-knife.

Farther upriver, men are rolling out onto their wharf
big solid barrels of a mealy wetness
and others with axes are dismembering downed cattle
in jarring sight of yarded herds. They heave the pieces
into huge smoking trypots. It is the boiling-down,
a kind of inland sealing.
The boiled-out meat is pitched down a cloacal gully.

All that can be exported of the squatter's cattle,
of the spinster Kelly's cattle and the others',
is their tallow, for candles.
Lights for the sickroom, lustre for pianoforte sconces.
Cattle distilled to a fluted wax, and sea creatures
sublimated to a liquor light the readers
of Charles Darwin and Charles Dickens.
On sleeping skins, snorting boys drip melted cattle.

Now the gently wrecking cornfields relax, and issue
parents and children. What do families offer us?
Some protection from history,
a tough school of forgiveness.
After the ship has twitched minutely out of
focus and back, as many times as there were barrels
and night has assumed the slab huts and sawn houses,
the faces drinking tea by their various lights
include some we had thought modern. The mask of unappeasable
rage is there, and those of scorn's foundling aristocracy,
among the timeless sad and contented faces,
the vacant and remote faces. Only the relative
licensing of expressions is wholly different.
Blame is not yet privileged.

And, walking on that early shore in our bodies
(perhaps the only uncowardly way to do history)
if we asked leading questions, we might hear,
short of a ringing ear,
something like: We do what's to be done
and some things because we can.
Don't be taking talk out of me.

Such not only from the haughtily dreaming,
intelligent, remorseless, secretly amused still face
of Isabella Kelly.
As the Highlandman said
eating his first meal of fresh beef and cornmeal porridge
after landing today:
*Thig lá choin duibh fhathast.* The black dog will have his day yet.
Not every dog, as in English, but the black dog.

# THE DREAM OF WEARING SHORTS FOREVER

To go home and wear shorts forever
in the enormous paddocks, in that warm climate,
adding a sweater when winter soaks the grass,

to camp out along the river bends
for good, wearing shorts, with a pocketknife,
a fishing line and matches,

or there where the hills are all down, below the plain,
to sit around in shorts at evening
on the plank verandah –

If the cardinal points of costume
are Robes, Tat, Rig and Scunge,
where are shorts in this compass?

They are never Robes
as other bareleg outfits have been:
the toga, the kilt, the lava-lava
the Mahatma's cotton dhoti;

archbishops and field marshals
at their ceremonies never wear shorts.
The very word
means underpants in North America.

Shorts can be Tat,
Land-Rovering bush-environmental tat,
socio-political ripped-and-metal-stapled tat,
solidarity-with-the-Third-World tat tvam asi,

likewise track-and-field shorts worn to parties
and the further humid, modelling negligée
of the Kingdom of Flaunt,
that unchallenged aristocracy.

More plainly climatic, shorts
are farmers' rig leathery with salt and bonemeal,
are sailors' and branch bankers' rig,
the crisp golfing style
of our youngest male National Costume.

Mostly loosely, they are Scunge,
ancient Bengal bloomers or moth-eaten hot pants
worn with a former shirt,
feet, beach sand, hair
and a paucity of signals.

Scunge, which is real negligée
housework in a swimsuit, pyjamas worn all day,
is holiday, is freedom from ambition.
Scunge makes you invisible
to the world and yourself.

The entropy of costume,
scunge can get you conquered by more vigorous cultures
and help you to notice it less.

Satisfied ambition, defeat, true unconcern,
the wish and the knack for self-forgetfulness
all fall within the scunge ambit
wearing board shorts or similar;
it is a kind of weightlessness.

Unlike public nakedness, which in Westerners
is deeply circumstantial, relaxed as exam time,
artless and equal as the corsetry of a hussar regiment,

shorts and their plain like
are an angelic nudity,
spirituality with pockets!
A double updraft as you drop from branch to pool!

Ideal for getting served last
in shops of the temperate zone
they are also ideal for going home, into space,
into time, to farm the mind's Sabine acres
for product or subsistence.

Now that everyone who yearned to wear long pants
has essentially achieved them,
long pants, which have themselves been underwear
repeatedly, and underground more than once,
it is time perhaps to cherish the culture of shorts,

to moderate grim vigour
with the knobble of bare knees,
to cool bareknuckle feet in inland water,
slapping flies with a book on solar wind
or a patient bare hand, beneath the cadjiput trees,

to be walking meditatively
among green timber, through the grassy forest
towards a calm sea
and looking across to more of that great island
and the further topics.


## AT THE AQUATIC CARNIVAL

Two racing boats seen from the harmonic railing
of this road bridge quit their wakes,
plane above their mirroring shield-forms
and bash the river, flat out, their hits batts of appliqué
violently spreading, their turnings eiderdown
abolishing translucency before the frieze of people,
and rolled-over water comes out to the footings of the carnival.

Even up drinking coffee-and-froth in the town
prodigious sound rams through arcades and alleyways
and burrs in our teeth, beneath the slow nacelle
of a midsummer ceiling fan.
No wonder pelicans vanish from their river at these times.
How, we wonder, does that sodden undersized one
who hangs around the Fish Co-op get by?
The pert wrymouth with the twisted upper beak.

It cannot pincer prey, or lid its lower scoop,
and so lives on guts, mucking in with the others
who come and go. For it to leave would be death.
Its trouble looks like a birth defect, not an injury,
and raises questions.
There are poetics would require it to be pecked
to death by fellow pelicans, or kids to smash it with a stick,
preserving a hard cosmos.

In fact it came with fellow pelicans, parents maybe,
and has been around for years. Humans who feed it
are sentimental, perhaps – but what to say
of humans who refused to feed a lame bird?
Nature is not human-hearted. But it is one flesh
or we could not imagine it. And we could not eat.

Nature is not human-hearted. So the animals
come to man, at first in their extremity:
the wild scrub turkeys entering farms in drought-time,
the done fox suddenly underfoot among dog-urgers
(that frantic compliment, that prayer never granted by dogs)
or the shy birds perching on human shoulders and trucks
when the mountains are blotted out in fiery dismemberment.


## THE SLEEPOUT

Childhood sleeps in a verandah room
in an iron bed close to the wall
where the winter over the railing
swelled the blind on its timber boom

and splinters picked lint off warm linen
and the stars were out over the hill;
then one wall of the room was forest
and all things in there were to come.

Breathings climbed up on the verandah
when dark cattle rubbed at a corner
and sometimes dim towering rain stood
for forest, and the dry cave hunched woollen.

Inside the forest was lamplit
along tracks to a starry creek bed
and beyond lay the never-fenced country,
its full billabongs all surrounded

by animals and birds, in loud crustings,
and something kept leaping up amongst them.
And out there, to kindle whenever
dark found it, hung the daylight moon.


TROPICAL WINDOW

Out through a long bright window
are three headlands ruched together
on an ivory drawstring of beach. Salad and jade
over freckled pancake rock, each
is washed at foot by noonday suds intermittently
and some yachts are pinned with tall spears to the bay.

This horizontal window
is lamp and sole brilliant picture
to a shadowy cane room
where people stir instant drinks. There is the man
with sunglasses at his throat like sleek electrodes
or a very high tech bow tie
and the woman with the luminous
ruby signet of the smoker. And another
figure saying We need more passive verbs:

I am sneezed, for example (and just try to resist!) or:
You are coughed. More coughed about than coughing –
But the windowed littoral
distracts them again and again. The motionless
shellburst palms, on the skyline, over the golf course,
the sea's lucent linoleum,
the near trees with green-ants' nests
square-folded out of living leaves, like Japanese packages.

If the three stepped out
into that scene, humidity and glare would sandbag them,
make them fretful tourists.
Not coated glass but simple indoor contrast
has tuned the hyaline
to a sourceless cerebral light
and framing has made the window photo-realist,
a style of art everybody now feels they have been
in. And will be in again
at any immortal democratic moment.


LOUVRES

In the banana zone, in the poinciana tropics
reality is stacked on handsbreadth shelving,
open and shut, it is ruled across with lines
as in a gleaming gritty exercise book.

The world is seen through a cranked or levered
weatherboarding of explosive glass
angled floor-to-ceiling. Horizons which metre
the dazzling outdoors into green-edged couplets.

In the louvred latitudes
children fly to sleep in triplanes, and
cool nights are eerie with retracting flaps.

Their houses stand aloft among bougainvillea,
covered bridges that lead down a shining hall
from love to mystery to breakfast,
from babyhood to moving-out day

and visitors shimmer up in columnar gauges
to touch lives lived behind gauze
in a lantern of inventory,
slick vector geometries glossing the months of rain.

There, nudity is dizzily cubist, and directions
have to include: stage left, add an inch of breeze
or: enter a glistening tendril.

Every building of jinked and slatted ledges
is at times a squadron of inside-out
helicopters, humming with rotor fans.

For drinkers under cyclonic pressure, such
a house can be a bridge of scythes –
groundlings scuffing by stop only for dénouements.

But everyone comes out on platforms of command
to survey cloudy flame-trees, the plain of streets, the future:
only then descending to the level of affairs

and if these things are done in the green season
what to do in the crystalline dry? Well
below in the struts of laundry is the four-wheel drive

vehicle in which to make an expedition
to the bush, or as we now say the Land,
the three quarters of our continent
set aside for mystic poetry.

# THE EDGELESS

Floodwater from remote rains has spread out
of the riverine scrub, resuming its mirages.
Mostly shallow, mild water
it ties its hidden drowning strains
taut around odd trees, in that low forest
whose skinny shade turns the water taupe. Nests float
and the vaster flat shine is cobbled at wave-shadow points
with little brown melons, just starting to smell rank.

The local station manager, his eyes
still squinting from the greenest green on the place,
the computer screen, strolls out of his office
onto the verandah. Tiny native bees
who fly standing up, like angels, shimmer the garden.
His wife points out their dog Boxer,
pads slipping, tongue slipping out, nails
catching in unseen lurch mineshafts, gamely
teetering along the round top rail of the killing yard.

Where does talk come from? the two ask each other
over teacups. – From the same place as the world.
We have got the word and we don't understand it.
It is like too much. – So we made up a word of our own
as much like nothing else as possible
and gave it to the machines. It made them grow –
And now we can't see the limits of that word either.

Come down off there, Boxer! Who put you up there?


# THE DRUGS OF WAR

On vinegar and sour fish sauce Rome's legions stemmed avalanches
of whirling golden warriors whose lands furnished veterans' ranches;
when the warriors broke through at last, they'd invented sour mash
but they took to sugared wines and failed to hold the lands of hash.

By beat of drum in the wars of rum flogged peasant boys faced front
and their warrior chiefs conversed coolly, attired for the hunt,
and tobacco came in, in a pipe of peace, but joined the pipes of war
as an after-smoke of battle, or over the maps before.

All alcohols, all spirits lost strength in the trenches, that belt-fed country
then morphine summoned warrior dreams in ruined and would-be gentry;
stewed tea and vodka and benzedrine helped quell that mechanized fury –
the side that won by half a head then provided judge and jury.

In the acid war the word was Score; rising helicopters cried Smack! Smack!
Boys laid a napalm trip on earth and tried to take it back
but the pot boiled over in the rear; fighters tripped on their lines of force
and victory went to the supple hard side, eaters of fish sauce.

The perennial war drugs are made in ourselves: sex and adrenalin,
blood, and the endomorphias that transmute defeat and pain
and others hardly less chemical: eagles, justice, loyalty, edge,
the Judas face of every idea, and the fish that ferments in the brain.


LETTERS TO THE WINNER

After the war, and just after marriage and fatherhood
ended in divorce, our neighbour won the special lottery,
an amount then equal to fifteen years of a manager's
salary at the bank, or fifty years' earnings by
a marginal farmer fermenting his clothes in the black
marinade of sweat, up in his mill-logging paddocks.

The district, used to one mailbag, now received two
every mailday. The fat one was for our neighbour.
After a dip or two, he let these bags accumulate
around the plank walls of the kitchen, over the chairs,
till on a rainy day, he fed the tail-switching calves,
let the bullocks out of the yard, and, pausing at the door
to wash his hands, came inside to read the letters.

Shaken out in a vast mound on the kitchen table
they slid down, slithered to his fingers. *I have 7 children
I am under the doctor if you could see your way clear
equal Pardners in the Venture God would bless you lovey
assured of our best service for a mere fifteen pounds down
remember you're only lucky I knew you from the paper straightaway.*

Baksheesh, hissed the pages as he flattened them, baksheesh!
*mate if your interested in a fellow diggers problems
old mate a friend in need* – the Great Golden Letter
having come, now he was being punished for it.
*You sound like a lovely big boy we could have such times
her's my photoe Doll Im wearing my birthday swimsuit
with the right man I would share this infallible system.*

When he lifted the stove's iron lid and started feeding in
the pages he'd read, they clutched and streamed up the corrugated
black chimney shaft. And yet he went on reading,
holding each page by its points, feeling an obligation
to read each crude rehearsed lie, each come-on, flat truth, extremity:
*We might visit you the wise investor a loan a bush man like you*

*remember we met on Roma Street for your delight and mine
a lick of the sultana* – the white moraine kept slipping
its messages to him *you will be accursed* he husked them like cobs
*Mr Nouveau Jack old man my legs are all paralysed up.*
Black smuts swirled weightless in the room *some good kind person*
like the nausea of a novice free-falling in a deep mine's cage
*now I have lost his pension* and formed a sticky nimbus round him

but he read on, fascinated by a further human range
not even war had taught him, nor literature glossed for him
since he never read literature. Merely the great reject pile
which high style is there to snub and filter, for readers.
That his one day's reading had a strong taste of what he and war
had made of his marriage is likely; he was not without sympathy,

but his leap had hit a wire through which the human is policed.
His head throbbed as if busting with a soundless shout
of immemorial sobbed invective *God-forsaken, God-forsakin*
as he stopped reading, and sat blackened in his riches.


## THE CHINA PEAR TREES

The power of three China pear trees
standing in their splintery timber bark
on an open paddock:

the selector's house that staked and watered them
in Bible times, beside a shaded patch,
proved deciduous; it went away in loads,

but after sixty years of standing out,
vanishing in autumn, blizzarding in spring,
among the farmlands' sparse and giant furniture,

after sixty crops gorged on from all directions,
so that no windfalls, fermenting, shrank to lizard-skinned
puree in the short grazed grass,

the trees drew another house, electrified and steaming
but tin-roofed as before for blazing clouds to creak over
and with tiny nude frogs upright again on lamplit glass;

they drew another kitchen garden, and a dam
half scintillating waterlily pleasance, half irrigation,
an ad hoc orchard, Christmas pines, a cud-dropping mower;

they drew a wire fence around acres of enclosure
shaped like a fuel tin, its spout a tunnel of trees
tangled in passionflower and beige-belled wonga vine,

down inside which a floodtime waterfall churns
millet-sized gravel. And they called lush water-leaved trees
like themselves to the stumpholes of gone rainforest

to shade with four seasons the tattered evergreen
oil-haloed face of a subtle fire landscape
(water forest versus fire forest, ancient war of the southern world).

It was this shade in the end, not their coarse bottling fruit
that mirrored the moist creek trees outward, as a culture
containing the old gardener now untying and heaping up

one more summer's stems and chutneys,
his granddaughter walking a horse the colour of her boots
and his tree-shaping son ripping out the odd failed seedling,
'Sorry, tree. I kill and I learn.'


# THE VOL SPRUNG FROM HERALDRY

Left wing, right wing:
two wings torment our lives,
two wings without a body,
joined, turkey wing and vulture wing

like the badge of an airborne army.
Each has its clients to enfold
and shed lice on. It gets quite underarm
and the other wing lashes at them.

Two wings without a bird –
is called a *vol* in heraldry –
spinning, fighting, low to the ground,
whomping up evil dusts for our breath.

Two wings, longing for a body:
left wing, right wing, flexing
still from the noble secret spring
that launched, propels and will exhaust them:

that everything in the end grows boring.

# THE MEGAETHON: 1850, 1906–29

I.M. LEO PORT

Farmer Cleve, gent., of the Hunter
Valley has ordained that his large
Sydney-built steam engine shall be walked
home under its own power, on iron
shoes serially laid beneath its wheels.
Making four miles a day, it's no fizzer.
He has christened it the Megaethon,
Greek for the Ruddy Big Fiery Thing.

On black iron plates that lean down
and flatten successively, imprinting
rectangular billets of progression
it advances on the Hawkesbury district
hissing, clanking, stoked by freed men.
People run from oat-field and wash-house,
from pot-house and cockpit to gape
at its shackled gait, its belt-drive pulsation:

'Look, Mother, it walks on its knees!' 'Aye,
it's praying its way to Wiseman's Ferry,
coughing black smoke out of its steeple!'
Sparks canter by it, cracking whips. Small
native children scream 'Buggy-buggy!'
and the iron gangs straighten from their sad
triangular thoughts to watch another
mighty value approach along their spadework.

In that last, dissolving convict year
what passes their wedged grins is a harbinger
not merely of words like *humdinger*, but
of stumpjump ploughs, metal ores made float,
ice plants, keel wings, a widening vote,
the world's harvesters, the utility truck, rotary
engines pipemoulds lawnmowers – this motor the
slaves watch strikes a ringing New World note.

As, tilting, stayed with ropes and pulleys,
the Megaethon descends a plateau edge,
casting shoes, crushing sandstone, only
the poorest, though, watching from dry bush
in that chain-tugging year, last before the gold rush,
know that here is a centre of the world
and that one who can rattle the inverted
cosmos is stamping to her stamping ground.

Not guided by such truth, the Megaethon
veers towards rum-and-opium stops,
waits, cooling, beside a slab bordello
and leans at last in upland swamp,
flat-footed, becoming salvage,
freight for ribald bullockies. Its polygonal
rhythms will engender no balladry;
it won't break the trench-lines at Vicksburg.

The engine goes home to make chaff
and the idea of the Megaethon
must travel underground. Stockmen gallop
above it. It travels underground.
Secret ballots and boxkites are invented,
unions form, national purposes gather
above it. It travels underground;
for fifty years it travels underground

losing its first name. It surfaces
in Melbourne at last, in the mind
of one Frank Bettrill, who calls
his wheel of three sliding plates
the Pedrail or Dreadnaught wheel
'for travelling across country in all
conditions, where roads may be absent.'
In all but name, the Megaethon

is abroad again, now clearing country,
now ploughing the new farms. Its jointed
wheel-plates go to war on artillery
lashing back the Ottoman Empire
from Suez to Damascus. The monster
guns of Flanders advance and recoil
on many-slatted wheels. Tanks grind by them,
collateral descendants of the Megaethon

which itself remains in innocent
rebirth in its own hemisphere.
Its largest example, Big Lizzie
spends the mid-war years crossing Victoria
and following the Murray through Gunbower,
Mystic Park and Day Trap to Mildura.
From its cab eighteen feet above ground
crews wave to the river paddlesteamers:

'Gutter sailors! Our ship don't *need* water!'
Submarine in the mallee forests
Big Lizzie leaves a shattered wake;
she wades marsh, crosses grass fires' negative
landscape: black ground, bleached rattling trees;
her slamming gait shuts the earth down
but her following ploughs reopen it
in long rising loaves. Soldiers follow her

and turn into farmers sewing full
wheat bags with a large darning needle.
Giant workhorse born between the ages
of plodding feet and highway speeds
it takes lorries a decade to catch
and relegate Lizzie's oil-engined shuffle.
The Megaethon thus re-enters quaintness
at two miles an hour, having,

though ponderous, only lightly existed
(twice so far) and never directly
shed blood. And there, repaired with wire
from strict fences, it still walks the trackless,
slow as workaday, available for metaphor,
laying down and picking up the squeezed-
fragrant iron suit-cards of its patience,
crews making mugs of tea from its boiler.


## FASTNESS

I am listening for words the eldest
of three brothers must have uttered
magically, out of their whole being,

to make a sergeant major look down
at the stamped grass, and not have them stopped
as they walked, not trooped, off his shouting
showground parade, in the brown
fatal clothes and pink boots they'd been given,

to retrieve their own horses and vanish
bearing even the unloaded strap rifles
the Government would still be pursuing
a decade later, along with the brothers.

I have come as far as officials
and sergeants ever came, telling their
hillbilly yarns: the boy-headed calf,

the barbed wire across the teenage bedroom,
the dead wife backpacked forty miles
in a chaff bag, but gutted to save weight.
I have passed where their cars' spoke wheels
slid and stopped, and the silent vines hung.

Since beyond the exact words, I need
the gesture with which they were said,
the horizons and hill air that shaped them,
the adze-faceted timbers of the kitchen
where they were repeated to the old people

who, having heard nothing about war,
had sent the boys three days round trip
in to town for saltpetre and tobacco.
I need the angle of cloud forest
visible through that door, the fire chains
and the leaf tastes of tank water there.

I will only have history, lacking these,
not the words as they have to be
spoken out, in such moments:

centrally, so as to pass the mind
of cheerful blustering authority
and paralyse it in its dream –
right in the unmeant nick of time
even as the rails were shutting
on the wide whooping yard of adventure
and making it a cattle chute
that led through jokes and accoutrements
to the long blood trail a-winding.

I need not think the brothers were
unattracted by a world venture
in aid of the woman Belgium
or not drawn by herd-warmth towards
the glorious manhunting promised them
by fellows round pipe-drawing fires
outside the beast-pavilions they slept in.

I need remember only the angel
poverty wrestles with in vast places
to know the power of abandon
people want, with control, to touch
when they tell hillbilly stories

and knowing it well, to uncover
how the brothers missed their legendary
Anzac chance, I need only
sit on this rusty bedstead, on a known
vanished sleepout verandah and reflect

how the lifelong lordly of space
might speak, in discernment of spirits
at the loud surcingled overseer's
very first bawled genial insult
to any of theirs. Not the camel's-back-
breaking, trapped slight, but the first.


## 1980 IN A STREET OF FEDERATION HOUSES

In 1980, in a street of Federation houses
a man is brushing his hair inside a car
while waiting for his children. It is his access day.

Men down the street – one perched high
as an oldtime sailor, others hauling long lines –
are dismantling a tree, from the top down. A heavy
branch drops, out of keen gristing noise, and runs
dragging all the stumpy hauliers
inwards on their ropes, then hangs swinging.

In 1964, the same man, slightly plumper,
is proclaiming in the Union bar *Now let
us watch the angels dance on the head of a pill!*
He does not mean, but swallows, a methedrine tablet.

In the same year he consents for the first time
to find the woodchoppers at the Easter Show
faintly comical, in their cricketing whites and singlets,

starting in handicap order to knock on wood:
one chopper, two choppier, then a clobbering
increment of cobbers, down in the grunting arena –

he assigns them to 1955, an obsolete year,
and the whole Labor Movement
shifts and re-levels in his mind
like mercury, needing new calibrations.

In 1824 in another country
present to his albums, small children run all day
breathing lint in a cavernous tropic factory
lit by weak globes on which older lint has caramelled.

They work from dawn to palm-frond-clattering dark
loading bales of packaged shirts onto trucks
driven by tribesmen who smoke, as they do themselves,
like the Industrial Revolution, paper chimneys in their cursing mouths.

Upcountry, men of the Thirties in 1950s uniform
instruct youths and girls of the starving fourteen hundreds
how to conjure with rifles the year 1792.
Their ammunition is the first packaged goods they have handled.

*To reproduce yourself is to admit defeat!*
His dashing friend had said it, in the year
he was told about cadmium fish, and blamed for the future.
To reproduce oneself? Who ever did that?

Most perhaps, before the Industrial Revolution
but then permanent death came in; all the years,
all the centuries now had to fit into one lifetime.

As did Heaven. Which drew Hell.
The Bomb and the Club Méditerranée had to lie
down together –. He begins to see his educators
as missionaries of the new unending death.

He shifts to another year, along the band
of his car's stereo, and his children are playing
in a tent on sandy grass;
can there be a time in which this scene is not a bibelot?

Now that up the suburban street that leads to the past
a figure is leading not greyhounds but Afghan hounds
and on the beach beyond, women who enter the surf
shielding a web of dusty lint emerge
and each is wearing a feather!


## THE MILK LORRY

Now the milk lorry is a polished submarine
that rolls up at midday, attaches a trunk and inhales
the dairy's tank to a frosty snore in minutes

but its forerunner was the high-tyred barn of crisp mornings,
reeking Diesel and mammary, hazy in its roped interior
as a carpet under beaters, as it crashed along potholed lanes

cooeeing at schoolgirls. Long planks like unshipped oars
butted, levelling in there, because between each farm's
stranded wharf of milk cans, the work was feverish slotting

of floors above floors, for load. It was sling out the bashed
paint-collared empties and waltz in the full,
stumbling on their rims under ribaldry, tilting their big gallons

then the schoolboy's calisthenic, hoisting steel men man-high
till the glancing hold was a magazine of casque armour,
a tinplate 'tween-decks, a seminar engrossed

in one swaying tradition, behind the speeding doorways
that tempted a truant to brace and drop, short of town,
and spend the day, with book or not, down under

the bridge of a river that by dinnertime would be
tongueing like cattledogs, or down a moth-dusty reach
where the fish-feeding milk boat and cedar barge once floated.

# THE BUTTER FACTORY

It was built of things that must not mix:
paint, cream and water, fire and dusty oil.
You heard the water dreaming in its large
kneed pipes, up from the weir. And the cordwood
our fathers cut for the furnace stood in walls
like the sleeper-stacks of a continental railway.

The cream arrived in lorried tides; its procession
crossed a platform of workers' stagecraft: *Come here
Friday-Legs! Or I'll feel your hernia* –
Overalled in milk's colour, men moved the heart of milk,
separated into thousands, along a roller track – *Trucks?
That one of mine, son, it pulls like a sixteen-year-old* –
to the tester who broached the can lids, causing fat tears,
who tasted, dipped and did his thin stoppered chemistry
on our labour, as the empties chattered downstage and fumed.

Under the high roof, black-crusted and stainless steels
were walled apart: black romped with leather belts
but paddlewheels sailed the silvery vats where muscles
of the one deep cream were exercised to a bullion
to be blocked in paper. And between waves of delivery
the men trod on water, hosing the rainbows of a shift.

It was damp April even at Christmas round every
margin of the factory. Also it opened the mouth
to see tackles on glibbed gravel, and the mossed char louvres
of the ice-plant's timber tower streaming with
heavy rain all day, above the droughty paddocks
of the totem cows round whom our lives were dancing.

# ROMAN CAGE-CUPS

Polish, at a constant curving interval, within
a layer of air between the inner and outer
skins of a glass beaker, leaving only odd struts integral.

Pause, and at the same ablative atom-
by-atom rate, sculpt the outer shell to an openwork
of rings, or foliage, or a muscular Elysium –

It made for calm paste and a steady file
that one false stroke, one twitch could cost a year's time,
a good billet, your concubine. Only the cups were held noble.

Plebs and immigrants fashioned them, punters
who ate tavern-fried pike and talked Vulgate.
The very first might have been made as a stunt, as

the life-gambit of a slave. Or a joke on the feasting scene:
a wine-bowl no one coarsely drunk could handle
nor, since baseless, easily put down,

a marvel of undercutting, a glass vessel
so costly it would exact that Roman gravity,
draw blood, and feud, if grasped without suavity.

The one depicting Thracian Lycurgus
strangled by amorous vines for slighting Bacchus
could hardly have survived an old-time bacchanal.

The glass flowers of Harvard, monks' micro pen-lace, a chromosome
needled to grow wings on a horse (which they'd also have done),
the freely moving ivory dragons-inside-a-dragon

ball of Cathay – the impossible is a groove:
why else do we do it? Even some given a choice
would rather work the metaphors than live them, in society.

But nothing, since sparkle became permanent in the thumbs
and rib-cages of these craftsmen, has matched their handiwork
for gentleness, or edge. They put the gape into agapé,

these factory products, of all Rome's underground Gothic:
cups transfigured by hand, too delicate to break.
Some, exported beyond the Rhine as a *miss-*

*ion civilisatrice,* have survived complete and unchipped
a sesquimillennium longer than the trumpets (allude,
allude) of the arena. Rome's very hardest rock.


## THE LAKE SURNAMES

There are rental houseboats down the lakes now.
Two people facing, with drinks, in a restaurant party
talk about them: *That idiot, he ran us aground
in the dark! These fishermen rescued us,
towed us off the mudbank. They were frightening actually,
real inbred faces, Deliverance people
when we saw them by torchlight in their boat* –

   For an instant, rain rattles at the glass
   and brown cardboards of a kitchen window
   and drips lamplight-coloured out of soot
   in the fireplace, hitching steam off stove-iron.

   Tins of beeswax, nails and poultice mixture
   stick to shelves behind the door. Triangular
   too, the caramel dark up under rafters
   is shared, above one plank wall, by the room

   where the English housekeeper screamed
   at a crisp bat on the lino. Guest room,
   parents' room, always called *the room*
   with tennis racquet and rifle in the lowboy.

   Quick steps jingle the glassed cabinet
   as a figure fishes spoons from scalding water
   ('what's not clean's sterilised') in the board-railed
   double triangle of a kerosene-tin sink,

a real Bogan sink, on the table.
The upright wireless, having died when valves vanished,
has its back to the wall. It is a *plant* for money
guarded by a nesting snake, who'll be killed when discovered.

The new car outside, streaming cricket scores,
is a sit-in radio, glowing, tightly furnished
but in the Auburn wood stove, the fire laps
and is luxury too, in one of them flood years.

– With only the briefest pause, the other
answers: *There aren't that many full-time
surnames down the lakes. If you'd addressed them
as Mr Blanche, Mr Woodward, Mr Legge,
Mr Bramble, or Palmer, your own surname,
you'd probably have been right. And more at ease.*


# NOCTURNE

Brisbane, night-gathered, far away
estuarine imaginary city
of houses towering down one side
of slatted lights seen under leaves

confluence of ranginess with lush,
Brisbane, of rotogravure memory
approached by web lines of coke and grit
by sleepers racked in corridor trains

weatherboard incantatory city
of the timber duchess, the strapped port
in Auchenflower and Fortitude Valley
and bottletops spat in Vulture Street

greatest of the floodtime towns
that choked the dictionary with silt
and hung a navy in the tropic gardens.
Brisbane, on the steep green slope to war

brothel-humid headquarters city
where commandos and their allies fought
down café stairs, belt buckle and boot
and once with a rattletrap green gun.

In midnight nets, in mango bombings
Brisbane, storied and cable-fixed,
above your rum river, farewell and adieu
in marble on the hill of Toowong

by golfing pockets, by deep squared pockets
night heals the bubbled tar of day
and the crab moon, rising, reddens above
Brisbane, rotating far away.


## LOTUS DAM

Lotus leaves, standing feet above the water,
collect at their centre a perfect lens of rain
and heel, and tip it back into the water.

Their baby leaves are feet again, or slant lips
scrolled in declaration; pointed at toe and heel
they echo an unwalked sole in their pale green crinkles

and under blown and picket blooms, the floor
of floating leaves rolls light rainwater marbles
back and forth on sharkskins of anchored rippling.

Each speculum, pearl and pebble of the first water
rides, sprung with weight, on its live mirroring skin
tipped green and loganberry, till one or other sky

redeems it, beneath bent foils and ferruled canes
where cupped pink bursts all day, above riddled water.

# AT MIN-MIN CAMP

In the afternoon, a blue storm walloped and split
like a loose mainsail behind us. Then another
far out on the plain fumed its corrugated walls.

A heavy dough of cloud kept rising, and reached us.
The speeding turbid sky went out of focus, fracturing
continually, and poured. We made camp on a verandah

that had lost its house. I remembered it: pitsawn pine
lined with newspaper. People lived on treacle and rabbit
by firelight, and slept under grain-bag quilts there.

It was a lingering house. Millions had lived there
on their way to the modern world. Now they longed for and feared it.
It had been the last house, and the first.

Dark lightnings tore the ground as we ripped up firewood
and when the rain died away to conversation, and parted
on refreshed increasing star-charts, there arose

an unlikely bushfire in the ranges. The moon leaped from it,
slim, trim in perfect roundness. Spiderwebs palely yellow
by firelight changed sides, and were steel thread, diamante.

Orange gold itself, everything the moon gave, everywhere
was nickel silver, or that lake-submerged no-colour
native to dreams. Sparse human lights on earth

were solar-coloured, though: ingots of a homestead,
amoebae that moved and twinned on distant roads
and an unfixed anomaly, like a star with land behind it.

We were drinking tea round a sheet-iron fire on the hoards
bearing chill on our shoulders, like the boys who'd slept
on that verandah, and gone to be wandering lights

lifelong on the plains. You can't catch up to them now
though it isn't long ago: when we came from the Rift Valley
we all lived in a small star on the ground.

From the Rift we also carried the two kinds of fear
humans inherit: the rational kind, facing say weapons,
and the soul's kind, the creeps. Awe, which warns of law.

The two were long bound together, in the sacred
cultures of fright, that called shifting faces to the light's edge:
none worse than our own, when we came dreaming of houses.

Then the sacred turned fairytale, as always. And the new thing,
holiness, a true face, constant in all lights,
was still very scattered. It saved some. It is still scattered.

Many long for the sacred lights, and would renew their lore
in honoured bantustans – no faery for the laager of the lagerphone –
but they are unfixed now, and recede, and suddenly turn pale as

an escaped wife dying of a dread poem. Or her child
who sniffs his petrol, and reels like a shot kangaroo:
something else, and not the worst, that happens in a shifting light.

Holiness is harder to inhale, for adventure or desperation.
It cleanses awe of fear, though not of detailed love,
the nomads' other linkage, and maps the law afresh with it.

We left that verandah next day, and its ruined garden
of wire and daylilies, its grassy fringe of ancient pee scalds,
and travelled further west on a truck that had lost its body.


## HEARING IMPAIRMENT

Hearing loss? Yes, loss is what we hear
who are starting to go deaf. Loss
trails a lot of weird puns in its wake, viz.
Dad's a real prism of the Left –
you'd like me to repeat that?

# THE SAD SURREALISM OF THE DEAF.

It's mind over mutter at work
guessing half what the munglers are saying
and society's worse. Punchlines elude to you
as Henry Lawson and other touchy drinkers
have claimed. Asides, too, go pasture.
It's particularly nasty with a wether.

First you crane at people, face them
while you can still face them. But grudgually
you give up dinnier parties; you begin
to think about Beethoven; you Hanover
next visit here on silly Narda Fearing – I SAY
YOU CAN HAVE AN EXQUISITE EAR
AND STILL BE HARD OF HEARING.

It seems to be mainly speech, at first,
that escapes you – and that can be a rest,
the poor man's escape itch from Babel.
You can still hear a duck way upriver,
a lorry miles off on the highway. You
can still say boo to a goose and
read its curt yellow-lipped reply.
You can shout SING UP to a magpie,

but one day soon you must feel
the silent stopwatch chill your ear
in the doctor's rooms, and be wired
back into a slightly thinned world
with a faint plastic undertone to it
and, if the rumours are true, snatches
of static, music, police transmissions:
it's a BARF minor Car Fourteen prospect.

But maybe hearing aids are now perfect
and maybe it's not all that soon.
Sweet nothings in your ear are still sweet;
you've heard the human range by your age
and can follow most talk from memory;

the peace of the graveyard's well up
on that of the grave. And the world would
enjoy peace and birdsong for more moments

if you were head of government, enquiring
of an aide Why, Simpkins, do you tell me
a warrior is a ready flirt?
I might argue – and flowers keep blooming
as he swallows his larynx to shriek
our common mind-overloading sentence:
I'M SORRY, SIR, IT'S A RED ALERT!


## AT THUNDERBOLT'S GRAVE IN URALLA

The New England Highway was formed
by Christian men who reckoned
Adam and Eve should have been
sodomized for the curse of work
they brought on humankind,
not drudgery, but work.
No luxury of distinctions.

None ever went to Bali. Some set out.
But roads were game reserves to Thunderbolt
when a bridge was a leap, and wheels
were laborious, trundling through the splashways.
There were two heights of people: equestrians
and those foreshortened on foot.
All were more dressed, because more naked.

That German brass band that Thunderbolt,
attended by a pregnant boy,
bailed up on Goonoo Goonoo Gap:
'Gentlemen, if you are that poor
I'll refund your twenty pound, provided
a horse I mean to shake wins at Tenterfield.'
And it did, arching its neck, and he did
by postal note at Warwick.
Hoch! Public relations by trombone!

No convict ever got off Cockatoo
Island by swimming except Thunderbolt.
His lady, Yellow Long or Long Yella,
whichever way the name points, swam
the channel from Balmain before him
bringing tucker and clothes, and she got
him past the sharks when he swam for it.

But who wouldn't swim, and wear trousers
for a man pinched and bearded as the nine
lions on the courthouse coat of arms
with their tongues saying languish and lavish,
who took her from men who gasped romance
into her lungs and offered sixpence,
from her own heart-gelded tribesfolk
and white women's dreadful eyes?

Though Uralla creek is floored with planks now
the amethystine light of New England
still seems augmented from beneath
both horizons; tin outside chimneys
still squeeze woodsmoke into the air
but the police cars come wailing their
unerotic In-Out In-Out,
red-shifting over Goonoo Goonoo.

Of all the known bushrangers,
those cropped in the floggers' gulag,
those jostled by its Crown guards,
the bolters and the hoods were merely shot
or ironed or hanged. Only three required
frenzied extermination, with rituals:
Jackey Westaway, made monstrous by torture,
Fred Ward shot and head-pulped, Ben Hall
shot dead, and for several minutes afterwards.

All three were thieves. They likely never met.
All three stole the Crown's magic pallium
and trailed it through the bush, a drag
for raging pursuit. On every snag
they left some white or blue – the red part
they threw away at once, disdaining murder.
*Robbery with mock menaces? Why that is subsidy!*
The part they died hard for was the part
they wouldn't play, not believing the game worth murder.

Criminal noncomplicity! It was something nameless
above all stations, that critical magic
haloed in laughter. *Tell Fred I need to be robbed Friday
or I'm jiggered!* A deadly style suddenly felt lumbering,
battered with a slapstick. Our only indigenous revolution.
It took Ned Kelly to reassure policemen.

Why don't we kill like Americans?
We started to. The police were pushing it
but we weren't a republic for bringing things to a head
and these, even dying – *Are you a married man?*
cried Ward, and fired wide – helped wrong-foot mortal drama
and leave it decrepit, a police atmosphere.
In a few years, the game was boss and union.
Now society doesn't value individuals
enough for human sacrifice.

You were a cross swell, Fred. You alone never
used a gang. Those always kill, as Hall learned.
I hope your children found your cache
and did good with it. They left some on deposit.

# INFRA RED

FOR PROF. FRED HOYLE AND THE *IRAS* TELESCOPE

Dark stars that never fire,
brown dwarfs, whose deepening collapse
inward on themselves never tightens to fuse glory,
scorched dust the size of worlds, and tenuous
sandbars strung between the galaxies,
a universe dull with life:

with the eye and eye-adjuncts
mind sees only what is burning, the peak nodes of fury
that make all spiralling in on them
or coronally near, blowing outward from them,
look eager, intense, even brave. Most of the real
however is obscurely reflective, just sauntering along,
yarning across a ditch, or watching television,
vaguely dreaming, perhaps about pubic stuff,

getting tea ready. This absorbs most of the light
but is also family. It impoverishes to unreality
not to consider the dim, cannon fodder of stardom,
the gravities they are steepening to,
the unfathomable from which the trite is spoken.
And starry science is an evening-paper astrology
without the unknown bodies registered
only by total pain, only by dazzled joy,
the transits marked by a tight grip of the heart.

That the visible stars are suburbs and slow towns
hyped to light speed is the testimony of debris
and the serious swarms at rest in migrant trajectories.
Brilliance stands accused of all their losses.
Presence perhaps, and the inference of presence,
not light, should found a more complete astronomy.

264

It will draw in absence, too:
the pain-years between a love and its fulfilment,
the intricate spiral space of suppressed tradition
and all the warmth, whose peaks aren't those of heat,
that the white dwarfs froze out of their galaxies.


## POETRY AND RELIGION

Religions are poems. They concert
our daylight and dreaming mind, our
emotions, instinct, breath and native gesture

into the only whole thinking: poetry.
Nothing's said till it's dreamed out in words
and nothing's true that figures in words only.

A poem, compared with an arrayed religion,
may be like a soldier's one short marriage night
to die and live by. But that is a small religion.

Full religion is the large poem in loving repetition;
like any poem, it must be inexhaustible and complete
with turns where we ask Now why did the poet do that?

You can't pray a lie, said Huckleberry Finn;
you can't poe one either. It is the same mirror:
mobile, glancing, we call it poetry,

fixed centrally, we call it a religion,
and God is the poetry caught in any religion,
caught, not imprisoned. Caught as in a mirror

that he attracted, being in the world as poetry
is in the poem, a law against its closure.
There'll always be religion around while there is poetry

or a lack of it. Both are given, and intermittent,
as the action of those birds – crested pigeon, rosella parrot –
who fly with wings shut, then beating, and again shut.

# INVERSE BALLAD

Grandfather's grandfather rode down from New England
that terrible steep road. One time there, his horse
shat over his shoulder. It's not so steep now.
Anyway he was riding, and two fellows came
out of the brush with revolvers pointed at him:

Bail up! What joy have you got for the poor, eh?
Bail up? Ye're never bushrangers? Wad ye shoot me?
My oath we'd shoot yer – . He looked them up and down,
poor weedy toerags both. Ye'd really shoot, then?
Masel, I never find it necessary.

Eh? You're on our lay, are you? – Aye, I am.
Ward's the name. – Not Thunderbolt? By Hell. Hmm.
They muttered some asides. Well, Mister Ward, you
are money on the hoof. A thousand's a fair screw
for turning you in. Dead *or* alive, so ride!

We're going to town to sell your pretty hide.
It must have felt lonely, riding ahead of them
knowing they could just as easily turn you in,
head lolling and blood dripping, strapped over your saddle.
When they reached the police post, the old sergeant listened

a moment, then snapped: Ye'll gie me thae barkers;
hand them over! Constable, handcuff yon men!
Ye ignorant puir loons, did ye no ken
Thunderbolt's no Scots. He disnae talk like me.
Ye'll hae time tae regret bailing up Mister Murray!

Ward's wintertime employer, had the police or he known.

# RELICS OF SANDY

Beside the odd gene
just three pictures remain
of Uncle Sandy Beattie,
big fair man:

He used to swim his horse
through the flooded rivers
with bags tied on the saddle
when he was the mailman;
he'd hang on to its tail:
he couldn't swim at all.

Once for a bet he
humped a ton of iron
sheets up from the jetty
to the pub at Tinonee
and found a man had ridden
up, clinging on the load:
Ye've bowed my legs, laddie.

A loudmouth in the pub
was needling Sandy
one night, talking fight,
all the men he'd stiffened,
how the big raw ones were easy.
Yes, McMahon, I hear ye.
He finished his beer.
It's hard to take, McMahon,

and I'll not take any more.
Barman, give me a room key.
And he took the bareknuckle man
upstairs to the room,
pushed him in, locked the door:
Now, man, it's what you wanted,
no audience, we're private.
Just you and me for it!

There was thunder up there.
All the bottles jinked about
in the bar, and the fighter
squealed like a poor rabbit.
The barman got a pound
when Sandy came downstairs:
Yon man shouldn't have to
pay twice, for accommodation.
Sandy Beattie. Big fair man.


## JOKER AS TOLD

Not a latch or lock could hold
a little horse we had
not a gate or paddock.

He liked to get in the house.
Walk in, and you were liable
to find him in the kitchen
dribbling over the table
with a heap behind him

or you'd catch a hoof
right where it hurt bad
when you went in your bedroom.

He grew up with us kids,
played with us till he got rough.
Round then, they cut him,
but you couldn't ride him:
he'd bite your bum getting on,
kick your foot from the stirrup

and he could kick the spurs off
your boots. Almost hopped on with you,
and if he couldn't buck you
he'd lie down plop! and roll
in his temper, and he'd squeal.

He was from the Joker breed,
we called him Joker;
no joke much when he bit you
or ate the Monday washing.

They reckon he wanted to be
human, coming in the house.
I don't think so, I think he
wanted something people had.
He didn't do it from love of us.

He couldn't grow up to be a
full horse, and he wouldn't be a slave one.
I think he was looking for his childhood,
his foalhood and ours, when we played.

He was looking for the Kingdom of God.


## WRITER IN RESIDENCE

I was good at the Common Room game
but when Dr X dropped a name
it hung in the air
like a parachute flare
far over my head, to my shame.


## A PUBLIC FIGURE

To break the Judaeo-Christian mould was his caper
but the ethic he served torched him with its newspaper.

## THE YOUNG WOMAN VISITOR

I never heard such boasting.
For two whole days while I was there
he never let up. He was the best axeman,
driver, horsebreaker, farmer, bullocky and judge
of standing timber 'that ever God put guts in'.
He's also had the best dog, the best car,
the best crop of corn and the very best eight-day clock
and he'd been the best psalm-singer in his church, too.
Someone had let a little boy grow old;
I saw that all these things were a posy of flowers
snatched out of a funeral wreath and offered
to me, or to anyone,
not a wreath that would lie heaped on his grave
but the little special one that would go down
diminishing past clay, and trembling, on his coffin.


## THE GRANDMOTHER'S STORY

Just a few times in your life, you speak
those strange words. Or they speak themselves
out of you, before you can bite your tongue.
They are there, like a dream. You're not sure you've spoken
but you see them hit the other person
like a stone into floodwater. No splash much
but they go right to the bottom. To the soul.
No use saying you're sorry, or didn't mean them.

I never liked Ted Quarrie. Partly the way
he treated women. More, and it's the same,
the way he made poor Annie behave like him,
drinking and dribbling with Harold's whisky friends,
falling on the floor. The way they drank it:
Heere's luck! and pitch it down like castor oil;
they almost held their noses. They were like that at the show
when Ted sneaked up and pinched me. Hard, to hurt

and I hit him. Not slapped him. Shut my fist
and flattened him, in front of the whole showground.
I'd lumped more iron camp ovens, butter churns, and logs too
than ever he had. He stayed out for minutes.
When he came around, he cursed me. Called me every kind
of low-bred bitch. That's when I said – that other.
What did I say? That doesn't matter. I silenced him.
It would be a sin to do on purpose. To practise.

He hated me, ever after. And he hung round home
so I'd see him and know. But I've got a strong back;
I could bear it. You could still buy revolvers then
and he had one. But it took him years to creep away
round the verandahs, one Sunday, from where they were drinking
and lean in at our window, where I lay sick in bed.
He opened his coat, took out that thieves' gun, said
*See this, Emily? It's for you.* Poor thing. I nearly laughed.

Of course, I might have been shot for that. So I had to
look frightened, when really I was sick and tired
of the whole silliness. He went away, but my third boy
heard him, and followed. He was only seventeen
and Ted was a grown man. But he made him hand over
that gun in front of everyone. Harold never spoke, as usual.
The boys climbed up and dropped the thing down inside
the walling of this kitchen. It's still rusting there, I fancy.


## THE LINE

Opium and vitriol and a plug of twist
added to the rum have left the Tiger prostrate,
snoring on his stripes in the sun.
              Mickeen and Hoojah
step gingerly around him. Their own headache-bones
wince at the long saw's bare-fanged undulant clangour.

At the palace of a felled tree's crown, they strike up a fire,
share a pannikin of tea, then mix burnt bark with the dregs
and immerse a string in it.
       *Hold your end, Mickeen!*
They walk either side of the sawdust-mealy pit
and pass the string above a chocked log. Precisely as Mercator

the wet black twine hovers half an inch above
the timber's knocked continents, tautens, is minutely
aligned. Then Hoojah plucks it.
       The whipped note lays the first
straight line of a city, the first rectilinear thought
realised on that landscape. And marks it for division.

*Down in the hole, now. Sheeus late, a Vickeen!*\*
*And keep yer feet on the ground, ye Fenyan bolter!*
The black blade angles down,
       is gripped: a rhythmic chaff
starts modelling sweat, choking ripe Donegal curses.
As each plank slats off, the saw sings its future as cattlebells.

The line has been printed six times, when the Tiger stumbles
across from their tent with bread and three pounds of salt beef
stuck on a bayonet.
       At least it's not the poisonous snake
he slung into the pit last time the rum clawed at him.
Belching after a feed, he rips the handles downward

as if to pull the merciful saw through himself
or drag work itself down on his anguish, like Samson.
*Don't jerk a woman*
       *right through the cut, there, Tiger!*
Shouts Hoojah, laughing, *or I'll be narrer and flat.*
Taste, reverence and polemic close over the gang after that.

\* Down with you, Mickey! (Anglicised Irish)

# EXTRACT FROM A VERSE LETTER
# TO DENNIS HASKELL

Dear Dennis,
               Warm thanks for your letter
in verse. It's very much better,
nicer and more thoughtful than those
postcards packed with minuscule prose
I write even to friends, like the harassed
editor I once was. I'm impressed.
Moved, too, that you should miss my company
– I never quite expect that, perhaps funnily,
of people. Yes, too much ochre
separates us now, joker from joker.
It's a bore that the width of the continent
can't be secretly folded or bent
so's to let us yarn here on the crest
of Deer's Hill, watching sunsets on Rottnest,
or strolling, well fed, by the Swan
as it flows beside our vegie garden.
I think you'd like it here, in our glade
of fruit saplings that now nearly manage shade
and soft grass, beside the lotus dam
and our other trees. Some year you must see them.
Trees, space, waterbirds – things of that ilk,
plus people of my own kind, are the milk
and honey I came home for. Not dairying,
that drudgery, poor, imprisoning, unvarying.
At eighteen, I made a great vow
I'd never milk another bloody cow.
It was only after I won my battle
to be free of them, that I came to love cattle.
Few dairy here now, anyway. It's gone largely bung.
I'm forty-eight next week. I won't die a dairyman. Or young.
The bush permits allusion, not illusion:
I didn't come for any past that's gone.
More for Dad, who had stopped getting on
and was getting old and sick. Our eldest children
too had already missed a country childhood

and we didn't think the younger three should
have to. Also there was this choice I had:
get out of Yuppie City or go mad.
No perhaps in that either. But enough.
Life here is scarcely tough:
Valerie's wryly and happily learning bush ways
and would have mastered the harder ones, too, of the old days.
She's on leave from teaching. Alec goes to special school by bus,
Clare to a local school. I'm running my export business
out of this room from which, well, four bean rows
and two of turnips are visible. Peter, our smallest boy,
is enjoying his babyhood, but sometimes gets wistful for Sydney.
Dad's had a cataract op. and sees well for his age
but now he's got shingles, nailed not to rafters but his rib-cage.
Ouch! Still, spring here delivers days you could dance to,
given a chance to. And that is our news.


## MAX FABRE'S YACHTS

Towers of swell fabric
leaning on the ocean
go about in salt haze
to race for the rocked gun.

Straining theory makes the world
equivocal as miracles
ever were. Between spear and sphere
here tussle in purified war

the souls of rich men,
of syndicates and winch-winders
but no longer do they skate
on a sunk ice of ambition.

Nothing turns on a blade: all
now glide on a lucky trefoil,
a trinitarian trifoil,
vision of a drowning man

and first unveiled off Newport:
Hermes, messenger of Heaven,
speeding with one winged foot
dipped in the ocean.


Max Fabre, of Sydney, made pioneering designs in the early 1960s of
trifoil 'winged' keel forms for ocean racing yachts.


## ASPECTS OF LANGUAGE AND WAR
## ON THE GLOUCESTER ROAD

I travel a road cut through time
by bare feet and boots without socks,
by eight-year-old men droving cattle,
by wheels parallel as printed rhyme
over rhythms of hill shale and tussocks.
    In the hardest real trouble of my life
    I called this Gloucester road to mind,
      which cuttings were bare gravel, which rife
      with grass, which ones rainforest-vined.
The road starts at Coolongolook
which means roughly Leftward Inland
from *gulunggal*, the left hand,
runs west between Holdens' and James'
where new people have to paint names
on their mailboxes, and stumps have board-slots
from when tall trees were jibbed like yachts
and felled above their hollow tones.
Later logs lie about like gnawed bones.
The road comes on through Sawyers Creek
where the high whaleback ridge becomes a peak
and where my father, aged nine years,
faced down the Bashing Teacher, a Squeers
who cut six-foot canes in the scrub
and, chewing his tongue in a sub-
jective ecstasy, lashed back-arching children.
*Mind your mhisness! – Time someone chipped you! –*

Short blazed at tall – and the knobbed cane withdrew.
My father was cheered shoulder-high in the playground then
and the flogging rods vanished. But previously slack
parents loomed, shouting. And behind them, the sack.

    Here too a farmer heard *Give up*
    *cigarettes or your life!* He coughed a sup
    of Flanders gas, cried *Jesus Christ and that,*
    *Doctor, I'll give up my life!* And what
    was burning inside him smouldered on
    for decades, disclosed only once
    in '39, teaching dodges to his sons.
    (1939, smiles an aunt, *the year*
    *when no woman had to stay a spinster.*)

The road runs through Bunyah, meaning bark
for shelters, or firelighters' candlebark
blown on in a *gugri* house, a word
for fire-hut that is still heard
though few farms still use a googery.
Few? None now. I was gone a generation.
Even parrot-eating's stopped: – *The buggers,*
*they'd been eating that wild-tobacco berry:*
*Imagine a soup of boiled cigars!* –

    I'm driving to Gloucester station
    to collect my urban eldest from the train,
    and there are the concrete tips
    of bridge piles, set like a tank trap
    up a farm entryway. The huge rap
    of a piledriver shivered few chips
    off the bedrock when they were banged stubbornly
    by an engineer who would not be told
    *Black rock at eight feet'll stop you cold!*
    What did locals know, lacking a degree?
    I loved the old bridge, its handrails,
    ballast logs and deck, an inland ship.
    Kids watched how floods' pewter rip
    wracked limbs over it. Floods were our folktales.
    Now we drive above missed schooldays, high
    on the Shire's concrete second try.

There at the hall, drums and accordions

still pump, and well-lit dancers glide.
In the dark outside move, single and duo,
the angrily shy and the bawdy ones:
blood and babies from the dancing outside.
    We held Free Church services too, though,
    in that hall. For months I'd cry aloud
    at the rise in the east of any cloud
    no bigger than a man's hand.
    A cloud by day led me out of Babyland
    about when Hiroshima had three years to go.
The Free Church, knuckle-white on its ridge,
now looks north at the Lavinia Murray Bridge,
at my great-grandmother's Chinese elm tree
and the Dutchman tractoring peaceably.
That faint scar across the creek is butts
of a range for aligned wartime rifle shots.
    What fearsome breach of military law
    sent you, Lieutenant Squance, to command
    that platoon of worried men-on-the-land
    the Bunyah Volunteer Defence Corps
    in those collapsing months after Singapore,
    brassbuttoned fathers, deadly afraid
    for life and family? Your British parade
    manner gave them some diversion:
    milky boots, casual mutiny, aspersion,
    your corporal raving death-threats in your face
    for calling his clean rifle a disgrace,
    brownpaper sandwiches sent to you with tea
    after parade one Saturday –
    I think, though, you'd have stayed and defended
    us, and died as our world ended,
    Mr Squance. Belated thanks are extended.
There's a house where I had hospitality
without fuss for years when I needed it.
Now it's dying, of sun-bleach, of shadowed
scarlet lichen, the poisons of abandonment.
I'm thinking, over the next rises,
of children who did not have their lives,
who died young, and how one realises

only at home that, unknown to younger wives,
faces lie in wait in finger-felted albums'
gapless groupings of family. The sums
of those short lifetimes add to one's own age,
to its weight, having no light yarns to lift them.
Peace or war, all die for our freedom.
The innocent, the guilty, the beasts, all die for our freedom.
I was taught the irreparable knowledge
by a baby of thirty next door in his wheelchair
who'd thrash and grimace with happiness when I went there.
I see the road, and many roads before,
through a fawn snap of him as a solemn little boy
before meningitis. And it is first for him
that I insist on a state where lives resume.

    The squatter style grinds eastward here, or 'down'
    (both *baarung* in the old language) and spreads out from town.
    One property here was Something Downs for a bit:
    over there through the hills I can glimpse part of it
    just short of the pines round my gone one-teacher school
    with its zigzag air raid trench and morning flagpole;
    from there I remember birthdays, and how to shin
    fast over fence rails: *You're last! – I'll be first in Heaven!*
    I pass by Lavinia's gate,
    the first woman Shire President in the State
    and not dowager at eighty, but reigning, in her fox fur,
    descending on Parliament, ascending with the cropduster
    whose rent for an airfield was shopping flights to Gloucester.
A flagman stops me with a circled word.
I halt beside him, wait till he can be heard
over a big steel roller's matt declensions
as it tightens gravel down into two dimensions.
He points at a possum curled like an ampersand
around a high dead branch, spending the day
miserably where its light caught her away
from her cache of darkness. – *There's her baby's hand
out of her pouch. – She's dreaming. – Wonder if we
are in her dream? – Wonder if she's ever seen a hill? –
What lights would we have, on what cars, if we were nocturnal?
Look lower, native bees.* – Round a knothole spout

a thought-balloon of grist breathes in and out.
*Look, one on your arm. – Their mixture must need salt.*
*Hell will have icecream before this road gets asphalt.*

    I drive off, on what sounds like a shore.
    In Upper Bunyah there are more
    settlers without nicknames, or
    none they know. The widower on that hill
    used to have one (and he was the raving corporal).
    He once had some evangelists staying
    in his house, demonstratively praying,
    so one day his two dozen cats annoyed him
    and he took the small rifle and destroyed them,
    shot them off rafters, sniped eyes under his bed –
    cups exploded in the kitchen as poor Tibby fled –
    the men of prayer too ran headlong from his charity.
    Sweet, for one, are the uses of barbarity.
His later wife had a chequebook and painted in France.
Why does so much of our culture work through yarns
equivalent to the national talent for cartoons?
It is an old war brought from Europe
by those who also brought poverty and landscape.
They had scores to settle, even with themselves. Tradition
is also repeating oneself, expecting inattention,
singing dumb, expecting scorn. Or sly mispronunciation
out of loyalty to the dead: *You boiling them bikinis*
*in that Vichy sauce?* We were the wrong people risen
– forerunners in that of nearly everyone –
but we rose early, on small farms, and were family.
A hard yarn twangs the tension
and fires its broad arrow out of a grim space
of Old Australian smells: toejam, tomato sauce,
semen and dead singlets the solitary have called peace
but which is really an unsurrendered trench. Really prison.

    It is a reminder all stories are of war.
    Peace, and the proof of peace, is the verandah
    absent from some of the newer houses here.
    It is also a slight distance – as indeed
    grows between me and the farm of my cousin
    who recently was sold treated seed grain

in mistake for cattle-feed grain:
it killed cows, but he dared not complain
or sue the feed merchant, for fear
he'd be barred as a milk supplier
to the Milk Board, and ruined, and in consequence
see his house become somebody's rural residence.
Such things can make a farmer look down, at his land
between his boots, and dignity shrink in his hand.
Now the road enters the gesture of the hills
where they express geologic weather
and contend with landscape in spills
of triangular forest down fence lines
and horse-and-scoop dams like filled mines.
What else to say of peace? It is a presence
with the feeling of home, and timeless in any tense.

    I am driving *waga*, up and west.
    Parting cattle, I climb over the crest
    out of Bunyah, and skirt Bucca Wauka,
    A Man Sitting With Knees Against His Chest:
    *baga waga*, knees up, the burial-shape of a warrior.
Eagles flying below me, I will ascend Wallanbah,
that whipcrack country of white cedar
and ruined tennis courts, and speed up on the tar.
In sight of the high ranges I'll pass the turnoff to Bundook,
Hindi for musket – which it also took
to add to the daylight species here, in the primal 1830s of our numbered Dreamtime

    and under the purple coast of the Mograni
    and its trachyte west wall scaling in the sky
    I will swoop to the valley and Gloucester Rail
    where boys hand-shunted trains to load their cattle
    and walk on the platform, glancing west at that country
    of running creeks, the stormcloud-coloured Barrington,
    the land, in lost Gaelic and Kattangal, of Barandan.

# THE IDYLL WHEEL:
## CYCLE OF A YEAR AT BUNYAH,
## NEW SOUTH WALES,
## APRIL 1986–APRIL 1987

PREFACE

An east-running valley where two hooded creeks make junction
and two snoring roads make a rainguttered cross of function:

there, each hamlet of house-and-sheds stands connected and alone
and the chimneys of old houses are square bottles cut from iron.

Gum forest is a solid blue cloud on the hills to the south
and bladygrass and chain rust round its every wheeltracked mouth.

Being back home there, where I am all my ages,
I wanted to trace a year through all its stages.

I would start after summer, to catch a subtly vernal effect
(April is also when I conceived the project).

At one poem per month, it would take a baker's dozen
to accommodate the stretch and overlap of season

into season, in any single year –
and to be real, the year had to be particular

since this wasn't to be a cyclic calendar
of miniature peasantry painted as for a proprietor.

No one can own all Bunyah. Names shouted over coal-oil lamps
cling to their paddocks. Bees and dingoes tax the cattlecamps.

As forefather Hesiod may have learned too, by this time,
things don't recur precisely, on the sacred earth: they rhyme.

To illuminate one year on that known ground
would also draw light from the many gone underground

with steel wedges and glass and the forty thousand days lost or
worked, daylight to dark, there between Forster and Gloucester.

*So: as grass tips turn maroon in a further winter*
*I present how time revolved through the spiral of a year*

*average, says experience, in erosions and deposit of seeds.*
*I thank Rosalind Atkins, whose burin opens up further leads*

*into the heart of it, making the more exquisite lines –*
*and I thank Alec Bolton for a book that dresses ours to the nines.*


APRIL


## Leaf Spring

The long-limbed hills recline high
in Disposals khaki boiled in tankwater
or barbed-wire-tattered navy wool.
A dust of oil blues the farther air.

Crotches of black shade timber
thicken, and walled sky insets;
friezes of the one tree are repeated
along ridgelines, and the gesture of the heights

continues beneath the valley floor,
outcrops stepping toward the roofed creeks'
greener underground forest, spacing
corrugated corn flats. Contour-line by contour

cattle walk the hills, in a casual-seeming
prison strung from buried violins.
Sparse houses sit unpacked for good, each
among sheds, in its wheeltracked star.

Hobnail and elastic-side, bare and cloven feet:
you can't know this landscape in shoes, or with ideas
like relevance. It is a haughty pastoral
bent fitfully to farming's fourteen-hour days.

Disked-up ground in unseasonable heat
burns purple, and the tracks of a foam-white
longed-for watersnake are brown down every incline.
Season of smoke and parrots pecking the road,

half-naturalized autumn. Fruit is almost done
though few deciduous imports have yet decided;
no rain, and the slow tanks fill with dew;
nothing flowering, yet colour is abundant:

it is leaf spring, that comes on after heat.
The paperbark trees that suck on swampy clay
are magnified in skims of leek and sherry.
Though growth's gone out of grass, and cattle nose

green from underneath its tawny pelt,
the creek trees cluster, showered with pale expansion
from inside themselves, as if from dreams of rain;
heightening gum trees are tipped bronze and citrine

and grey-barked apple trees are misted round
with rosy blue – the aged angophora trees
that sprout from every live part of themselves
and drop their heavy death along the ground

on just such a still day here
as shade broadens south of everything
and fugitive whisky-bottle blink
and windscreen glance point the paddock air.


MAY


*When Bounty is Down To Persimmons and Lemons*

In May, Mary's month,
when snakes go to sleep,
sunlight and shade lengthen,
forest grows deep,

wood coughs at the axe
and splinters hurt worse,
barbed wire pulls through
every post in reverse,

old horses grow shaggy
and flies hunker down
on curtains, like sequins
on a dead girl's ball gown.

Grey soldier-birds arrive
in flickers of speed
to hang upside down
from a quivering weed

or tremble trees' foliage
that they trickle down through.
Women's Weekly summer fashions
in the compost turn blue.

The sun slants in under things
and stares right through houses;
soon pyjamas will peep, though,
from the bottoms of trousers.

Night-barking dogs quieten
as overcast forms
and it rains, with far thunder,
in queer predawn storms;

then the school bus tops ridges
with clay marks for effort,
picking up drowsy schoolkids,
none of them now barefoot,

and farmers take spanners
to the balers, gang ploughs
and towering diesel tractors
they prefer to their cows.

## The Kitchens

*This deep in the year, in the frosts of then*
*that steeled sheets left ghostly on the stayed line,*
*smoked over verandah beds, cruelled water taps rigid,*
*family and visitors would sit beside the lake*
*of blinding coals, that end of the detached kitchen,*
*the older fellows quoting* qoph *and* resh
*from the Book of Psalms, as they sizzled phlegm*
*(some still did it after iron stoves came*
*and the young moved off to cards and the radio)*
*and all told stories. That's a kind of spoken video:*

> We rode through from the Myall
> on that road of the cedarcutter's ghost.
> All this was called Wild Horses Creek then;
> you could plait the grass over the pommel
> of your saddle. That grass don't grow now.
> I remember we camped on Waterloo that night
> there where the black men gave the troopers a hiding.

The garden was all she had: the parrots were at it
and she came out and said to them, quite serious
like as if to reasonable people They are *my* peas.
And do you know? They flew off and never come back.

> If you missed anything: plough,
> saddle, cornplanter, shovel,
> you just went across to Uncle Bob's
> and brought it home. If he
> was there, he never looked ashamed:
> he'd just tell you a joke,
> some lies, sing you a poem,
> keep you there drinking all night –

Bloody cruel mongrels, telling me the native bear
would grow a new hide if you skun it alive.
Everybody knows that, they told me. I told them
if I caught any man skinning bears alive
on my place, he'd bloody need a new hide himself.

    Tommy Turpin the blackfellow said to me More better
    you walk behind me today, eh boss.
    Might be devil-devil tell me hit you with the axe
    longa back of the head. I thought he was joking
    then I saw he wasn't. My word I stayed behind
    that day, with the axe, trimming tongues on the rails
    while he cut mortises out of the posts. I listened.

I wis eight year old, an Faither gied me the lang gun
tae gang doon an shuit the native hens at wis aitin
aa oor oats. I reasoned gin ye pit ae chairge
i the gun, pouder waddin an shot, ye got ae shot
sae pit in twa, ye'd get twa. Aweel, I pit in seven,
liggd doon ahint a stump, pu'd the trigger – an the warld
gaed milky white. I think I visited Scotland
whaur I had never been. It was a ferlie I wis seean.
It wis a sonsy place. But Grannie gard me gang back.
Mither wis skailan watter on ma heid, greetin. Aa they found
o the gun wis stump-flinders, but there wis a black scour thro the oats,
an unco ringan in ma ears, an fifteen deid native hens.

    Of course long tongue she laughed about that other
    and they pumped her about you can guess and hanging round there
    and she said He's got one on him like a horse, Mama,
    and I like it. Well! And all because of you know –

Father couldn't stand meanness.
When Uncle you-know-who
charged money for milking our cows
that time Isabel took bad
Father called him gutless,
not just tin-arsed, but gutless.
Meanness is for cowards, Father reckoned.

The little devil, he says to the minister's wife
Daddy reckons we can't have any more children,
we need the milk for the pigs. Dear I was mortified –

Poor Auntie Mary was dying Old and frail
all scroopered down in the bedclothes pale as cotton
even her hardworking old hands Oh it was sad
people in the room her big daughters performing
rattling the bedknobs There is a white angel
in the room says Mary in this weird voice And then
NO! she heaves herself up Bloody no! Be quiet!
she coughed and spat Phoo! I'll be damned if I'll die!
She's back making bread next week Lived ten more years.

Well, it was black Navy rum; it buggered Darcy.
Fell off his horse, crawled under the cemetery fence.
Then some yahoos cantered past Yez all asleep in there?
All but me, croaks Darcy. They off at a hand gallop,
squealing out, and his horse behind them, stirrups belting it.

The worst ghost I ever saw
was a policeman and (one of the squatters)
moving cattle at night.
I caught them in my headlights.
It haunted me. Every time
I went in to town after that
somehow I'd get arrested –

I'll swear snakes have got no brains!
The carpet snake we had in the rafters
to eat rats, one day it et a chook.
I killed it with the pitchfork, ran a tine
through the top of its head, and chucked it
down the gully. It was back in a week
with a scab on its head and another under its chin.
They bring a house good luck but they got no brain.

Then someone might cup his hand short of the tongue
of a taut violin, try each string to be wrung
by the bow, that spanned razor of holy white hair
and launch all but his earthly weight into an air
that breathed up hearth fires strung worldwide between
the rung hills of being and the pearled hills of been.
In the language beyond speaking they'd sum the grim law,
speed it to a daedaly and foot it to a draw,
the tones of their scale five gnarled fingers wide
and what sang were all angles between love and pride.


JULY


## Midwinter Haircut

Now the world has stopped. Dead middle of the year.
Cloud all the colours of a worn-out dairy bucket
freeze-frames the whole sky. The only sun is down
intensely deep in the dam's bewhiskered mirror
and the white-faced heron hides in the drain with her spear.

Now the world has stopped, doors could be left open.
Only one fly came awake to the kitchen heater
this breakfast time, and supped on a rice bubble sluggishly.
No more will come inside out of the frost-crimped grass now.
Crime, too, sits in faraway cars. Phone lines drop at the horizon.

Now the world has stopped, what do we feel like doing?
The district's former haircutter, from the time before barbers, has shaved
and wants a haircut. So do I. No longer the munching hand clippers
with locks in their gears, nor the scissors more pointed than a beak
but the buzzing electric clipper, straight from its cardboard giftbox.

We'll sit under that on the broad-bottomed stool that was
the seat for fifty years of the district's only sit-down job,
the postmistress-telephonist's seat, where our poor great-aunt
who trundled and spoke in sour verdicts sat to hand-crank
the tingling exchange, plugged us into each other's lives

and tapped consolation from gossip's cells as they unlidded.
From her shrewd kind successor who never tapped in, and planes
along below the eaves of our heads, we'll hear a tapestry
of weddings funerals surgeries, and after our sittings
be given a jar of pickle. Hers won't be like the house

a mile down the creek, where cards are cut and shuffled
in the middle of the day, and mortarbombs of beer
detonate the digestion, and they tell world-stopping yarns
like: I went to Sydney races. There along the rails,
    all snap brims and cold eyes, flanked by senior police

and other, stony men with their eyes in a single crease
stood the entire Government of New South Wales
watching Darby ply the whip, all for show, over this fast colt.
It was young and naïve. It was heading for the post in a bolt
while the filly carrying his and all the inside money

strained to come level. Too quick for the stewards to note him
Darby slipped the colt a low lash to the scrotum.
It checked, shocked, stumbled – and the filly flashed by.
As he came from weighing in, I caught Darby's eye
and he said *Get out of it, mug,* quite conversationally. –


AUGUST


*Forty Acre Ethno*

The Easter rains are late this year
at this other end of a dry hard winter.
Low clouds grow great rustling crops of fall
and all the gully-courses braid and bubble,
their root-braced jugs and coarse lips pour
and it's black slog for cows when, grass lake to puddle,
a galloping dog sparks on all four.
It'll be plashy England here for a while
or boggy Scotland, by the bent straw colour
and the breaks of sun mirror-backed with chill.


289

Coming home? It was right. And it was time.
I had been twenty-nine years away
after books and work and society
but society vanished into ideology
and by then I could bring the other two home.
We haven't been out at night since we came
back, except last month, in the United Kingdom.
The towns ranged like footlights up the highway
and coastline here rehearse a subtle play
that's only staged in private by each family.

Sight and life restored by an eye operation
my father sits nightly before the glass screen
of a wood-burning slow combustion stove. We see
the same show, with words, on television.
Dad speaks of memories, and calls his fire homely:
when did you last hear that word without scorn
for something unglossy, or some poor woman?
Here, where thin is *poor*, and fat is *condition*,
'homely' is praise and warmth, spoken gratefully.
Its opposite lurks outside in dark blowing rain.

Horses are exposed to it, wanly stamping out
unglazed birth ware for mosquitoes in the coming season
and already peach trees are a bare wet frame
for notional little girls in pink dots of gingham.
Cars coming home fishtail and harrow the last mile,
their undersea headlights kicking gum trees around eerily;
woodducks wake high in those trees, and peer from the door
they'll shove their ducklings out of, to spin down in their down,
sprawl, and swim to water. Our children dog the footsteps of their grandfather, learning their ancient culture.

## Mercurial

Preindustrial haze. The white sky rim
forecasts a hot summer. Burning days
indeed are rehearsed, with flies and dinnertime fan,
but die out, over west mountains
erased with azure, into spring-cool nights
and the first flying insects
which are the small weeds of a bedroom window.

Early in the month, the valley was a Friesian cow:
knobbed black, whitened straw.
Alarming smokes bellied up behind the heights of forest.
Now green has invested fires'
fixed cloud-shadows; lower gum boughs are seared chestnut.
Emerald kingparrots, crimson-breasted, whirr
and plane out of open feed sheds.

Winds are changeable. We're tacking.
West on rubbed blue days,
easterlies on hot, southerly and dead calm for rain.
Mercury is near the moon, Venus at perigee
and frogs wind their watches all night on swampy stretches
where waterhens blink with their tails at dusk, like rabbits
and the mother duck does her cripple act.

Dams glitter like house roofs again.
The first wasp comes looking for a spider to paralyse:
a flimsy ultralight flier
who looks like a pushover, but after one pass lifts
you, numb, out of your trampoline. Leaves together
as for prayer or diving, bean plants erupt
into the grazing glory. Those unnibbled spread their arms.

Poddy calves wobbling in their newborn mushroom colours
ingest and make the pungent custard of infancy.
Sign of a good year, many snakes lie flattened
on the roads again. Bees and pollens drift
through greening orchards. And next day it pours rain:
smokes of cloud on every bushland slope,
that opposite, wintry haze. The month goes out facing backwards.


OCTOBER


## Freshwater and Salt

It's the opening of the surf season
thirty miles away east;
most things speak a different dialect
over there on the coast.

Here, the rising wave comes as
grass. The animals drink it
thirstily. It's a sweetwater ocean.
If your house is fenced in, it'll sink it.

Fire and snakes swim in it;
you have to slash and mow.
Time for rotary blades, and weeping salt water
with your whole skin as you make them go.

It isn't in fact such a whelming
tide. But it's an ever-swelling one
you have to keep in balance, like the Dutch.
Much worse when it doesn't run.

Between us and the saltwater breakers
there's that rind, too, of chip-frying city
twelve thousand miles long, that locals
will come home from soon with gritty

trunksful and running shoes full
of ground bottle, ground coral, ground shell.
I guess we're all flesh of that shell
and will broach it by New Year, and wade gingerly

up to our nacres in salt swirl,
even we freshwater pearlers
and privately pale herbage hurlers
happiest on the grassed forms of groundswell.


NOVEMBER


## The Misery Cord

IN MEMORY OF F.S. MURRAY

Misericord. The Misery Cord.
It was lettered on a wall.
I knew that cord, how it's tough to break
however hard you haul.

My cousin sharefarmed, and so got half:
half dignity, half hope, half income,
for his full work. To get a place
of his own took his whole lifetime.

Some pluck the misery chord from habit
or for luck, however they feel,
some to deceive, and some for the tune –
but sometimes it's real.

Milking bails, flannel shirts, fried breakfasts,
these were our element,
and doubling on horses, and shouting Score!
at a dog yelping on a hot scent –

but an ambulance racing on our back road
is bad news for us all:
the house of community is about
to lose a plank from its wall.

293

Grief is nothing you can do, but do,
worst work for least reward,
pulling your heart out through your eyes
with tugs of the misery cord.

    I looked at my cousin's farm, where he'd just
    built his family a house of their own,
    and I looked down into Fred's next house,
    its clay walls of bluish maroon.

Just one man has broken the misery cord
and lived. He said once was enough.
A poem is an afterlife on earth:
Christ grant us the other half.


DECEMBER


*Infant Among Cattle*

Young parents, up at dawn, working. Their first child can't
be his own babysitter, so as they machine the orphaned milk
from their cows, he must sit plump on the dairy cement,
the back of his keyhole pants safetypinned to a stocking

that is tied to a bench leg. He studies a splotch of cream,
how the bubbles in it, too thick to break, work like
the coated and lucid gravels in the floor. On which he then dings
a steel thing, for the tingling in it and his fingers

till it skips beyond his tether. As the milkers front up
in their heel-less skiddy shoes, he hangs out aslant
on his static line, watching the breeching rope brace them
and their washed udders relieved of the bloodberry ticks

that pull off a stain, and show a calyx of kicking filaments.
By now the light stands up behind the trees like sheet iron.
It photographs the cowyard and dairy-and-bails in one vast
buttery shadow wheel on the trampled junction of paddocks

where the soil is itself a concrete, of dust and seedy stones
and manure crustings. When his father slings a bucketful
of wash water out the door, it wallops and skids
and is gulped down by a sudden maw like the cloth of a radio.

Out and on out, the earth tightens down on the earth
and squeezes heat up through the yellow grass
like a surfaceless fluid, to pool on open country,
to drip from faces, and breed the insect gleams of midday.

Under the bench, crooning this without words to his rag dog,
he hears a vague trotting outside increase – and the bull
erupts, aghast, through the doorway, dribbling, clay in his curls,
a slit orange tongue working in and out under his belly –

and is repulsed, with buckets and screams and a shovel.
The little boy, swept up in his parents' distress, howls then
but not in fear of the bull, who seemed a sad apparition:
a huge prostrate man, bewildered by a pitiless urgency.


JANUARY


*Variations on a Measure of Burns*

When January is home to visit her folks
and official work is a public hoax,
soy sprouts dotting the serpentine strokes
    ploughs combed in the lacquered
hill soil that each afternoon's rainstorm soaks
    weave a green jacquard

and zucchini and wart squash and Queensland Blues
(not the dog, but the pumpkin) squeak together like shoes
in tractor trailers, and nectarines bruise
    from being awaited,
but the grizzled haze over mountain views
    looks faintly methylated

because Drought, who's in on every forced sale,
thought he may have seen the farmers granted bail
this summer, has the continent in his entail.
    Even smashed, he's seen you:
that old man up a back road fumbling his mail
    gets letters from El Niño.

Disappointment, holiday and heatwave shilly-shally
round this snaky time of year. Stock prices plunge and rally
but the government's retreated for keeps from this valley:
    the flash brick erstwhile
Whitlam toilet block lacks its school, and stands orphaned on its gully;
the PO's a closed file.

We retain a public phone and some dirt main roads
on whose corners part-time squatters tip sprawling loads
of gravel for drunk drivers who for lifetimes and by codes
    like Whoa car! and hug-the-crown
miraculously get home to treat their families like toads
    or finish upside down

    in the dark, miles from town,
standing on my scalp with the rain's sparks falling upward,
    windscreen a collective noun,
delighted by the spinning tyre slowing above the cupboard
and the glare-path through inverted trees – myself as I could
have been, through brutal labour for a bare livelihood,

    myself on that quest
few families dare acknowledge, let alone go with you on,
    the hunger for the Rest
when mortgage world time politics, everything's on top of one
and the teenage girl you married is not months but decades gone:
I'm sorry for myself in his sideburns and cardigan.

O he will like that,
murmurs his wife, wrestling farm accounts, steering above the rocks,
then bundling the children off to bed, switching off the box:
    Television makes you fat!
Our concern cuts away at once. Moorhen and flying fox
outside creak identical rusty keys in their vocal locks
    and the dark stands pat.


FEBRUARY

*Feb*

        Seedy drytime Feb,
        lightning between its teeth,
        all its plants pot-bound.

        Inside enamelled rims
        dams shrink their mirroring shields,
        baking the waterlilies.

        Days stacked like clay pigeons
        squeezed from dust and sweat.
        Two cultures: sun and shade.

        Days dazed with actuality
        like a bottle shot
        sniping fruit off twigs,

        by afternoon, portentous
        with whole cloud-Atlantics
        that rain fifteen drops.

        Beetroot and iron butter,
        bread staled by the fan,
        cold chook: that's lunch with Feb.

Weedy drymouth Feb, first cousin of scorched creek stones,
of barbed wire across gaunt gullies, bringer of soldered
death-freckles to the backs of farmers' hands. The mite-struck

foal rattles her itch on fence wires, like her mother,
and scraped hill pastures are grazed back to their charred
bulldozer stitchings. Dogs nip themselves under the tractor

of needy Feb, who waits for the raw eel-perfume
of the first real rain's pheromones, the magic rain-on-dust
sexual scent of Time itself, philtre of all native beings –

> Lanky cornhusk Feb,
> drilling the red-faced
> battalions of tomatoes
>
> through the grader's slots:
> harvest out of bareness,
> that semidesert mode.
>
> Worn grasshopper month
> suddenly void of children;
> days tucking their tips in
>
> with blackberry seeds to spit
> and all of life root-bound;
> stringy dryland Feb.

MARCH

*Masculeene, Cried the Bulls*

Bang! it was autumn,
right on the first of the month,
cool overcast after scorchers
and next day it poured.

Four and a half inches
of rise in the dams, of wet in garden soil:
we know how long you were, rain,
four and a half deep inches.

As fresh green abolished
this summer's only white-blond month
the first autumnal scents
were ginger and belladonna

and as beds resumed their blankets
at the mopoke hour, bulls sang.
Among cattle, the more masculine
the higher the voice is pitched.

Our pumpkins took
first prize at Nabiac Show,
where a horse named Danielle
pirouetted, and posed on a tub,

and men raced through solid timber
backwards, with aimed steel strides,
and we met the Anglo-Nubian
tree-climbing goat, maker of,

and sheep of, the desert.
This was the weekend after clocks
jerked the sun an hour forward,
and all the time, leafage

of various winebottle colour
sprouted on the roses and lemon trees
and dew twinkled for longer
on the lengthening paddocks.

APRIL

## The Idyll Wheel

And so we've come right round the sun
to April again. It's unique again
like each month, each year. Much less of summer
reached April this year. Yet grass burgeoned after Easter.
Now fenced cultivations rug up, blue and tan
and old fruit trees declare themselves russet
along the creeks, or that dismantling brown
of cedars long ago spied from a mountain.

Into blue dimensionless as an ideal
with a Y-shaped prop, Mavis hoists the unreal
statures, flat and wet, of her whole family
for her glance and the warm sun to re-fill
above the pleats and hoed flickers of their hill
where Jack and her father move bent, keeping busy.
This isn't that year. But their names are there still
with Careys, Monks, Arnolds, the farms of surnames gone.

Here, roads have different names coming and going.
Over Bulby kinks one the Murrays rode along
into the hard-to-discern ruins of an idyll,
beige, drab with new bush, country emptied and unshaven.
On went Johnnie and Bella, east went Mina and Jimmy
whose family milked squatting so as not to get lazy,
Uncle Hughie, Aunt Grace – *us girls say Mrs Murray!* –
and years turned with handles were the first farming wheel.

This month, this year, Hiles' cattle mar the air
with saleyards' caked music. Before dinner, Charlie sang
*The old folk had their reasons* over the horizontal
queer hang of his guitar. Then we who say muttai
ate the last of this year's, boiled. Those who say corn
didn't all fly Macquarie Street dachas, though, here:
many are as poor as settlers ever were.
Now small frogs turn bronze. With the Post Office gone

nowhere's left for district people to meet by accident.
It has to be by knowledge. Ellen Harris, who taught me
to walk, Joyce new-widowed, and Vera and Norm
bail up cows, or watch milk suffuse the machine-glass
like a blizzarding idea. And I'm visible to them
on this wheel that was our Law, once. I haven't milked,
again, and it's sundown. They are the last to dairy.
Still, farmlets and cattle-spreads also live by touches,
a stump burning, dam scoopings, new wire stitches
and unstated idylls had driving to and from.


## THE TRANSPOSITION OF CLERMONT

After the Big Flood, we elected
to move our small timber city
from the dangerous beauty of the river
and its fringed lagoons
since both had risen to destroy us.

Many buildings went stacked on wagons
but more were towed entire
in strained stateliness, with a long groyning sound,
up timber by traction engines.

Each moved singly. Life went on round them;
in them, at points of rest.
Guests at breakfast in the Royal Hotel, facing
now the saddlery, now the Town Hall.

We drank in the canted Freemasons
and the progressive Shamrock, but really
all pubs were the Exchange. Relativities
interchanged our world like a chess game:

butcher occluded baker, the police
eclipsed both brothels, the dance hall
sashayed around the Temperance Hall,
front doors sniffed rear, and thoughtfully ground on.

Certain houses burst, and vanished.
One wept its windows, one trailed mementoes up the street.
A taut chain suddenly parted and scythed down
horses and a verandah. Weed-edged black rectangles
in exploded gardens yielded sovereigns and spoons.

That ascent of working architecture
onto the pegged plateau was a children's crusade
with lines stretching down to us.
Everything standing in its wrong accustomed place.
My generation's memories are intricately transposed:

butcher occluding dance music, the police
eclipsed by opportunity, brothels sashaying royally
and, riding sidesaddle up shined skids, the Town Hall.
Excited, we would meet on streets that stayed immutable

sometimes for weeks; from irrecoverable corners
and alleys already widening, we'd look
back down at our new graves and childhood gardens,
the odd house at anchor for a quick tomato season
and the swaying nailed hull of a church going on before us.

And many allotments left unbought, or for expansion
never filled up, above, as they hadn't below.
What was town, what was country stayed elusive
as we saw it always does, in the bush,
what is waste, what is space, what is land.


# THE FALL OF APHRODITE STREET

So it's back to window shopping
on Aphrodite Street
for the apples are stacked and juicy
but some are death to eat.

For just one generation
the plateglass turned to air –
when you look for that generation
half of it isn't there.

An ugliness of spirit
leered like a hunting dog
over the world. Now it snarls and whines
at its fleshly analogue.

What pleased it made it angry:
scholars Score and Flaunt and Scene
taught that everything outstanding
was knobs on a skin machine.

Purer grades of this metaphysic
were sold out of parked cars
down alleys where people paired or reeled
like desperate swastikas.

Age, spirit, kindness, all were taunts;
grace was enslaved to meat.
You never were mugged till you were mugged
on Aphrodite Street.

God help the millions that street killed
and those it sickened too,
when it was built past every house
and often bulldozed through.

Apples still swell, but more and more
are literal death to eat
and it's back to window shopping
on Aphrodite Street.

# TWO RAINS

Our farm is in the patched blue overlap
between Queensland rain and Victorian rain
(and of two-faced droughts like a dustbowl tap).

The southerly rain is skimmed and curled
off the Roaring Forties' circuit of the world.
It is our chased Victorian silver

and makes wintry asphalt hurry on the spot
or pauses to a vague speed in the air,
whereas, lightning-brewed in a vast coral pot

the tropical weather disgorges its lot
in days of enveloping floodtime blast
towering and warm as a Papuan forest,

a rain you can sweat in, it steams in the sun
like a hard-ridden horse, while southern rain's absorbed
like a cool, fake-colloquial, drawn out lesson.


# TO THE SOVIET AMERICANS

The working class, the working class,
it is too radiant to see through.
More claim to come from the working class
than admit they do.

Between syruping mailed brutes in flattery
and translating the world into litmag terms
those equivalent modes of poetry
there comes this love of the working class

who never set out to be a class
or the subject forever of exams
they're not allowed to take or pass
or else they're no longer the working class,

and in the forest, a working man
must say, *Watch out for the ones in jeans*
*who'll stop you smoking and stop you working:*
*I call them the Soviet Americans.*

*I used to have work and a family here*
*but both them have shot through.*
*Now that trees belong to the working class*
*I don't suppose I do.*


## LOW DOWN SANDCASTLE BLUES

You can't have everything, I said as we drank tea.
No, you can't have everything. And I sipped my tea.
    You can't have anything, my friend answered me.

Yes, I've wrestled with an angel: there is no other kind.
I wrestled with an angel: that wrestling's the only kind.
    Any easier wrestling finally sends you blind.

Trouble's a stray dog that's mighty hard to lose:
if he latches on to you, he's mighty hard to lose
    but not even a dog joins in when you sing the blues.

A man told me I've no right to what I need.
He told me Oh yes, I've no right to what I need.
    He had all his rights and quivered under them like a reed.

If you've got the gift of seeing things from both sides
– it's an angel-wound, that curse of seeing things from both sides –
    then police beat you up in a sandcastle built between tides.

# THE EMERALD DOVE

We ought to hang cutout hawk shapes
in our windows. Birds hard driven
by a predator, or maddened by a mirrored rival
too often die zonk against the panes'
invisible sheer, or stagger away from
the blind full stop in the air.
It was different with the emerald dove.
In at an open sash, a pair

sheered, missile, in a punch of energy,
one jinking on through farther doors, one
thrown, panicked by that rectangular wrong copse, braked
like a bullet in blood, a full-on splat of wings
like a vaulter between shoulders, blazed and calliper,
ashriek out of jagbeaked fixe fury, swatting wind,
lights, keepsakes, panes, then at the in window out, gone.
A sparrowhawk, by the cirrus feathering.

The other, tracked down in a farther room
clinging to a bedhead, was the emerald dove,
a rainforest bird, flashed in beyond its world
of lice, sudden death and tree seeds. Pigeon-like,
only its eye and neck in liquid motion,
there, as much beyond us as beyond
itself, it perched, barefoot in silks
like a prince of Sukhothai, above the reading lamps and cotton-buds.

Modest-sized as a writing hand, mushroom fawn
apart from its paua casque, those viridescent closed wings,
it was an emerald Levite in that bedroom
which the memory of it was going to bless for years
despite topping our ordinary happiness, as beauty
makes background of all around it. Levite too
in the question it posed: sanctuary without transformation,
which is, how we might be,

plunged out of our contentment into evolved strange heaven,
where the need to own or mate with or eat the beautiful
was bygone as poverty,
and we were incomprehensibly, in our exhaustion,
treasured, cooed at, then softly left alone
among vast crumples, verticals, refracting air,
our way home barred by mirrors, our splendour unmanifest
to us now, a small wild person, with no idea of peace.


## CAVE DIVERS NEAR MOUNT GAMBIER

Chenille-skinned people are counting under the countryside
on resurrections by truck light off among the pines.

Here in the first paddocks, where winter comes ashore,
mild duckweed ponds are skylights of a filled kingdom

and what their gaze absorbs may float up districts away.
White men with scorches of hair approach that water,

zip into black, upturn large flap feet and free-fall
away, their mouths crammed full. Crystalline polyps

of their breathing blossom for a while, as they disturb
algal screens, extinct kangaroos, eels of liquorice colour

then, with the portable greening stars they carry under,
these vanish, as the divers undergo tight anti-births

into the vaults and profound domes of the limestone.
Here, approaching the heart of the poem they embody

and thereby make the gliding cavern-world embody,
they have to keep time with themselves, and be dull often

with its daylight logic – since to dream it fully
might leave them asprawl on the void clang of their tanks,

their faceplates glazing an unfocused dreadful portrait
at the apex of a steeple that does not reach the day.

# THE TIN WASH DISH

Lank poverty, dank poverty,
its pants wear through at fork and knee.
It warms its hands over burning shames,
refers to its fate as Them and He
and delights in things by their hard names:
rag and toejam, feed and paw –
don't guts that down, there ain't no more!
Dank poverty, rank poverty,
it hums with a grim fidelity
like wood-rot with a hint of orifice,
wet newspaper jammed in the gaps of artifice,
and disgusts us into fierce loyalty.
It's never the fault of those you love:
poverty comes down from above.
Let it dance chairs and smash the door,
it arises from all that went before
and every outsider's the enemy –
Jesus Christ turned this over with his stick
and knights and philosophers turned it back.
Rank poverty, lank poverty,
chafe in its crotch and sores in its hair,
still a window's clean if it's made of air,
not webby silver like a sleeve.
Watch out if this does well at school
and has to leave and longs to leave:
someone, sometime, will have to pay.
Shave with toilet soap, run to flesh,
astound the nation, rule the army,
still you wait for the day you'll be sent back
where books or toys on the floor are rubbish
and no one's allowed to come and play
because home calls itself a shack
and hot water crinkles in the tin wash dish.

# THE INVERSE TRANSPORTS

Two hundred years, and the bars
reappear on more and more windows;
more people have a special number to ring.
This started with furious strange Christians:
they would have all things in common,
have morals superseded by love –
truth and Christ they rejected scornfully.

More people sell and move to the country.
The bush becomes their civil city.
What do they do there? Some make quilts
sewing worn and washed banknotes together.
What romantic legends do they hear there?
Tales of lineage, and of terrible accidents:
the rearing tractor, the sawmills' bloody moons.

Accident is the tiger of the country,
but fairytale is a reserve, for those rich only
in that and fifty thousand years here.
The incomers will acquire those fifty thousand
years too, though. Thousands of anything
draw them. They discovered thousands,
even these. Which they offer now, for settlement.

Has the nation been a poem or an accident?
And which should it be? America, and the Soviets
and the First and Third Reich were poems.
Two others, quite different, have been Rome's.
We've been through some bloody British stanzas
and some local stanzas where 'pelf'
was the rhyme for 'self' – and some about police,

refuge, ballots, space, the Fair Go and peace.
Many strain now to compose a National Purpose,
some fear its enforcement. Free people take liberties:
inspired government takes liberty itself.

Takes it where, court to parliament to bureaucracy
to big union to gaol, an agreed atmosphere
endures, that's dealt with God and democracy.

Inside convict ships that Christ's grace inverted
hanging chains end in lights. Congregations
approach the classless there. But the ships are being buried
in tipped dirt. Half the media denies
it's happening, and the other half justifies
this live burial – and the worshippers divide likewise
in their views of the sliding waves of garbage

in which their ships welter and rise
beneath towers with the lyric sheen of heroin
that reach skyward out of the paradox
that expression and achievement are the Prize
and at the same time are indefensible privilege.
Two hundred years, and the bars
appear on more and more windows.


## THE NARRABRI RESERVATION

On the road to the Nandewars
there was a slab of dead
enfolded in a green gumtree
and a nectar-blackened hole in it
at which bees hovered and appeared –

Still unfocused from the dream-prolonging
shower, this man sops lather,
stipples his face, then grades off
the Santa-wool of his shave
with flicks and whittlings.

Despite back yard and front garden
his children watch breakfast television
like Japanese in a miniature apartment
on the fiftieth floor. They
don't know a bywash from a bore-drain.

Splashed cologne won't sting the thought away.
It bothers him, knotting the tie
that will serve him for a beard
expounding lines in the boardroom:
his children don't come from his country.

Fatal, that in his own childhood
he walked up mortised stays
to the tops of strainer posts
on the coast of a wheat ocean.
It seeded in him the Narrabri reservation

with which he'll hear every scheme put forward today.
Also by midday, when downtown wears the aspect
of towering sets left over from a nighttime
private-eye series, he'll recall how at midnight
the same buildings appear left over from the day

and will feel toward them the Narrabri reservation.
Not being the only person in his family
he won't start reading the Farm and Station ads
but will listen to the irony colleagues bring
to items in the paper: Ted's is the Katanning,

Laurel's will be the Gayndah reservation –
On the worn brakes of the city
all these instants of light friction.

# THE UP-TO-DATE SCARECROW

FOR MELISSA GORDON

With my mouldy felt hat and my coat pinned shut
I'd soon frighten nothing; birds'd sit on me – but
with some builders' plastic sheeting and a Coles bag on my head
I can dance standing still in a garden bed.
Ah, raggy plastic sheets! They're my favourite fad!
the best new idea the gardeners have had
for an old scarecrow (we scarecrows are born old):
they give me a voice, and the birds get told!
In any sort of breeze, in my polythene clothes
I can make crows vanish and men swear oaths –
fair crack of the whip! – when I put an elastic
snap to the air with a crinkle of my plastic,
and give me a wind blowing as wind can
I can crackle like eggs in a giant's frying pan!


# THE POLE BARNS

Unchinked log cabins, empty now, or stuffed with hay
under later iron. Or else roofless, bare stanzas of timber
with chars in the text. Each line ends in memorial axemanship.

With a hatch in one gable end, like a cuckoo clock,
they had to be climbed up into, or swung into
from the saddle of a quiet horse, feet-first onto corn.

On logs like rollers these rooms stand on creek flat and ridge,
and their true roofs were bark, every squared sheet a darkened
huge stroke of painting, fibrous from the brush.

Flattened, the sheets strained for a long time to curl again:
the man who slept on one and woke immobilised
in a scroll pipe is a primal pole-barn story.

The sound of rain on bark roofing, dotted, not pointed,
increasing to a sonic blanket, is millennia older than walls
but it was still a heart of storytelling, under the one lantern

as the comets of corn were stripped to their white teeth
and chucked over the partition, and the vellum husks shuffled down
round spooky tellers hunched in the planes of winter wind.

More a daylight thinker was the settler who noticed the tide
of his grain going out too fast, and set a dingo trap
in the servery slot – and found his white-faced neighbour,

a man bearded as himself, up to the shoulder in anguish.
Neither spoke as the trap was released, nor mentioned that dawn ever.
Happiest, in that iron age, were sitting aloft on the transom

unscrewing corn from cobs, making a good shower for the hens
and sailing the barn, with its log ram jutting low in front.
Like all the ships of conquest, its name was Supply.


## THE 1812 OVERTURE AT TOPKAPI SARAY

The Rosary in Turkish, and prayers for the Sultān.
Through the filigree perforations of a curtain wall
a vagrant breeze parts a hanging mist of muslin
behind the Dowager Wife seated in her pavilion.

For fourteen hundred Sundays she has commended
to the Virgin's Son a fluctuating small congregation
of those who, like herself, had no choice about virginity:
concubines and eunuchs with the faces of aged children.

For perhaps thirteen hundred she has prayed for the Sultān,
both him to whom she was sent as a captured pearl
by the Bey of Algiers, and their son who reigns now in succession
beneath the inscriptions which, though she reads them fluently, still

at moments resemble tongues involved with a pastille,
or two, or three. The bitterest to her own taste
was never to succeed in stopping the trade in eunuchs
whereby little boys, never Muslim on the cutting day,

must be seated crying in hot, blood-stanching sand.
A sorrowful mystery. The traffic in bed-girls is another,
but there were eventually also joyous days
when the sea of Martinique yielded to the Marmara's glitter.

Now a messenger approaches the Executioner's House
beyond which only one entire man may pass
into this precinct on the headland of the city,
this Altai meadow of trees and marble tents.

An indifferent face is summoned to the grille
and the letter the messenger brings goes speeding on
to the woman concluding Glory Be among the cushions.
The rest withdraw, rustling, as she reads the superscription:

From the Commander of the Faithful to the Most Illustrious
Lady of the Seraglio – Mother, I have today
made a treaty with the Tsar, ceding one province
and retaining two we had also certainly lost.

These favourable terms arise from the Tsar's great need
of his army to face an invasion by the man Bonaparte,
Commander of the Faithless, to borrow your title for him.
Prospects for the Empire are improved at last

by this invasion, which will come. Russia is very great
but Bonaparte may defeat her. He may be Chinghiz Khan.
Our mightiest enemy would thereby be nullified
and such a victory might well ensnare the victor.

On the other hand, Bonaparte may lose – and then I think
with his legend broken, all Europe would turn on him
with Russia in the van, and engaged in that direction.
I must add, mother, that as I released the Tsar

for this coming contest, I had in mind our cousin
the Empress Josephine, dear playmate of your childhood
whom the Viper of the Nile so shamefully cast off
two years ago, in his quest for a Habsburg connection.

I was holding an exact balance: the choice was mine
to release the Tsar, or keep him engaged a while longer –
our treacherous Janissaries beat their spoons for this option.
If I held him, destruction of our old foe was assured:

I savoured that a little. Then I savoured his shielding us from
the spirit that drives France. As you taught me, the spirit is inseparable –
thus the honour of two wronged ladies tipped my decision.
Such moments, not I, are the shadow of God upon Earth. –

Aimée Dubucq de Rivéry, mother of the Sultan
walks in her pavilion, her son's letter trailing in her hand
and the carpets are a beach far beyond the Barbary pirates.
There she skips with Marie-Josèphe, her poor first cousin

but *poor* concerns parents only. A black manservant
attends each girl, as they splash filigree in the tide-edge
and gather it, as coral and pierced shells, which the men receive
for in that age young women are free, and men are passive.


## GLAZE

Tiles are mostly abstract:
tiles come from Islam:
tiles have been through fire:
tiles are a sacred charm:

After the unbearable parallel
trajectories of lit blank tile,
figure-tiles restore the plural,
figuring resumes its true vein.

Harm fades from the spirit as tiles
repeat time beyond time their riddle,
neat stanzas that rhyme from the middle
styles with florets with tendrils of balm.

Henna and mulberry mos-
aics controvert space:
lattice on lattice recedes
through itself into Paradise

or parrot starbursts framing themes
of stars bursting, until they salaam
the Holy Name in sprigged consonants
crosslaced as Welsh metrical schemes.

Conjunct, the infinite doorways
of the mansions of mansions amaze
underfoot in a cool court, with sun-blaze
afloat on the hard water of glaze.

Ur shapes under old liquor
ziggurats of endless incline;
cruciform on maiolica
flourishes the true vine.

Tulip tiles on the grate of Humoresque
Villa join, by a great arabesque
cream boudoirs of Vienna, then by left-
handed rhyme, the blue pubs of Delft

and prominence stands in a circle
falling to the centre of climb:
O miming is defeated by mime:
circles circle the PR of ominence.

Cool Mesach in fused Rorschach,
old from beyond Islam,
tiles have been to Paradise,
clinkers of ghostly calm.

# FARMER AT FIFTY

He could envisage
though he didn't invent
the breeze-steered dam
in its khaki pug,
cattle twinned at their drinking
and the baby frogs
still in their phlegm.

Woodducks drowsing on their feet
enriching the dam wall,
he could foresee them,
but not the many jets
of the native waterlily
burning Bunsen-blue
on many a high stem

out of leaf-clouds
on the anchored stream.
He didn't know they'd come.
But: what he'd done, stopping
erosive water's hurry
had also been to build
a room for them.

The same with home.
He could foresee
daily bunting on the line,
white, pink, swallowtail and square
flags announcing a baby
but not what came then,
nor who had come;

not the childhoods he'd be in
and left in, eventually.
On the dam wall, the dog
sits beside its tail
and turns its head with him
as he looks into the tops
of the trees downstream.

# THE TUBE

FOR ANN MOYAL AND ROB CRAWFORD

Many resemble Henry Sutton
in sleevelinks in Ballarat
who invented television;
later several would do that
but not in eighteen eighty seven.

'Telephany' – he named it well:
his Greek was more correct.
His design was theoretical
but: Nipkow disc and Kerr effect
and selenium photocell,

all were there. It would have worked
and brought the Melbourne Cup alive
to Ballarat, which was his object –
but no one had yet sent an aerial wave
and wire had this defect:

signals couldn't race so fast
along it that they'd sustain a picture.
Only when the horse-drawn age was past
could horses surge into the air
with music and gunfire, galloping broadcast.

Tremendous means, and paltry vision:
some will dare ask you about that
in your interview, Henry Sutton,
in Ballarat, in your floreat,
standing telephanous on your front lawn.

## SHALE COUNTRY

Watermelon rinds around the house,
small gondolas of curling green
lined with sodden rosy plush;
concrete paths edged with kerosene,

tricycles and shovels in the yard
where the septic tank makes a fairy ring;
a wire gate leads into standing wheat,
cream weatherboard overlaps everything –

and on the wheatless side, storm-blue
plaques curl off the spotted-gum trees
which, in new mayonnaise trunks, stand over
a wheelbarrow on its hands and knees.


## BARRENJOEY

Along Sydney's upraised finger
diced suburbs mass and hide
in bush, or under brilliant towels
that swirl – or brace and glide
man-hung out over blue horizons
that roll in on the land.
Twinned dips, with imprinted nipples
or not, cool in the sand,
and castles top odd headlands
and rarely a shark-bell rings;
loud-hailers honk French: Cardin! Croissants!
and detectives wear G-strings.

Where the poet Brennan wandered
the soaked steeps of his mind
now men and women warily
strike deals that can't be signed.
Where once in salt sheet-iron days
a girl might halt her filly
under posies atop cornstalks three yards high,
groves of the Gymea lily,
the northward sandstone finger, knobbed
with storms and strange injections
has beckoned Style, and Porsche windscreens
glimmer with cool deflections –

but Pittwater's still a quiver of masts
and Broken Bay in the sun
is seamed with tacking arrowheads
and that's always gone on.
Modest wealth's made a paradise garden
of that range and its green sound
so to throw sand in the evil eye
some scandal must be found.
To flesh a bone for envy's pup
now scandals must be found.


## THE INTERNATIONAL TERMINAL

Some comb oil, some blow air,
some shave trenchlines in their hair
but the common joint thump, the heart's spondee
kicks off in its rose-lit inner sea
like an echo, at first, of the one above
it on the dodgy ladder of love –
and my mate who's driving says *I never
found one yet worth staying with forever.*
In this our poems do not align.

*Surely most are if you are*, answers mine,
and I am living proof of it,
I gloom, missing you from the cornering outset –
and hearts beat mostly as if they weren't there,
rocking horse to rocking chair,
most audible dubbed on the tracks of movies
or as we approach where our special groove is
or our special fear. The autumn-vast
parking-lot-bitumen overcast
now switches on pumpkin-flower lights
all over dark green garden sites
and a wall of car-bodies, stacked by blokes,
obscures suburban signs and smokes.
Like coughs, cries, all such unlearned effects
the heartbeat has no dialects
but what this or anything may mean
depends on what poem we're living in.
Now a jet engine, huge child of a gun,
shudders with haze and begins to run.
Over Mount Fuji and the North Pole
I'm bound for Europe in a reading role
and a poem long ago that was coming for me
had Fuji-san as its axle-tree.
Cities shower and rattle over the gates
as I enter that limbo between states
but I think of the heart swarmed round by poems
like an egg besieged by chromosomes
and how out of that our world is bred
through the back of a mirror, with clouds in its head
– and airborne, with a bang, this five-hundred-seat
theatre folds up its ponderous feet.


## GRANITE COUNTRY

Out above the level
in enormous room
beyond the diagram fences
eggs of the granite loom.

In droughts' midday hum,
at the crack of winter,
horizons of the tableland
are hatched out of them

and that levelling forces
all the more to rise
past swamp, or thumbwhorled ploughing,
tor, shellback, cranium

in unended cold eruption.
Forces and strains of granite
ascended from a kingdom
abandon over centuries

their craft on the sky-rim,
sprung and lichened hatches,
as, through gaps in silence, what
made itself granite goes home.


## THE OCEAN BATHS

Chinning the bar or Thirties concrete rim
of this ocean baths as the surf flings velleities of spray
brimming the bright screen
I am in not the sea but the sea's television.

As the one starfish below me quivers up
through a fictive kelp of diffraction, I'm thinking of workers
who made pool-cementing last, neap tide by neap,
right through the Depression,

then went to the war, the one that fathered the Bomb
which relegated war to the lurid antique new nations
of emerging television. All those appalling horizontals
to be made vertical and kept the size of a screen –

I duck out of focus
down chill slub walls in this loud kinking room
that still echoes *Fung blunger* the swearwords *Orh you Kongs*
of men on relief for years, trapping ocean in oblongs,

and check out four hard roads tamed to a numinous
joke on it all, through being stood up side-on
and joined at their stone ends by bumper-smokers who could,
just by looking up, see out of relegation –

here the sky, the size of a mirror, the size of a fix
becomes imperative: I explode up through it beneath
a whole flowering height of villas and chlorine tiled pools
where some men still swear hard
to keep faith with their fathers
who are obsolete and sacred.


## THREE LAST STANZAS

That's the choice: most
as failures and tools
or an untrustworthy host
of immortal souls.

      o

The owl who eats living
mice in the gloom
is still in the long
rehearsals for your freedom.

      o

Absolutely anything
is absolute to those
who see the poem in it.
Relegation is prose.

# MIRROR-GLASS SKYSCRAPERS

Jade suits pitched frameless up the sky
drift all day with sheer weather,
annexed cubes ascend and blend
at chisel points away high
on talc-green scintillant towers,

diurnal float-glass apparitions:
through their aspects airliners flow,
their decoration's anything that happens.
Even their height above suburb
is reflected. Perfect borrowers' rococo!

Outside, squared, has finally gone in,
closed over like steadying water,
to quote storms, to entertain strapped gondolas
and loose giants swimming in contour.
Inside yearning out isn't seen;

work's turned its back on sweat brilliantly –
but when they start to loom, these towers
disappear. Dusk's lightswitches reveal
yellow Business branching kilotall
and haloed with stellar geometry.


# THE LIEUTENANT OF HORSE ARTILLERY

Full tilt for my Emperor and King, I
galloped down the moonlit roads of Hungary
past poplar after Lombardy poplar tree
in our dear multicultural Empi-

re alas! on a horse I didn't know
had been requisitioned from a circus. Without fail
he leaped every tree-shadow lying like a fox's tail
over the road, O despite whip, despite Whoa!

unswerving, he hurdled them. My leather shako jerked,
my holster slapped my hip, my despatch case too,
every leap! I was clubbed black and blue
inside my tight trousers. So many shadows lurked

to make him soar and me cry out, taking wing
every fifty metres the length of a desperate ride
for my Emperor and King, as our Empire died
with its dream of happy cultures dancing in a ring.


## DOG FOX FIELD

*The test for feeblemindedness was, they had to make up a sentence using the
words* dog, fox *and* field.

— *Judgement at Nuremberg*

These were no leaders, but they were first
into the dark on Dog Fox Field:

Anna who rocked her head, and Paul
who grew big and yet giggled small,

Irma who looked Chinese, and Hans
who knew his world as a fox knows a field.

Hunted with needles, exposed, unfed,
this time in their thousands they bore sad cuts

for having gaped, and shuffled, and failed
to field the lore of prey and hound

they then had to thump and cry in the vans
that ran while stopped in Dog Fox Field.

Our sentries, whose holocaust does not end,
they show us when we cross into Dog Fox Field.

# HASTINGS RIVER CRUISE

I.M. RUTH AND HARRY LISTON, D. PORT MACQUARIE 1826

Getting under way in that friendly suburb of balconies
we were invited to imagine up to thirty woollen ships
and timber ships and beef ships with fattening sails
along the one-time quay. Then down Heaven-blued
olive water of the estuary, we saw how ocean's crystal
penned up riverine tinctures. On our coast, every river
is a lake, for lack of force, and lives within its colour bar.

Upstream, past the bullock-faced and windjammer-ballasted shore
we passed where men in canary flannel were worked barefoot
on oystershells in shark tides. No one's walked in Australia
since, for pride and sympathy. Sheds lay offshore, pegged to the water
and lascivious oysters, though they are nearly all tongue
didn't talk drink, on their racks of phlegm, but lived it.
Opposite lay the acre where Queensland was first planted

as the pineapple of cropped heads in hot need of sugar walls.
There too, by that defiance, were speedboat mansions up canals
and no prescriptive ulcers or divorces apparent in them
though one, built late in life perhaps, spilled grapefruit down its lawns.
And the river curved on, and a navy-backed elephant stood
in the mountains for mission boys who stepped right up, through the drum,
and belted blue eyes into red-leather Kingdom Come.

At the highway bridge, in sight of plateaux, we turned back
and since the shore of the present was revetments and raw brick
or else flood-toppled trees with mullet for foliage, I looked
over at the shore of the past. Rusty paddocks, with out-of-date palms,
punt ramps where De Sotos crossed; there, in houses patched with tan,
breezeways wound to green bedrooms with framed words like He Moaneth,
the sort of country I might traverse during death.

Returning downstream, over the Regatta Ground's liquid tiling,
we passed through the place where, meeting his only sister
in a new draft to the Port, the tugged escapee snatched the musket
of a redcoat captor, aimed and shot her dead –
and was saluted for it, as he strangled, by the Commandant.
In sight of new motels, this opposite potential stayed defined
and made the current town look remote, and precarious, and kind.


## GUN-E-DARR

The red serpent of cattle, that eclipsed the old dreaming serpents,
there it still is, the first stock route, winding out of far lilac ranges
onto the grassed sea-floor of the plain. The shortest distance
between two points being, in life, the serpentine,
it was dissimulation to have angled it to a crankshaft
of official roads. I see it now, smoking high and raw with dust
as it curved and lengthened in its first days. And if taking
the continent was no walkover, then there were brave men
on both sides, amid the bellowing, the scattering whipcrack undulations
and sleepy flooding onward of the blood-red cattle serpent,
destroyer of sacred dance circles, and equally of little hoed farms.


## WORDS OF THE GLASSBLOWERS

In a tacky glass-foundry yard, that is shadowy and bright
as an old painter's sweater stiffening with light,

another lorry chockablock with bottles gets the raised thumb
and there hoists up a wave like flashbulbs feverish in a stadium

before all mass, nosedive and ditch, colour showering to grit,
starrily, mutually, becoming the crush called cullet

which is fired up again, by a thousand degrees, to a mucilage
and brings these reddened spearmen bantering on stage.

Each fishes up a blob, smoke-sallow with a tinge of beer
which begins, at a breath, to distil from weighty to clear

and, spinning, is inflated to a word: the paraison
to be marvered on iron, box-moulded, or whispered to while spun –

*Sand, sauce-bottle, hourglass – we melt them into one thing:*
*that old Egyptian syrup, that tightens as we teach it to sing.*


## HIGH SUGAR

Honey gave sweetness
to Athens and Rome,
and later, when splendour
might rise nearer home,

sweetness was still honey
since, pious or lax,
every cloister had its apiary
for honey and wax

but when kings and new doctrines
drained those deep hives
then millions of people
were shipped from their lives

to grow the high sugar
from which were refined
frigates, perukes, human races
and the liberal mind.

## LEVITIES OF THE SHORT GIANT

Afternoon, and the Short Giant takes his siesta
on a threadbare ruby sofa which, being shorter than he,
curves him into the half moon or slice-of-pawpaw position,
hull down, like a deep-timbered merchantman, with both hands on deck,
his stubbed head for poop and lantern, and at the bow
twin figureheads: bare feet with soles the earthen green
of seed potatoes, rimmed with old paintings' craquelure.
Massive mosquito-scabbed legs slope down into dungaree;
asleep in his own arms, he makes odd espresso noises.

This man, who warms cold ground by lying on it, who hand-parks his car,
who knows in his shoulders crab from scissors from flying mare
is most of all the man who attaches the thick wheels
and coins of weight, the bronzes and black steels,
and hoists (tingling) them, from knees to arrh! collarbone to full
extension overhead, the left and the right, bending his milled bar
– I breathe them up, shutting my thighs, and those fat ladies sing
to crack my spine's teeth. O but when I drop them, they ding
the stage hollow, jolt gravity itself, and chuck me in the air.


## ON REMOVING SPIDERWEB

Like summer silk its denier
but stickily, o ickilier,
miffed bunny-blinder, silver tar,
gesticuli-gesticular,
crepe when cobbed, crap when rubbed,
stretchily adhere-and-there
and everyway, nap-snarled or sleek,
glibly hubbed with grots to tweak:
ehh weakly bobbined tae yer neb,
spit it Phuoc Tuy! filthy web!

# THE ASSIMILATION OF BACKGROUND

Driving on that wide jute-coloured country
we came at last to the station,
its homestead with lawn and steel awnings
like a fortress against the sun.
And when we knocked, no people answered;
only a black dog came politely
and accompanied us round the verandahs
as we peered into rooms, and called brightly
Anyone home? The billiard room,
shadowed dining room, gauze-tabled kitchen
gave no answer. Cricket bats, ancient
steamer trunks, the chugging coolroom engine
disregarded us. Only the dog's very patient
claws ticked with us out of the gloom
to the grounds' muffling dust, to the machine shed
black with oil and bolts, with the welder
mantis-like on its cylinder of clocks
and then to the stallion's enclosure.
The great bay horse came up to the wire,
gold flares shifting on his muscles, and stood
as one ungelded in a thousand
of his race, but imprisoned for his sex,
a gene-transmitting engine, looking at us
gravely as a spirit, out between
his brain's potent programmes. Then a heifer,
Durham-roan, but with Brahman hump and rings
around her eyes, came and stood among us
and a dressy goat in sable and brushed fawn
ogled us for offerings beyond
the news all had swiftly gathered from us
in silence, and could, it seemed, accept.
We had been received, and no one grew impatient
but only the dog, host-like, walked with us
back to our car. The lawn-watering sprays
ticked over, and over. And we saw
that out on that bare, crusted country
background and foreground had merged;
nothing that existed there was background.

330

## ARAUCARIA BIDWILLI

Big leaves of the native tamarind,
vein-gathered, spread coppery black-green.

Finger-bone beads, refreshing, sour-sweet,
are the amber berries of the native tamarind.

Nearby to far up kink invisibly winging
calls, above vine-strung palisade tracks

and over steep gullies, on the ringing mountain:
stupendous, racial green, the first crosstreed soaring

allosaur-skinned primeval pines, their shrapnel
cones dizzying above gullies, on the rayed mould mountain,

lanterns of fitted flour, that can drop to kill
on once-sacred gullies, along the two-peaked mountain.

These are the trees that teach me again
every tradition is a choke on metaphor

yet the limits to likeness don't imprison its ends,
climbing above gullies, through mote-drift on the mountain.


## SPRING

A window glimmering in wheeltracked clay
and someone skipping on the windowsill;
spins of her skipping-rope widen away.
She is dancing light and water
out of the cold side of the hill
and I've brought rhyme to meet her;
rhyme has been ill.

## ACCORDION MUSIC

A backstrapped family Bible that consoles virtue and sin,
for it opens top and bottom, and harps both out and in:

it shuffles a deep pack of cards, flirts an inverted fan
and stretches to a shelf of books about the pain of man.

It can play the sob in Jesus!, the cavernous *baastards* note,
it can wheedle you for cigarettes or drop a breathy quote:

it can conjure Paris up, or home, unclench a chinstrap jaw
but it never sang for a nob's baton, or lured the boys to war.

Underneath the lone streetlight outside a crossroads hall
where bullocks pass and dead girls waltz and mental gum trees fall

two brothers play their plough-rein days and long gone spoon-licked
    nights.
The fiddle stitching through this quilt lifts up in singing flights,

the other's mourning, meaning tune goes arching up and down
as life undulates like a heavy snake through the rocked accordion.


## EXPERIENTIAL

Rubbish! As the twig is bent the tree does not grow, at all.
In fact, on the high side of the bend small new twigs appear
and the strongest becomes a new trunk, and restores the vertical.


## THE GREENHOUSE VANITY

Sea-perch over paddocks. Dunes. Salt light everywhere low down
just like the increasing gleam between Bass Strait hills
nine thousand years ago. In an offshore crumbling town
the Folk Museum moans of a stormy night, and shrills:

You made the oceans rise! Nonsense, it was you!
The Pioneers Room and Recent Times are quarrelling.
By day the flannelled drone: up at daylight, lard and tea,
axe and crosscut till black dark, once I shot a ding-

o at the cradle, there at fifteen, the only white woman
ploughing by hand, parrot pie, we sewed our own music –
Recent Times blink and hum; one bends to B-cup a pair,
each point the rouge inside a kiss; one boosts the tape-deck:

> Hey launder your earnings with a Green gig: show you care!
> > Rock millionaire,
> When every city's Venice we'll all go to Venus, yeah!
> > Smoke green shit there

– till coal conveyors rattle and mile-high smokestacks pant
Beige! Beige! on every viewscreen. This should re-float your Hardships,
despoiler, black-shooter! – Nature's caught up with you, Trendywank! –
So. We changed the weather. – Yep. Humans. We made and unmade
  the maps.


## SLIP

*This week, one third of Australia is under water.*
                    – *Sydney newspaper report, 9 April 1989*

Over the terra cotta
speeds a mirrored sun
on bare and bush-mossed water
as a helicopter's stutter
signals a stock-feed run,

and cubic fodder-bombs splash
open on sodden islands
in their yolk of orange squash,
tugging out each mud galosh,
sheep climb those twenty-inch highlands,

and vehicles at a miles-wide rushing
break in the human map
stare mesmerised at the whooshing
pencil strokes that kink where a crushing
car rolls, and turns on like a tap.

A realised mirage reaches
into tack-sheds and yards
and laps undreamed-of beaches
wadded with shock-tranced creatures.
Millennia of red-walled clouds

have left the creekbeds unable
to let the spreading glaze
spill off the water table,
though here and there a cable
braids light between crumbling cays.

Hand-milling tobacco, each dent
in his bronze oilskin adrip,
the scraped owner surveys the extent
of death-slog when the red-ware continent
glistens next week in its slip,

and when all the shapes and shallows
of inland ocean turn grass
and scarlets and purples and yellows,
when lizards eat clouds in jammed hollows
and horizons turn back into glass.


# AIRCRAFT STRESSED-SKIN BLOWOUT MID-PACIFIC

(UNITED AIRLINES FLIGHT 811)

The miles-high bubble civility
ruptured, and instantly the tear
stormed with a jetlike volatility
of baggage shoes people into air

darkly white and shrilling as the pole
that every unbuckled thing was whirling to.
Windmilling toward seats already nowhere
a member of the cabin crew
was going with the West out the hole
when legs in a scissor lock around her
and male hands in her clothes before the blue
absolute mastered it, raped her of fall
then, under restored equal pressure,
gestured in a tear-halo with joking humility.


## ARIEL

Upward, cheeping, on huddling wings,
these small brown mynas have gained
a keener height than their kind ever sustained
but whichever of them fails first
falls to the hawk circling under
who drove them up.
Nothing's free when it is explained.


## POLITICS AND ART

Brutal policy,
like inferior art, knows
whose fault it all is.


## MAJOR SPARRFELT'S TRAJECTORY

*Öland, Southern Baltic, 1 June 1676*

Our ship was a rope-towered town
built inside its own wall;
carved Romans, niches, mantlings in gilt
made its stern a palace, a Popish cathedral.

335

That day as we joined battle
my sword swung so wide with the tilt
our mighty *Crown* assumed, turning
that my crossed right hand missed its hilt

as from lidded and horsecollar ports
the ponderous ship's cannon ran back:
shrieks mingled with bronze thunder below
– all life then split upward with the crack

of glare that stripped my rational mind
and left me in the one mind of animals.
I flew above crosstrees, over lightning-defined
tangling and clubbed recoil of ships,

every cannon-hit a tube of mortal screams
burrowed deep in a closing gun-wall;
soldiers' massed steel heads bent to muskets
thick as cart-shafts, which squirted a blue pall.

Swordsmen, blood-seekers, crisscrossed everywhere,
letting some from one, from another all,
blood of men, as of fowls and beasts; these *pompiers*
*funèbres* in their leaping Aztec skill

were true limbs of perpetual motion.
Remembrance never touched me, overhead,
angel to fragments, that I too was such a one.
Removed, I watched as from the dead,

orbiting the royal park of mastheads
like a soul through war's updraft of souls,
above where men flared flintlocks intently,
flung, plunged, hung seeping in cloth scrolls

above a chipped sea of continual white tussocks,
of drifting fires, collapsed floats, drinking men,
Swedish blue, Danish red – a cloud-wide bolster
of foresail canvas caught me then

and I slid, grabbed, tumbled to the deck
of our own king's frigate *Draken*.
By a singular grace of the Almighty
lifted out of death by the rays of detonation,

I lived fifty-four more years, fought the Tsar,
saw great-grandchildren, was Münchhausen's uncle, governed Gotland,
but never attained the disembodying era
of television, that I'd foreshadowed. Yet in my life of command

a similar vantage of death would never leave me.
Red health and fierce moustaches
still served their turn, and were true
in the world of acts, but no longer could deceive me;

as a smiling woman said once: Colonel, you
I imagine saying *I'll miss me when I'm gone.*
I partly have, but there's true foretaste and gain
in times even fear's tight wig does not stay on.


## A TORTURER'S APPRENTICESHIP

Those years trapped in a middling cream town
where full-grown children hold clear views
and can tell from his neck he's really barefoot
though each day he endures shoes,

he's what their parents escaped, the legend
of dogchained babies on Starve Gut Creek;
be friends with him and you will never
be shaved or uplifted, cool or chic.

He blusters shyly – poverty can't afford instincts.
Nothing protects him, and no one.
He must be suppressed, for modernity,
for youth, for speed, for sexual fun.

Also, believing as tacitly as he
that only dim Godly joys are equal
while the competitive, the exclusive
class pleasures are imperative evil

they see him as a nascent devil,
wings festering to life in his weekly shirt,
and daily go for the fist-and-finger
hung at the arch of keenest hurt.

Slim revenge of sorority. He must shoot birds,
discard the love myth and search for clues.
But for the blood-starred barefoot spoor
he found, this one might have made dark news.


## THE BALLAD OF THE BARBED WIRE OCEAN

No more rice pudding. Pink coupons for Plume. Smokes under the lap
    for aunts.
Four running black boots beside a red sun. Flash wireless words like
    Advarnce.
When the ocean was wrapped in barbed wire, terror radiant up the
    night sky,
exhilaration raced flat out in squadrons; Mum's friends took off sun-hats
    to cry.

Starting south of the then world with new showground rifles being
    screamed at and shown
for a giggle-suit three feeds a day and no more plans of your own,
it went with some swagger till God bless you, Tom! and Daddy come back!
    at the train
or a hoot up the gangways for all the girls and soon the coast fading
    in rain,

but then it was flared screams from blood-bundles whipped rolling as
    iron bombs keened down
and the insect-eyed bombers burned their crews alive in off-register
    henna and brown.
In steep ruins of rainforest pre-affluent thousands ape-scuttling mixed
    sewage with blood
and fear and the poem played vodka to morals, fear jolting to the mouth
    like cud.

It was sleep atop supplies, it was pickhandle, it was coming against the
    wall in tears,
sometimes it was factory banter, stoking jerked breechblocks and filing
    souvenirs,
or miles-wide humming cattleyards of humans, or oiled ship-fires
    slanting in ice,
rag-wearers burst as by huge War Bonds coins, girls' mouths full of
    living rice.

No one came home from it. Phantoms smoked two hundred daily.
    Ghosts held civilians at bay,
since war turns beyond strut and adventure to keeping what you've
    learned, and shown,
what you've approved, and what you've done, from ever reaching
    your own.
This is died for. And nihil and nonsense feed on it day after day.


MIDNIGHT LAKE

Little boy blue, four hours till dawn.
Your bed's a cement bag, your plastic is torn.

Your breakfast was tap water, dinner was sleep;
you are the faith your olds couldn't keep.

In your bunny rug room there were toys on the floor
but nothing is obvious when people get poor

and newspaper crackles next to your skin.
You're a newspaper fairytale now, Tommy Thin,

a postnatal abortion, slick outer space thing,
you run like a pinball BING! smack crack BING!

then, strung out and spotty, you wriggle and sigh
and kiss all the fellows and make them all die.


## ANTARCTICA

Beyond the human flat earths
which, policed by warm language, wreathe
in fog the limits of the world,
far out in space you can breathe

the planet revolves in a cold book.
It turns one numb white page a year.
Round this in shattering billions spread
ruins of a Ptolemaic sphere,

and brittle-beard reciters bore
out time in adamant hoar rods
to freight where it's growing short,
childless absolutes shrieking the odds.

Most modern of the Great South Lands,
her storm-blown powder whited wigs
as wit of the New Contempt chilled her.
The first spacefarers worked her rope rigs

in horizontal liftoff, when to climb
the high Pole was officer class.
Total prehuman pavement, extending
beyond every roof-brink of crevasse:

Sterility Park, ringed by sheathed animals.
Singing spiritoso their tongueless keens
musselled carollers fly under the world.
Deeper out, our star's gale folds and greens.

Blue miles above the first flowered hills
towers the true Flood, as it was,
as it is, at the crux of global lattice,
and long-shod humans, risking diamond there,
propitiate it with known laws and our wickedness.


## DISTINGUO

Prose is Protestant-agnostic,
story, discussion, significance,
but poetry is Catholic:
poetry is presence.


## THE PAST EVER PRESENT

Love is always an awarded thing
but some are no winners, of no awarding class.
Each is a song that they themselves can't sing.

For months of sundays, singlehanded under iron, with the flies,
they used to be safe from that dizzying small-town sex
whose ridicule brought a shamed evasion to their eyes.

Disdaining the relegated as themselves, they eyed the vividest
for whom inept gentleness without prestige was *slow*.
Pity even the best, then, when they're made second best.

Consider the self-sentenced who heel the earth round with shy feet
and the wallflower who weeps not from her eyes but her palms
and those who don't master the patter, or whom the codes defeat.

If love is always an awarded thing
some have cursed the judging and screamed off down old roads
and all that they killed were the song they couldn't sing.

# LIKE THE JOY AT HIS FIRST LIE

Paradises of limitation, charm
of perpetual doughy innocence –
how quickly the reality
scrubs such stuff from mind.
Today, at eleven and a half,
he made his first purchase:
forty cents, for two biscuits, no change
but a giant step into mankind.


# BLUE ROAN

FOR PHILIP HODGINS

As usual up the Giro mountain
dozers were shifting the road about
but the big blue ranges looked permanent
and the stinging-trees held no hint of drought.

All the high drill and blanket ridges
were dusty for want of winter rains
but down in the creases of picnic oak
brown water moved like handled chains.

Steak-red Herefords, edged like steaks
with that creamy fat the health trade bars
nudged, feeding, settling who'd get horned
and who'd horn, in the Wingham abattoirs

and men who remembered droughttime grass
like three days' growth on a stark red face
described farms on the creeks, fruit trees and fun
and how they bought out each little place.

Where farm families once would come just to watch
men knock off work, on the Bulliac line,
the fear of helplessness still burned live brush.
Dirty white smoke sent up its scattered sign

and in at the races and out at home
the pump of morale was primed and bled:
'Poor Harry in the street, beer running out his eyes,'
as the cousin who married the baker said.


## THE ROAD TOLL

FOR THOSE MOST RECENTLY SLAUGHTERED ON THE ROADS

Toll. You are part of the toll
government causes, and harps on, and exacts
as more toll. The word means both death and taxes.

Trains are government, so they don't pay, toll. Trucks pay
and pay, and pay. Speed narrows the wrecked highway
as fines, based on the death toll, are increased continually.

So you justify, and your stretchers drip, the toll
we must pay for the juggernaut Government,
for every Crown careerist's inner greasy pole,
for the logic of swift movement –

It's crocodile tears, toll, except from those who loved you.
Your death taps us for revenue. You were driving on the railway
and we'll all be fined for it. You were a tin boat on the sea
and a ship ran over you. A fleeing merchantman, toll.


## AN ERA

The poor were fat and the rich were lean.
Nearly all could preach, very few could sing.
The fashionable were all one age, and to them
a church picnic was the very worst thing.

# THE GAELIC LONG TUNES

On Sabbath days, on circuit days,
the Free Church assembled from boats and gigs
and between sermons they would tauten
and, exercising all they allowed of art,
haul on the long lines of the Psalms.

The seated precentor, touching text,
would start alone, lifting up his whale-long tune
and at the right quaver, the rest set sail
after him, swaying, through eerie and lorn.
No unison of breaths-in gapped their sound.

In disdain of all theatrics, they raised
straight ahead, from plank rows, their beatless God-paean,
their giving like enduring. And in rise
and undulation, in Earth-conquest mourned
as loss, all tragedy drowned, and that weird
music impelled them, singing, like solar wind.


# WAGTAIL

Willy Wagtail
sings at night
black and white
Oz nightingale
    picks spiders off wall
    nest-fur and eyesocket
    ticks off cows
    cattle love that
Busy daylong
eating small species
makes little faeces
and a great wealth of song
    Will and Willa Wagtail
    indistinguishable
    switchers, whizzers
    drinkers out of scissors

weave a tiny unit
    kids clemming in it
Piping in tizzes
two fight off one
even one eagle
    little gun swingers
    rivertop ringers
    one-name-for-all
    whose lives flow by heart
    beyond the liver
    into lives of a feather
Wag it here, Willy
pretty it there
flicker and whirr –
if you weren't human
how many would care?


## SANDSTONE COUNTRY

Bush and orchard forelands stop sheer
with stencilled hands under mossed cliff eaves
and buried rain peeing far down off balconies
stains ink-dark and slows into leaves.

Bleached rusting country, where waterfalls
reanimate froth and stripped-out cars
in hills being cleft for shopping malls.
If sex and help never dawned on Mars

maybe they're unique, and yet to spread
and Sun and Moon and barren stars
revolve round the scrub Earth after all,
pale handprints climbing an old smoked wall.

# MANNERS OF THE SUPRANATION

Along our hills, before the first star
arises the glow of Meruka,
the clearer, brighter, more focused nation
we enter to rest from contemplation.

There songs are for watching, and sexy as war
and truth is what there is footage for.
Most death is by contract, though. And people kiss a lot
but reproduce by zoom and gunshot.

Night and Day are lighting terms. There are no cycles.
Seasons and epochs there are locales.
Breasts and faces are matte. Chests and horses shine
and everything spoken is a line,

and actorly spoken – though in sport, men, not women
may talk like blokes. The lit bowl all swim in
streams fact, the shortest urban myth:
cholesterol, radon, IQ, coprolith.

Square-muscled as chocolate bars, sirens give tongue
but their fountain of youth is just for the young.
The authentic, from hoeing dry earth to raise rent,
stare into the wash cycle where their children went.

Very few are fat there; all are reduced;
poverty looks applied when it is produced.
The red neck, in country that never gets dark,
is curbed by young nobles from the National Park.

Labour's dim-sacred, business sinister, trade sly:
the only chic enterprise is private eye.
There the one book in everyone is filmed and on show
but its strange truths are trimmed to what viewers may know;

in spy series, the knowing may rise to despair
which is noblest and deadliest, above savoir faire.
Also Meruka loves animals, but hers have no smell
so those in the animal world can't tell,

but ads shine through satire like poems through critique
and to win on the replay is mortal technique
as, name-starred, the monolith from 2001
lies half sunk at right angles in Washington.

Meruka, death's babysitter, hearth fire of cool
the ads are in Hamlet and he's in Play School:
now you're First. Second's us, where we glance or lie curled,
and where anything still happens, that is the Third World.


KIMBERLEY BRIEF

With modern transport, everywhere you go
the whole world is an archipelago,
each place an island in a void of travel.
In our case, cloud obscured the continent's whole gravel
of infinite dot-painting, as we overflew zones and degrees
toward the great island of the Kimberleys.
It was dusk when we slanted into Broome
to be checked in, each with a bungalow for a room.

Town of bougainvillea, of turmeric dust, of tin
geometric solids that people run tourist shops in,
of pastels and lattice, of ghosts with dented heads
and porthole eyes, whose boats recline on beds
of tidal concentrate, to resurrect, if ever, when aquamarine
re-engorges the mangroves, the raw Romance has been,
where a recent Shire President was Mr Kimberley Male
and pearls shower upward through shops like inverse hail.

In that town restrained from lovingly demolishing its past
I saw fewer brown faces than when I'd been there last,
Malay Afghans, Chinese Aborigines, or Philippine Celts,
and Euro Australians, with hind paws stuck in their belts
and a bumless tail dressed as two moleskin legs from there down
must have hopped to Derby for the races, or moved out of town,
but the sun off Cable Beach, entering the ocean's hold
ran its broad cable hot with incoming traffic of gold.

Deeper levels were anchored with many-fathomed ropes
knotted with old murder and world-be-my-oyster hopes;
jerseyed grandsons of the neck-chained took marks, or kicked a goal
while a great painter of theirs sat in jail for jumping parole
and it was dry months till some mouthless cave-coloured one
would don cloudy low-pressure dress and dance a cyclone –
Why tell this in verse? For travelling, your reasons can be
the prosiest prose. As a tourist, though, you come for the poetry.

Slot-car racing in a groove deep-cut by a grader through dust
I asked my mate *'This low bush we're in, this pubic forest:*
*is it all picture, or all detail?' 'You could die in it, resolving that.'*
Our bus seemed to climb all day, the land was so flat.
The Kimberley was once mooted as a National Home for the Jews,
in the late Thirties. Even then, they felt constrained to refuse.
In Palestine were their Dreamings, in Vilna and Krakow their roots.
Midmorning, then, we came to an Aboriginal kibbutz,

with real children, barefoot ones. The square we weren't to stray from
contained a mud-brick church we hated to come away from,
since inside were Mosaic scale-armour and celestial wicket gates,
the table of God, His kitchen, His dresser of plates
each a lucent pearl shell; above that, His concrete city, rose-pearled
with all the arch-shells' mundane sides facing out of the world
and their lustre cupped our way. And over all, full span,
hung the Reader among characters: God, sacrificed to man.

The Stations had been painted by Sisters from Mainz and Bavaria,
the sort who seized children to educate and ran hands-on leprosaria
when leprosy was AIDS, but less pitied. The Carpenter who
taught Oscar Wilde, and millions before him too,
that the opposite of a platitude is more likely true
moves through sheets of action that are echoing with energy, like Munch
but often stronger, till he tilts like a plank off a shed
in hue and rigour, with one arm hinged hanging, dead

and helplessly ready to stand all death on its head.
That peninsula, named for a pirate who hated the place,
had no kangaroos to stand with handcuffed paws and belly-face,
no emus, no sheep, but featureless termite men instead.
We lunched under tamarinds planted by some Macassar crew
to refresh them when harvesting the sea, as most peoples there do.
If Australia is part of Asia, as some fervently declare,
why were we never kamponged, paddied, pagoda'd from there?

It was Europe's blood-watering let Asian Australia take root.
We had sights of more sites, and bought tourist stuff as the tribute
such trips vaguely exact. I had wanted to visit Tunnel Creek
and Wolf Creek crater, where huge iron in full spacefall
treated Earth like tar; one mile-wide ripple forms a ring-wall.
Those will have to wait. Instead, our hospitable week
next saw us in Kununurra where, Israel again, the dry earth
is irrigated to supply winter vegie markets, in this case Perth.

There we cruised on a river perennially full to the brim,
that old Outback longing; we heard of Stumpy Michael, of Kim,
and where we landed to buy stuff a square-bearded crow
perturbed our spirits with its wire-prisoned frantic *Hello.*
And far trees meshed antennae along the ridgelines, like ants;
the sunset, like all the light, was factual; I felt underdreamt.
Chemicals were imprinted with catfish, spouses, cormorants –
how naturally random recording edges into contempt.

Kind people explained about Development and suicide;
which race drank indoors, and which is seen drunk outside.
The lost sounded not dissimilar, whatever their skin.
I saw no squalor. Some houses looked lived around, some in.
It was still four-wheel-drive country. Artefacts and lean beef
were the style, not muddied tractors. No pub was called the Sheaf.
Then past inverted trees and umber hills with slopes of pale cowhair
we were off to Purnúlulu, the Bungles, to camp two nights there.

En route, we were shown the creamy shitwood tree,
named long ago by stockmen, as it would be,
and near it, two such ringers, men with the remote eyes
of those who meet with scant gentleness, who live on supplies,
whose little screw horses perform superbly or get shot –
the sort who took Australia, and founded the good life we've got.
And then we reached the Bungles, a massif of roofless caves
made of rock-brittle, like brick skin after a lifetime's shaves.

Chasms munched underfoot. Long palm trees from primeval
Australia, where we live, emplumed niches near the sky
as if lowered in there by their rotors. In a retrieval
of hobohood that night, I spread my sleeping bag atop dry
grass whose merciless needled spirochaetes of seed
still infest my clothes. I, sex slave to a weed!
On the massif's other side, striped towers of profiteroles
hid chasms with similar stained flumes and limestone swallow-holes.

Over one of these quivered water-shine from a pool long void.
Gaudí palisades spoke of wet-seasons by which a near-destroyed
otherworld, that long ago was this world, is dissolving.
As we left, tourist dust was a pillar by day, revolving,
and we heard of the crazed hunter, here on human-safari some years ago
who shot several, and died riddled. Rangers told campers that although
guns were outlawed in the park, they were okay for self-protection
and an arsenal emerged: revolvers, assault rifles, a black-powder gun ...

Next day on the Dam road, unaccountable miles from water,
a snake-bird showed its prongs to two eagles planning its slaughter.
We netted it, in a jacket. Next monster to devour it was our bus.
It lay in cloth-dark, intensely alive, without fuss,
as we visited the Durack homestead on the ridge where that'd found
Ararat when their grass castle wasn't blown away, but drowned.
In one room leaned a real spear, not tourist junk, but straitly thin,
tense as if in slung flight, like the legend-shaft Windinbin.

There too hung a kite-framed headdress, coloured in concentric twine:
that's true Kimberley, and can't be bought, unless you're Lord McAlpine.
At the dam, we reimmersed the darter bird, who instantly sounded
(with no notion of cross-species help, it seemed unastounded)
and then we regarded the nine-times-Sydney-Harbour expanse
where nine tipsy Joe Lynches might embrace deep mischance
and ferry the wrecked moonlight down a diminishing spoor
of bubbles between nine Empires' chained men-o'-war –

that is, if it weren't desert water, that has not softened
its stark mountain poundage, nor summoned any arbour,
villa, folly or hamlet to make its shores less bare:
merely warnings about crocodiles, by whom you can be leather-coffined.
Our guide showed us the green Ord River in its downstream pose
and the gold kapok flower, and the veal-coloured Kimberley rose.
We learned later about diamonds and their blue clay arcana
and we heard of the scrub cattle who found someone's marijuana.

In Broome, I didn't revisit, as they're now a guidebook draw,
the headstones of Japanese who once trod the sea floor
sending its clamped crockery skywards out of floury detail
and hung nightly in shark-heaven to still their blood's crippling ale.
Every cemetery's a fleet of keels. We checked out the Zoo
with its high wired cupola, walked the catwalk in full view
of many endangered species – and beyond them, more and more
dying distinctive towns, looking up in hopes of rescue.

Land of pearl and plain, where just one man now goes for baroque
and is mostly liked for it; of seeping pink gorges and smoke,
where whites run black shops since, as my aunt found at Bunyah,
deny credit to your own poor and your world will shun you,
where great films await making, perhaps not for Southern television
(most Oz comedy dismays us, we agreed, with its terrible derision),
where bush balladry has set rock hard, with decrepitations,
as a means to silence poetry, and a finger stuck up at denigrations,

since most modern writing sounds like a war against love.
We were grateful for our week, and experiences that brought
bottom lip to top teeth, in that f that betokens thought.
The true sign of division, in that land of the boab tree,
lies perhaps between those who must produce and those who must be.
But the nacre of cloud had formed over the earth again, above,
and the rust and dents were gone that say the Kimberleys are
a splendid door ripped off the Gondwanaland car.


## EQUINOCTIAL GALES AT HAWTHORNDEN CASTLE

The tidal wind through Drummond's gorge
washed treetops coralline in its surge
and keyed every reed the house had
hid in its pink quoins overhead.
Allegedly beneath its steeps wound the deep Pict
cave where the Bruce once lay, licked,
watching a bob spider cast, time on time,
its whole self after the slant rhyme
of purchase needed to stay its transverse
then radial map of the universe
and all the tiny mixed krill that
too would jewel the king as he burst out.


## ULTIMA RATIO

TRANSLATED FROM THE GERMAN OF
FRIEDRICH GEORG JÜNGER (1945)

Like vapour, the titanic scheme
is dissipated,
everything grows rusty now
that they created.

They hoped to make their craze
the lasting Plan,
now it falls apart everywhere,
sheet steel and span.

Raw chaos lies heaped up
on wide display.
Be patient. Even the fag-ends
will crumble away.

Everything they made contained
what brought their fall
and the great burden they were
crushes them all.


## NORTH COUNTRY SUITE

White, towering, polished as an urn,
with blue-winking escort, a cabin cruiser sails
not affluent waters yet, but the coast highway
and swimming pools pass it, stacked like cake-pans.

Even at speeds where landscape is cursory
butter-works have yielded to dozer and nursery.
White volleyed trees like arrested rain
have slumped and burnt and shot green again.

Each river bridge once had a wheel-topped tower
from which a thick stone table hung:
this was when the dead ate midday dinner
and smokes were holy, and trees were rung.

Now a long bridge crosshatching smoke and river-shine
ends, and slowing cars divide.
A man at the lights does what men do alone
and children cheer him from the van alongside.

*That bed, with stirrups,* their mother relates
*when the nurse ran in, Kay was already born.*
*I was reaching down, singing out, for fear she might*
*be hanging by her cord like a little telephone!*

Textures of men on the courthouse steps
are those of car seat and packing shed
and a busy barrister floats between them
wearing a dried brain on her head.

Paddocks to sell, swamps, creeks to sell:
plateglass and gingerbread shops are tiled
with rectangles of country the colour of soldiers
that old farmers grow and realtors sell.

*You not have to leave, Mrs Newell, I bought*
*your farm, not your home.* The Polish farmer is distressed.
*My wife and I build own house. You stay for life!*
She doesn't stay. You don't. But she dies still impressed.

On furrows that once grew hansom-cab fuel
the post-employed fit formwork to their dreams;
their welcome is a finger lifted off a steering wheel
and city and wilderness are extremes.

Some never become cousins. When work died
they moved up to live on a rug-weave hillside.
They love the quiet, the birds, the sun.
There they know everything and no one.

Gathered at a dangerous crux of life
smokers stand around it, all backs, looking down.
A wobble at the centre is help with emotion.
A hollow there is two letting silence have a turn.

Children in that schoolroom, stripped of its brim,
that now teeters in low range out of the hills
were deprived into innocence by family and space.
The world is emptying as it fills,

but even at speeds where the human is cursory
grandchildren of those who left on a bursary
may see, where logs were bloodied with hand tools,
new rainforest, or truckloads of swimming pools.


## PRESENCE: TRANSLATIONS FROM
## THE NATURAL WORLD


### Bats' Ultrasound

Sleeping-bagged in a duplex wing
with fleas, in rock-cleft or building
radar bats are darkness in miniature,
their whole face one tufty crinkled ear
with weak eyes, fine teeth bared to sing.

Few are vampires. None flit through the mirror.
Where they flutter at evening's a queer
tonal hunting zone above highest C.
Insect prey at the peak of our hearing
drone re to their detailing tee:

*ah, eyrie-ire, aero hour, eh?*
*O'er our ur-area (our era aye*
*ere your raw row) we air our array,*
*err, yaw, row wry – aura our orrery,*
*our eerie ü our ray, our arrow.*

*A rare ear, our aery Yahweh.*


### Eagle Pair

We shell down on the sleeping-branch. All night
the limitless Up digests its meats of light.

The circle-winged Egg then emerging from long pink and brown
re-inverts life, and meats move or are still on the Down.

Irritably we unshell, into feathers; we lean open and rise
and magnify this meat, then that, with the eyes of our eyes.

Meat is light, it is power and Up, as we free it from load
and our mainstay, the cunningest hunter, is the human road

but all the Down is heavy and tangled. Only meat is good there
and the rebound heat ribbing up vertical rivers of air.


## Layers of Pregnancy

Under eagle worlds     each fixed in place
it is to kangaroo     all fragrant space
to feed between long feet     to hop
from short to ungrazed sweet     to stop
there whittling it     down between eyed knees
cocked to propel     away through shadow trees
as Rain the father     scented ahead through time
greens into motherhood     expels a blood-clot to climb
wet womb     to womb of fur
and implants another     in the ruby wall.


## Strangler Fig

I glory centennially slow-

ly in being Guugumbakh the

strangular fig bird-born to overgrow

the depths of this wasp-leafed stinging-tree

through muscling in molten stillness down

its spongy barrel crosslacing in overflow

even of myself as in time my luscious fat

leaves top out to adore the sun forest high

and my shade-coldest needs touch a level that

discovered as long yearned for transmutes

my wood into the crystal mode of roots

and I complete myself and mighty on

buttresses far up in combat embraces no

rotted traces to the fruiting rain surface I one.


## Two Dogs

Enchantment creek underbank pollen, are the stiff scents he makes,
hot grass rolling and rabbit-dig but only saliva chickweed.
Road pizza clay bird, hers answer him, rot-spiced good. Blady grass,
she adds, ant log in hot sunshine. Snake two sunups back. Orifice?
Orifice, he wriggles. Night fox? Night fox, with left pad wound.
Cement bag, hints his shoulder. Catmeat, boasts his tail, twice enjoyed.
Folded sapless inside me, she clenches. He retracts initial blood.
Frosty darks coming, he nuzzles. High wind rock human-free howl,
her different law. Soon. Away, away, eucalypts speeding –
Bark! I water for it. Her eyes go binocular, as in pawed
hop frog snack play. Come ploughed, she jumps, ground. Bark tractor,
white bitterhead grub and pull scarecrow. Me! assents his urine.


## Cockspur Bush

I am lived. I am died.
I was two-leafed three times, and grazed,
but then I was stemmed and multiplied,
sharp-thorned and caned, nested and raised,
earth-salt by sun-sugar. I am innerly sung
by thrushes who need fear no eyed skin thing.
Finched, ant-run, flowered, I am given the years
in now fewer berries, now more of sling
out over directions of luscious dung.
Of water the crankshaft, of gases the gears

my shape is cattle-pruned to a crown spread sprung
above the starve-gut instinct to make prairies
of everywhere. My thorns are stuck with caries
of mice and rank lizards by the butcher bird.
Inches in, baby seed-screamers get supplied.
I am lived and died in, vine-woven, multiplied.


## Lyrebird

Liar made of leaf-litter, quivering ribby in shim,
hen-sized under froufrou, chinks in a quiff display him
or her, dancing in mating time, or out. And in any order.
Tailed mimic aeon-sent to intrigue the next recorder,
I mew catbird, I saw crosscut, I howl she-dingo, I kink
forest hush distinct with bellbirds, warble magpie garble, link
cattlebell with kettle-boil; I rank ducks' cranky presidium
or simulate a triller like a rill mirrored lyrical to a rim.
I ring dim. I alter nothing. Real to real only I sing,
Gahn the crane to Gun the chainsaw, urban thing to being,
Screaming woman owl and human talk: eedieAi and uddyunnunoan.
The miming is all of I. Silent, they are a function
of wet forest, cometary lyrebirds. Their flight lifts them barely a semitone.


## Shoal

Eye-and-eye eye an eye
each. What blinks is I,
unison of the whole shoal. Thinks:
a dark idea circling by –
again the eyes' I winks.
Eye-and-eye near no eye
is no I, though gill-pulse drinks
and nervy fins spacewalk. Jinx
jets the jettisoned back into all,
tasting, each being a tongue,
vague umbrations of chemical:
this way thrilling, that way Wrong,
the pure always inimical,

compound being even the sheer thing
I suspend I in, and thrust
against, for speed and feeding,
all earblades for the eel's wave-gust
over crayfishes' unpressured beading,
for bird-dive boom, redfin's gaped gong –


## Prehistory of Air

Fish, in their every body
hold a sac of dry
freeing them from gravity
where fish go when they die.
It is the only dryness,
the first air, weird and thin –

but then my beak strikes from there
and the world turns outside-in.
I'm fishes' horror, being
crushed into dimensions,
yet from their swimming bladder
hatched dry land, sky
and the heron of prehensions.


## The Gods

There is no Reynard fox. Just foxes.
I'm the fox who scents this pole.
As a kit on gravel, I brow-arched Play? to a human.
It grabbed to kill, and gave me a soul.

We're trotting down one hen-stalk gully.
Soul can sit up inside, and be.
I halt, to keep us alive. Soul basks in
scents of shadow, sound of honey.

*Call me the lover in the dew*
*of one in his merriment of blur.*
*Fragile as the first points of a scent*
*on the mind's skin settle his weights of fur.*

*A light not of the sky attends*
*his progress down the unleaped dim –*
There's a young false-hoofed dog human coming
and the circling gunshot scent of him

eddies like sickness. I freeze, since their
ears point them, quicker than a wagtail's beak.
I must be Not for a while, *repressing*
*all but the low drum of the meek.*

*Dreams like a whistle crack the spring;*
*a scentless shape I have not been*
*threads the tall legs of deities*
*like Hand, and Colour, and Machine.*


## Cattle Ancestor

Darrambawli and all his wives, they came feeding from the south east
back in that first time. Darrambawli is a big red fellow,
terrible fierce. He scrapes up dust, singing, whirling his bullroarers
in the air: he swings them and they sing out Crack! Crack!
All the time he's mounting his women, all the time more *kulka*,
more, more, smelling their *kulka* and looking down his nose.
Kangaroo and emu mobs run from him, as he tears up their shelters,
throwing the people in the air, stamping out their fires.
Darrambawli gathers up his brothers, all making that sad cry *mar mar*:
he initiates his brothers, the Bulluktruk. They walk head down in a line
and make the big blue ranges. You hear their clinking noise in there.
Darrambawli has wives everywhere, he has to gallop back and forth,
mad for their *kulka*. You see him on the coast, and on the plains.
They're eating up the country, so the animals come to spear them:
You have to die now, you're starving us. But then Waark the crow
tells Darrambawli Your wives, they're spearing them. He is screaming,
frothing at the mouth, that's why his chest is all white nowadays.

Jerking two knives, he screams *I make new waterholes! I bring the best song!*
He makes war on all that mob, raging, dotting the whole country.
He frightens the water-snakes; they run away, they can't sit down.
The animals forget how to speak. There is only one song
for a while. Darrambawli must sing it on his own.


## Mollusc

By its nobship sailing upside down,
by its inner sexes, by the crystalline
pimplings of its skirts, by the sucked-on
lifelong kiss of its toppling motion,
by the viscose optics now extruded
now wizened instantaneously, by the
ridges grating up a food-path, by
the pop shell in its nick of dry,
by excretion, the earthworm coils, the glibbing,
by the gilt slipway, and by pointing
perhaps as far back into time as
ahead, a shore being folded interior,
by boiling on salt, by coming uncut over
a razor's edge, by hiding the Oligocene
underleaf may this and every snail sense
itself ornament the weave of presence.


## Cattle Egret

Our sleep-slow compeers, red and dun,
wade in their grazing, and whirring lives
shoal up, splintering, in skitters and dives.
Our quick beaks pincer them, one and one,
those crisps of winnow, fats of air,
the pick of chirrup – we haggle them down
full of plea, fizz, cark and stridulation,
our white plumes riffled by scads going spare.
Shadowy round us are lives that eat things dead
but life feeds our life: fight is flavour,

stinging a spice. Bodies still electric play for
my crop's gravel jitterbug. I cross with sprung tread
where dogs tugged a baa-ing calf's gut out, fold on fold.
Somewhere may be creatures that grow old.


## The Snake's Heat Organ

Earth after sun is slow burn
as eye scales darken.
                          Water's no-burn.
Smaller sunlives all dim slowly
to predawn invisibility
but self-digesters constantly glow-burn.
Their blood-coals fleet
                          glimmering as I spin
lightly over textures.
                          Passenger of my passage
I reach round upright leaf-burners, I
reach and follow under rock balances,
I gather at the drinking margin.
Across the nothing there
                          an ardency
is lapping blank, which segments serially up
beneath the coruscating braincakes
                                     into the body,
three skin-sheddings' length of no-burn negatively
coiled in a guttering chamber:
                          a fox,
it is pedalling off now,
a scintillating melon,
                     gamboge in its hull
                     round a dark seed centre
and hungry as the sun.

*Great Bole*

Needling to soil point
lengthens me solar,
my ease perpendicular
from earth's mid ion.

Health is hold fast,
infill and stretch.
Ill is salts lacking,
brittle, insect-itch.

Many leaves numb
in tosses of sear,
bark split, fluids caramelled,
humus less dear,
barrel borer-bled.

Through me planet-strain
exercised by orbits.
Then were great holding,
earth-give and rain,
air-brunt, stonewood working.

Elements water brought
and solar, outwards sharing
its all-pollen of heats
enveloped me, spiralling.

In no one cell
for I am centreless
pinked a molecule
newly, and routines

so gathered on
that I juice away all
mandibles. Florescence
suns me, bees and would-bes.
I layer. I blaze presence.

## Echidna

Crumpled in a coign I was milk-tufted with my suckling
till he prickled.
He entered the earth pouch then
and learned ant-ribbon,
the gloss we put like lightning on the brimming ones.
Life is fat is sleep. I feast life on and sleep it,
deep loveself in calm.
I awaken to spikes of food-sheathing, of mulling fertile egg,
of sun, of formic gravels,
of worms, dab hunting, of fanning under quill-ruff when budged:
all are rinds, to sleep.
Corner-footed tongue-scabbard, I am trundling doze
and wherever I put it
is exactly right. Sleep goes there.


## Yard Horse

Ripple, pond, liftoff fly. Unlid the outswallowing snorter
to switch at fly. Ripples over day's gigantic peace.
No oestrus scent, no haem, no pung of other stallion,
no frightening unsmell of sexless horses,
the unbearable pee-submissive ones who are not in instinct.
Far off blistering grass-sugars. Smoke infinitesimal in air
and, pond gone, his dense standing now would alert all mares
for herded flight. Fire crowds up-mountain swift as horses,
teeters widening down. Pond to granite to derelict
timber go the fur-textures. Large head over wire
contains faint absent tastes, sodichlor, chaff, calc.
The magnified grass is shabby in head-bowed focus, the earth
it grows from only tepidly exists, blots of shade are abyssal.
In his mind, fragments of rehearsal: lowered snaking neck
like goose-speech, to hurry mares; bounced trot-gait of menace
oncoming, with whipping headshake; poses, then digestion.
Moment to moment, his coat is a climate of mirrorings
and his body is the word for every meaning in his universe.

## The Octave of Elephants

Bull elephants, when not weeping need, wander soberly alone.
Only females congregate and talk, in a seismic baritone:

Dawn and sundown we honour you, Jehovah Brahm,
who allow us to intone our ground bass in towering calm.

Inside the itchy fur of life is the sonorous planet Stone
which we hear and speak through, depending our flugelhorn.

Winds barrel, waves shunt shore, earth moans in ever-construction
being hurried up the sky, against weight, by endless suction.

We are two species, male and female. Bulls run to our call.
We converse. They weep, and announce, but rarely talk at all.

As presence resembles everything, our bulls reflect its solitude
and we, suckling, blaring, hotly loving, reflect its motherhood.

Burnt-maize-smelling Death, who brings the collapse-sound *bum-bum*,
has embryos of us on its free limbs: four legs and a thumb.

From dusting our newborn with puffs, we assume a boggling pool
into our heads, to re-silver each other's wrinkles and be cool.


## The Masses

The masses encroach on all of bare, and grow
down every side of earth, and into shadow.
To fit more bodies, we sprout in two dimensions.
The rest of air-life is islanded in our extensions.
We thicken by upper grazing, fatten palely under dung,
we burn to spring innumerable – only water is so sprung.
Blindly we invented space from denial of height
and colonisation was the true mass movement.
Massing held water. We calmed cataclysm to green.
Short rebound of raindrops, we make of our deaths a sun screen,
of our sex we make darts, glue, drunken cities. Tied in fasces,
dead, living, still we rule. No god is bowed to like grass is.

## That Evolution Proceeds by Charity and Faith

Not bowing, but a full thrown back upreach
of desperate glorying totter took a fibre-scabbed
ravenous small lizard out to a hold on the air
beyond possibility.
                     Which every fledgeling re-attains
and exceeds, past the spills it recalls from that forebear
but soon beats down under memory, breaking out
into the sky opening
                     – though it will groggily cling
a few times yet, as if listening to the far genetic line
confirm the presented new body-idea first embraced
that noon, the epoch-lurch of it, all also still plotted there.


## Queen Butterfly

In his frenzy to use
what I am to refuse
from a belly-puff he strews
fine powder on my joins
which, filtering inside, coins
a splendour more eye-bugged than the three
deaths I have died had ever given me:
sweller than digestion, flitter than wings
or witting as selves all glitterings
in the coloured perfumes of panoply –
while the liquid rings
he is threading bend
his body at my breeding end.


## Pigs

Us all on sore cement was we.
Not warmed then with glares. Not glutting mush
under that pole the lightning's tied to.
No farrow-shit in milk to make us randy.

Us back in cool god-shit. We ate crisp.
We nosed up good rank in the tunnelled bush.
Us all fuckers then. And Big, huh? Tusked
the balls-biting dog and gutsed him wet.
Us shoved down the soft cement of rivers.
Us snored the earth hollow, filled farrow, grunted.
Never stopped growing. We sloughed, we soughed
and balked no weird till the high ridgebacks was us
with weight-buried hooves. Or bristly, with milk.
Us never knowed like slitting nor hose-biff then.
Not the terrible body-cutting screams up ahead.
The burnt water kicking. This gone-already feeling
here in no place with our heads on upside down.


## The Cows on Killing Day

All me are standing on feed. The sky is shining.

All me have just been milked. Teats all tingling still
from that dry toothless sucking by the chilly mouths
that gasp loudly in in in, and never breathe out.

All me standing on feed, move the feed inside me.
One me smells of needing the bull, that heavy urgent me,
the back-climber, who leaves me humped, straining, but light
and peaceful again, with crystalline moving inside me.

Standing on wet rock, being milked, assuages the calf-sorrow in me.
Now the me who needs mounts on me, hopping, to signal the bull.

The tractor comes trotting in its grumble; the heifer human
bounces on top of it, and cud comes with the tractor,
big rolls of tight dry feed: lucerne, clovers, buttercup, grass,
that's been bitten but never swallowed, yet is cud.
She walks up over the tractor and down it comes, roll on roll
and all me following, eating it, and dropping the good pats.

The heifer human smells of needing the bull human
and is angry. All me look nervously at her
as she chases the dog me dream of horning dead: our enemy
of the light loose tongue. Me'd jam him in his squeals.

Me, facing every way, spreading out over feed.

One me is still in the yard, the place skinned of feed.
Me, old and sore-boned, little milk in that me now,
licks at the wood. The oldest bull human is coming.

Me in the peed yard. A stick goes out from the human
and cracks, like the whip. Me shivers and falls down
with the terrible, the blood of me, coming out behind an ear.
Me, that other me, down and dreaming in the bare yard.

All me come running. It's like the Hot Part of the sky
that's hard to look at, this that now happens behind wood
in the raw yard. A shining leaf, like off the bitter gum tree
is with the human. It works in the neck of me
and the terrible floods out, swamped and frothy. All me make the Roar,
some leaping stiff-kneed, trying to horn that worst horror.
The wolf-at-the-calves is the bull human. Horn the bull human!

But the dog and the heifer human drive away all me.

Looking back, the glistening leaf is still moving.
All of dry old me is crumpled, like the hills of feed,
and a slick me like a huge calf is coming out of me.

The carrion-stinking dog, who is calf of human and wolf,
is chasing and eating little blood things the humans scatter
and all me run away, over smells, toward the sky.

## MeMeMe

Present and still present don't yet add up to time
but oscillate at dew-flash speed, at distance speed. Me me me
a shower of firetail (me me) finches into seed grass
flickers feeding (me) in drabs and red pinches of rhyme.
All present is perfect: an eye on either side
of hard scarlet nipping the sexual biscuits of plants,
their rind and luscious flour. It is a heart-rate of instants,
life with no death, only terror, no results, just prudence –
all vacuumed back up, onto low boughs, by a shift in shimmer,
present and still-present bringing steps that mute crickets' simmer.


## Puss

I permit myself to be
neither ignored nor understood.
The shivered sound you tin-belching giant cloth birds
sometimes point at me unnatures me. I'm both your sexes to you.
I tread the thin milk of sentiment
out of you, I file off your most newly-dried skins –
but electric with self-possession
I must then turn over inside my own skin to be free of you.
One passion at a time, and your dry-licking one suddenly
sickens me, till next time. I go to rehearse my killing.
I pose on long wood to groove on one crazy food-tin:
a real blood rabbit, hunched throbbing
round his knotty vegetable tube!
Aaa, the peaks of his dying, neck-bitten. The ripping hind feet
slowing to automatic. Dirt not being washed from his stare –
This loveliness scoots my body up indoor stumps, spilling smashers,
my every move paced
to the cat who is always everywhere.

## Shellback Tick

Match-head     of groins
nailhead     in fur
blank     itch     of blank
the blood     thereof
is the strength thereof is
the jellied life-breath     is O the
sweet incision     so the curdy reed
floodeth sun-hot liquor the only ichor the only
thing which existeth wholly alley-echoing
duple rhythmic feed which same of great yore turned
my back on every other thing the mothering thereof
the seed whereof in need-clotting strings
of plaque I dissolve with reagent drool
that doth stagger swelling's occult throb.
O one tap of splendour turned to me –
blank years     grass grip
sun     haggard     rain
shell to that all.


## Cell DNA

I am the singular
in free fall.
I and my doubles
carry it all:

life's slim volume
spirally bound.
It's what I'm about,
it's what I'm around.

Presence and hungers
imbue a sap mote
with the world as they spin it.
I teach it by rote

but its every command
was once a miscue
that something rose to,
Presence and freedom

re-wording, re-beading
strains on a strand
making I and I more different
than we could stand.


## Sunflowers

I am ever fresh cells who keep on knowing my name
but I converse in my myriads with the great blast Cell
who holds the centre of reality, carries it behind the cold
and on out, for converse with a continuum of adorers:

The more presence, the more apart. And the more lives circling you.
*Falling, I gathered such presence that I fused to Star, beyond all fission –*
We face our leaves and ever-successive genitals toward you.
*Presence is why we love what we cannot eat or mate with –*

We are fed from attachment and you, our futures draw weight from both,
    and droop.
*All of my detached life lives on death or sexual casings –*
The studded array of our worship struggles in the noon not to lose you.
*I pumped water to erect its turning, weighted its combs with floury oil –*

You are more intense than God, and fiercely dopey, and we adore you.
*Presence matches our speed; thus it seems not flow but all arrivals –*
We love your overbalance, your plunge into utterness – but what is
    presence?
*The beginning, mirrored everywhere. The true indictment. The end all
    through the story.*

371

## Goose to Donkey

My big friend, I bow help;
I bow Get up, big friend:
let me land-swim again beside your clicky feet,
don't sleep flat with dried wet in your holes.


## Spermaceti

I sound my sight, and flexing skeletons eddy
in our common wall. With a sonic bolt from the fragrant
chamber of my head, I burst the lives of some
and slow, backwashing them into my mouth. I lighten,
breathe, and laze below again. And peer in long low tones
over the curve of Hard to river-tasting and oil-tasting
coasts, to the grand grinding coasts of rigid air.
How the wall of our medium has a shining, pumping rim:
the withstood crush of deep flight in it, perpetual entry!
Only the holes of eyesight and breath still tie us
to the dwarf-making Air, where true sight barely functions.
The power of our wall likewise guards us from
slowness of the rock Hard, its life-powdering compaction,
from its fissures and streamy layers that we sing into sight
but are silent, fixed, disjointed in. Eyesight is a leakage
of nearby into us, and shows us the tastes of food
conformed over its spines. But our greater sight is uttered.
I sing beyond the curve of distance the living joined bones
of my song-fellows; I sound a deep volcano's valve tubes
storming whitely in black weight; I receive an island's slump,
song-scrambling ship's heartbeats, and the sheer shear of current-forms
bracketing a seamount. The wall, which running blind I demolish,
heals, prickling me with sonars. My every long shaped cry
re-establishes the world, and centres its ringing structure.

## Honey Cycle

Grisaille of gristle lights, in a high eye of cells,
ex-chrysalids being fed crystal in six-sided wells,
many sweating comb and combing it, seating it sexaplex.
The unique She sops lines of descent, in her comedown from sex
and drones are driven from honey, having given their own:
their oeuvre with her ova or not, he's re-learn the lone.
Rules never from bees but from being give us to build food
then to be stiff guards, hairtrigger for tiffs with non-Brood.
Next, grid-eyes grown to gathering rise where a headwind bolsters
hung shimmering flight, return with rich itchy holsters
and dance the nectar vector. Bristling collectors they entrance
propel off, our stings strung. And when we its advance
beyond wings, or water, light gutters in our sight-lattice
and we're eggs there again. Spent fighting-suits tighten in grass.


## The Dragon

It was almost not born.
The lioness stopped short from full
gallop, at a black apparitional
onrush of glare and jag horn
stark as day's edge on the moon.

With râles of fury she conceded
a step – the herd's meat slipped her pride,
a step – and the bull only needed
to keep sure, and encroaching, deadly-eyed,
facing her, facing her down.

The dragon was nearly not born
*but the herd's gone silence shakes me*
*to wavering, to need of more me –*
*my teeth through his tongue, he moans in me.*
*I have crushed shut his mouth bone –*

Dust torn aloft by hooves, by pads
is fanning wings over how they shorten,
twist, wrest, re-elongate the dragon,
their bubbling Stokes, their gasps Cheyne,
the snake they make has lived for chiliads.

From under like-tasselled tails, one gas
blows oppositely, in the soundless burning
blare of urinary language. Turning
on their needs, on their agony, like a windlass
tightening life and all contested goodness,

gored power draining splintered blood-froth
toward dirt death for one, or both,
the dragon spirals, straining, over eight legs to
where there never was a dragon
and all such beasts exist like God, or you.


*Animal Nativity*

The Iliad of peace began
when this girl agreed.
Now goats in trees, fish in the valley
suddenly feel vivid.

Swallows flit in the stable as if
a hatchling of their kind,
turned human, cried in the manger
showing the hunger-diamond.

Cattle are content that this calf
must come in human form.
Spiders discern a water-walker.
Even humans will sense the lamb,

He who frees from the old poem
turtle-dove and snake
who gets death forgiven
who puts the apple back.

Dogs, less enslaved but as starving
as the poorest humans there
crouch, agog at a crux of presence
remembered as a star.


## Stone Fruit

I appear from the inner world, singular and many, I am
the animals of my tree, appointed to travel and be eaten
since animals are plants' genital extensions, I'm clothed in luscious
dung but designed to elicit yet richer, I am modelled on the sun,
dry shine shedding off mottled surface but having like it a crack seed,
I am compact of laws aligned in all their directions, at behests I tip
over from law to law, I am streamy inside, taut with sugar meats, circular,
my colours are those of the sun as understood by leaf liquor cells
and cells of deep earth metal, I am dressed for eyes by the blind,
perfumed, flavoured by the mouthless, by insect-conductors who kill
and summon by turns, I'm to tell you there is a future and there are
consequences, and they are not the same, I emerge continually
from the inner world, which you can't mate with nor eat.


## Deer on the Wet Hills

As anywhere beyond the world
it is always the first day.

Smell replaces colour
for these ones, who are loved
as they are red: from within.

Bed brightening into feed,
the love stays hooves on steep.

History is unforgiveness.
Terse, as their speech would be,
food-rip gets widespread.

Tuned for stealth and sudden
ones' senses all point, chewing
uninterest as anguish flaps one wing.

Day-streak, star-cinders.
Black sky. Pale udders forming there.

Ones' nap spooned in licks
like mutual silent sentences,
bulk to mirrored bulk.

One forgets being male
right after the season.


*Raven, sotto voce*

Stalk's so unlike      every other flight, or walk
a casual so pitched      it's out of whack
with all lives around.      Its head has eyes
in the neck, in the back.      Its stick is a gun,
its mind's read from its knees.
                              This prime of lies
stills normal sound:      wing-sink, vague trot,
the closing tack      alone, in on the heat
of fellow-life      makes loosely shared flesh speak
in flashed silence, in whirrs,
                              the first pan-warmblood talk.
The gun's a stick      when eyes come out of stalk.


*Cuttlefish*

Spacefarers past living planetfall
on our ever-dive in bloom crystal:
when about our self kin selves appear,
slowing, rubber to pulp, we slack from spear,
flower anemone, re-clasp and hang, welling
while the design of play is jelling,

then enfolding space, jet
every way to posit some essential set
of life-streaks in the placeless,
or we commune parallel, rouge to cerulean
as odd proposals of shape and zip floresce
– till a jag-maw apparition
spurts us apart into vague as our colours shrink,
leaving, of our culture, an ectoplasm of ink.


## Migratory

I am the nest that comes and goes,
I am the egg that isn't now,
I am the beach, the food in sand,
the shade with shells and the shade with sticks.
I am the right feeling on washed shine,
in wing-lifting surf, in running about
beak-focused: the feeling of here, that stays
and stays, then lengthens out over
the hill of hills and the feedy sea.
I am the wrongness of here, when it
is true to fly along the feeling
the length of its great rightness, while days
burn from vast to a gold gill in the dark
to vast again, for many feeds
and floating rests, till the sun ahead
becomes the sun behind, and half
the little far days of the night are different.
Right feelings of here arrive with me:
I am the nests danced for and now,
I am the crying heads to fill,
I am the beach, the sand in food,
the shade with sticks and the double kelp shade.

## From *Where We Live on Presence*

A human is a comet streamed in language far down time; no other
living is like it. Beetlehood itself was my expression.
It was said in fluted burnish, in jaw-tools, spanned running, lidded shields
over an erectile rotor. With no lungs to huff hah! or selah!
few sixwalkers converse. Ants, admittedly, headlong flesh-mobbers,
     meeting,
hinge back work-jaws, part their food-jaws, merge mouths in communion
and taste their common being; any surplus is message and command.
Mine signal, in lone deposits; my capsule fourth life went by clues.
I mated once, escaped a spider, ate things cooked in wet fires of decay
but for the most part, was. I could not have put myself better,
with more lustre, than my presence did. I translate into segments,
     laminates,
cachou eyes, pungent chemistry, cusps. But I remain the true word for me.


## Possum's Nocturnal Day

The five-limbed Only One
in bush that bees erect as I curb glare-bringing mistletoe
can alight, parachute, on any bird's touchdown,
perch eating there,
cough scoff at other Only Ones, drop through
reality and flicker at tangents clear to its crown
but then, despite foliage,
my cool nickel daytime bleaches into light
and loses me the forest genes' infinite air of sprung holds.
My eyes all hurt branchings
I curl up in my charcoal trunk of night
and dream a welling pictureless encouragement
that tides from far but is in arrival me
and my world, since nothing is apart enough for language.

## HOME SUITE

Home is the first
and final poem
and every poem between
has this mum home seam.

Home's the weakest enemy
as iron steams starch –
but to war against home
is the longest march.

Home has no neighbours.
They are less strong
than the tree, or the sideboard.
All who come back belong.

No later first-class plane
flies the sad quilt wings.
Any feeling after final
must be home, with idyll-things.

Love may be a recent,
and liquid enough term
to penetrate and mollify
what's compact in home.


## THE FELLOW HUMAN

Beside Anchor Flour school frocks dimmed with redknuckle soaps
poverty's hardly poverty nowadays, here.
The mothers who drive up under tortoiseshell pines to the school
are neat in jeans and track tops
and have more self and presence on hand in the car.

Their four-wheeled domains are compound of doors to slam
but only their children do. Drama is private, for home.
Here, the tone is citizenly equal.
The woman with timber-grey braids and two modelled in cold-cream
chat through and minutely modulate their opening wry smile.

Another, serene, makes a sad-comic mouth beneath glasses
for her fine-necked rugby-mad boy, also in glasses,
and registers reed notes in the leatherhead birds' knotty music
who unpick a red-gold judge's wig of bloom
in the silky-oak tree above the school's two classes.

To remodel the countryside, in this post-job age of peace,
women have slept with trucks, raised houses by hammer and telephone,
plucked sopping geese and whitened them to stone,
and suddenly most sex writing seems slave-era boasting, in the face,
living mousseline, never-shaved, of the fellow human.

The ginger local woman alighting from the saddle of her van
talks to a new friend who balances a baby on one hip
and herself on the other. The two nod upwards, and laugh.
Not for heavy old reasons does the one new here go barefoot
but to be arrived, at home in this dust-warm landscape.


# THE WEDDING AT BERRICO

CHRISTINA AND JAMES, 8TH FEBRUARY 1992

To reach your watershed country
we've driven this summer's green climbs
and the creekwater film spooling over
causeways got spliced many times
with its boulders like ice under whisky,
tree pools mirrory as the eyes of horses.
Great hills above, the house *en fête*:
we've parked between soaring rhymes
and slipped in among brilliant company.

Here are your gifts. I see God's sent
all your encounters so far with him:
life. Landscape. Unfraught love. Some poetry.
Risk too, with his star rigger Freedom,
but here's poise, for whatever may come.
What's life wish you? Sound genetics, delight,
long resilience against gravity, the sight
of great-grandchildren, a joint sense of home.

Hey, all these wishes in smart boxes! Fun,
challenges, Meaning, work-satisfaction –
this must be the secular human lot: health
till high old age, children of character,
dear friendships. And the testing one: wealth.
Quietly we add ours: may you
always have each other, and want to.

Few poems I've made mention our children.
That I write at all got you dork names.
More might have brought worse. Our jealous nation...
I am awed at you, though, today,
silk restraining your briskness and gumption,
my mother's face still hauntingly in yours

and this increase, this vulnerable beauty.
James is worthy of his welcome to our family.
Never would I do, or he ask
me to do what no parental memories
could either: I won't give you away.

But now you join hands, exchanging
the vows that cost joyfully dear.
They move you to the centre of life
and us gently to the rear.

# CRANKSHAFT

Buildings, like all made things
that can't be taken back
into the creating mind,
persist as reefs of the story
which made them, and which someone
will try to drive out of fashion.

On a brown serpentine road,
cornice around a contour
into steep kikuyu country,
the Silver Farm appears
hard-edged on its scarp of green
long-ago rainforest mountain.

All its verandahs walled in,
the house, four-square to a pyramid
point, like an unhit spike head
bulks white above the road
and the dairy and cowyard
are terraced above, to let
all liquid waste good spill down
around windowless small sheds, iron
or board, alike metallised with silverfrost,
to studded orange trees, hen-coops,
wire netting smoky with peas,
perched lettuce, tomato balconies.

The story that gathers into
such pauses of shape isn't often
told to outsiders, or in words.
It might be poisoned by your hearing it,
thinking it just a story.
It is for its own characters
and is itself a character.

The Silver Farm has always been
self-sufficient, ordering little in.
Two brothers and respective wives
and children, once, live there quietly
in the one house. At dawn,
the milking done, the standing wife
knits by the roadside, watching
small spacy-eyed caramel Jersey
cows graze the heavy verges,
and the sitting wife, on a folding stool
hidden by her blanket, reads
two turns of the road further on.
Men, glimpsed above in the dairy,
flit through the python fig tree.

A syphoned dam, a mesh room –
and the Silver Farm closes
behind a steep escutcheon pasture
charged with red deer. New people:
unknown story. Past there
is where the lightning struggled
all over the night sky like bared Fact
ripping free of its embodiments, and
pronged the hillside, turning
a rider on his numbed horse
to speechless, for minutes, rubber.

Above is a shrine house, kept
in memory of deep childhood
whitewash-raw, as it always was
despite prosperity. No stories
cling to the mother, many
to the irascible yeoman heir
blown by a huff, it seems his own,
a lifetime's leap from Devonshire:
*Quiet, woman, I am master here!*

*No high school for our boys:*
*it would make them restless.*
Children of this regimen,
touchy well-informed cattlemen
and their shrine-tending sister
remember their father's pride
in knowing all of Pope by heart:
*Recited those poems till he died!*
The proper study of mankind
is weakness. If good were not
the weaker side, how would
we know to choose it?

Shrine-houses are common here,
swept on visits, held
out of time by feeling.
I leave this one's real story
up its private road, where
it abrades and is master.
I'm glad to be not much deeper
than old gossip in it. Fiction-deep.
A reverence for closed boxes is returning.
Left standing, still grouped readably
in the countryside, with trees,
they may be living communities.

How does the house of the man
who won his lands in a card game
come to have the only slate roof
in all these hills? Was it
in hopes of such arrived style
that when the cards' leadlight smile
brightened, his way, his drawl didn't
waver, under iron and tongue-and-groove?
No one knows. He attracted no yarns.
Since all stories are of law, any
about him might have rebounded,
like bad whisky, inside the beloved losers.

Keenly as I read detective fiction
I've never cared who done it.
I read it for the ambiences:
David Small reasoning rabbinically,
Jim Chee playing tapes in his tribal
patrol car to learn the Blessing Way,
or the tweed antiquaries of London,
fog from the midriff down,
discoursing with lanthorn and laudanum.

    I read it, then, for the stretches
    of presence. And to watch analysis
    and see how far author and sleuth
    can transcend that, submitting
    to the denied whole mind, and admit it,
    since the culprit's always the same:
    the poetry. Someone's poem did it.

This further hill throws another
riffle of cuttings, and a vista
sewn with fences, chinked with dams
and the shed-free, oddly placed
brick houses of the urban people
who will be stories if they stay.

    There's a house that was dying
    of moss, sun-bleach and piety –
    probate and guitar tunes revived it.
    Down the other way, seawards, dawn's way,
    a house that was long alive
    is sealed. Nailgunned shut
    since the morning after its last day.

And it was such an open house:
You stepped from the kitchen table's
cards and beer, or a meal of ingredients
in the old unmixed style, straight
off lino into the gaze of cattle
and sentimental dogs, and beloved

385

tall horses, never bet on. This was
a Turf house: that is, it bet on men.
Men sincere and dressy as detectives
who could make time itself run dead.

Gaunt posthumous wood that supported
the rind-life of trees still stands
on that property. The house is walled
in such afterlife sawn. Inside it
are the afterlives of clothes, of plates,
equestrienne blue ribbons, painted photos,
of childlessness and privacy.
Beef-dark tools and chain out in the sheds
are being pilfered back into the present.

Plaintive with those she could
make into children, and shrewd
with those she couldn't, the lady
sits beautifully, in the pride
of her underlip, shy of naming names
as that other lot, the Irish, she canters
mustering on Timoshenko with a twig of leaves.

When urban dollars were already
raining on any country acre, her husband
with the trickle of smoke to his wall eye
from his lip-screw of tobacco
sold paddocks to a couple of nephews.

The arm a truck had shattered
to a crankshaft long ago trembled,
signing. He charged a fifth of what
he could have. A family price,
and used the grazing rights,
which we had thrown in, to make sure
we didn't too greatly alter
their parents' landscape till he
and she were finished with it.

Now they, who were cool midday East
to my childhood, have moved on into
the poem that can't be read
till you yourself are in it.


## THE FAMILY FARMERS' VICTORY

FOR SALVATORE ZOFREA

White grist that turned people black,
it was the white cane sugar
fixed humans as black or white. Sugar,
first luxury of the modernising poor.

It turned slavery black to repeat it.
Black to grow sugar, white to eat it
shuffled all the tropic world. Cane sugar
would only grow in sweat of the transported.

That was the old plantation,
blackbirding ship to commissar.
White teeth decried the tyranny of sugar –
but Italian Australians finished it.

On the red farm blocks they bought
and cleared, for cane-besieged stilt houses
between rain-smoky hills on the Queensland shore,
they made the black plantation obsolete.

When they come, we still et creamed spaghetti cold, for pudding,
and we didn't want their Black Hand on our girls.
But they ploughed, burnt, lumped cane: it shimmied like a gamecock's tail.
Then the wives come out, put up with flies, heat, crocodiles, Irish clergy,
and made shopkeepers learn their lingo. Stubborn Australian shopkeepers.
*L'abito, signora, voletelo in sargia, do you?*
Serge suits in Queensland? Course. You didn't let the white side down.

Shorts, pasta, real coffee. English only at school. But sweet biscuits,
cakes, icing – we learnt all that off the British and we loved it!
Big families, aunts, cousins. You slept like a salt tongue, in gauze.
Cool was under the mango tree. Walls of cane enclosed us and fell:
sudden slant-slashed vistas, burnt bitter caramel. Our pink roads
were partings in a world of haircut. I like to go back. It's changed now.
After thirty years, even Sicilians let their daughters work in town.

> Cane work was too heavy for children
> so these had their childhoods
> as not all did, on family farms,
> before full enslavement of machines.
>
> But of grown-up hundreds on worked estate
> still only one of each sex can be adult.
> Likewise factory, and office, and concern:
> any employee's a child, in the farmer's opinion.


## A BRIEF HISTORY

We are the Australians. Our history is short.
This makes pastry chefs snotty and racehorses snort.
It makes pride a blood poppy and work an export
and bars our trained minds from original thought
as all that can be named gets renamed away.

A short history gets you imperial scorn,
maintained by hacks after the empire is gone
which shaped and exiled us, left men's bodies torn
with the lash, then with shrapnel, and taught many to be
lewd in kindness, formal in bastardry.

Some Australians would die before they said Mate,
though hand-rolled Mate is a high-class disguise –
but to have just one culture is well out of date:
it makes you Exotic, i.e. there to penetrate
or to ingest, depending on size.

Our one culture paints Dreamings, each a beautiful claim.
Far more numerous are the unspeakable Whites,
the only cause of all earthly plights,
immigrant natives without immigrant rights.
Unmixed with these are Ethnics, absolved of all blame.

All of people's Australia, its churches and lore
are gang-raped by satire self-righteous as war
and, from trawling fresh victims to set on the poor,
our mandarins now, in one more evasion
of love and themselves, declare us Asian.

Australians are like most who won't read this poem
or any, since literature turned on them
and bodiless jargons without reverie
scorn their loves as illusion and biology,
compared with bloody History, the opposite of home.


## WHERE HUMANS CAN'T LEAVE AND MUSTN'T COMPLAIN

FOR BECKI AND CLARE

Where humans can't leave and mustn't complain
there some will emerge who enjoy giving pain.

Snide universal testing leads them to each one
who will shrivel reliably, whom the rest will then shun.

Some who might have been chosen, and natural police,
do routine hurt, the catcalling, the giving no peace,

but dull brilliance evolves the betrayals and names
that sear dignity and life like interior flames.

Hormones get enlisted, and consistency rehearsed
by self-avengers and failures getting in first,

but this is the eye of fashion. Its sniggering stare
breeds silenced accomplices. Courage proves rare.

This models revolution, this draws flies to stark pools.
This is the true curriculum of schools.


## GREEN ROSE TAN

Poverty is still sacred. Christian
and political candles burn before it
for a little longer. But secretly

poverty revered is poverty outlived:
childhoods among bed-ticking midnights
blue as impetigo mixture, through the grilles,

cotton-rancid contentments of exhaustion
around Earth's first kerosene lamp
indoors out of wet root-crop fields.

Destitution's an antique. The huge-headed
are sad chaff blown by military bohemians.
Their thin metal bowls are filled or not

from the sky by deodorised descendants
of a tart-tongued womb-noticing noblesse
in the goffered hair-puddings of God's law

who pumped pioneer bouillons with a potstick,
or of dazzled human muesli poured from ships
under the milk of smoke and decades.

The mass rise into dignity and comfort
was the true modern epic, black and white
dwarfing red, on the way to green rose tan.

Green rose tan that the world is coming to,
land's colour as seen from space
and convergent human skin colour, it rises

out of that unwarlike epic, in the hours
before intellect refracts and disdains it,
of those darker and silver-skinned, for long ages

humbly, viciously poor, our ancestors,
still alive in India, in Africa, in ghettoes.
Ancestors, ours, on the kerb in meshed-glass towns.


## THE SAY-BUT-THE-WORD CENTURION
## ATTEMPTS A SUMMARY

That numinous healer who preached Saturnalia and paradox
has died a slave's death. We were manoeuvred into it by priests
and by the man himself. To complete his poem.

He was certainly dead. The pilum guaranteed it. His message,
unwritten except on his body, like anyone's, was wrapped
like a scroll and despatched to our liberated selves, the gods.

If he has now risen, as our infiltrators gibber,
he has outdone Orpheus, who went alive to the Shades.
Solitude may be stronger than embraces. Inventor of the mustard tree,

he mourned one death, perhaps all, before he reversed it.
He forgave the sick to health, disregarded the sex of the Furies
when expelling them from minds. And he never speculated.

If he is risen, all are children of a most high real God
or something even stranger called by that name
who knew to come and be punished for the world.

To have knowledge of right, after that, is to be in the wrong.
Death came through the sight of law. His people's oldest wisdom.
If death is now the birth-gate into things unsayable

in language of death's era, there will be wars about religion
as there never were about the death-ignoring Olympians.
Love, too, his new universal, so far ahead of you it has died

for you before you meet it, may seem colder than the favours of gods
who are our poems, good and bad. But there never was a bad baby.
Half of his worship will be grinding his face in the dirt

then lifting it to beg, in private. The low will rule, and curse by him.
Divine bastard, soul-usurer, eros-frightener, he is out to monopolise hatred.
Whole philosophies will be devised for their brief snubbings of him.

But regained excels kept, he taught. Thus he has done the impossible
to show us it is there. To ask it of us. It seems we are to be the poem
and live the impossible. As each time we have, with mixed cries.


## DEAD TREES IN THE DAM

Castle scaffolding tall in moat,
the dead trees in the dam
flower each morning with birds.

It can be just the three resident
cormorants with musket-hammer necks, plus
the clinician spoonbill, its long pout;

twilight's herons who were almost too lightfoot
to land; pearl galahs in pink-fronted
confederacy, each starring in its frame,

or it may be a misty candelabrum
of egrets lambent before saint Sleep –
who gutter awake and balance stiffly off.

Odd mornings, it's been all bloodflag
and rifle green: a stopped-motion shrapnel
of kingparrots. Smithereens when they freaked.

Rarely, it's wed ducks, whose children
will float among the pillars. In daytime
magpies sidestep up wood to jag pinnacles

and the big blow-in cuckoo crying
Alarm, Alarm on the wing is not let light.
This hours after dynastic charts of high

profile ibis have rowed away to beat
the paddocks. Which, however green, are
always watercolour, and on brown paper.


## ROCK MUSIC

Sex is a Nazi. The students all knew
this at your school. To it, everyone's subhuman
for parts of their lives. Some are all their lives.
You'll be one of those if these things worry you.

The beautiful Nazis, why are they so cruel?
Why, to castrate the aberrant, the original, the wounded
who might change our species and make obsolete
the true race. Which is those who never leave school.

For the truth, we are silent. For the flattering dream,
in massed farting reassurance, we spasm and scream,
but what is a Nazi but sex pitched for crowds?

It's the Calvin SS: you are what you've got
and you'll wrinkle and fawn and work after you're shot
though tears pour in secret from the hot indoor clouds.

# THE ROLLOVER

Some of us primary producers, us farmers and authors
are going round to watch them evict a banker.
It'll be sad. I hate it when the toddlers and wives
are out beside the fence, crying, and the big kids
wear that thousand-yard stare common in all refugees.
Seeing home desecrated as you lose it can do that to you.

There's the ute piled high with clothes and old debentures.
There's the faithful VDU, shot dead, still on its lead.
This fellow's dad and grandad were bankers before him, they sweated
through the old hard inspections, had years of brimming foreclosure,
but here it all ends. He'd lent three quarters and only
asked for a short extension. Six months. But you have to

line the drawer somewhere. You have to be kind to be cruel.
It's Sydney or the cash these times. Who buys the Legend of the Bank
any more? The laconic teller, the salt-of-the-earth branch accountant
it's all an Owned Boys story. Now they reckon he's grabbed a gun
and an old coin sieve and holed up in the vault, screaming
about his years of work, his identity. Queer talk from a bank-johnny!

We're catching flak, too, from a small mob of his mates,
inbred under-manager types, here to back him up. Troublemakers,
land-despoiling white trash. It'll do them no good. Their turn
is coming. They'll be rationalised themselves, made adapt
to a multinational society. There's no room in that for privileged
traditional ways of life. No land rights for bankers.

## LATE SUMMER FIRES

The paddocks shave black
with a foam of smoke that stays,
welling out of red-black wounds.

In the white of a drought
this happens. The hardcourt game.
Logs that fume are mostly cattle,

inverted, stubby. Tree stumps are kilns.
Walloped, wiped, hand-pumped,
even this day rolls over, slowly.

At dusk, a family drives sheep
out through the yellow
of the Aboriginal flag.


## CORNICHE

I work all day and hardly drink at all.
I can reach down and feel if I'm depressed.
I adore the Creator because I made myself
and a few times a week a wire jags in my chest.

The first time, I'd been coming apart all year,
weeping, incoherent; cigars had given me up;
any road round a cliff edge I'd whimper along in low gear
then: cardiac horror. Masking my pulse's calm lub-dup.

It was the victim-sickness. Adrenalin howling in my head,
the black dog was my brain. Come to drown me in my breath
was energy's black hole, depression, compère of the predawn show
when, returned from a pee, you stew and welter in your death.

The rogue space rock is on course to snuff your world,
sure. But go acute, and its oncoming fills your day.
The brave die but once? I could go a hundred times a week,
clinging to my pulse with the world's edge inches away.

Laugh, who never shrank around wizened genitals there
or killed themselves to stop dying. The blow that never falls
batters you stupid. Only gradually do
you notice a slight scorn in you for what appals.

A self inside self, cool as conscience, one to be erased
in your final night, or faxed, still knows beneath
all the mute grand opera and uncaused effect –
that death which can be imagined is not true death.

The crunch is illusion. There's still no outside world
but you start to see. You're like one enthralled by bad art –
yet for a real onset, what cover! You gibber to Casualty,
are checked, scorned, calmed. There's nothing wrong with your heart.

The terror of death is not afraid of death.
Fear, pure, is intransitive. A Hindenburg of vast rage
rots, though, above your life. See it, and you feel flogged
but like an addict you sniffle aboard, to your cage,

because you will cling to this beast as it gnaws you,
for the crystal in its kidneys, the elixir in its wings,
till your darlings are the police of an immense fatigue.
I came to the world unrehearsed but I've learned some things.

When you curl, stuffed, in the pot at rainbow's end
it is life roaring and racing and nothing you can do.
Were you really God you could have lived all the lives
that now decay into misery and cripple you.

A for adrenalin, the original A-bomb, fuel
and punishment of aspiration, the Enlightenment's air-burst.
Back when God made me, I had no script. It was better.
For all the death, we also die unrehearsed.

# SUSPENDED VESSELS

FOR JOANNA GOODING AND SIMON CURTIS

Here is too narrow and brief:
equality and justice, to be real,
require the timeless. It argues
afterlife even to name them.

I've thought this more since that morning
in barren country vast as space-time
but affluent with cars
at the fence where my tightening budget
denied me basket-room
under the haunches of a hot-air balloon

and left thirteen people in it,
all ages, teens to grans,
laughing excitedly as the dragon nozzle
exhaled hoarse blazing lift, tautening it,
till they grabbed, dragged, swayed
up, up into their hiatus.

Others were already aloft
I remember, light bulbs against the grizzled
mountain ridge and bare sky,
vertical yachts, with globe spinnakers.

More were being rigged, or offering
their gape for gusts of torch.
I must have looked away –
suddenly a cry erupted everywhere:

two, far up, lay overlapping,
corded and checked as the foresails of a ship
but tangled, and one collapsing.

I suppress in my mind
the long rag unravelling, the mixed
high voice of its spinning fall,
the dust-blast crash, the privacies
and hideous equality without justice
of those thirteen, which running helpers,
halting, must have seen
and professionals lifted out.

Instead, I look at coloured cash and plastic
and toddlerhood's vehement equities
that are never quite silenced.
Indeed, it prickles, and soon glares
if people do not voice them.


## THE WATER COLUMN

We had followed the catwalk upriver
by flowering trees and granite sheer
to the Basin park crying with peacocks.

After those, we struck human conversation.
A couple we'd thought Austrian proved to be
Cape Coloured. Wry good sense and lore

and love of their strange country
they presented us with, cheerfully.
They were eager 'to get home for the riots'.

As we talked, shoes dreamily, continually
passed above us on the horizontal chairlift.
It was Blundstones and joggers that year,

cogwheel treads with faces between them.
That was also the year I learned
the Basin was a cold crater lake:

swimmers whacking above ancient drownings –
'it's never been plumbed, in places'.
I thought of a rock tube of water

down, down levels too frigid for upwelling,
standing at last on this miles-deep
lager head, above a live steam layer

in impossible balance, facing
where there can't be water, the planet's
convecting inner abortive iron star.


## THE BENEFICIARIES

Higamus hogamus
Western intellectuals
never praise Auschwitz.
Most ungenerous. Most odd,
when they claim it's what finally
won them their centuries-
long war against God.


## THE MAENADS

Four captured a man. When he grasped what they meant to do,
he stole the one's credit card and hid it in his shoe –
by which they were traced, after their butchery and howls,
and given a housewifely twenty years folding towels.

# THE PORTRAIT HEAD

FOR JONATHAN HIRSCHFELD

How Jews may have pioneered sculpture under Pharaoh's knout:
how atheism is sometimes a greater strictness about
the Second Commandment – ideas the massed green Tuileries
heard us stroll with, amid family lore, values by Worth and fooleries,
pooped after your third session of translating my head into clay
preparatory to bronze. Not as Nature will do it someday.

Your intent travel through my features, transposing them to wet,
had half detached me from them. But I wouldn't start a new set
in that late headhunting capital. We came then to a netting-and-lath
builders' yard full of pedestals, giant jardinières, torsoed wrath,
marble nymphs acid-eaten to plaster, bare matte heroes
standing whitely to reason, or weeping into their elbows.

It was so forlorn we couldn't help grinning. Poor cracked
discards of the ambient *gloire*, removed and stacked.
Did all universals, still expounding themselves with a clenched,
didactic or flat upsloped hand, get trucked there when retrenched,
to be one with lopped heads, trophies of arms, carven terebinths?
There were no portraits in that corral of plinths.

No gargoyles either. Leaf-roofed, walled in high iron bars,
the grand dank gardens released us by a river of cars
streaming and cross-eddying, with sunk water in stanzas between.
Itching from the Shakespeare bookshop, I paused. Evolution seen
end on is creation. As often, every object seemed a case:
the great Louvre. Leash-dogs fighting. Six p.m. Back, impaled
in your studio, bulked our unbloodied milk-cocoa work face.

400

## IN PHRYGIA, BIRTHPLACE OF EMBROIDERY

When Midas, no less deserving of mercy or better for
being a king dope, had lost all faith in the gods,
either they or their haughty absence sent him metaphor,

an ever-commencing order that can resemble a philosophy
but is more charming faster, like a bird that stars into flight,
like rhyme, its junior, like edgings of the clinker-built sea –

The gold was a symbol, like a need to prize things. I'm smarter
now! he cried. I'm enlightened, as befits a great king!
My silver age will not seize the taramosalata!

But his court worked like stuff he'd learned through nonhuman ears
and like a gold effigy entitled The Hug his first daughter
stood in the strongroom. Age was like age, tears like tears,

his palace equalled his design for it, and looked no nobler tiled,
his desire for slave girls was like when he could slake it,
his wife was like an aged queen, and his heir like a child.


## LIKE WHEELING STACKED WATER

Dried nests in the overhanging limbs
are where the flood hatched eggs of swirl.
*Like is* unscary milder love. More can be in it.

The flood boomed up nearly to the door
like a taxiing airliner. It flew past all day.
Now the creek is down to barley colour
waist deep on her, chest on him,
wearing glasses all around them, barely pushing.

Down under stops of deadwood pipe in living
branches, they move on again. The bottom
is the sunk sand cattle-road they know
but hidden down cool, and mincing
magically away at every step, still going.

The wide creek is a tree hall decorated
with drowned and tobacco ribbons,
with zippy tilting birds, with dried snakes hanging
over the doorways everywhere along.

They push on. *Say this log I'm walking*
*under the water's a mast like off a*
*olden day ship – .* Fine hessian shade
is moistening down off cross-trees,

and like wings, the rocking waterline
gloving up and down their bodies
pumps support to their swimmy planet steps.

They've got a hook and bits
of bluebottle line from salt holidays.
They had a poor worm, and crickets automatic in a jar
but they let all them off fishing.

They're taking like to an adventure instead,
up past there where the undercut bank
makes that bottling noise, and the kingfisher's
beak is like the weight he's thrown by
to fly him straight.

By here, they're wheeling stacked-up water.
It has mounted like mild ice bedclothes to
their chest and chin. They have to tiptoe
under all the white davits of the bush.

But coming to the island, that is like the pupil
in acres of eye, their clothes pour water
off like heavy chain. They toil, and lighten
as they go up on it. All this is like the past
but none of it is sad. It has never ended.

# THE SAND COAST SONNETS

*Wallis Lake Estuary*

FOR VALERIE

A long street of all blue windows,
the estuary bridge is double-humped
like a bullock yoke. The north tide
teems through to four arriving rivers,
the south tide works the sinus channel
to the big heart-shaped real estate lake.
Both flood oyster farms like burnt floor joists
that islands sleep out among like dogs.

Glorious on a brass day the boiling up
from the south, of a storm above these paddocks
of shoal-creamed, wake-dolphined water.
Equally at dusk, when lamps and pelicans
are posted, the persistence of dark lands
out there on the anodised light void.


*Twin Towns History*

The northern shore used to be framed up
in shipbuilding's tap-tap and tar.
South across the wide celeste gap
where Lipariote fishermen, Fazio and Sciacca

bagged nets, were a beacon, more shops, scallop
arches of a lattice pub, in another shire.
The Colonial Secretary, way back, gave not a rap
for that side's name, the Learning Place – blacks, hey? –

and wrote in his own name on the map,
but Pacific men, who'd built the North Coast railway
became Koori there, warned off Town Beach by the cop.

On a punt like a fruit crate braced with wire
cars would balance for the crossing trip,
but the north side kept its name: Fish Shoaling in the Bay.


## The Sand Dingoes

Long before bridges, the old men who are hills now
were woken by the mopoke owl. And each had become an island,
ringed salt-white, like the *bora*. 'Older sister, younger sister,'
they sang out, 'you have drowned all our eastern country!'
'Yes, that Mopoke raped us! We turned him into a night bird
and dug up the salt water.' The old men started whistling
and big sandy dingoes ran down from the blue plateau
far south, beyond the Wattagan. They streamed out past Barrenjoey
and swam all up the new coast. They yarded that wild ocean
to be lakes and swamps for the people's fishing, they lay down
around the old men on a cold night and still sleep there,
being new country in their pelts of tea-tree and palm,
there east of Left Hand, and Mixing Bowl, up east of Brisbane.
Those blue south mountains were halved in height, and the sisters
took their sea-digging sticks and camped with the Cross in the sky.


## On Home Beaches

Back, in my fifties, fatter than I was then,
I step on the sand, belch down slight horror to walk
a wincing pit edge, waiting for the pistol shot
laughter. Long greening waves cash themselves, foam change
sliding into Ocean's pocket. She turns: ridicule looks down,
strappy, with faces averted, or is glare and families.
The great hawk of the beach is outstretched, point to point,
quivering and hunting. Cars are the surf at its back.
You peer, at this age, but it's still there, ridicule,
the pistol that kills women, that gets them killed, crippling men
on the towel-spattered sand. Equality is dressed, neatly,
with mouth still shut. Bared body is not equal ever.
Some are smiled to each other. Many surf, swim, play ball:
like that red boy, holding his wet T-shirt off his breasts.

## Leash Chain

The pelican of urban myth swooping
away with syllables of chihuahua
leash-chain trickling from its beak
at the owner crying down the beach
can't have been more hunter-insouciant
than this wadded water-skier in bikers
jacket wings now braking to assume
its seat on the lunchtime peak of tide.

Does that child's sock of dog, though, dropped
for its very chain, get pulled by it down
a boggling counter-chain to drowned zero?
Or does it rock back, tickling asphalt after
jerking fans across the floor of the palms'
idling forest of helicopter feathers?


## From Bennett's Head

The absolute blue ocean is scaled and smoothed.
Fur seals, absolute until they die, ruche through it.

The headland mounts raked strata with a white-fronted
sea eagle angling along them. Inland, blue

medicinal scrublands are being bared and squared.
The wind brings a sense of shiplap and cream clinker.

It is the suburbs, broadcast in colour from Metropolis
and received along the coast by loans and savings,

the sort of money, not nobly notorious, which literary
language curls to ironise. But the sky is bare

of human class hatred. I mirror a blacktop street,
biscuit walls, Roman numeral balustrades, inner shadow

and a plastic pedal car, all fronting a vast minute clarity
of lives assuming brick, and not as a performance.

405

# THE BOHEMIAN OCCUPATION

Take back Bohemia, Havel; take back the name.
Wrap it round the Hradčany, weight it with linden hills,
goose ponds and lozengy punchbowls. Let depression
find itself a new game.

Take back Bohemia, Vaclav. Don't supply a noun
to that dreamy world empire of unpaid and sexual police
where the tanks still are, green under boredom and garlands,
and fathers get mown down.

Take back Bohemia, dear President. Disclaim
the coffee machines whose every snort is *Bourgeois!*
where all non-Bohemians are cattle to brand, and all
difference is the same.

You alone, colleague, can close Bohemia back
down over Brno guns, plates of fox-with-juniper-berries
and that strategist of race whom Hindenburg's Bohemian corporal
sent upon you in black.

Reclaim Bohemia, Havel, and also Bohème
from that sweet soil, avid for barbed wire again,
where poetry is made a progressive model prison.
Now that Philistine is Palestine once more
take back your good name!


# THE FOSSIL IMPRINT

The impress of a whelk
in hard brown rock,

fluted as a plinth.
Its life gone utterly,

throb, wet and chalk,
left this shape-transmission,

a kin boat of fine brick.
Just off centre is a chip

healed before its death.
Before some credit help

this glazed biographee
beat surf-smash, stone rap,

maybe even saurid bite
in a swamp Antarctic.

Here, and where you are,
have been Antarctic.


## ON THE PRESENT SLAUGHTER OF FERAL ANIMALS

It seems that merciless human rearrangement
of the whole earth is to have no green ending.
In khaki where nothing shoots back, rangers pose,
entering a helicopter with its sniping door removed.
In minutes, they are over drab where buffalo flee
ahead of dust – beasts rotund and beetle brown, with rayed

handlebar horns – or over shine that hobbles them in spray.
The rifle arrests one's gallop, and one more, and one,
cow, calf, bull, the two tons of projectile
power riding each bullet's invisible star
whipcrack their plunging fluids. Poor caked Asian cattle,
they lie, successive, like towns of salt stench on a map.

Passionate with altruism as ever inquisition was,
a statistical dream loads up for donkeys, cats, horses.
The slab-fed military rifles, with lenses tubed on top,
open and shut. A necked bulging cartridge case and animal
both spin to oblivion. Behind an ear, fur flicks,
and an unknowable headlong world is abolished.

But so far as treetops or humans now alive know
all these are indigenous beings. When didn't we have them?
Each was born on this continent. Burn-off pick and dusty shade
were in their memory, not chill fall, not spiced viridian.
Us against species for bare survival may justify
the infecting needle, the pig rifle up eroded gullies,

but this luxury massacre on landscapes draining of settlement
smells of gas theory. The last thing brumby horses hear
is that ideological sound, the baby boom.
It is the hidden music of a climaxing native self-hatred
where we edge unseeing around flyblown millions toward
a nonviolent dreamtime where no one living has been.


## MEMORIES OF THE HEIGHT-TO-WEIGHT RATIO

I was a translator in the Institute back
when being accredited as a poet
meant signing things against Vietnam.
For scorn of the bargain I wouldn't do it.

And the Institute was after me
to lose seven teeth and five stone in weight
and pass their medical. Three years I dodged
then offered the teeth under sacking threat.

From five to nine, in warm Lane Cove,
and five to nine again at night,
an irascible Carpatho-Ruthenian strove
with ethnic teeth. He claimed the bite

of a human determined their intelligence.
More gnash-power sent the brain more blood.
In Hungarian, Yiddish or Serbo-Croat
he lectured emotional fur-trimmers good,

clacking a jointed skull in his hand
and sent them to work face-numbed and bright.
This was my wife's family dentist. He
looked into my mouth, blenched at the sight,

eclipsed me with his theory of occlusion
and wrested and tugged. Pausing to blow
out cigarette smoke, he'd bite his only
accent-free mother tongue and return below

to raise my black fleet of sugar-barques
so anchored that they gave him tennis elbow.
Seven teeth I gave that our babies might eat
when students were chanting Make Love! Hey Ho!

But there was a line called Height-to-Weight
and a parallel line on Vietnam. When a tutor
in politics failed all who crossed that, and wasn't
dismissed, scholarship was back to holy writ.

Fourteen pounds were a stone, and of great yore so,
but the doctor I saw next had no schoolyard in him:
*You're a natural weight-lifter! Come join my gym!*
Sonnets of flesh could still model my torso.

Modernism's not modem: it's police and despair.
I wear it as fat, and it gnawed off my hair
as my typewriter clicked over gulfs and birch spaces
where the passive voice muffled enormity and faces.

But when the Institute started afresh
to circle my job, we decamped to Europe
and spent our last sixpence on a pig's head.
Any job is a comedown, where I was bred.

# WATER-GARDENING IN AN OLD FARM DAM

Blueing the blackened water
that I'm widening with my spade
as I lever up water tussocks
and chuck them ashore like sopping comets
is a sun-point, dazzling heatless
acetylene, under tadpoles that swarm
wobbling, like a species of flies
and buzzing bubbles that speed
upward like many winged species.

Unwettable green tacos are lotus leaves.
Waterlily leaves are notched plaques
of the water. Their tubers resemble
charred monstera trunks. Some I planted,
some I let float. And I bought
thumb-sized mosquito-eating fish
for a dollar in a plastic amnion.
'Wilderness' says we've lost belief
in human building: our dominance
now so complete that we hide from it.

Where, with my levered back,
I stand, too late in life,
in a populous amber, feet deep
in digesting chyle over clays,
I love green humanised water
in old brick pounds, water carried
unleaking for miles around contour,
or built out into, or overstepping
stonework in long frilled excess.

The hands' pride and abysmal
pay that such labour earned,
as against the necks and billions
paid for Nature. But the workers
and the need are gone, without reaching
here: this was never canal country.
It's cow-ceramic, softened at rain times,

where the kookaburra's laugh
is like angles of a scrubbing toothbrush
heard through the bones of the head.

Level water should turn out of sight,
on round a bend, behind an island,
in windings of possibility, not
be exhausted in one gesture, like an avenue.
It shouldn't be surveyable in one look.
That's a waterhole. Still, the trees
I planted along this one bend it
a bit, and half roof it, bringing
its wet underearth shadow to the surface
as shade. And the reeds I hate,

mint sheaves, human-high palisades
that would close in round the water,
I could fire floating petrol among them
again, and savage but not beat them,
or I could declare them beautiful.

## THE SUSPENSION OF KNOCK

Where will Australia be held?
Ethnics who praise their home ground
while on it are called jingo chauvinists.
All's permitted, though, when they migrate;
the least adaptable are the purest then,
the narrowest the most multicultural.

Where will we hold Australia,
we who have no other country?
Not Indigenous, merely born here,
shall we be Australian in Paraguay
again, or on a Dublin street corner?
Some of them like us in Dublin.

We were the proletarian evolution,
a lot of us. We've been the future
of many snobbish nations,
but now the élite Revolution
that rules unsullied by elections
has no use for us. Our experience
and presence, unlike theirs, are fictive
ideological constructions.

When we are made fully nothing
by our own, at home and abroad,
where will we hold Australia?
In con-men's scams? In overdone slang?
In great shifting floods and rescue?
In the hand-high spaces that doctors
crawled through beneath a wrecked train?
In the very uniqueness of a racism
practised only against ourselves?

For the moment, a salamander identity
is permitted us in fire, in the tones
that say Well we got all the kids out;
the house was only property;
where the unsleeping blood-eyed run
their hoses toward full nightmare,
saving strangers and strangers' houses
from the Other Flower of the gum tree,
feral highrise, blizarding, total orange,
oncoming in shot azure, glorious as an air raid,
our recurrent Blitz, hideout of values.


## IT ALLOWS A PORTRAIT IN LINE SCAN AT FIFTEEN

He retains a slight 'Martian' accent, from the years of single phrases.
He no longer hugs to disarm. It is gradually allowing him affection.
It does not allow proportion. Distress is absolute, shrieking, and runs him
     at frantic speed through crashing doors.
He likes cyborgs. Their taciturn power, with his intonation.

It still runs him around the house, alone in the dark, cooing and laughing.

He can read about soils, populations and New Zealand. On neutral
topics he's illiterate.

*Arnie Schwarzenegger is an actor. He isn't a cyborg really, is he, Dad?*

He lives on forty acres, with animals and trees, and used to draw it
continually.

He knows the map of Earth's fertile soils, and can draw it freehand.

He can only lie in a panicked shout *SorrySorryIdidn'tdoit!* warding off
conflict with others and himself.

When he ran away constantly it was to the greengrocers to worship
stacked fruit.

His favourite country was the Ukraine: it is nearly all deep fertile soil.

Giggling, he climbed all over the dim Freudian psychiatrist who told us
how autism resulted from 'refrigerator' parents.

When asked to smile, he photographs a rictus-smile on his face.

It long forbade all naturalistic films. They were Adult movies.

*If they* (that is, he) *are bad the police will put them in hospital.*

He sometimes drew the farm amid Chinese or Balinese rice terraces.

When a runaway, he made uproar in the police station, playing at three
times adult speed.

Only animated films were proper. *Who Framed Roger Rabbit* then
authorised the rest.

Phrases spoken to him he would take as teaching, and repeat.

When he worshipped fruit, he screamed as if poisoned when it was fed
to him.

A one-word first conversation: *Blane. – Yes! Plane, that's right, baby! – Blane.*

He has forgotten nothing, and remembers the precise quality of
experiences.

It requires rulings: Is *stealing very playing up, as bad as murder?*

He counts at a glance, not looking. And he has never been lost.

When he ate only nuts and dried fruit, words were for dire emergencies.

He knows all the breeds of fowls, and the counties of Ireland.

He'd begun to talk, then returned to babble, then silence. It withdrew
speech for years.

When he took your hand, it was to work it, as a multi-purpose tool.

He is anger's mirror, and magnifies any near him, raging it down.

It still won't allow him fresh fruit, or orange juice with bits in it.

He swam in the midwinter dam at night. It had no rules about cold.

He was terrified of thunder and finally cried as if in explanation *It – angry!*
He grilled an egg he'd broken into bread. Exchanges of soil-knowledge are
    called landtalking.
He lives in objectivity. I was sure Bell's palsy would leave my face only
    when he said it had begun to.
*Don't say word!* when he was eight forbade the word 'autistic' in his
    presence.
Bantering questions about girlfriends cause a terrified look and blocked
    ears.
He sometimes centred the farm in a furrowed American Midwest.
*Eye contact, Mum!* means he truly wants attention. It dislikes I-contact.
He is equitable and kind, and only ever a little jealous. It was a relief
    when that little arrived.
He surfs, bowls, walks for miles. For many years he hasn't trailed his left
    arm while running.
*I gotta get smart!* looking terrified into the years. *I gotta get smart!*


PERFORMANCE

I starred last night, I shone:
I was footwork and firework in one,

a rocket that wriggled up and shot
darkness with a parasol of brilliants
and a peewee descant on a flung bit;
I was busters of glitter-bombs expanding
to mantle and aurora from a crown,
I was fouettés, falls of blazing paint,
para-flares spot-welding cloudy heaven,
loose gold off fierce toeholds of white,
a finale red-tongued as a haka leap:
that too was a butt of all right!

As usual after any triumph, I was
of course inconsolable.

# WAR SONG

TRANSLATED FROM THE GERMAN OF
MATTHIAS CLAUDIUS 1740–1815

It's war! O angel of God, restrain
    It: lift up your voice!
It's war, alas – and unbearable pain
    If any think it my choice!

How would I endure it if, bloody and wan,
    The slaughtered came to me in sleep,
All those mourning spirits, and began
    Around me to weep?

If valiant men, maimed in the dust, near death,
    Who had gone seeking fame,
Writhed before me, and with their dying breath
    Cursed my very name?

If millions of poor fathers, mothers, wives,
    So glad before the war,
Now brought the wreck, the misery of their lives,
    Crying, to my door?

If famine, evil plague and their affliction
    Smote friend and foe the same,
Then stood up on a corpse to crow the fiction
    Of my glorious fame?

Neither in crown nor honour, lands nor gain
    Could I ever rejoice!
It's war, alas – and unbearable pain
    If any think it my choice!

# AUSTRALIAN LOVE POEM

FOR JENNIFER STRAUSS

A primary teacher taking courses,
he loved the little girls,
never hard enough to be sacked:
parents made him change schools.

When sure this was his life sentence,
he dropped studies for routine:
the job, the Turf papers, beer,
the then-new poker machine.

Always urbane, he boarded happily
among show-jump ribbons, nailed towels,
stockwhip attitudes he'd find reasons for
and a paddock view, with fowls.

Because the old days weren't connected
the boss wouldn't have the phone.
The wife loved cards, outings, *Danny Boy*,
sweet malice in a mourning tone.

Life had set his hosts aside, as a couple,
from verve or parenthood.
How they lived as a threesome enlivened them
and need not be understood.

Euchre hands that brushed away the decades
also fanned rumour
and mothers of daughters banned the teacher
in his raceday humour,

but snap brim feigning awe of fat-cattle brim
and the henna rinse between them
enlarged each of the three to the others, till
the boss fell on his farm.

Alone together then, beyond the talk,
he'd cook, and tint, and curl,
and sit voluble through rare family visits
to his aged little girl.

As she got lost in the years
where she would wander,
her boy would hold her in bed
and wash sheets to spread under.

But when her relations carried her,
murmuring, out to their van,
he fled that day, as one with no rights,
as an unthanked old man.


## INSIDE AYERS ROCK

Inside Ayers Rock is lit
with paired fluorescent lights
on steel pillars supporting the ceiling
of haze-blue marquee cloth
high above the non-slip pavers.
Curving around the cafeteria
throughout vast inner space
is a Milky Way of plastic chairs
in foursomes around tables
all the way to the truck drivers' enclave.
Dusted coolabah trees grow to the ceiling,
TVs talk in gassy colours, and
round the walls are Outback shop fronts:
the Beehive Bookshop for brochures,
Casual Clobber, the bottled Country Kitchen
and the sheet-iron Dreamtime Experience
that is turned off at night.

A high bank of medal-ribbony
lolly jars presides over
island counters like opened crates,
one labelled White Mugs, and covered with them.
A two-dimensional policeman
discourages shoplifting of gifts
and near the entrance, where you pay
for fuel, there stands a tribal man
in rib-paint and pubic tassel.
It is all gentle and kind.
In beyond the children's playworld
there are fossils, like crumpled
old drawings of creatures in rock.


## EACH MORNING ONCE MORE SEAMLESS

Mother and type of evolution,
the New Testament of the scholars
may be likened to a library catalogue
of the old type, a card index console
of wooden drawers, each a verse.
And you never know which ones are out,
stacked up, spilt, or currently back
in, with some words deleted
then restored. And it never ends.

Reputations slide them out,
convictions push them in.
Speculations look backwards once
and stiffen to salt-crystal proofs.
Dates grow on palms in the wilderness
and ferment in human minds –
and criticism's prison for all poems
was modelled on this traffic.

Most battered of all are the drawers
labelled Resurrection, The.
Bashed, switched, themselves resurrected
continually. Because it is impossible,
as the galaxies were, as life was,
as flight and language were. The impossible,
· evolution's prey, shot with Time's arrow.
But this one is the bow of time.

Shadowy at a little distance tower
other banks of card-index drawers,
other myriad shelves, jammed with human names.
Some labelled in German are most actively
worked over, grieved, and reinserted.
More stretch away in Eastern scripts,
scarcely visited. Dust softens their headwords.
Yet the only moral reason to leave any
in silence fragments and reassembles
in the swarmed over, nagged, fantasised
word-atoms of the critics' testament.


## CONTESTED LANDSCAPE AT FORSAYTH

The conquest of fire-culture
on that timber countryside
has broadcast innumerable
termite mounds all through
the gravel gold rush hills
and the remnant railhead town,
petrified French mustards
out of jars long smashed.

Train platform and tin Shire
are beleaguered in nameless cemetery.
Outworks of the Dividing range
are annulled under Dreaming-turds.
It's as if every place a miner
cursed, or thought of sex,

419

had its abraded marker. Mile
on mile of freckled shade,
the ordinary is riddled by
cylinder-pins of unheard music.

On depopulated country
frail billions are alive
in layered earthen lace.
Their every flight is
a generation, glueing towers
which scatter and mass
on a blind smell-plan.
Cobras and meta-cobras
in the bush, immense black vines
await monsoon in a world
of clay lingam altars.

Like the monuments to every
mortal thing that a planet without God
would require, and inscriptionless
as rage would soon weather those,
the anthills erupt on verges,
on streets, round the glaring pub,
its mango trees and sleeping-fridges,
an estuary of undergrounds,
dried cities of the flying worm.


THE SHIELD-SCALES OF HERALDRY

Surmounting my government's high evasions
stands a barbecue of crosses and birds
tended by a kangaroo and emu
but in our courts, above the judge,
a lion and a unicorn still keep
their smaller offspring, plus a harp,
in an open prison looped with mottoes.

Coats of arms, plaster Rorschach blots,
crowned stone moths, they encrust Europe.
As God was dismissed from churches
they fluttered in and cling to the walls,
abstract comic-pages held by scrolled beasts,
or wear on the flagstones underfoot.
They pertain to an earlier Antichrist,

the one before police. Mafiose citadels
made them, states of one attended family
islanded in furrows. The oldest
are the simplest. A cross, some coins,
a stripe, a roof tree, a spur rowel,
bowstaves, a hollow-gutted lion,
and all in lucid target colours.

Under tinned heads with reveries tied on,
shields are quartered and cubed by marriage
till they are sacred campaign maps
or anatomy inside dissected mantling,
glyphs minutely clear through their one
rule, that colour must abut either
gold or silver, the non-weapon metals.

The New World doesn't blazon well –
the new world ran away from blazonry
or was sent away in chains by it –
but exceptions shine: the spread eagle
with the fireworks display on its belly
and in the thinks-balloon above its head.
And when as a half-autistic

kid in scrub paddocks vert and or
I grooved on the cloisons of pedigree
it was a vivid writing of system
that hypnotised me, beyond the obvious
euphemism of force. It was eight hundred
years of cubist art and Europe's dreamings:
the Cup, the Rose, the Ship, the Antlers.

High courage, bestial snobbery,
neither now merits ungrace from us.
They could no longer hang me,
throttling, for a rabbit sejant.
Like everyone, I would now be lord
or lady myself, and pardon me
or myself loose the coronet-necked hounds.


## THE YEAR OF THE KILN PORTRAITS

I came in from planting more trees.
I was sweating, and flopped down aslant
on the sofa. You and Clare were sitting
at the lunch table, singing as you do
in harmony even I hear as beautiful,
mezzo soprano and soprano,
for anything Arno. You winked at me
and, liquescent as my face was,
I must have looked like the year
you painted all our portraits, lovingly,
exquisitely, on ceramic tiles
in undrying oil, just one
or at most two colours at a time
and carried them braced oblique, wet,
in plastic ice-cream boxes to town.
It was encaustic painting,
ancient Rome's photography, that gets
developed in successive kiln firings
till it lives, time-freed, transposed
in behind a once-blank glaze.
Afterwards, you did some figured tiles
for our patchwork chimney, then stopped.
In art, you have serious gifts. But it's
crazy: you're not driven. Not obsessive.

# UNDER THE BANANA MOUNTAINS

At the edge of the tropics
they cut on the hills
raw shapes of other hills
and colour them banana.
One I used to see towering
each time I came away
climbed up and up, dressed in
a banana-tree beach shirt
with bush round its shoulders
like thrown-back jersey sleeves
and the rimmed sea below
drawing real estate to it.
Two islands were named Solitary
and the town wharf was crumbling
but surfers climbed sea-faces
on their boards, hand over hand.
The perched banana farms
mounted thousandfold stands
of room-long Chinese banners
or green to yellow lash-ups
of quill pens, splitting-edged,
their ink points in scrap vellum
each time I came away,
shiplapped fruit in blue mantles
all gaslit by the sun
and men drove tractors sidelong
like fighter planes, round steeps
worse than killed Grace Kelly.
Their scale came down to us
or caught round high-set houses.
I had shining hospitality
in dimmed subtropic rooms,
I unveiled a pastel school
and swift days keep passing
since I came away.

# A STAGE IN GENTRIFICATION

Most Culture has been an East German plastic bag
pulled over our heads, stifling and wet,
we see a hotly distorted world
through crackling folds and try not to gag.

Sex, media careers, the Australian republic
and recruited depression are in that bag
with scorn of God, with self-abasement studies
and funding's addictive smelling-rag.

Eighty million were murdered by police
in the selfsame terms and spirit which nag
and bully and set the atmosphere
inside the East German plastic bag.

It wants to become our country's flag
and rule by demo and kangaroo court
but it's wearing thin. It'll spill, and twist
and fly off still rustling Fascist! Fascist!

and catch on the same fence as Hitler, and sag.


# EARTH TREMOR AT NIGHT

Stopped by an earthquake on the North Coast line
in moonless dark, and thrumming, between Mount George
and Charity Creek, passengers become neighbours, worry,
peer out through mirrored selves. Opened doors reveal
steep winter canebrakes and the wide skinned scent
of the upper Manning River in a time of drought.
At the train's lit head, talk clangs like obscure tools.

Away over past a window is Kimbriki,* tribal estate
of one dignified slim old man and the farm of another,
my great great grandfather. Both occupied the same land
amicably. Smoke rose beside separate bark roofings.
In the next generation, no tribal heir appeared.
What you presume concerning this will tell you
the trend of your life. The sky is bumper with stars:

each like a snowflake, if seen through reading glasses.
The crew still knocking out words up along the train,
the people beg for radios, telephones. It's an earthquake!
Miles out to the south my family already has news
but here we're baulked of action. All dark hills, no road.
Alarm is like childhood, when love was from before thinking.
Beyond choice, we see our loves as indigenes see land.


* Kimbriki: pronounced KIM-brik-ai


## WAKING UP ON TOUR

Almost surprised to have been
delivered to the same house
as I went to sleep in, I unglue
my mouth, and flap back the bedclothes.

Brickwork is dawning, and pooled streets
which are floors of that red sea.
Time enough, for descending stair-depths
on a smile, dispelling hosts' privacy.

The salmon were scabbard and blade
in the delis of Ireland;
mist formed like manna on dusk fields.
Glassed prison cells jutted singly

425

there, nuclei filled with soldiers
inside cubed membranes of mesh.
Wales was reached across tuned
high strings, and the proud black red cream

towns of England go orange at nightfall,
still being rammed by lorries,
all those cities that exiled and hanged
the present, when it was their future.


## TYMPAN ALLEY

Adult songs in English,
avoiding schmaltz,
pre-twang:
the last songs adults sang.

When roles and manners wore
their cuffs as shot as Or-
tega y Gasset's,
soloists sang

as if a jeweller raised
pinches of facets
for hearts as yet unfazed
by fatty assets.

Adult songs with English;
the brilliantine long-play
records of the day
sing of the singlish,

the arch from wry to rue,
of marques and just one Engel,
blue, that Dietrich played;
euphemism's last parade

with rhymes still on our side
unwilling to divide
the men from the poise,
of lackadays and lakatois –

and always you,
cool independent You,
unsnowable, au fait,
when Us were hotly two,

not lost in They.


## A LEGO OF DRIVING TO SYDNEY

Dousing the campfire with tea
you step on the pedal and mount
whip-high behind splashboard and socket.
Your burnished rims tilt and rebound
among bristling botany. Only
a day now to the Port,
to bodices in the coffee palace,
to metal-shying razors in suits
and bare ships towing out, to dress
and concentrate in the wind.

> Motoring down the main roads,
> fenced wheeltrack-choices in forest,
> odd scored beds of gravel,
> knotwood in the ground –
> you will have to wrestle
> hand and foot to reach Sydney
> and win every fall.
> River punts are respites.

Croak-oak! the horsedung roads
aren't scented any more, but tasted.
Paved road starts at Chatswood:
just one ferry then, to stringing
tramcars and curl the mo,
to palms in the wonderful hotels.

Blazing down a razorback
in slab dark, in a huge
American car of the chassis age
to rescue for pleated cushions
a staring loved one who'll sway
down every totter of the gangway
on cane legs. Petrol coupons
had to be scrounged for this one:
they have seen too much railway.

Queuing down bloody highways
all round Easter, crawling in
to the great herbed sandstone bowl
of tealeaf scrub and suburbs,
hills by Monier and Wunderlich
in kiln orange, with cracks of harbour,
coming down to miss the milking
on full board, with baked Sundays,
life now to be neat and dry eyed,
coming down to be gentrified.

One long glide down the freeway
through aromatic radar zones,
soaring Egyptian rock cuttings
bang into a newsprint-coloured
rainstorm, tweeting the car phone
about union shares and police futures.
Driving in in your thousands
to the Show, to be detained
half a lifetime, or to grow rental
under steel flagpoles lapping
with multicoloured recipes.

# BURNING WANT

From just on puberty, I lived in funeral:
mother dead of miscarriage, father trying to be dead,
we'd boil sweat-brown cloth; cows repossessed the garden.
Lovemaking brought death, was the unuttered principle.

I met a tall adopted girl some kids thought aloof,
but she was intelligent. Her poise of white-blonde hair
proved her no kin to the squat tanned couple who loved her.
Only now do I realise she was my first love.

But all my names were fat-names, at my new town school.
Between classes, kids did erocide: destruction of sexual morale.
Mass refusal of unasked love; that works. Boys cheered as seventeen-
year-old girls came on to me, then ran back whinnying ridicule.

The slender girl came up on holidays from the city
to my cousins' farm. She was friendly and sane.
Whispers giggled round us. A letter was written as from me
and she was there, in mid-term, instantly.

But I called people 'the humans' not knowing it was rage.
I learned things sidelong, taking my rifle for walks,
recited every scene of *From Here to Eternity*, burned paddocks
and soldiered back each Monday to that dawning Teen age.

She I admired, and almost relaxed from placating,
was gnawed by knowing what she came from, not who.
Showing off was my one social skill, oddly never with her
but I dissembled feelings, till mine were unknown to me too

and I couldn't add my want to her shortfall of wantedness.
I had forty more years, with one dear remission,
of a white paralysis: she's attracted it's not real nothing is enough
she's mistaken she'll die go now! she'll tell any minute she'll laugh –

Whether other hands reached out to Marion, or didn't,
at nineteen in her training ward she had a fatal accident
alone, at night, they said, with a lethal injection
and was spared from seeing what my school did to the world.

# THE LAST HELLOS

Don't die, Dad –
but they die.

This last year he was wandery:
took off a new chainsaw blade
and cobbled a spare from bits.
Perhaps if I lay down
my head'll come better again.
His left shoulder kept rising
higher in his cardigan.

He could see death in a face.
Family used to call him in
to look at sick ones and say.
At his own time, he was told.

The knob found in his head
was duck-egg size. Never hurt.
Two to six months, Cecil.

*I'll be right*, he boomed
to his poor sister on the phone
*I'll do that when I finish dyin.*

       o

Don't die, Cecil.
But they do.

Going for last drives
in the bush, odd massive
board-slotted stumps bony white
in whipstick second growth.
*I could chop all day.*

*I could always cash*
*a cheque, in Sydney or anywhere.*
*Any of the shops.*

Eating, still at the head
of the table, he now missed
food on his knife side.

*Sorry, Dad, but like*
*have you forgiven your enemies?*
*Your father and all of them?*
All his lifetime of hurt.

*I must have* (grin). *I don't*
*think about that now.*

o

People can't say goodbye
any more. They say last hellos.

Going fast, over Christmas,
he'd still stumble out
of his room, where his photos
hang over the other furniture,
and play host to his mourners.

The courage of his bluster
firm big voice of his confusion.

Two last days in the hospital:
his long forearms were still
red mahogany. His hands
gripped steel frame. *I'm dyin.*

On the second day:
*You're bustin to talk but*
*I'm too busy dyin.*

o

Grief ended when he died,
the widower like soldiers who
won't live life their mates missed.

Good boy Cecil! No more Bluey dog.
No more cowtime. No more stories.
We're still using your imagination,
it was stronger than all ours.

Your grave's got littler
somehow, in the three months.
More pointy as the clay's shrivelled,
like a stuck zip in a coat.

Your cricket boots are in
the State museum! Odd letters
still come. Two more's died since you:
Annie, and Stewart. Old Stewart.

On your day there was a good crowd,
family, and people from away.
But of course a lot had gone
to their own funerals first.

Snobs mind us off religion
nowadays, if they can.
Fuck thém. I wish you God.


OPENING IN ENGLAND

All days were work days on the farm:
respite and dreaming were in them,
so holidays, I reasoned in childhood
must be hollow-days. Which people filled
with hotels, cars, wincing parade sand.
Now my plane is keening in to land
from Hollywood, supreme human judging-ring.

I only looked. Poets are nothing

in that profit vortex. Entertainment
and all the decorations of satiety
were craft, but poetry was a gent
always, regaled with gifts, not money.
Ancient shame, to pay for love or the sacred.
Deny the sacred, and we are owed pay.

Wage justice for poets, a living
like that of all who live off our words:
surreal notions from the lecture I'm giving
uphill from the concrete Liver birds –
then, feasted by kind hosts, I'm away
under Springtime's wind-hoed Mersey
to make holiday amid the ballpoint Spires

for new friends and hearers, be well dined
in an ormolu hall, with more good talk in London
till I die of reaction. Not theirs: mine.
Rising, I unzip more high-speed shires,
tour a mansion lovely as an unenraged mind,
nod with narrowboat windows and dipped tyres
and surface with my family near the Wye, at Hay.


## MY ANCESTRESS AND THE SECRET BALLOT

1848 AND 1851

Isabella Scott, born eighteen-oh-two,
grows gaunt in a cottage on Cheviot side,
the first and last house in Scotland, its view
like a vast Scottish flag, worn linen and blue
with no warmth in it. When her man died
it's what she and ten children could afford,
out of the village, high in the wind.

433

Five years before, in Paterson town,
a corpse stains the dust on voting day.
Rioters kicked him to death for the way
he was known to vote; more were struck down.
The way you voted being known
can get you sacked and driven away.
The widened franchise is a fizzer, folk say.

Isabella Scott, when Scotch wives kept
their surnames, has letters from her cousin
in New South Wales, Overseer of Free Men:
*Send me your grown lads. If they adapt*
*to here, come out yourself with the children.*
In those sunburnt colonies, in more than one mind,
how to repair the ballot's been divined.

Put about, wee ship, on your Great Circle course,
don't carry Bella's Murray daughter and boys
to the British Crown's stolen Austral land.
In ten years the Secret Ballot will force
its way into law in those colonies.
If the poor can just sit on their non-smoking hand
till they're old, help will come from Labor policies

and parties, sprung worldwide from that lag idea
which opens, by evading duellisms of the soul,
the only non-murderous route to the dole.
Don't sail, don't sail, Great-grannie(cubed) dear:
wait just a century and there'll be welfare
in full, and you won't play the Settler role.
The polling booth will be a closet of prayer.

## COMETE

Uphill in Melbourne on a beautiful day
a woman was walking ahead of her hair.
Like teak oiled soft to fracture and sway
it hung to her heels and seconded her
as a pencilled retinue, an unscrolling title
to ploughland, edged with ripe rows of dress,
a sheathed wing that couldn't fly her at all,
only itself, loosely, and her spirits.
                    A largesse
of life and self, brushed all calm and out,
its abstracted attempts on her mouth weren't seen,
nor its showering, its tenting. Just the detail
that swam in its flow-lines, glossing about –
as she paced on, comet-like, face to the sun.


## DRY WATER

My sleep, that had gone astray,
flying home, turned up at last,
developing in the brain's red room
like film of crowding and woollies,
but builders were tapping the house
and I couldn't lie down, not
while they worked. I still can't
do privilege. So I fed the fowls

and pottered round the dead-tree dam
which lay stilled under water fern,
matte as the rough side of masonite
with trails of swimming birds
through it like fading tyre-tracks
and gaps re-coalescing. The cud
of azolla, scooped up, was tiny green
rockery plants, brown only in total.

Wind impulses quivering the water
were damped under that blanket level
which would floor it till next flood.
It made me think of other
dry water. Dry bath water
magicked out of lustrous fine gravel
in the Roman military museum
at Caerleon, in Old South Wales.

The mealiness and illusory slick
of minute stones there evoke steam,
soldier-scrapings and olive oil
worked to motionless ripples, as they fill
the excavated real masonry pools.
Sunproofed water, safety water – yawn.
Imprisoning the actual in commentary:
will that get us sex after death?

Our one-eyed fowl lay on his side
to peck at grain in two dimensions
and, still nailing the house's scansions
and line lengths, the only people
who abash me – *Not a working model,
our bloke! No.* – kept me from bed,
atoning for poetry's slight sacredness
and the deep shame of achievement.


LIFE CYCLE OF IDEAS

An idea whistles with your lips,

laughs with your breath.
An idea hungers for your body.

An alert, hot to dissemble and share,
it snatches up cases of its style
from everywhere, to start a face.

An idea is a mouth that sells
as it sucks. It lusts to have
loomed perpetual in the night colours:
an idea is always a social climb.

Whether still braving snorts,
ordering its shootings, or at rest
among its own charts of world rule,
a maturing idea will suddenly want

to get smaller than its bearers.

It longs to be a poem:
earthed, accurate immortal trance,
buck as stirrups were,
blare as the panther.

Only art can contain an idea.


## COTTON FLANNELETTE

*Shake the bed,* the blackened child whimpers,
*O shake the bed!* through beak lips that never
will come unwry. And wearily the iron-
framed mattress, with nodding crockery bulbs,
jinks on its way.
                   Her brothers and sister take
shifts with the terrible glued-together baby
when their unsleeping absolute mother
reels out to snatch an hour, back to stop
the rocking and wring pale blue soap-water
over nude bladders and blood-webbed chars.

Even their cranky evasive father
is awed to stand watches rocking the bed.
Lids frogged shut, *O please shake the bed,*
her contour whorls and braille tattoos
from where, in her nightdress, she flared

out of hearth-drowse to a marrow shriek
pedalling full tilt firesleeves in mid air,
                              are grainier with repair
than when the doctor, crying *Dear God, woman!*
*No one can save that child. Let her go!*
spared her the treatments of the day.

*Shake the bed.* Like: count phone poles, rhyme,
classify realities, bang the head, any
iteration that will bring, in the brain's forks,
the melting molecules of relief,
and bring them again.
                              *O rock the bed!*
Nibble water with bared teeth, make lymph
like arrowroot gruel, as your mother grips you
for weeks in the untrained perfect language,
till the doctor relents. Salves and wraps you
in dressings that will be the fire again,
ripping anguish off agony,
                              and will confirm
the ploughland ridges the gum joins
in your woman's skin, child saved by rhythm
for the sixty more years your family weaves you
on devotion's loom, rick-racking the bed
as you yourself, six years old, instruct them.


## THE TRANCES

We came from the Ice Age,
we work for the trances.
The hunter, the Mother,
seers' inside-out glances

come from the Ice Age,
all things in two sexes,
the priest man, the beast man,
I flatten to run
I rise to be human.

438

We came from the Ice Age
with the walk of the Mothers
with the walk of the powers
we walked where sea now is

we made the dry land
we told it in our trances
we burnt it with our sexes
but the tongue it is sand
see it, all dry taste buds
lapping each foot that crosses
every word is more sand.

Dup dup hey duhn duhn
the rhythm of the Mothers.
We come from the Ice Ages
with the tribes and the trances
the drum's a tapped drone
dup dup hey duhn duhn.

We come from the Ice Age,
poem makers, homemakers,
how you know we are sacred:
it's unlucky to pay us.

Kings are later, farmers later.
After the Ice Age, they
made landscape, made neuter,
they made prose and pay.

Things are bodied by the trances,
loved, analysed and scorned:
a true priest's loved in scorn,
how you know he is sacred.

We're gifted and pensioned.
Some paid ones were us:
when they got their wages
ice formed in their mouths
chink chink, the Ice Age.

A prose world is the Ice Age
it is all the one sex
and theory, that floats land
we came over that floe land

we came from the Ice Age
we left it by the trances
worlds warm from the trances
duhn duhn hey dup dup
it goes on, we don't stop
we walk on from the Ice Age.


## THE DEVIL

I must have heard of the Devil
in our splintery church
but the earliest I remember him
is when, as a bullocky's child
in a clan of operatic swearers,
I first essayed the black poetry.

My mouth-farting profanities
horrified Barney McCann,
the Krambach carpenter staying
with us to rebuild our bails:
*Lord, I won't sleep on that verandah*
*where you sleep! Not tonight.*
*After what you just said*
*the old Devil's sure to come for you.*
*O he's bad, with his claws and tail.*
My parents smiled uneasily.

Bats flitted, the moon shone in.
*Will the old Devil get me?*
I quavered, four years old, through the wall,
*Will he get me?* The agile long-boned man
of pure horror, clinging to the outside
weatherboards like the spur-shouldered
hoatzin bird in my mother's
encyclopedia books. *Not if you
knock off swearing. Go to sleep, Leslie.*

But the carpenter was soldering iron
gutterings, dipping flux with a feather
from a yellow bottle. *Spirits of salts:
it'll eat through everything. Only
this bottle can hold it. A drop
on your head would sizzle right down
through you, burn on into the ground –
fearful stuff.* Then he flicked the feather
at me, and leaned away with a grin
from my wept hysteric shower of oaths.
*That's it! I won't sleep in your house now.
He'll take everybody tonight.*
I was cured. It became a funny yarn.

But over the next years
I sneaked back, in daylight first,
to the insulted people's language
that made me feel so thrillingly
alone and empty of heart
that the church's doctrines and
the snootiest dismissals of them
would both need to be true
at once, to come near it.
It fitted the future easily.

# THE NEARLY DEPARTED

TRANSLATED FROM THE GERMAN OF
HEINRICH HEINE 1797–1856

In my breast I've seen expire
every worldly vain desire,
even, among things dead in there,
hatred of evil, likewise any care
for my or others' hour of need –
only Death lives in me indeed.
   The curtain falls, the play is done,
and my dear German public as one
saunters yawning in homeward throngs.
The good folk, enjoying laughs and songs
aren't such fools, I have to allow,
supping and boozing and making a row –
It's true, that speech of the noble hero's
long ago in the book Homeros:
the lot of the meanest live Philistine
in Stuttgart-on-Neckar is happier than mine,
I, son of Peleus, dead champ whose shade is
prince of shadows in gloomy Hades.


# THE WARM RAIN

Against the darker trees or an open car shed
is where we first see rain, on a cumulous day,
a subtle slant locating the light in air
in front of a Forties still of tubs and bike-frames.

Next sign, the dust that was white pepper bared
starts pitting and re-knotting into peppercorns.
It stops being a raceway of rocket smoke behind cars,
it sidles off foliage, darkens to a lustre. The roof
of the bush barely leaks yet, but paper slows right down.

Hurrying parcels pearl but don't now split
crossing the carparks. People clap things in odd salute
to the side of their heads, yell wit, dance on their doubles.
The sunny parallels, when opposite the light, have a flung look
like falling seed. They mass, and develop a shore sound;
fixtures get cancelled, the muckiest shovels rack up.

The highway whizzes, and lorries put spin on vapour;
soon puddles hit at speed will arch over you like a slammed sea.
I love it all, I agree with it. At nightfall, the cause
of the whole thing revolves, in white and tints, on TV
like the Crab nebula; it brandishes palm trees like mops,
its borders swell over the continent, they compress the other
nations of the weather. Fruit bumps lawn, and every country dam

brews under bubbles, milky temperas sombering to oils.
Grass rains upward; the crêpe-myrtle tree heels, sopping crimson,
needing to be shaken like the kilt of a large man.
Hills run, air and paddocks are swollen. Eaves dribble like jaws
and coolness is a silent film, starring green and mirrors.
Tiny firetail finches, quiet in our climber rose, agree to it
like early humans. Cattle agree harder, hunched out in the clouds.
From here, the ocean may pump up and up and explode
around the lighthouses in gigantic cloak sleeves, the whole book
of foam slide and fritter, disclosing a pen shaft. Paratroops

of salt water may land in dock streets, skinless balloons
be flat out to queue down every drain, and the wind race
thousands of flags. Or we may be just chirpings, damped
under calm high cornfields of pour, with butter clearings

that spread and resume glare, hiding the warm rain
back inside our clothes, as mauve trees scab to cream
and grey trees strip bright salmon, with loden patches.

# DEMO

No. Not from me. Never.
Not a step in your march,
not a vowel in your unison,
bray that shifts to bay.

Banners sailing a street river,
power in advance of a vote,
go choke on these quatrain tablets.
I grant you no claim ever,

not if you pushed the Christ Child
as President of Rock Candy Mountain
or yowled for the found Elixir
would your caste expectations snare me.

Superhuman with accusation,
you would conscript me to a world
of people spat on, people hiding
ahead of oncoming poetry.

Whatever class is your screen
I'm from several lower.
To your rigged fashions, I'm pariah.
Nothing a mob does is clean,

not at first, not when slowed to a media,
not when police. The first demos I saw,
before placards, were against me,
alone, for two years, with chants,

every day, with half-conciliatory
needling in between, and aloof
moral cowardice holding skirts away.
I learned your world order then.

## DEAF LANGUAGE

Two women were characters, continually
rewriting themselves, in turn, with their hands
mostly, but with face and torso too
and very fast, in brushwork like the gestures
above a busy street in Shanghai.


## REVERSE LIGHT

Man was a mug, really,
to give them his right age:
I could have gone on
being the lighthouse keeper
for another ten years. Fishing,
lighting her, keeping her clean,
end-for-ending the tablecloth.

A small whale beached below
once. I cut it up for the dogs.
It was good out on the bo'sun's
chair, slathering on paint
with my safety ladder going up,
thinking about cows, and seals,
sand dollars and my wives and stuff.

Queerest thing about the job,
the light that jabs away out
at night, and rides the horizons
comes out of just a bulb
inside this turntable rack
of like thick glass saucers.

When I'd switch her off
of a summer morning
and polish those ridgy lenses
I had to draw the curtains

round the windows facing inland
or else the sun could spike in
through them, the lenses, and make
rays, and set all the bush alight.


# THE GENETIC GALAXY

FOR SIR JOHN GUISE, FIRST GOVERNOR GENERAL
OF PAPUA NEW GUINEA

A chart, wider than the world
which would diagram with sober truth
the parentage of everyone, named
and linked with their real kin
across all of time and space:

Strips and fragments of this chart
are the snigger of community
often waved at Identity overdone,
thst is, underdone with intent –
wives have hung them out with the smalls.

Plenty, could they get this chart,
would display it entire
to howls of revised posh, burning wills,
unspoken people, death rays
of Whititude and Negritude,

anguish of men out of whose children
other men peer innocently,
shock historical non-maternities
and the stratosphere-tightening
gasp at incest seen in full.

Glorious to see a hero car-bomber
or kulak-shooter sunk by wrong ancestry,
a Klan klutz awed by his colours of descent
and much sheer joy of disinheritance.
Sadder, an adoptee's frantic name-thirst,

446

but a million years' unreachable blamed dead
might stun revenge, sheer wealth of tangents
swamp destiny and victimhood,
Aborigines in the House of Windsor
and of Worth, where they always belonged.

Names rising from deep time
by the new propulsion of anecdote,
all descent-lines nine tenths tribesfolk
then odder that reincarnation's princess-tales
and far wilder than the genome

which may be their first rough lens.
When complete the Chart will need
to hang in space, to be safe from us
like the relativised stars
once also made by love.


## BLOWFLY GRASS

The houses those suburbs could afford
were roofed with old savings books, and some
seeped gravy at stitches in their walls;

some were clipped as close as fury,
some grimed and corner-bashed by love
and the real estate, as it got more vacant

grew blady grass and blowfly grass, so called
for the exquisite lanterns of its seed
and the land sagged subtly to a low point,

it all inclined way out there to a pit
with burnt-looking cheap marble edges
and things and figures flew up from it

like the stones in the crusher Piers had
for making dusts of them for glazes:
flint, pyroclase, slickensides, quartz, schist,

447

snapping, refusing and spitting high
till the steel teeth got gritty corners on them
and could grip them craw-chokingly to grind.

It's their chance, a man with beerglass-cut arms
told me. Those hoppers got to keep filled. A girl,
edging in, bounced out cropped and wrong-coloured

like a chemist's photo crying. Who could blame her
among in-depth grabs and Bali flights and phones?
She was true, and got what truth gets.


## DREAMBABWE

Streaming, a hippo surfaces
like the head of someone
lifting, with still entranced eyes,
from a lake of stanzas.


## BELOW BRONTE HOUSE

The children pouring down,
supervised, into the ravine
and talking animatedly all over
each other like faces in a payout
of small change, now come in
under a vast shadowy marquee
of native fig and tree of heaven.
In their indigo and white
they flow on down, glimpsed
between the patisserie trunks
of green coral trees, and as
they go on towards the ocean
they are still tangling and grabbing
at an elusive bright string
that many want to pick off others

and off themselves. It is
of course childhood, which they
scorn as a disabling naïveté
as they approach where waves
of sand bulge up through shaved grass.


## THE HEAD-SPIDER

Where I lived once, a roller coaster's range
of timber hills peaked just by our backyard cliff
and cars undulated scream-driven round its seismograph
and climbed up to us with an indrawn gasp of girls.

Smiles and yelling could be exchanged as they crested
then they'd pitch over, straining back in a shriek
that volleyed as the cars were snatched from sight
in the abyss, and were soon back. Weekdays they rested,

and I rested all days. There was a spider in my head
I'd long stay unaware of. If you're raped you mostly know
but I'd been cursed, and refused to notice or believe it.
Aloof in a Push squat, I thought I was moral, or dead.

Misrule was strict there, and the Pill of the day only ever
went into one mouth, not mine, and foamed a Santa-beard.
I was resented for chastity, and slept on an overcoat.
Once Carol from upstairs came to me in bra and kindness

and the spider secreted by girls' derision-rites to spare
women from me had to numb me to a crazed politeness.
Squeals rode the edge of the thrill building. Cartoonist Mercier
drew springs under Sydney. Push lovers were untrue on principle.

It's all architecture over there now. A new roller coaster
flies its ups and downs in wealth's face like an affront.
I've written a new body that only needs a reader's touch.
If love is cursed in us, then when God exists, we don't.

449

## AMANDA'S PAINTING

In the painting, I'm seated in a shield,
coming home in it up a shadowy river.
It is a small metal boat lined in eggshell
and my hands grip the gunwale rims. I'm
a composite bow, tensioning the whole boat,
steering it with my gaze. No oars, no engine,
no sails. I'm propelling the little craft with speech.
The faded rings around my loose bulk shirt
are of five lines each, a musical lineation
and the shirt is apple-red, soaking in salt birth-sheen
more liquid than the river. My cap is a teal mask
pushed back so far that I can pretend it is headgear.
In the middle of the river are cobweb cassowary trees
of the South Pacific, and on the far shore rise
dark hills of the temperate zone. To these, at this
moment in the painting's growth, my course is slant
but my eye is on them. To relax, to speak European.


## ONE KNEELING, ONE LOOKING DOWN

Half-buried timbers chained corduroy
lead out into the sand
which bare feet wincing Crutch and Crotch
spurn for the summer surf's embroidery
and insects stay up on the land.

A storm engrossing half the sky
in broccoli and seething drab
and standing on one foot over the country
burrs like a lit torch. Lightning
turns air to elixir at every grab

but the ocean sky is untroubled blue
everywhere. Its storm rolls below:
sand clouds raining on sacred country
drowned a hundred lifetimes under sea.
In the ruins of a hill, channels flow,

450

and people, like a scant palisade
driven in the surf, jump or sway
or drag its white netting to the tide line
where a big man lies with his limbs splayed,
fingers and toes and a forehead-shine

as if he'd fallen off the flag.
Only two women seem aware of him.
One says *But this frees us. I'd be a fool –*
*Say it with me*, says the other. *For him to revive*
*we must both say it. Say Be alive. –*

*But it was our own friends who got*
*him with a brave shot, a clever shot. –*
*Those are our equals: we scorn them*
*for being no more than ourselves.*
*Say it with me. Say Be alive. –*

*Elder sister, it is impossible. –*
*Life was once impossible. And flight. And speech.*
*It was impossible to visit the moon.*
*The impossible's our summoning dimension.*
*Say it with me. Say Be alive again. –*

The younger wavers. She won't leave
nor stop being furious. The sea's vast
catchment of light sends ashore a roughcast
that melts off every swimmer who can stand.
Glaring through slits, the storm moves inland.

The younger sister, wavering, shouts *Stay dead!*
She knows how impossibility
is the only door that opens.
She pities his fall, leg under one knee
but her power is his death, and can't be dignified.

# BOTTLES IN THE BOMBED CITY

MANCHESTER 1996

They gave the city a stroke. Its memories
are cordoned off. They could collapse on you.

Water leaks into bricks of the workers' century
and every meaning is blurred. No word in Roget

now squares with another. If the word is Manchester
it may be Australia, where that means sheets and towels.

To give the city a stroke, they mixed a lorryload
of henbane and meadowsweet oil and countrified her.

Now Engels supports Max, and the British Union
of beautiful ceramics is being shovelled up,

blue-green tiles of the Corn Exchange,
umber gloss bricks of the Royal Midlands Hotel.

Unmelting ice everywhere, and loosened molecules.
When the stroke came, every bottle winked at its neighbour.


# THE MARGIN OF DIFFERENCE

One and one make two,
the literalist said.
So far they've made five billion,
said the lateralist, or ten
times that, if you count the dead.

# A RETICENCE

After a silver summer
of downpour, cement-powder autumn
set in its bag. Lawns turned crunchy
but the time tap kept dribbling away.

The paddocks were void as that evening
in early childhood when the sun
was rising in the west,
round and brimming as the factory furnace door,

as I woke up after sickness.
Then it was explained to me
that I'd slept through from morning
and I sobbed because I'd missed that day,

my entire lovely day.
Without you, it might have been a prophecy.


# TRAVELS WITH JOHN HUNTER

We who travel between worlds
lose our muscle and bone.
I was wheeling a barrow of earth
when agony bayoneted me.

I could not sit, or lie down,
or stand, in Casualty.
Stomach-calming clay caked my lips,
I turned yellow as the moon

and slid inside a CAT-scan wheel
in a hospital where I met no-one
so much was my liver now my dire
preoccupation. I was sped down a road

of treetops and fishing-rod lightpoles
toward the three persons of God
and the three persons of John Hunter
Hospital. Who said We might lose this one.

Twenty days or to the heat-death
of the Universe have the same duration:
vaguely half an hour. I awoke
giggling over a joke

about Paul Kruger in Johannesburg
and missed the white court stockings
I half remembered from my prone
still voyage beyond flesh and bone.

I asked my friend who got new lungs
How long were you crazy, coming back?
Five days, he said. Violent and mad.
Fictive Afrikaner police were at him,

not unworldly Oom Paul Kruger.
Valerie, who had sat the twenty days
beside me, now gently told me tales
of my time-warp. The operative canyon

stretched, stapled, with dry roseate walls
down my belly. Seaweed gel
plugged views of my pluck and offal.
Some accident had released flora

who live in us and will eat us
when we stop feeding them the earth.
I'd rehearsed the private office of the grave,
ceased excreting, made corpse gases

all while liana'd in tubes
and overseen by cockpit instruments
that beeped or struck up Beethoven's
Fifth at behests of fluid.

I also hear when I lay lipless
and far away I was anointed
first by a mild metaphoric church
then by the Church of no metaphors.

Now I said, signing a Dutch contract
in a hand I couldn't recognise,
let's go and eat Chinese soup
and drive to Lake Macquarie. Was I

not renewed as we are in Heaven?
In fact I could hardly endure
Earth gravity, and stayed weak and cranky
till the soup came, squid and vegetables,

pure Yang. And was sane thereafter.
It seemed I'd also travelled
in a Spring-in-Winter love-barque of cards,
of flowers and phone calls and letters,

concern I'd never dreamed was there
when black kelp boiled in my head.
I'd awoken amid my State funeral,
nevermore to eat my liver

or feed it to the Black Dog, depression
which the three Johns Hunter seem
to have killed with their scalpels:
it hasn't found its way home,

where I now dodder and mend
in thanks for devotion, for the ambulance
this time, for the hospital fork lift,
for pethidine, and this face of deity:

not the foreknowledge of death
but the project of seeing conscious life
rescued from death defines and will
atone for the human.

## DROUGHT DUST ON THE CROCKERY

Things were not better
when I was young:
things were poorer and harsher,
drought dust on the crockery,
and I was young.


## THE HARLEYS

Blats booted to blatant
dubbin the avenue dire
with rubbings of Sveinn Forkbeard
leading a black squall of Harleys
with Moe Snow-Whitebeard and

Possum Brushbeard and their ladies
and, sphincter-lipped, gunning,
massed leather muscle on a run,
on a roll, Santas from Hell
like a whole shoal leaning

wide-wristed, their tautness stable
in fluency, fast streetscape dwindling,
all riding astride, on the outside
of sleek grunt vehicles, woman-clung,
forty years on from Marlon.

# AURORA PRONE

The lemon sunlight poured out far between things
inhabits a coolness. Mosquitoes have subsided,
flies are for later heat.
Every tree's an auburn giant with a dazzled face
and the back of its head to an infinite dusk road.
Twilights broaden away from our feet too
as rabbits bounce home up defiles in the grass.
Everything widens with distance, in this perspective.
The dog's paws, trotting, rotate his end of infinity
and dam water feels a shiver few willow drapes share.
Bright leaks through their wigwam re-purple the skinny beans
then rapidly the light tops treetops and is shortened
into a day. Everywhere stands pat beside its shadow
for the great bald radiance never seen in dreams.


# BEST WESTERN

The calm couple have no objection
and the baby, he looks keen
to see a smoker hunch in from the snow
and fatten a patchwork quilt in the straw
of their kerbsite Nativity scene.


# THE INSTRUMENT

Who reads poetry? Not our intellectuals;
they want to control it. Not lovers, not the combative,
not examinees. They too skim it for bouquets
and magic trump cards. Not poor schoolkids
furtively farting as they get immunized against it.

Poetry is read by the lovers of poetry
and heard by some more they coax to the cafe
or the district library for a bifocal reading.
Lovers of poetry may total a million people
on the whole planet. Fewer than the players of *skat*.

What gives them delight is a never-murderous skim
distilled, to verse mainly, and suspended in rapt
calm on the surface of paper. The rest of poetry
to which this was once integral still rules
the continents, as it always did. But on condition now

that its true name is never spoken: constructs, feral poetry,
the opposite but also the secret of the rational.
And who reads that? Ah, the lovers, the schoolkids,
debaters, generals, crime-lords, everybody reads it:
Porsche, lift-off, Gaia, Cool, patriarchy.

Among the feral stanzas are many that demand your flesh
to embody themselves. Only completed art
free of obedience to its time can pirouette you
through and athwart the larger poems you are in.
Being outside all poetry is an unreachable void.

Why write poetry? For the weird unemployment.
For the painless headaches, that must be tapped to strike
down along your writing arm at the accumulated moment.
For the adjustments after, aligning facets in a verb
before the trance leaves you. For working always beyond

your own intelligence. For not needing to rise
and betray the poor to do it. For a non-devouring fame.
Little in politics resembles it: perhaps
the Australian colonists' re-inventing of the snide
far-adopted secret ballot, in which deflation could hide

and, as a welfare bringer, shame the mass-grave Revolutions,
so axe-edged, so lictor-y.
Was that moral cowardice's one shining world victory?
Breathing in dream-rhythm when awake and far from bed
evinces the gift. Being tragic with a book on your head.


## OUR WEEK IN GRAND LUXE

After Waterloo, the Channel
Tunnel was eventless experience:
we sloped down out of a Picardy
called Kent, talked beside blur
and emerged in a Kent called Picardy
but then the train began
to outrun nearby cars and
stop aeroplanes in the sky.
It began flying on earth
towards the portals of Paris
and everything, hamlets, trees, fields
was left in an arrowy fallback
that only the suburbs could restrain.
Then we tumbled in a *valse*
*à mille temps* across the city,
paid off the taxi and rolled out
on a wingless plane for Avignon
over prairies and bisected hills
and sat up for hours where nothing
could join us from outside
without killing us, till we were in
the Province where pale rock has windows
and mortise-holes for coffins in it
and bubble-powdered speedy water
is guttered to carry cool through towns
built in a language they've stopped speaking.

There was knocking of steel boules
in shade until, in gloved unison,
domes of polished metal were raised
on Sèvres of festivity, on picnics
with galantines and counter-tenor,
on buses up a teetering road
to the high mountaintop where Petrarch,
first to climb a mountain just to write of it,
glimpsed the vision of tourism
and down to an evening-green
roof of fruiting cherry branches,
dense-spattered in human grazing reach
before more ortolans, more cabernets.
There was never snobbery, from our expert
carers. Friendly and artisanal,
their menus carried credits like films.
And when it was all achieved,
laudations, responses, evening brain-fag
from speaking literary languages,
we saw the Popes' emptied donjon and
St Bénézet's bridge, that stops short.


## SPITAL TOWER

I.M. SORLEY MacLEAN 1911–96

A cloister below
the Cheviot Hills
once sheltered lepers
but the Church dissolved
and the lepers died.
All over Northern Europe
the helpless died.

The cloister reared up
on end, against raiders,
then sank to a farmstead.
Murrays were in it
but poverty blew us
out of peasanthood
toward the Antipodes.

To no part of Europe
is our country antipodal:
its counter-foot
is the mid-Atlantic.

Where the great Gaelic poet
has gone, that's Antipodes,
Antipodes to everywhere.
Horror to the fortunate,
to the helpless, harbour:
death makes us all emigrants.

I pray where he is
excels modern doctrine
as his lines left on earth
out-glory his Spain.

I mourn, MacGillEain,
that my sleep under scalpels
meant I missed reading with you.
Now turning your pages
will be as if I riffled
the Northern Lights
and heard their language.

## RODD ISLAND WEDDING

On your wedding day, women were seated
on the Harbour, resting their oars.
Single sculls, in the grace of that spelling,
their canoes, slim as compass needles
pointed at sandstone black with water,
at balconies and wharves and houses,
at sunny bays and lawn-set madhouses,
those chateaux of the upper Harbour,
at the tensioned bridges and their opposites.

Aqaba! A snorkel cleared its throat
and there you were, facing castanets of focus
on your wedding island. Since you'd become happy,
you told me, you'd stopped writing poems.
I should wish you a long silence. I do,
I do, if you mean it. The ribbed iron
feast-hall cruised through courses and clapping
like an airship under fans. The sportswomen
bent, and reached for distance like thistledowns.


## MUSIC TO ME IS LIKE DAYS

Once played to attentive faces
music has broken its frame
its bodice of always-weak laces
the entirely promiscuous art
pours out in public spaces
accompanying everything, the selections
of sex and war, the rejections.
To jeans-wearers in zipped sporrans
it transmits an ideal body
continuously as theirs age. Warrens
of plastic tiles and mesh throats
dispense this aural money
this sleek accountancy of notes
deep feeling adrift from its feelers

462

thought that means everything at once
like a shrugging of cream shoulders
like paintings hung on park mesh
sonore doom soneer illy chesh!
they lost the off switch in my lifetime
the world reverberates with Muzak
and Prozac. As it doesn't with poe-zac
(I did meet a Miss Universe named Verstak).
Music to me is like days
I rarely catch who composed them
if one's sublime I think God
my life-signs suspend. I nod
it's like both Stilton and cure
from one harpsichord-hum:
penicillium –
then I miss the Köchel number.
I scarcely know whose performance
of a limpid autumn noon is superior
I gather timbre outranks rhumba.
I often can't tell days apart
they are the consumers, not me
in my head collectables decay
I've half-heard every piece of music
the glorious big one with voice
the gleaming instrumental one, so choice
the hypnotic one like weed-smoke at a party
and the muscular one out of farty
cars that goes Whudda Whudda
Whudda like the compound oil heart
of a warrior not of this planet.


## COOLONGOLOOK TIMBER MILL

Down a road padlocked now
steel discs and weeds sprawled
in a room whose rusty hair
was iron cornrows, and its brow

463

a naily timber lintel
under which I'd gaze across
the river at Midge Island
as the tide turned on its pintle

and atoms would be dancing
like mayflies in the dusk
at the exact same speed as
gold roubles once spread glancing

around inch-freeboard puntloads
of sleepers axe trimmed
for Wittgenstein and Company
building the Siberian railroads

and black saws' sharkmouth edges
kept pipe-stuffers careful
up skids from sawdust-sized
shimmering of midges

then living drills were screwed
from punk wood to eat
by men wearing genitals; their
fish spears twitched like sedges

and the ocean sprawled in sight
gull-squealing, then weeks away
and the night sky quivered
with the vanished river's fleet

*– a city man bought*
*the mill land for ten times*
*its price, and let the mill*
*fall down. But I have kept it.*

# INCUNABULAR

Tom Fisher was my Grail King:
he endowed the Gothic library
to which my life had been pointing.
His high sandstone box held the Culture
bush folk were scorned for lacking.

On its milk-glass stack levels I still
hear stiletto heels clacking,
glass floors for the light to perfuse,
not for voyeurs: you could only
make out the sex of shoes.

The lipsticked gargoyle downstairs
kissed much social ascent.
Above, I'd browse beside the point
power made, for the points it didn't.
Reflex, more than intent.

The reading-room beam supported heraldry
and a roof like a steep tent.
Mine was a plan-free mass querying
of condensed humans off the shelves,
all numbered, the tribal, the elderly.

Knowledge was the gait of compressed selves
and poetry seemed windows of italic
inset in grievous prose
which served it and mastered it:
few grapes for many rows.

Students murmured airily of the phallic
they were going to be marked by
but the shelvers book-trolleys were parked by
closed gaping tomes and stood them drily back,
vogue, value, theory.

The stacks clanged down metal stairs
to floors below reality,
to books in dragon-buckram, books like dreams,
antiphonaries and grimoires,
philologies with pages still uncut:

my blade made a sound like *rut*.
I never used the catalogue,
it held no serendipities.
The lateral book's the tip: it is
the seminal one near the one set.

You must range real shelves to find it.
Continuous assessment could have
excluded me; soon it did weed out my sort.
Critique closed over poetry,
the hip proved very straight.

What our donjon of kisses and cribs held
they say now will go on line.
This does not light my taper.
Others may have my joys at home? Fine.
But I surfed the true paper.


## A DEPLOYMENT OF FASHION

In Australia, a lone woman
is being crucified by the Press
at any given moment.

With no unedited right
of reply, she is cast out
into Aboriginal space.

It's always for a defect in weeping:
she hasn't wept on cue
or she won't weep correctly.

There's a moment when the sharks are
still butting her, testing her protection,
when the Labor Party, or influence,

can still save her. Not the Church,
not other parties. Even at that stage
few men can rescue her.

Then she goes down, overwhelmed
in the feasting grins of pressmen,
and Press women who've moved

from being owned by men
to being owned by fashion,
these are more deeply merciless.

She is rogue property,
she must be taught her weeping.
It is done for the millions.

Sometimes the millions join in
with jokes: how to get a baby
in the Northern Territory? Just stick

your finger down a dingo's throat.
Most times, though, the millions
stay money, and the jokes

are snobbish media jokes:
Chemidenko. The Oxleymoron.
Spittle, like the flies on Black Mary.

After the feeding frenzy
sometimes a ruefully balanced last lick
precedes the next selection.

# PRIME NUMBERS

What are you doing now, Les?

Normally I live in the country,
work, garden, parry thrusts from the *Herald*,
but two days a week I fly in
to a cubicle in the Stacked City,
an every-coloured brick university
that is built on top of itself
like a brain's lobes and evolutionary layers
on the last rock before Botany Bay.

The inner streets of this oppidum
are paved with grey carpet, and inmates
lie on them for cool negotiations
or to write in big pads. Footsteps with vocal
animate the stairs and little squares;
odd walls not yet built over
catch sun and frecklings of leaves;
a coffee shop may form round a stairwell.

My cubicle briefly bears my name
but no dates yet. Today I compose
in there about a former madhouse,
still meshed and brass-keyed when I met
all three of a shattered great poet.
He died before they let the mad out
to home like themes in family novels,
to swap locked for liberated hells.

Now the place is ochre, after cream,
and writers read there, beneath airliners
that brew up from under the horizon
and score prodigious hyphens through poems.

My dapper friend Philip appeared there,
nine years up-ramp in his wheelchair
from a stroke, to a dry chin, to language,
to his first new poem, just written.

The same week, a boy-man who didn't
speak for years told me *Cars in the mirror
drive on the right, the noon sun's south:
mirrors are like the Northern hemisphere.*
A million self-rescues so vertical
don't multiply. Each one is the shining one.
Love poured out on them also doesn't
subtract from the numbers they've attained.

Back above the racehorse-named streets
in Overlap City, I'm really a specimen,
a mountain to geographers. But Louise's friend
Sarah yarned with me, Annette too (God and Mary to her!)
and poet Hazel, and Peter the biographer –
all these the day after the burial
of Mother Theresa, whose real grace
lay in knowing how little to generalise.


## TO ME YOU'LL ALWAYS BE SPAT

Baby oyster, little grip,
settling into your pinch of shape
on a flooded timber rack:

little living gravel
I'm the human you need,
one who won't eat you,

not with much relish, even
when you're maturely underexercised
inside your knuckle sandwich.

Bloodless sheep's eye, never
appear in a bottle. Always bring
ice, lemon and your wonky tub.

You have other, non-food powers:
your estuaries are kept clean as crystal,
you eat through your jacuzzi,

469

you make even the non-sexy
think of a reliable wet
machine of pleasure,

truly inattentive students
of French hope they heard right,
that you chant in the arbours.

Commandant-of-convicts Wallis
who got the Wallis name unfairly
hated, had you burnt alive

in millions to make mortar.
May you now dance in the streets
and support a gross of towns!


## THE DISORDERLY

We asked How old will you be
in the year Two Thousand?
Sixty two. Sixty. Fifty nine.

Unimaginable. We started running
to shin over the sliprails
of a wire fence. You're last! –

It's all right: I'll be first in Heaven!
and we jogged on to school
past a yellow-flowering guinea vine.

Cattle stood propped on the mountain.
We caught a day-blind glider possum
and took him to school. Only later

at the shoe-wearing edge of our world
did we meet kids who thought everything
ridiculous. They found us incredible.

Cream-handed men in their towns
never screamed Christ-to-Jesus! at the hills
with diabetes breath, nor talked fight

or Scotch poetry in scared timber rooms.
Such fighters had lost, we realised
but we had them to love

or else we'd be mongrels.
This saved our souls later on,
sometimes, crossing the cousinless

detective levels of the world
to the fat-free denim culture,
that country of the Attitudes.


## FIVE POSTCARDS

Having run herself up out of
plush, the white-cheeked wallaby
sits between her haunches
like an old-country tailor behind
her outstretched last yard, her tail,
and hems it with black fingers.

o

Cosmic apples by Cézanne:
their colours, streaming, hit
wavelengths of crimson and green
in the yellowy particle-wind.
Slant, parallel and pouring,
every object's a choke-point of speeds.

o

The kitchens of this 18th century
Oxford college are ten metres high
by the squinch-eyed cooks basting
tan birds spiked in hundreds all over
the iron griddle before hellfire.
Below high lozengy church windows
others flour, fill, pluck. And this too
was the present once, that absolute of fools.

o

1828. Timber slums of the future
top a ship of the line, which receives
more who might have stormed St James's.
Cheery washing lines signal they're bound
for the world's end, to seize there
the lands of unclothed aristos
rich in myth and formal grammar.

o

A mirrory tar-top road across
a wide plain. Drizzling sky.
A bike is parked at a large book
turned down tent-fashion on the verge.
One emerging says *I read such crazy
things in this book. 'Every bird
has stone false teeth and enters
the world in its coffin.' That's in there.*


## THE INTERNATIONALE

Baron Samedi, leaving the House of Lords,
shrugs on his shoulders and agrees to come.
*Have you observed,* he asks, *dat a tarantula
is built like, but nimbler than, a Rugby scrum?*

472

The Manche blows East like a billion tabloid pages,
annoying the Baron: *Sheer prose, dese Narrow Seas!*
but a cohort of Lundys leaps out of Leemavaddy
on an intricate tuning of spring steel in their knees.

Mardi, now svelte, hoists up a horizontal ballad
and ascends its couplets because the fire's at the top
but Macready with a wheedle of a reedy pitch-pipe conjures
the cobra whose head will fit his wet eye-socket. Pop!

Jeu d'Esprit and Jeu de Paume grace our company
and the Countess von Dredy informs us with some pain
that in Gold-Orange-Land is now the sour gherkin season.
She'd rather complete a Seminar than a Semaine.

*Yall need some time on the low horse!* Mardi cries
as they all skip around us with Sha-na-na and Boom!
*Our energy shorten your lease of joy,* cries the Baron.
*But having summoned we, do you wish we trudge in gloom?*


## MORE THAN AN OBITER DICHTER

FOR PETER PORTER

Peter, you're in the dictionary!
It doesn't say what you mean
but you're noted for urbane wit in
the Macquarie, second edition.

Another friend's daughter found my
name in there, and the year I died
already past. With that behind me,
hey, I'm invincible, I cried.

It's right, as you know: our true
poetry follows our deaths.
It's fun to write the rest alive, though,
bibbling among the shibboleths,

weaving between our epitaphs.
Like a fast waterbird leading the dawn
in a string of musket-flashes across Garda
what we have written we have drawn.

May you reach your own century from this one.
Thank you for much hospitality.
A pillar of good talk all night
you were, and of company by day.

Master poet, Peter, you're this rock
tickled by roses in their climb;
you're our blue-edged flag, our fore-runner
first off the adzed blocks of home.

Be Italy and music for all readers:
Australia's no place to be Australian.
Let's tussle in a jar again sometime.
Thank you for my start in London.


## THE WATER PLOUGH

That was the Iron Age all right.
I'm glad it's in the museum.
Like that iron dam-sinking scoop
the weight of an Indian Chief motorbike
in there, from back before dozers.
I trained on that, cleaning dams.

Every five or ten years
you had to scoop out the silt
and stinking slop from a dam
or you'd have a paddy, not a pond.
First thing, you'd break through the wall
and let the water go like a culvert
you hoped you could seal up again.

The horse you yoked for the scooping
had to be a goer, but smart
enough to stop short at a word.
The trace-chains came off a swingle-tree
way ahead at his heels, and the timber
steering-shafts stretched you like flying,
your hands were so far apart.

You'd skim round the edges first,
shaving off the lashes of reeds
and dumping them with a twist over
and a twist back to keep the chains
uncrossed. And then you'd face
the dam bottom, the eel jelly.

What you did in there wasn't walk
nor swim, it was trail belly-down
with stabs for purchase with your boots
and curses and sprawls and swerving
as your big two-handed cruet
filled and piled and overflowed
and you'd lie down on the shafts
to keep its front edge up and clear
and swim it out to the paddock
to spill there, and the eels kicking
like nerves in it, biting at the dogs.

And that was when it went right.
However it went, you'd come up
out of the lost bedsteads and bones
with a suit of slime all over you
the colour of a Box Brownie photo
and thick as beef, smelling aluminium,
or yellow pug with leeches hooked like bait to you.
You'd glop around, weighing tons.
No hose, no showers then. A mate
or your wife might bucket your face
clear for tea and a smoke
as you caked and stiffened, then back:
*Into it, son: you wasn't born dry!*

475

Making the dams in the first place,
that was the bastard of a job.
You'd be stagger-walking, on dry land
at least, but the scoop might
stop curling the dirt and nosedive
for Hell any minute, and stick
and break the harness or your shoulders.
A quick enough kick-up of the shafts
could toss you over them like over
the horns of a bullock at the Show
and it was iron, that ridge ground.

The edge of a dragline scoop got
so sharpened, grinding gravel and stone,
it could have cut a man in two
easily if he got in front of it.
No wonder it glided purring through
spewy stuff, and snoring through
the better loam and clay, and left them
all polished like tiles, on a good day.
Butchered like shellholes on a bad day
groaning and screaming like them, too.

From the off you had to keep separate
the loam and leaf-mould so they didn't
get into the clay wall that you keyed,
levelled with just your eye, which is water
after all, and walked the horse over
and over, and hand-rammed, and hoped would hold
and half the time it didn't hold.

You got the blind staggers from tiredness
but I admit I liked the work, odd times,
spreading the hard knuckles of ridges
to fit a dam between, or giving
full play to a soak. Building with the country,
not on it. Building and reshaping it,
cuttings and bywashes and ramps,
finding the walls it would agree to,
stopping the chainsaws of erosion-water,

arresting them to spoons of sky light
for cattle and dingoes and birds
and turtles and blue lilies with leaves
like the tin stump-caps of houses.

Now the green bulldozer dams everywhere
are lakes to the puddleholes we made.
Fly over the country with the sun low
and it's all like gripped with fingernails:
gleams hang up on every allotment
to be some family's park pond
but it's still our idea
of making flood rain stay and perform
before it got off the continent
or deep into it, to the great still swirls.


## THE GREAT HALL OF CHLORINE

It is the great hall of Chlorine,
the Aquatic Centre. Light shaking all over the walls,
people of bleach and biscuit pad on raw feet
and children splat diamante. Many intently surge
out of deep trampolines of wavering.
Women adjust harness, some karate-chop at speed;
men exude their inner showers on the sauna's wooden shelves.
Heads are calm in the laundry-boiling of the spa
and a rare drip falls bling!
from the loose leaves of the ceiling.

A nonwhite family comes in, and glances vaguely,
aware some may still notice. The mother
picks at her plastic wrist-tie, her entry ticket.
Hardly anyone looks; no children do,
but through being of an age, or an education,
a few are subtly forced to notice. Many
of the white people, so called, are darker, from the sun,
but this is Race. This carries accusation.
Intellectuals invented race, and for centuries supplied

477

the terrible theory which deflected chains and conquest
away from the Modern, onto Primitives.
Now they turn the same weapon on their poor relations.
Anything these brown folk say, any hurt in their eyes
may be used against us.

Imagery has stopped. We're furtive in our minds.
What reaches of Gondwanaland are ancestral to these
I don't know. Whatever Race is, I read it poorly.
If their forebears once stood behind trees on their shore
watching nightmare develop like a Polaroid from seaward, what
stopped them charging, burning its stores, clubbing, killing
in that last window moment? That it was also riveting?
Occasionally some were decisively conservative
but it always came to that same moment again:
you had been after game, or making men, and the
excreting spirits were back, with their offering hands.

When the Martians come, they're like a university.
Their genes wink to instinct, their flashes shiver the gods.
Every mind intuits its escape from a perfect world.
But it goes on. The Martians are setting exams
in their own language. The Fail mark is terrible: epidemic,
the swerving muskets, death in a bag of flour.
The ancient poetry totters – but new laughs get learned,
jobs tried, worlds pictured, and brave ambitious women
come to borrow seed at the edge of spaceship tents,
things better known on the low horse than the high horse.

Few horses come into the great hall of the Chlorine:
better not to bring them.
Nothing in the water feeds Race. A little of the sun
pouring in through wiped walls may be kin to it,
but that family the Race dog followed in has merged
in the swimming noise of this mall, handling blue and yellow
floats that mark the lapping lanes. They plunge under ropes
and separate into their ages, over by the wheelchair hoist.
If I met them, we might become good friends
if we could cross that land, proxy-farmed for indignation,
that lies between us.

## A DOG'S ELEGY

The civil white-pawed dog who'd strain
to make speech-like sounds to his humans
lies buried in the soil of a slope
that he'd tear down on his barking runs.

He hated thunder and gunshot
and would charge off to restrain them.
A city dog too alive for backyards,
we took him from the pound's Green Dream

but now his human name melts off him;
he'll rise to chase fruit bats and bees;
the coral tree and the African tulip
will take him up, and the prickly tea trees.

Our longhaired cat who mistook him
for an Alsatian flew up there full tilt
and teetered in top twigs for eight days
as a cloud, distilling water with its pelt.

The cattle suspect the Dog lives
but three kangaroos stood in our pasture
this daybreak, for the first time in memory,
eared gazing wigwams of fur.


## LÁSZLÓ

One crepe-myrtle tree's already mirrored
in the grass by bloom it has shed,
tissue flowerets the exact mauve of gloves
that adjust the coffined dead.

Now it's evening. Cuisine on television:
artful pinches in Republic-flag liquid
on vast plates. I thought I would find
thistles in Scotland, too, but I never did.

479

Last night I met Lesley Murray.
She was my junior. Logically so.
Male Leslies crashed with Leslie Howard
in '43. And he was a László.

My friend's mother, seeing a woman shot,
split, and knew detachment from then on.
I marvelled She remembers when hers started! –
I watch myself writing this down.


## BIG SHAME

When Dad and I first drove to Sydney
we shared billy tea by the kerb
brewed with water a housewife boiled for us.
Too flash for him, a cafe in a suburb,

though he could charm them dewy when he tried.
Same with all Up Home advice, where to eat
or stay, in the Big Smoke: it's always
cheap holes where slurs die of defeat.

One dictionary awards rural-poor speech
entire to the Black folk who share it:
box up, walk off, bad friends, Poor, growl,
cheeky, hollow, in with, hunt, quiet –

Define me all those, or spare the Proletariat.
It's called Big Shame, my poison-brother fellow
says, this feeling abashed by proper people.
Before Racist and Beaut Authentic, we were Low

for which you get sentenced to the past
– you never see the court –
to smokes, to single beds in plywood rooms,
to union legends, to sashcord round your port.

* *poison-brother* – (Aboriginal English) brother-in-law.
An avoidance relationship in the Aboriginal kinship system.

# THE SUNRAYSIA POEMS

## Asparagus Bones

Thirstland talc light
haunted the bush horizons
all day. As it softened
into blusher we drove out
through gardens that are farms
past steeped sultana frames
to a red-earth dune
flicked all over with water
to keep it tightly knitted
in orange and avocado trees
black-green and silver green
above trickling dust. My friend
fetched a box of fossil bones
from the unlocked half-million
of the coolroom there: asparagus
for his banquet kitchen,
no-one around, no dog,
then we drove where biceps
of river water swelled
through a culvert, and bulges
of turbulence hunted swirls
just under their moon skin,
and we mentioned again
unsecured farm doors, open
verandahs, separate houses,
emblems of a good society.

## Oasis City

Rose-red city in the angles of a cut-up
green anthology: grape stanzas, citrus strophes,
I like your dirt cliffs and chimney-broom palm trees,

your pipe dream under dust, in its heads of pressure.
I enjoy your landscape blown from the Pleistocene
and roofed in stick forests of tarmacadam blue.

Your river waltzed round thousands of loops to you
and never guessed. Now it's locked in a Grand Canal,
aerated with paddlewheels, feeder of kicking sprays,

its willows placid as geese outspread over young
or banner-streamed under flood. Hey, rose-red city
of the tragic fountain, of the expensive brink,

of crescent clubs, of flags basil-white-and-tomato,
I love how you were invented and turned on:
the city as equipment, unpacking its intersections.

City dreamed wrongly true in Puglia and Antakya
with your unemployed orange-trunks globalised out of the ground,
I delight in the mountains your flat scrub calls to mind

and how you'd stack up if decanted over steep relief.
I praise your camel-train skies and tanglefoot red-gums
and how you mine water, speed it to chrome lace and slow it

to culture's ingredients. How you learn your tolerance
on hideous pans far out, by the crystals of land sweat.
Along high-speed vistas, action breaks out of you,

but sweeter are its arrivals back inside
dust-walls of evergreen, air watered with raisins and weddings,
the beer of day pickers, the crash wine of night pickers.

## Closer Links with Sunraysia

Hoofed beasts are year-round fires
devouring as high as they can reach,
hopeless to put out. Pink smoke
lifts off their terra cotta

but all fences have been torn out
and flocks, herds and horses banished
from this apricot country. Here
they've finished with the pastoral.

Downstream of this sprinkled terrain
merged desert rivers stop-go to Ocean
but the real Australian river,
the one made of hard labour and launched

with a tilt of a Chinese pole-bucket,
that one sets out for the human mouth
down a thousand asphalt beds
in squeaky crates and marshalled vintages.


## The Bulb of the Darling Lily

Sitting round in the Grand Hotel
at Festival time. Another year
that Philip Hodgins can't be here.
Naming the festival after him
almost confirms that. But like his fine
drypoint poems, it lets him be somewhere.

Sitting around in the Grand
with the stained glass in the gaming room
an upwelling pattern of vivid cards
and the T-shaped lolly-coloured logo
of the TAB everywhere, the Tabaret.
All Victoria's become one casino.

Sitting around the Grand Hotel
adding antipasto to the impasto
of my mortal likeness, writing postcards
instead of going on the guided
Lake Mungo tour. Too reverential,
too sacred. No grinners out there laugh.

So, sitting around in the Grand
yarning with Mario, with Donna and Stefano
and descending to the lower kitchen
to meet Leopardo Leopardi, who isn't
posing in languor on a thorn-tree limb
though he has the build, but making gnocchi.

Sitting around the Grand Hotel, yarning
about river cod as big as seals
and the de-snagged inland waters
being re-snagged to let them breed,
shovel-mouthed, with the beady gape
and rejecting clamp of a critic.


## THE NEWLY TRAGIC DODO

It's French for sleeping,
it's English for dead,
the first extinction
the regretful regretted.

Trustful island bird, flightless,
too long on its pat:
survivors-of-the-fittest
used to point to all that,

but approving any die-out's
now a thing you don't do;
evolution is racist
if you think it right through.

When we were tough
the dodo was grotesque,
fat, silly, comical –
now it's proud and brisk.

As any being becomes fashionable
its weight loses weight,
like the sea-supported whale
or the Carolina parrot.


## THE MOWED HOLLOW

When yellow leaves the sky
they pipe it to the houses
to go on making red
and warm and floral and brown
but gradually people tire of it,
return it inside metal, and go
to be dark and breathe water colours.

Some yellow hangs on outside
forlornly tethered to posts.
Cars chase their own supply.

When we went down the hollow
under the stormcloud nations
the light was generalised there
from vague glass places in the trees
and the colours were moist and zinc,
submerged and weathered and lichen
with black aisles and white poplar blues.

The only yellow at all
was tight curls of fresh butter
as served on stainless steel
in a postwar cafe: cassia flowers,
soft crystal with caraway-dipped tongues,
butter mountains of cassia flowers
on green, still dewed with water.

# TOWARDS 2000

As that monster the Twentieth Century
sheds its leathers and chains, it will cry

*Automatic weapons! I shot at*
*millions and they died. I kept doing it,*

*but most not ruled by uniforms ate well*
*in the end. And cool replaced noble.*

Nearly every black-and-white Historic figure
will look compromised by their haircut and cigar-

ette. And the dead will grow remoter
among words like *pillow-sham* and *boater.*

*You'll admit,* the old century will plead,
*I developed ways to see and hear the dead.*

Only briefly will TV restrain Hitler
and Napoleon from having an affair.

*I changed my mind about the retarded:*
*I ended great for those not the full quid.*

*You breathers, in your rhythmic inner blush,*
*you dismiss me, now I'm a busted flush,*

*but I brought cures, mass adventures* – no one's fooled.
A line called Last Century will be ruled

across all our lives, lightly at first,
even as unwiring bottles cough

their corks out, and posh aerosols burst
and glasses fill and ding, and people quaff.

# YOU FIND YOU CAN LEAVE IT ALL

Like a charging man, hit
and settling face down in the ringing,
his cause and panic obsolete,

you find you can leave it all:
your loved people, pain, achievement
dwindling upstream of this raft-fall,

back with the dishes that translated
beasts and croplands into the ongoing
self portrait your genes had mandated.

Ribbed fluorescent-panels flow
over you down urgent corridors,
dismissing midday outside. Slow,

they'd resemble wet spade-widths in a pit;
you've left grief behind you, for others;
your funeral: who'll know you'd re-planned it?

God, at the end of prose,
somehow be our poem –
When forebrainy consciousness goes

wordless selves it'd barely met,
inertias of rhythm, the life habit
continue the battle for you.

If enough of those hold
you may wake up in this world,
ache-boned, tear-sponged, dripped into:

*Do you know your name?* 'Yes' won't do.
It's Before again, with shadow. No tunnels.
You are a trunk of prickling cells.

It's the evening of some day. But it's also
afterlife from here on, by that consent
you found in you, to going where you went.

# THE DERELICT MILKY WAY

FOR TAREE CITY MILLENNIUM COMMITTEE

Those estuaries of the east coast
with burnish over their olives and tans
from a sun that reads its days from right
to left, the Arab and Hebrew way;

each river's a trumpet with a sand mute,
its valves are lift bridges at upstream towns;
receding outbreaks of violent hessian
map a long industry called The Highway

and little crosses turbaned in wreath
along its verges mark traffic death,
all because trumpets are no longer blown,
some reckon. Because there's no agreed tune.

This coast was a cheek the Millennium
kissed early, on both of its dawns
as the Black Armband tightened and loosened
round throats, on our moral proscenium.

Such stuff was all Town, though, way back
when milk-lorries stacked can on can
bringing us in to learn from Shakespeare's
fifteen acts against one fat man.

For pelicans over bottle-coloured lakes
time doesn't count to a climax
then re-start, from no egg, in mid air.
Eels scuttering on creek crossings don't care,

but a dog's nose snuggled to your bum
is a form of walking hand in hand
and all through the bricked enormous Hospital
cousins jink in wheeled beds from room to room.

I wish us all more truthful cousinship
of more races, in the centuries to come –
that's my boost. Beached lovers caress
like singing to each other in Braille

and *Wrong wrong!* the cattle grids shout
on sphinx-knee hills to the high plateau
and guitar-shaped helicopters peer, strumming,
for a pot crop in forests' cloud-shadow

but the big legal crop here is wilderness,
closing, in its solitudes and myriads,
on a Milky Way still settled by Australians
now portrayed kindly only in ads.


## LITERARY EDITOR

He sits rejecting poems,
saying too much no,
a black pen in his hand
to score their lack of lo!
but then a magic word stands up
off the page: *candelaborough* –

it throws him out of kilter.
*I've been too fine a filter.*
*Now see: the name of my true home.*
*It calls me! My native rococo!*
Snug in his stamped envelope,
folds grimed like those in verses,

he rejects himself, bites a wet lip
and steering with his paperclip
lifts off for their rendezvous:
*You edit me! You are my due!*
Above the cirrus he traverses
we hear his fading blip.

# THE RELATIVE GOLD

Most white people had no relations,
some had things to live up or live down;
in the days of Black Tommy McPherson
the country was more like the town.

Black Tom was a sport in New England
with his red Spanish boots and his sash
but among those who have no relations
respect is called credit. Bare cash

will get you supplies and survival
depending what stories are told –
so Black Tommy reached into New England
and drew out alluvial gold.

Places lightning had shattered in water
and still winked among pebbles were the source
of his drinking with duffers and teamsters;
all this drew the blue Police Force

who badgered him under suspicion
and questioned him where his claim lay
but the claims he half made and grinned off
truly tangled their snarling assay.

No trackers, no vertical riding
in gorges traced the washed vein of worth
with which he was buying up dignity.
Next thing, blacks'd be sharing the earth!

*Tom's one of the Tableland's richest men,*
smiled gold expert Henry Grob.
*Who'd begrudge a McPherson up here?* laughed Tommy,
*treat me right; I could give you a job.*

But someone who sought other favour
or had their own notions of class
sidled round in the Bald Nob barroom
and got their hand near Tommy's glass.

The spiked drink that sent Tommy reeling
across the dray road to fall down
gave him visions of two troopers gloating
*You look a real black now, you clown!*

Tom McPherson was never seen working;
he rode a high horse like a lord,
so the police who never worked either
had arranged, and now shared, a reward.

One put a bullet through a lung:
*That's for the times you got off!* –
*This is for Yugilbar sports day!*
Tom's wit drowned in his agonised cough.

As half of New England bewailed him,
diggers, carriers and Cobb and Co men
with relations and none declared Bald Nob Hotel
black, in the new jargon of then.

It broke and killed licensee McCormick,
it half starved his children and wife.
The tribal spouse Tommy had fought for
had more backup in her widowed life.

I was thinking about New England,
of the Buggs, the Wards and the Wrights,
how they'd all conjured gold from that country
by their different methods and lights.

I was thinking this when my credit cards
came up empty, and I was eyed
with that narrowed no-human-kin look
that would discount anything I tried.

All the gold I'd spun out of country
was imagery, remotely extolled,
but Tommy McPherson sported his with an air,
a black cousin with literal gold.

# THE ICE INDIGENE

Prone on its wrists, beige Bear
chins the ice, its shoulders a roll bar.
Its grand wheel-arch hindquarters

are flexed to propel this fur car
at you in a gallop
                    or bouncing in a lope
after oil seals who die for you.

Snow-mortared intelligent loner,
dope-eyed, with hair in his fur.
Abhor his sleeves upraised in preaching!

Arctos can drive on water
or canter the tilting platforms
amassed on the dome of ocean.

On the whitening blue-white, where landmarks
aren't made of land, and vanish,
she can live without help.

She wakes to motherhood. Gaffs
tip her gloves. Her diet is
all meat, with guts for vegetables.

She can wrest a red whale off Inuit,
appal their harpoons,
                      leave them Nunuvut.

Berg drifted to a grass shore, she'd
raven on Norsemen, those poetic terse men.
Caught flatfooted, the snowdrift garbageman

may totter cavern-voiced,
tall as tractor cabins
in the aurora's scope light,

then hibernate between divorcing
continents, in a helicopter sling.
He can be simple anywhere he's going.


## THE DAY I SLEPT LIKE A DOLPHIN

The day I slept like a dolphin
I'd flown the Atlantic twice over
and come down in snow-rimmed Denver.
There I filled in both entry papers
and got called back: *Hey! You, Buddy!*
*You didn't fill these out right!*
It was true. Only the right hand
side of the Immigration form
and of the Customs form had writing.
*I could explain that to you,* I marvelled,
as he impatiently did not,
he of La Migra.* *But I'd bore you,*
I added, and filled in the left questions.
Under an Atlantic of fatigue
one half of my brain had been sleeping
as the other kept watch and rose to breathe.
Next time, I'll peep, and get
a second, waking view of my dreams.


* La Migra: Mexican slang for the US Immigration Service.


## THE ROTTERDAM FLIGHT CAGE

Unexpected among Rotterdam's
steel-decked architectural cargo:
a flight cage three storeys high
built inside a theatre complex
and glazed on its snow-weather side.

493

It held a confetti of parrots
when I was there. Not burly
captains'-shoulder models, but small
taut pastel and nibble-mouthed Australians,
momentary foliage to polished stick boughs,

corellas, leeks, rosellas, budgerigars
which rose and jinked and showered
down again like crystalline themes
of badinage taken up and dropped
inside their day-and-night cylinder.

Well fed and I imagine all
European born, they were hardly
more imprisoned than most
little seed birds in the wild,
those whose aviary moves about

because it is the flock,
or ones whose whole life-territory
ranges from the verandah edge out
to the gloss-cardboard loquat tree,
or is two marsh fields a planet apart.

Safe from being frittered, in the powder
light of their deep tower they composed
in kinks, wing-leaves and creamy streaks
impressions of their inherent country,
like the stylised African moves

most humans now consciously do,
we being an African species.

## SMALL FLAG ABOVE THE SLAUGHTER

Perhaps a tribal kinship,
some indigenous skinship
is equivalent to the term our neighbour saw
fit to award his amiable then-fit successor,
now sick, whom he nurses:
*He is my husband-in-law.*


## DOWNHILL ON BORROWED SKIS

White mongrel I hate snow
wadded numbing mousse
grog face in a fur noose
the odd miraculous view
through glass or killing you
the only time I skied
I followed no skilled lead
but on parallel lent boards
fell straight down a hill
fell standing up by clenched will
very fast on toe-point swords
over logshapes and schist
outcrips crops it was no piste
nor had I had any drinks
wishing my ankles steel links
winging it hammer and Shazam
no stocks in afternoon mirk
every cloud-gap royally flash
like heading into a car crash
ayyy the pain! the paperwork!
my hands I didn't flail them
though neither left nor right
neither schuss nor slalom
my splitting splay twinned sled
pumping straining to spread
to a biplane wreck of snapped ligaments
all hell played with locked joints

but still I skidded down erect
in my long spill of grist
blinded hawk on a wrist
entirely unschooled unchecked
the worst going on not and not
happening no sprawl no bone-shot
till I stood on the flat
being unlatched and exclaimed at.


## THE HOLY SHOW

I was a toddler, wet-combed
with my pants buttoned to my shirt
and there were pink and green lights, pretty
in the day, a Christmas-tree party
up the back of the village store.

I ran towards it, but big sad people
stepped out. They said over me *It's just, like,
for local kiddies* and *but let him join in*;
the kiddies looked frightened
and my parents, caught off guard

one beat behind me, grabbed me up
in the great shame of our poverty
that they talked about to upset themselves.
They were blushing and smiling, cursing me
in low voices *Little bugger bad boy!*

for thinking happy Christmas undivided,
whereas it's all owned, to buy in parcels
and have at home; for still not knowing
you don't make a holy show of your family;
outside it, there's only parry and front.

Once away, they angrily softened to
me squalling, because I was their kiddie
and had been right about the holy show
that models how the world should be
and could be, shared, glittering in near focus

right out to the Sex frontier.


## THE GOOD PLATES

On the day of babyhood
the Christmas guest would come,
a soldier back from the war,
someone single, or far from home.

After new toys and ice cream,
midmorning those hot Decembers,
the family would turn ideal,
polite even to its members.

Still home, but genial, drought-free,
as the good plates came out;
angry topics winked as if forgiven
over cordials and Sheaf stout.

When all the Good Luck toasts failed
we in turn played guest
to old people in dark parlours
serving up their calm best,

then photos often show this person
among family, and loyal,
but chatting with some visible stranger
to mitigate the festival.

Passover night, Jews set a place
for Elijah the prophet.
If more than a twosome, perhaps,
no human circle is complete,

497

and one more's a way out of too many.
Come spirit, come witness:
family love's the point, or childhood,
but the guest is Christmas.


## A VERB AGREEMENT

After a windstorm, the first man
aloft in our broad silky-oak tree
was Andrew Lansdown the poet,
bearded and supple, nimbly
disinvolving wrecked branches
up where I couldn't clamber.

He asked for our chainsaw, but I
couldn't let him hazard an iamb or
a dactyl, nor far worse his
perched body of value and verses;
showering rubies were an image to terrify
even about an imagist so spry.

So, above my scattered choppings, he
hawked with a handsaw west-and-southerly
and went home to Susan with our thanks,
God-spared from caesuras or endstoppings.
The tree has twice since become
a Scala of ginger balconies, a palladium

as it does every October.
Birds with skin heads like the thumb
on a black hand interrogate its bloom
with dulcet commentary till it's sober
but, bat-nipped gold or greening out blue,
it glories like the kingdom within Andrew.

# AT THE SWAMPING OF CATEGORIES

WITH THANKS AND ACKNOWLEDGEMENTS TO IRIS CHANG

When the flag of the pool of blood
came up the Yangtze Valley
its soldiers were licensed to flow
into a great space of cruelty.
They filled canals with working men;

they transmitted their own DNA
then slaughtered the women who got it;
they widened the littlest girls
and halved them after with swords.
When the flag of the clot of blood

came up the Yangtze Valley
it flew above a tsunami
God waited for inertia or humans
to arrest, as with a wave of ocean.
When the red-dyed rice ball of the poor

fluttered below the walls of Nanjing
seven hundred thousand people
cowered, reassuring one another
as their own collapsed army changed clothes.
The Purple Mountain was burning

and the Emperor's troops entered the city
behind tracked one-eyed steel cars
that busted all bodies they reached
and the many more being made running.
This was old atomic war: humans as the atoms.

Of twenty seven Westerners in the city
most were missionaries. Of YH God.
To head-severing contests, to mass shootings,
to screaming flagrante with impalements
these opposed a refusal of awe.

With nonbelievers and mild Christmas-keepers,
armed only with prestige and shouts
they patrolled the two-square-mile bounds
of the Safety Zone Wilson Mills devised.
They ran between machine guns and ranked men;

their eyes were the Vietnam TV
of thirty years later, to Christmas bayonets.
Pure bluff, scorned at first, the Zone grew real:
some pronounced the reason *faith*, some *face*,
but John Rabe's swastika arm

day and night shielded a multitude.
Among Nazis, Oskar Schindler saved his thousand
and the Rabes their scores of thousands.
When the flag of the soldier's slapped face
sanctioned gut-pulling military dogs

Minnie Vautrin whose battery torch
was a light-sword to hack rapes apart,
James McCallum of the ambulance ploy,
Lewis Smythe, John Wilson the one surgeon,
these fought in the Iliad of peace,

Ernest Forster, John Magee who filmed it:
they were jostled, shot near, pitched down
HQ stairs, but their fiction held
the half of Nanjing that would survive
its slashed frosted-earth weeks of delirium.

Though all of Nanjing's twenty seven
were prosperous, in ways snobbish, and white,
they kept alive three hundred thousand
people seen then as not their colour,
got them mouthfuls, and their plight to the world.

Trade, ideological war, and the A-bomb
have buried the International Committee
but, each against armed lewd thousands,
by such very odds,
they turned a glamorous rage back into water.


## A RIDDLE

The tall Wood twins
grip each other everywhere:
'It's all right, we're only
standing in for Lady Stair.' *

* Answer: a ladder


## SOUND BITES

Attended by thousands, the Sun is opening

o

it's a body-prayer, a shower: you're
in touch all over, renewing, enfolded in a wing –

o

My sorrow, only ninety-five thousand
welcomes left in Scots Gaeldom now.

o

Poor cultures can afford poetry, wealthy cultures can't.

o

Sex is the ever-appeased class
system that defeats Utopias ...

o

but I bask in the pink that you're in (Repeat)

o

one day, as two continents are dividing
the whole length of a river turns salt.

o

What's sketched at light speed
thunder must track, bumbling, for miles

o

If love shows you its terrible face
before its beautiful face, you'll be punished.

o

People watching with their mouths
an increasing sky-birth of meteors

o

Y chromosomes of history, apologise to your Xes!

o


## YOUNG GENERAL MACARTHUR
## IN A COONSKIN COAT

Douglas MacArthur in a raccoon coat,
the Boy Brigadier with slackened cap-seam,
the Fighting Dude, his thin trench whip
and ten-foot scarf strike an English note:
he's the folksiest prince on this troopship.

502

Nothing here is irony. No returning to the grind
and camping up the glory one last drag time.
His eyes on the camera, his lips twinkle for them.
He'll always be a portrait disguised as a figure;
here he sails to the Jazz Age as the doughboys snigger.

He'll drive them from DC when their need scares him,
'It's the orders you disobey that make your reputation!'
yet be sparing with their sons in his bigger war.
As a remake of the Sun God he'll remake Japan,
demand another victory and get made an old man.

You can't see MacArthur past his MacArthur life.
We look from the future. It makes him monochrome
but he's just seen the Elephant, without reversal
and it's confirmed his genius: total rehearsal.
With himself on each arm he is Hero and Wife.


## IN THE COSTUME OF ANDALUSIA

Traditional costume puts you
anywhere in its span:
was it in the eighteenth
or the twentieth century
you were photographed, in colour,
at noonday in Seville?

Strolling with your sister
or your schoolfellow, perhaps,
and wearing for your *paseo*
the sash of a horsewoman,
the cropped black coatee
and the levelled flat hat.

That day was your perfection,
your tan face unwrinkled
as the rain-coloured skin
of the tiny pearls that buttoned
your ears and white collar.

503

You were photographed by a man,
a personable foreigner.
The total attention
in your olive eyes,
the stilled line of your mouth
all equally reveal it.

The windows of your perfectly
vertical nose inhale man
but you evince none
of the arts of cliché.
Your gaze photographs
the effect of his gaze and yours.

If you had a name, we might
imagine you strolling on
into all your private pictures,
the Sierra, the Range Rover,
into time's minute razors.

Here, where you still are
as you were then, briefly being
the temper of a people,
you don't know when you're kissed

or when your burnished horse
was brought, block by block,
shuddering happily in the sun.


CHANSON

The sun tunes out stars
when it shines the air blue
but the stars burn all day
and you're in their view

the star in your window
among the bow sashes
would itself be a beau
with glitter and dashes

he'd swim in through panes
framed up like the turrets
of old bombing planes
he'd intrude on your merits

as light on a diamond
of VVS grade
diamond's tender to light
brick and wool they are hard –

he's a daylight star though
from far back in time and
those vanish in sun-bleach
so he's all blast and reach

in illimitable night
he'd rather be a highlight
the stars burn beyond day
and you're in their view


## THE LONG WET SEASON

Poetry is apt to rise in you
just when you're on the brink
of doing something important,

trivially important, like flying
across the world tomorrow –
while here our paddock, waterlogged

from features and supplements of rain
smells to be making dark beer
out of rock oils afloat round its grass.

Paperbark trees sleep their lives here.
One supports a flowering constrictor
vine fit to muscle over a rainforest:

that tree's been allowed decades
of half life, being all the vine found,
and the ownerless local flock

of geese, spooked by something, all
glide off like Chinese pottery
spoons, rotating gloved feet.

Out of the sky, crackling and folding
like a spread of the *Australian*
a snowy egret arrives to spike water.

Nature, getting around like word.


## AUTUMN CELLO

Driving up to visit April
who lives on the Tableland
we were sorry for russet beef cattle
deciduous on pasture hills.

We'd had to shower off summer
to climb to the Tableland
where April would be breezily
scuffing her yellow shoes.

As we crossed the caramel river
that is walled in nettle trees
and drove up through black rainforest
the moon was in our mind

it being the dark of the moon
all day, as we went up to April,
the fat moon who saw it is children
who bring death into the world

and was exiled to the sky for it
before there was any April
to plant elm trees, or touch
amber glasses with a spoon.

Next night, the moon would rise
asleep in his brilliant rim
of cradle above bared trees
and April, having forgotten

she was once herself a moon
would feed cognac-coloured rosin
to her cello bow, and read us
story-feeling without the stories

and straight depth with no sides,
all from her tilted quatrain
of strings with its blunt prong
in her Wilton rug on the Tableland.


## THE NEW HIEROGLYPHICS

In the World language, sometimes called
Airport Road, a thinks balloon with a gondola
under it is a symbol for *speculation*.

Thumbs down to ear and tongue:
World can be written and read, even painted
but not spoken. People use their own words.

Latin letters are in it for names, for e.g.
OK and $H_2SO_4$, for musical notes,
but mostly it's diagrams: skirt-figure, trousered figure

have escaped their toilet doors. *I* (that is, *saya*,
*ego*, *watashi wa*) am two eyes without pupils;
those aren't seen when you look out through them.

*You* has both pupils, *we* has one, and one blank.
*Good* is thumbs up, thumb and finger zipping lips
is *confidential*. *Evil* is three-cornered snake eyes.

The effort is always to make the symbols obvious:
the bolt of *electricity*, winged stethoscope of course
for *flying doctor*. Pram under fire? *Soviet film industry*.

Pictographs also shouldn't be too culture-bound:
a heart circled and crossed out surely isn't.
For *red*, betel spit lost out to ace of diamonds.

*Black* is the ace of spades. The king of spades
reads *Union boss*, the two is *feeble effort*.
*If* is the shorthand Libra sign, the scales.

Spare literal pictures render most nouns and verbs
and computers can draw them faster than Pharaoh's scribes.
A bordello prospectus is as explicit as the action,

but everywhere there's sunflower talk, i.e.
*metaphor*, as we've seen. A figure riding a skyhook
bearing food in one hand is the pictograph for *grace*,

two animals in a book read *Nature*, two books
inside an animal, *instinct*. Rice in bowl with chopsticks
denotes *food*. Figure 1 lying prone equals *other*.

Most emotions are mini-faces, and the speech
balloon is ubiquitous. A bull inside one is dialect
for placards inside one. Sun and moon together

inside one is *poetry*. Sun and moon over palette,
over shoes etc. are all art forms – but above
a cracked heart and champagne glass? Riddle that

and you're starting to think in World, whose grammar
is Chinese-terse and fluid. Who needs the square-
equals-diamond book, the *dictionary*, to know figures

508

led by strings to their genitals mean *fashion?*
just as a skirt beneath a circle means *demure*
or a similar circle shouldering two arrows is *macho*.

All peoples are at times cat in water with this language
but it does promote international bird on shoulder.
This foretaste now lays its knife and fork parallel.


## ON THE BORDERS

We're driving across tableland
somewhere in the world;
it is almost bare of trees.

Upland near void of features
always moves me, but not to thought;
it lets me rest from thinking.

I feel no need to interpret it
as if it were art. Too much
of poetry is criticism now.

That hawk, clinging to
the eaves of the wind, beating
its third wing, its tail

isn't mine to sell. And here is
more like the space that needs
to exist around an image.

This cloud-roof country reminds me
of the character of people
who first encountered roses in soap.

# THE ANNALS OF SHEER

Like a crack across a windscreen
this Alpine sheep track winds
around buttress cliffs of sheer
no guard rail anywhere
like cobweb round a coat
it threads a bare rock world
too steep for soil to cling,
stark as poor people's need.

High plateau pasture must be great
and coming this way to it
or from it must save days
for men to have inched across
traverses, sometime since the ice age,
and then with knock and hammer
pitching reminders over-side
wedged a pavement two sheep wide.

In the international sign-code
this would be my pictograph for
cold horror, but generations

have led their flocks down and up
this flow-pipe where any spurt
or check in deliberate walking
could bring overspill and barrelling
far down, to puffs of smash, to ruin

which these men have had
the calm skills, on re-frozen
mist footing, to prevent
since before hammers hit iron.

# ERNEST HEMINGWAY AND THE LATEST QUAKE

In fact the Earth never stops moving.

Northbound in our millimetric shoving
we heap rainy Papua ahead of us
with tremor and fumarole and shear
but: no life without this under-ruckus.

The armoured shell of Venus doesn't move.
She is trapped in her static of hell.
The heat of her inner weight feeds enormous
volcanoes in that gold atmosphere

which her steam oceans boil above.
Venus has never known love:
that was a European error.
Heat that would prevent us gets expressed

as continent-tiles being stressed and rifted.
These make Earth the planet for lovers.
If coral edging under icy covers
or, too evolutionary slow

for human histories to observe it, a low
coastline faulting up to be a tree-line
blur landscape in rare jolts of travel
that squash collapsing masonry with blood

then frantic thousands pay for all of us.

# THE IMAGES ALONE

Scarlet as the cloth draped over a sword,
white as steaming rice, blue as leschenaultia,
old curried towns, the frog in its green human skin;
a ploughman walking his furrow as if in irons, but
as at a whoop of young men running loose
in brick passages, there occurred the thought
like instant stitches all through crumpled silk:

as if he'd had to leap to catch the bullet.

A stench like hands out of the ground.
The willows had like beads in their hair, and
Peenemünde, grunted the dentist's drill, Peenemünde!
Fowls went on typing on every corn key, green
kept crowding the pinks of peach trees into the sky
but used speech balloons were tacky in the river
and waterbirds had liftoff as at a repeal of gravity.


# ROOMS OF THE SKETCH-GARDEN

FOR PETER AND CHRISTINE ALEXANDER

Women made the gardens, in my world,
cottage style full-sun fanfares
netting-fenced, of tablecloth colours.

Shade is what I first tried to grow
one fence in from jealous pasture,
shade, which cattle rogueing into

or let into, could devour
and not hurt much. Shelter from glare
it rests their big eyes, and rests in them.

A graphite-toned background of air
it features red, focusses yellow.
Blue diffusing through it rings the firebell.

Shade makes colours loom and be thoughtful.
It has the afterlife atmosphere
but also the philosophic stone cool.

It is both day and night civilised,
the colour of reading, the tone
of inside, and of inside the mind.

I could call these four acres Hanlin
for the Chinese things they have nourished,
loquat, elm, mulberry, the hard pear

er ben lai. But other names would fit: Klagenfurt,
Moaner's Crossing, for the many things that die,
for worn-out farm soil, for the fruit fly.

Cloud shadows walking our pencilled roof
in summer sound like a feasting chook
or Kukukuku on about duk-duk

and this sketch garden's a retina for chance:
for floodwaters backing into the lower
parterres like lorryloads of mercury

at night, or level sepia by day,
for the twenty-three sorts of native vines
along the gully; for the heron-brought

igniting propane-blue waterlily,
for the white poplars' underworld advance
on the whole earth, out of my ignorance.

Tall Australians stand east of the house
and well north. The garden's not nationalist:
Australians burn, on winds from the west.

No birds that skim-drink, or bow
or flower in our spaces are owned now.
Jojo burrs make me skid my feet on lawn

being wary of long grass, like any bushman.
Begged and scavenged plants survived dry spells
best, back when I'd to garden in absentia:

Dad wouldn't grow flowers, or water ornamentals.
He mounded for the Iroquois three sisters,
corn beans and squash. And melons, and tomatoes.

Those years we'd plant our live Christmas tree
in January when it shed its brittle bells
and the drought sun bore down like dementia.

Now bloom-beds displace fox-ripped rooster plumes
in from paddocks, in our cattle-policed laager;
trampled weeds make wharves for the indigo waterhen.


## ANGOPHORA FLORIBUNDA

*That country seemed one great park*
*in which stood big bridal trees*
*raining nectar and white thread*
*as native things ate their blossom*
*like hills of wheaten bread*
*and we called them Apple trees*
*our homesickness being sore*
*if you took up land where they grew*
*it kept your descendants half poor ...*

but farmers rarely cut them down.
They survive from the Eden of the country
because the wood's useless and rots fast
and because they're the Eden of the country.

Slashed leaves feed stock in a drought
and the tree, in its dirt-coloured bark
and snakes-and-laddery branchage
often grows aslant, heeled over
like an apple-pie schooner aground
on the shores of a North Coast pig farm.

Aged ones get cancerous
with humps of termite nest.
They shed their rotted limbs
to lie around them like junk
which only decay can burn.
A chewed-paper termite city
set alight in an Apple trunk
will rage all night and never
ignite its crucible of wood.

A veteran may drop most of itself
in one crash autumn, and re-grow from its boot.
Uselessness, sprawl and resurrection
are this apple's fruit.


## AT THE FALLS

High mountain plateau edged
with vertical basalt cliffs
like black hung chain, like sprockets
conveying a continual footage
of water, abruptly curved
and whitening down into clouds.

On a damp earth track
to other viewing points, a
young wife twists her ankle.
She falls painfully. Her husband,
his eyes everywhere like a soldier,
mutters *Get up!* in a panic voice,
*Quick! There are people coming.*

She struggles up, furious,
spurning his hand. A cloud
like steam rises out of the gorge.
Over years, this memory
will distil its essence: fear

of the house her eccentric man
inhabits, and what is done
there, or away from there.
That she is the human he has married.


## TRUE YARN

A man approaches the edge
of his life, which has miscarried.

He looks down the enormous wall
of rock to the ocean-boulders
far below. They seem the teeth
in a white-green tidal blender
that won't fail him. He launches
off, just as the mightiest wave
ever recorded at Sydney gathers
lift in the chimney of the Gap like
a freight elevator, like the swelling
fore-smoke of a ballistic missile silo,
like a foam-faced cosmic air bag
that receives him, then drops back
so fast he not only can't sink
but has to cling to its narrowing
thunder-roof of drowning seagulls
and the collapse is so abundant
that, storeys above the death-studs,
he is surfed away in the wash
a mile clear of the cliffs
and left to the fast life boat.

More failure? Yet his rescue looked
like a wrathful peremptoriness.

# AN AUSTRALIAN LEGEND

It is the time of day
when shadows come in like animals
and shelter under their trees

when shade also tightens
in along the web of gullies
rehearsing old treelines and flood

all this drainage stops short
at a country of salt marsh
plodded in by dipping birds

this is the ancient sea shore
where the Aunt in her magic-propelled
boat carried off the younger brother

from the big island of men
to the island of left-handed women
who kill men on sight

wild mirror-image fighters
their arm doesn't cross their breasts
they strike from your own right side

it took obedience and discipline
for Younger Brother to hide prone in the boat
all day, then creep ashore at night,

lie pretending sleep and be felt
by furtive right hands, and so win
wives for his brother and himself

*Bro, these people are called Women*
people started to be born after that
along the coast here this happened

# THE ENGINEER FORMERLY KNOWN
# AS STRANGELOVE

Mein Führer, they called me Doctor Strangelove
in the 1960s. This now they'd dare not do.
Right and Left then thought in Perverts, like you
but now it's Doctor Preference, Doctor Paralimbic –

I've also quit the White race. The ac-
cident of pallor became not worth the flak.
I won't join another. Race is decadent.
I lay this wreath on your unknown grave, mein Führer.

In my third sunrise century, Germany
has re-conquered Europe on her knees.
Fighter planes still pull gravities, not levities
but the flag of the West is now a gourmet tablecloth.

The Cold War is a Dämmerung long since of dead Götter
but I am still in cutting-edge high tech.
In a think-tank up to my neck
I rotate, projecting scenarios.

In one, nearly every birth's a clone
of Elvis, of Guevara, of Marilyn
and many later figures. Few new people get born
then nostalgia for nostalgia collapses.

Of your own copies, one is a Trappist, to atone;
the other went through school and never heard of you.
He helps creased, off-register people who fade as they relax.
They are tourists travelling on the cheap, by 3D fax.

Marxists will resurge by squaring sex with equality.
Every wallflower will be subject to compulsory
fulfilment by the beautiful: deprivation makes Tory.
Evolution likewise, that condones and requires

extinctions will trip the moral wires
of Green thought and become a fascist outlaw.
Darwin will be re-read in tooth and claw.
In another projection, most of life goes Virtual.

War is in space, in the trenches, in chain armour:
for peace, just doff the Tarnhelm. But some maniac
will purloin a real nuke for his psychodrama –
and not the slow old-tech sort you developed, mein Führer.

In that model, too, the screen replaces school
and language (alas, English) regains the flavourful
and becomes again inventive, once post-intellectual.
Media story-selection and, in the end, all commentary

will be outlawed as censorship. Like fashion
they will be aspects of the crime Assault.
Direct filming of our underlit dreams will replace them
and poverty, sedulously never called a fault

will be stamped out by the United World Mafia.
Generals and tycoons will be excised like tumours
if they try to impede the conversion to consumers
of all their billionfold peons and garbage-sorters.

To forestall migration, all places will be Where the Action Is.
People will wear their showers, or dress in light and shade.
Australians will learn moral courage, disease will be cured –
Here the Doctor wallowed, and his speech became obscured.


## THE TIN CLOTHES

This is the big arrival.
The zipper of your luggage
growls *valise* round three sides
and you lift out the tin clothes.

## THE SUCCESSIVE ARMS

A drunk man in a rank shirt
unsteadily walks the street
begging, and arms flick up
dismissing him: Piss off!
Piss off mate. He recedes
far along, still groggily
reviewing backhand salutes
till you can trace him only
by the erupting stoic arms.


## JUDGED WORTH EVACUATING

Vertical war, north of my early childhood:

in pouring high forest, men labour,
deadly furniture in hand, on mud footholds.

They eye a youth strapped between shafts
and blanched with agony, being tenderly
levered down past them by Papuans.

A hammer of impatiens flowers got him.


## THE MOON MAN

Shadowy kangaroos moved off
as we drove into the top paddock
coming home from a wedding
under a midnightish curd sky

then his full face cleared:
Moon man, the first birth ever
who still massages his mother
and sends her light, for his having

been born fully grown.
His brilliance is in our blood.
Had Earth fully healed from that labour
no small births could have happened.


## SUCCOUR

Refugees, derelicts – but why classify
people in the wreck of their terms?
These wear mixed and accidental clothing
and are seated at long tables in rows.

It's like a school, and the lesson
has moved now from papers to round
volumes of steaming food
which they seem to treat like knowledge,

re-learning it slowly, copying it
into themselves with hesitant spoons.


## PREDAWN IN HEALTH

The stars are filtering through a tree
outside in the moon's silent era.

Reality is moving layer over layer
like crystal spheres now called laws.

The future is right behind your head;
just over all horizons is the past.

The soul sits looking at its offer.

# THE ANTIPODES OF INDIA

NORTH QUEENSLAND, DRY SEASON 1994

Out in country like a Lincolnshire
under Divine punishment, there was swimming
with harmless crocodiles in a sheathed
lava flume, the Copperfield River,
after which antique wooden carriages
lengthened on over jade and straw plain
volcano-shot with blackened boulders.

By next afternoon, the air was layered
with heat so ashen that liquids
weren't wet on cardboard lips.
Into that evening, the train
toiled up-range towards the lights of its own
weary loco. This was point-upwards India,
back of the Wet Tropics, and almost
unpeopled. Where town lights next flared
seemed a vacated maidan of the Raj.


# ROBERT FERGUSSON NIGHT

FOR THE COMMEMORATION AT
ST ANDREWS UNIVERSITY, OCTOBER 2000

All the Fergussons are black
I've heard said in the Outback.
Sub rosa, the Scots empire ranged wide.
I hope Scotland proportions her pride
now to the faith her lads kept with
all the subject folks they slept with.
I know for you this wasn't an issue.
Madness made a white man of you

disastrously young. You stayed alive
just long enough to revive
from Scottish models and kings
such mediaeval things
as documentary verse-television
and writing in Scots for the brain.
In that, you set the great precedent
for every vernacular and variant

the world-reach of English would present.
Now you're two hundred and fifty
and gin some power the giftie
gied ye of a writership-in-revenance
you'd find a death-cult called Romance
both selling and preserving a scrubbed Reekie
and the now-posh Highlands. Very freaky.
You might outdo Dr Johnson in polite

St Andrews now, that Reformation bombsite.
I fear you mightn't outdraw golf there:
golf keeps from the door the wolf there –
but no one does what you showed some aversion
to already in your time, poetical inversion.
Metrics too, now, are Triassic pent amateur
and 'Rhyme is for Negroes', I heard in Berlin:
the speaker was a literary Finn.

Such talk, now at last, is a sin
in place of much that wasn't. Madness
for instance. The Bedlams yielded to medicine:
even madness has, a little. Madness:
would you rise from the grave back through madness?
It took you and left us Burns
of the Night. Many jubilant returns:
this at last is Robert Fergusson Night.

## TO DYE FOR

A razor whetting silt and alluvium
off a neck in a mirror-doubled room
of soak and frizz and conversation
piling curlers and the hush-hush spray
and with the wide canny old shop broom
the work-experience schoolgirl hourly
angles and felts together
the one uncontentious human flag,
grey ginger lilac buff
black blonde and coherent brown.


## TOUCHDOWN

The great airliner has been filled
all night with a huge sibilance
which would rhyme with FORTH
but now it banks, lets sunrise
in in freak lemon Kliegs,
eases down like a brushstroke
onto swift cement, and throws out
its hurricane of air anchors.
Soon we'll all be standing
encumbered and forbidding in the aisles
till the heads of those farthest forward
start rocking side to side, leaving,
and that will spread back:
we'll all start swaying along as
people do on planks but not on streets,
our heads tick-tocking with times
that are wrong everywhere.

# THE CUT-OUT

In the shed it's bumped verticals,
tin and planking the colour of rain.

The sheep left their cloud inside
and two men lie wringing wet.

One man owns the flock, but neither
expects to wear the suitings.

The indoor storm of their work
earns a bit more survival, near home,

and each shearing-sling is a whale's
joined jawbones, dangling from a spring.


# HISTORY OF THE ENLIGHTENMENT

Faith was a dream technology
but one we couldn't master, or do cold
and it soon became equivocal again.
Mountains got moved by money or the lash
and we started to insult faith
as if it might be piqued and after all
kick in that sacred phase-shift
where cancers vanish, and the
golden brown in their antique clothes
enlarge from photograph size, walking
toward us, all welcoming, with secrets
the day it is Dreamtime in our streets.


# VISITOR

He knocks at the door
and listens to his heart approaching.

# MYTHOLOGY

A stupefying peak crack
across boiling air miles,
instantaneously annulled. That
was one of the Lightning brothers.
Brilliant longer than their lifetimes
they exist in orgasm only.
Between, they're air's memory
of climax. Death rays hid in hum.
Who'll fish the blind scrawl of lightning
out of Life's mouth, that old clay golem?
Eye-jabbing forerunners of live wire
their yield's that mirror perfume
mounting up to tame the Sun.


# CLOTHING AS DWELLING AS
# SHOULDERED BOAT

Propped sheets of bark converging
over skin-oils and a winter fire,
stitched hides of a furry rug-cloak
with their naked backs to the weather,
clothing as dwelling as shouldered boat
beetle-backed, with bending ridgelines,
all this, resurrected and gigantic:
the Opera House,
Sydney's Aboriginal building.


# STARRY NIGHT

In the late Nineteenth century
one is out painting landscapes
with spiralling sky
and helicopter lights approaching.

## THE KETTLE'S BUBBLE-MAKING FLOOR

Who remembers the bitter
smell of smoke still in the house
the sunny next afternoon?
So recently smoke was everyday.
Who remembers the woolly
pink inside a burning peat?
The taste of tank water boiled
in blanched, black-shelled cast iron?
The pucker of water heated with
ashy stones in a wooden dish?

## BIG BANG

If everything is receding
from everything, we're only
seeing the backs of the stars.

## WORKER KNOWLEDGE

The very slight S of an adze handle
or broadaxe handle are cut off square.
When adzes stopped licking timber ships
they were stubbed to scrape rabbit-trap setts.

But the worker's end of a felling axe
where the tapering upsweep levels down
to bulge, is cut slant, to the shape
of a thoroughbred's hoof pawing the ground.

## JELLYFISH

Globe globe globe globe
soft glass bowls upside down
over serves of nutty udder and teats
under the surface of the sun.


## TO FLY IN JUST YOUR SUIT

Humans are flown, or fall;
humans can't fly.
We're down with the gravity-lumpers,
rare, thick-boned, often basso.

Most animals above the tides are airborne.
Typically tuned keen, they
throw the ground away with wire feet
and swoop rings round it.

Magpies, listening askance
for their food in and under lawn,
strut so hairtrigger they almost
dangle on earth, out of the air.

Nearly anything can make their
tailcoats break into wings.


## THE GREAT CUISINE CLEAVER
## DANCE SONNET

Juice-wet black steel
rectangle with square bite
dock pork slice slice
candy pork mouth size
heel-and-toe work walk
thru greens wad widths
bloc duck bisect bone
facet glaze nick snake

slit wriggle take gallbladder
whop garlic shave lily-root
wham! clay chicken-crust
hiss wok plug flare
circling soy cringing prawn
blade amassing sideways mince.


## LACE CURTAIN

All politeness, all endearments
are known as palaver
once you are inside that love.
It is a compound
to keep out the world, and nearly everyone
even within it has a contempt-name.
You are in on a stare,
a style of looking down,
and what is counted worth saying
is what has turned all stuff
that housefly colour.


## CREOLE EXAM

How old were you when you first
lived in a weatherproof house?


## THE HEWERS

He used the older Irish profanity:
the hammer wriggled its bottom,
the heavens wore skimpy garish clothes,
the science of physics cruised men
who ogled it out of slow cars –
he put no limit to the fabulous
variety of entities
that might offer sex for money.

## LAGGAN CEMETERY

Sheep are like legal wigs
the colour of fissured cement
in that bleached country
and the few one-storey buildings
of the living can't dwarf the
absorbed marble chess of the dead.


## THE PAINT HOUSE

That house on the riverbank
below the high guillotine bridge
was of planking, but no light came out
through the joins. It didn't draw.
It turned a back on us like cheering
heard differently from year to year.

Gloss black on gut-pink with chartreuse
patched over both, all ignoring its house-shapes:
some said whatever remained in paint tins
was the design principle. Decades before hippiedom.
Next year it might be lime and navy blue
invading the cherry roof to big extents.
It was my first half dozen abstract paintings.

I hear the man who owned it was a Bird.


## HOON HOON

Hoon, hoon, that blowfly croon:
first a pimp and then a goon.
Sound of a prop plane crossing the moon.
The crack of noon from a can of beer
and a Viking is nothing but a rune hoon.

# A COUNTRYMAN

On the long flats north of the river
an elder in a leather jacket
is hitchhiking to his daughter's funeral.


# THE END OF SYMBOL

From a cinder in the far blue
a wedgetail eagle used to magnify
down into arrival, into belief,
matching speeds with a boy as he
rode his bike through suburban Melbourne,
then it would fold double and alight
on his handlebars, its inarguable expression
never ruffled, but its flickknife pinions
dilating around curves, and it would
chicken-peep near inaudibly when he
caressed it beneath the flames of its neck.


# THE SCORES

AUSTRALIA SINCE FEDERATION


## *1901*

When we were all servants
scrubbing off Madam's slurs
I gave up my baby
and the black girl kept hers.
When I got my own high horse
living things felt my spurs
and the flowers were all golden wattle.

## 1921

That weak word the *Battlers*:
I saw from the train
families punch hoods from wheat bags
to keep out the rain;
Tom said a seller's market
made Australian girls vain
and for Tom the flowers were poppies.


## 1941

Ar there, Ginger Meggs:
was it Susso tea and suet
put those calipers on your legs?
If Sister Kenny could do it
you'd walk again like a trooper,
left-right and left-right
and the wreaths would be Singapore orchids.


## 1961

*We came because here were no politics*
said your in-laws. *Sweet monotonous languor!*
and a *pill* was a sexless bore at school
but one brought bassinettes under control;
you were young and free for longer:
somehow this caused great anger
and soon flowers came by wire from America.

## 1981

You rose climbing up,
you rose going down
as snide peace with few imports
hung on in your home town.
When green learned to rust iron
dinners dared not be brown
and the flowers were flung gladioli.


## 2001

Fashion ruled, but another queen reigned.
Some flickers of nonsense remained:
*It's evening here, Nonna, so hey!*
*The world won't be ending today.*
One last war-trip, and none of ours killed!
Collective rights alone were instilled;
the singular was gagged and at bay
and the flowers were Olympic Gold roses.


## RECLAIM THE SITES

We are spared the Avenues of Liberation
and the water-cannoned Fifths of May
but I tire of cities clogged with salutes
to other cities: York, Liverpool, Oxford Streets
and memorial royalty: Elizabeth,
Albert, William, unnumbered George.
Give me Sallie Huckstepp Road, ahead of
sepia Sussex, or Argyle, or Yankee numbering
– and why not a whole metropolis
street-signed for its own life and ours:
Childsplay Park and First Bra Avenue,
Unsecured Loan, the Boulevard Kiss,
Radar Strip, Bread-Fragrance Corner,
Fumbletrouser, Delight Bridge, Timeless Square?

# THE CLEAR SALINE OF THEORY

Theory has done this:
orphans are filing into school
in the tropical 1940s
and every one of them has parents
living, who try to write to them.
Successive tides of theory
flood the poorest faces with salt.


# THE FAIR GO

A ginger-biscuit kelpie dog,
young, abandoned off the highway
up a gravel road. Livestock
and rifle country, so the big
harp of ribs in its mouth
as its start in life is
butcher-cut. To prove innocence.


# THE BELLWETHER BRUSH

As the painter Sali Herman discerns
and captures the iron-lace character
of what are still called slums then
he's unaware the bright haze his brush
confers is called Billions;
he delightedly thinks Beauty, Truth,
but fashion turns its head, and starts
walking clap-clap in the footsteps,
clap-clap, of his easel,
walking in twos, as coppers used to,
till the salt of the earth accept
hot offers for their bijou homes.

# IN A TIME OF CUISINE

A fact the gourmet
euphemism can't silence:
vegetarians eat sex,
carnivores eat violence.


# UPLANDS

Across silvering cobble
                into white-ant stump country.

Hills lie where they fell;
                boulders sultana their steeps.

Smoke wanders up from a couple of far places.

Crested trees pour their shade
                to one side on the ground.

Unplugging their weight,
                kangaroos hoist up, and bounce.

A hill's front becoming its back
                takes the sun all day.

Forest up some slopes,
                thin enough to see grass under.

Getting well out now
                back into the high country.

Mountains pregnant with hills in a white skim sky.

## THE PAY FOR FOSTERAGE

The carpenter could have stayed
hunched over, at work on his chagrin,
left everything to the hush-ups
and stone-evadings of women.
He could have escaped the thousands
of years of speculation. The horns.
But all that weakness was behind him.
The courteous presence had spoken
unearthly sense to its equal,
himself. As he would be from now
on into the world to come.


## THE MYRIADS

Resolute, you come to a cell
and its powers are all wrong.
It can never make your great tree
with you. And it was your chance.

Pine pollen on the water
making sallow jade islands
in the evening sun.


## A STUDY OF THE NUDE

Someone naked with you
will rarely be a nude.
A nude is never with just one.

Nude looks back at everyone
or no one. Aubergine or bluish rose,
a nude is a generalization.

Someone has given their name
and face to be face all over,
to be the face of something

that isn't for caressing
except with the mind's hand.
Nude is the full dress of undressing.


## IGUASSU

Shallow at brinks
with pouring tussocks
a bolt of live tan water
is continuously tugged
off miles of table
by thunderous white claws.


## PIETÀ ONCE ATTRIBUTED TO COSME TURA

This is the nadir of the story.

His mother's hairpiece, her *sheitel*,
is torn away, her own cropped hair looks burnt.
She had said the first Mass
and made Godhead a fact
which his strangeness had kept proving,
but what of that is still true
now, with his limp weight at her knee?
Her arms open, and withdraw,
and come back. That first eucharist
she could have been stoned to death for
is still alive in her body.

## THE KNOCKDOWN QUESTION

Why does God not spare the innocent?

The answer to that is not in
the same world as the question
so you would shrink from me
in terror if I could answer it.

## THE INSIDERS

What's in who for you?
Who's in you for himself?

## THE ONSET

Rain. Its breath a liquid dust
ages the brooding European
overcoat movie in the pond,
then it prickles, across the deep
windows there, then blinks
with excited eyelids, pinging
all rings like the dimples
on a steel-band drum, and soon
the closed velvet doors
of the still theatre have vanished
under shoal like tin lids dancing
massed pinches of potato water.

## THE DOG'S BAD NAME

My politics are like crop circles
that appear in angry wheat.

The sourest explanations of them
get force-fed to undefended minds.

I never know their outlines in advance;
all I know is, no group makes them.

What strikes me more is the frequent
wealth of the estates they afflict.


## POP MUSIC

Empty as a country town street
after five. Two or three crisp
high-heel walkers, and a pair
of little girls in a station wagon,
one bunging a pop bottle *boinc*
against her head and *bocc*
against the wagon. The other blows
music into hers: *Doe roe to hoe soon*
*but no throe for woe yet, moon!*


## THE BODY IN PHYSICS

The air has sides, in a house.
Birds, whacked from colliding, embrace
its sheer with umbrella-rib skiddings.
They gape silent death-cries when closed
in converging hands, or snatched out
of such parts of their theory as still fly.
Carried outside, they pause a beat
and drop upwards, into gravity that once more
blows as well as sucks. Fliers' gravity.


## FRUIT BAT COLONY BY DAY

High above its gloom
this forest is all hung
with head-down ginger bats
like big leather bees.

In sun to stay drowsy
daylong in slow dangle
chi-chi as monkeys
they blow on sad tin horns,
glide, nurture babies, sleep,
waiting for their real lives.


## COOL HISTORY

Identity oversimplifies humans.
It denies the hybrid, as trees can't.

Trees, which wrap height in pages
self-knitted from ground water and light

are stood scrolls best read unopened.
They lean to each other and away

in politics of sun-rivalry
or at knotted behests in the earth.

Billets cut from them are tight-bound
photocopies detailing food and ancestry.

Eons on, their concentric years
will be eloquent on suffering and old airs.


## THE MACHINE-GUNNING OF CHARM

Happy the city that stayed poorish
or unbombed through the twentieth century
and never rebuilt itself then.

All centuries back to the tenth
in the West, could put up more humane
ordinary and pretty-good buildings:

undercrofts, fat colonnades, gingerbread,
crooked corridors with much later privy,
street fronts bluff as God Save the King.

The twentieth century grew such icy
ambition and scorn that it built marvels
or else crap. Over charm's mass grave

its middle range gridded medicine's extra
billions in a punitive mediocrity.


## THE CLIMAX OF FACTORY FARMING

Farm gates were sealed with tape;
people couldn't stop shaking their heads.
Out on the fells and low fields
in twilight, it was the Satanic mills
come again: the farm beasts of Britain
being burnt inside walls of their feed.


## MASSACRE'S ALL-PARTY FUEL

The cones of the Wollemi pine
erupt at the ends of its branches
like the stars of the Eureka flag.
I grew up in the early country
and Libra put her sword up my nose
and taught me her values: *on the
other hand, but then on the third hand ...*

But my nose still pointed and discerned.
When humans lay stuck to their blood
en masse, under birches, on cobbles
or vibrated with heat on bush timber,
I'd heard the cause yip in dance halls
and in national brigand lore: blurts,

then licensings, of underdog revenge.

## FUSEE

A complex iron finial-head
still dazzling from the forge
smokes in its ash and sparkles
in the shadowy workshop –
but no:

in fact it's a feathered
intricate protea bloom
haloed in a dusty ray of sun,
which in turn evades the stark
truth

that it's an incandescent
missile tamped in the choke
of an 18th century mortar, aimed
to ignite a timber city.


## D.C.

City where aircraft are hung
as art, and security admits people
to the colonnaded floors
of horizontal beige skyscrapers
haunted by ideals and vast men.


## OUTSIDE OF THE IRON MASK

Was any ruler ever a twin?
Even now you never hear of it,

a consort suckling one infant
in tears, after successive labours

and the bundling out of linen
– *O Madam, it is the State* –

nor her comfort: a far apprentice
ribbed for his likeness to a coin.


## THE POISONS OF RIGHT AND LEFT

You are what you have got
and: to love, you have to hate.
Two ideas that have killed and maimed
holocausts and myriads.


## THE TOP ALCOHOL CONTENDER

An aircraft-engined kewpie doll
in chrome, with vast fat tyres,
stinks hotly of injection and rubdown
and little wheels splay at the far
end of its blood-red stick –
how else should it look,
the top alcohol contender?


## APSLEY FALLS

Abounding white water
details each stratum
on basalt stratum
down hundreds and hundreds
like bands of washed linen,
this mummy standing up
the height of its mountain
in an ink-wet corridor.

# TO ONE OUTSIDE THE CULTURE

Still ask me about adult stuff
when you want. But remember that day
in Madame Tussaud's basement
when all the grownups looked careful
and some young ones had to smirk?

You were right to cry out in horror
at the cut-off heads there
and the rusty dried trickles
shocked out of their eyes and ears.


# PORTRAIT OF A FELSPAR-COLOURED CAT

Plaintive, she named herself Min
in the reaching-down world.

Her texture manages itself;
her comet tail is Abyssinian.

All her intelligence
is elegance.

Never would soil she flicked up
persist in her belly fur.


# MARS AT PERIGEE

An apricot star
glittering, like a drop of desert rain
on the east night sky,
that was Mars at perigee;

the acrid sweet pulp around
the seed of a red passionfruit
was its taste on the mind

before any airtank thoughts.

## MORE PICTOGRAPHS

A beribboned question mark
is a *riddle*; one cut off sharp
and barbed is a *trick question*;

one bent over a magnifying glass
is *inspection*, or *investigation*
and one reversed is *answer*

but a tentacled octopus
with a human head
digesting life in its brain

is a mood. Which many have indulged
and there are hosts of words for
that mood, in the different lexicons.


## REFLECTION IN A MILITARY CAP BADGE

A pair of breasts in a window
as the Grenadiers marched by,
but were those breasts being displayed
by their own hands?


## EXPLAINING A CHEESE

Explaining a cheese
she spoke in Australian English
but her hands spoke Italian.

# NATIONAL DRESS

Ceremonial and truly ethnic
clothes may almost escape fashion.
For centuries on end
the hemlines of national costume
could allow women feet.

Before the Party or tourism
'national' meant local and peasant,
and in kingdom, tsardom
or *rzeczpospolita*, who needed
goose-satire on the train of a skirt?

Back before Hitler gave Poland
to his lawyer as a fee
for shameful relief
and got the fellow hanged,
who then wore national costume

daily and who once a year
mattered, in ways now lost.
Today, it's all identity,
all finery, with patterns a spring sun
might embroider in a park, and ribbons

in colours primary as principle,
but ancient mocking folk dance
sways in the light of forest
so deep it still breeds extinct
proto-cattle the shape of Lithuania.


# A SHRINE HOUSE

The past lives in a timber house
in off the road. A shrine house.

Tenants have never been let in there
and the car outside comes rarely now.

Paint from the first modern year
still strokes the shadowy best room

and in the silent talk of young parents
a slow broom isn't bunting cobwebs down.


## AT UNIVERSITY

Puritans reckoned the cadavers
in Anatomy were drunks off the street;
idealists said they were benefactors
who had willed their bodies to science,

but the averted manila-coloured
people on the tables had pinned-back
graves excavated in them
around which they lay scattered in the end
as if exhumed from themselves.


## THE YOUNG FOX

I drove up to a young fox
on the disused highway.
It didn't scare, but watched me
roll up to it along the asphalt.
I got out. Any poultry it would kill
wouldn't now be mine. No feud between us.

It watched quizzically, then bounded
away with an unmistakeable headshake
that says *Play with me!*
and stopped, waiting. I remember
how sharply perfumed the leaves were
that lay on the pavement in that world.

# EXPERIENCE

I heard a cat bark like a fox
because the car's larger purr
didn't soothe her, locked in a cat-box
and the hitchhiker said *We keep a snake
to eat our rats!* For heaven's sake.
I've heard a snake hiss like a man
I saw a goose sail like a bark
I heard a man wank like a goose.


# THE BARCALDINE SUITE

High on mountains worldwide they blow
on long wood trumpets in tones of psalm
summoning weirdness or cattle or calm
or play a wood horse with a horsehair bow
and the didgeridoo, that lowland shofar,
throttles where dancing and secrets are –

    Dance leaped from the Bang
    finding orbital speeds

    Life joined it underwater
    brought it skyward as reeds

    and half of dance air-dried
    into carolling and birds

    into drumming and howling
    and the human song, words –

Musicians mug outwards
dancing with their instruments
or stare deeply inward
communing with their instruments,
displaying the catch
or listening for the prey –

The band vamped along
to music pince-nez'ed to a tuba
and this woman stood in tears.
It was sunny Europe to her

and a Pentecost of tones
came to ignition over towns
getting nubs and gists uttered
that talk had often spattered –

Music is the great nonsense poem
written, for recital if at all,
in the old bonding lingo of cry
that we translate experience into
*dilly-O Johnny Ringo bye bye*
to check with the tree-nests of Home.

Music is the vast nonsense poem
our precisions float out on with emotion
to change and get poignant as they drown;
la Musique: it needs no translation.
It can back up, or send up, any Line;
it makes even the thought-police hum.

Tart angel that never lost Heaven
*O waly the faraway wine*
music is the great nonsense poem,
the religion no hard nose rejects,
not trapped in the medium of critics.
*O harmonium the zillion-armed Om* –

Being deeply moved
stops movement. Voice would be fur –

The soul is open. Something
always knew its key –

laughter and crying at once,
or rapt, or fainting to sleep –

549

        gooseflesh fades to shiver
        as the modern resumes –

I thought of ambient sounds that music has dipped up
in its silver ladle: heartbeats and hoofbeats, and trains
volleying with tipplers and Dopplers, or blue in the night,
drips in echoey spaces, wind through frightful places,
factory-crash heavy metal, the strung pluck of bows,
bells, whistles, the clinker coming at you across everything,
peaks peaks peaks of murder. And crowds, and the ocean snore.

It's a shortish list, even with the anvil and the cannon.
Has nobody scored the rippy un-tiling of a fish?
The colic in tennis courts? The blowfly race-call tune
that evokes no sex on a long flat saturday?
What about steamships, beyond the lorn siren to the barrel
and tumbledom of their nature, or the huge bulk gamelan
as hardwood logs collaborate into a keen sawmill?
Uneven steps rasping slowly, with rests, downhill?

        The weight of our weight
        the weight of our years –

I know the purist point isn't wild sound being redeemed
up into music, but what of music's own dimension
can be modulated into existence for the mind.
A body of its own for the mind, with no fixed visuals.
Without the beards and sweaters of hand-rolled wool
would work songs sound like politics? Would the symphonic,
without posh and penguin suits, still sound like a wall of money? –

        The weight of our weight
        the weight of our years
        the said and the shed and the
        stammered in tears
        and always this broadcast
        Otherworld at our ears –

Then, we'll be a tune
they'll put on and play
bits of and rarely
till our times pass away
and there's no one on earth
who knew us by heart.
Obsolete for all time
and that's just the start.


## THE MEANING OF EXISTENCE

Everything except language
knows the meaning of existence.
Trees, planets, rivers, time
know nothing else. They express it
moment by moment as the universe.

Even this fool of a body
lives it in part, and would
have full dignity within it
but for the ignorant freedom
of my talking mind.


## THE ABORIGINAL CRICKETER

MID-19TH CENTURY

Good-looking young man
in your Crimean shirt
with your willow shield
up, as if to face spears,

you're inside their men's Law,
one church they do obey;
they'll remember you were here.
Keep fending off their casts.

Don't come out of character.
Like you, they suspect
idiosyncrasy of witchcraft.
Above all, don't get out

too easily, and have to leave here
where all missiles are just leather
and come from one direction.
Keep it noble. Keep it light.


## THE GYMNAST VALERIA VATKINA

Legs counterposed like six o'clock, her stretch
is bowstave, sky foot to ground foot. A point shoe tips each.

She leans out around herself then, and gazes
intently past her hand at what she blazes:

a switchback trail of rainbow ribbon
that climbs stairs of air to her whipped baton

and equally shimmies down landings of allure
right-left right-left like a Caliph's signature.


## THE AZTEC REVIVAL

Human sacrifice has come back
on another city-island
and bloodied its high stepped towers.

Few now think the blood's redeemed
by red peppers, or turkey in chocolate.
Human sacrifice comes, now always,

in default of achievement,
from minds that couldn't invent
the land-galaxies of dot painting

or new breakthrough zeroes, or jazz.

552

# BRIEF, THAT PLACE IN THE YEAR

Brief, that place in the year
when a blossoming pear tree
with its sweet laundered scent
reinhabits wooden roads
that arch and diverge up
into its electronic snow city.


# THE AVERTED

The one whose eyes
do not meet yours
is alone at heart
and looks where the dead look
for a comrade in his cause.


# AT THE WIDENING OF A WAR

Everyone was frightened of the sky.

Each night, Mars emerged at the zenith.
A bleb of pure rage tore off the Sun.

For days, the living and the dead
hung in the air like dust
whirled aloft from tired roads.

The fuselage of a lobster lay abandoned.

The Isles of the Blest were receding
to their sailing distances
and the gunfire of tourist shoes was stilled.

Sports stadiums and crowds loomed from another age.

The blow struck now
would be weaker than the blow withheld.

## THE MUDDY TRENCH

In the dream, Clarrie Dunn
sits naked with many thousands
in the muddy trench. He is saying
The true god gives his flesh and blood.
Idols demand yours off you.

*– from The Boys who Stole the Funeral, Sonnet 88*

# INDEX OF FIRST LINES

557

# INDEX OF TITLES

577